# The Holy Spirit

## or

# Power From on High

**A. B. Simpson**
(1843 - 1919)

**Volumes 1 & 2**

Trumpet Press Edition, 2023

Copyright 2023 by Trumpet Press

Author: Simpson, Albert Benjamin

Title: The Holy Spirit or Power from on High

1. Holy Spirit 2. New Testament 3. Jesus

ISBN: 978-1-0882-0344-6

Trumpet Press is a Member of the *Christian Indie Publishing Association* (CIPA).

## Table of Contents

Brief Biography ................................................................... 5

## Volume 1

Chapter 1: Like a Dove ............................................................ 7
Chapter 2: The Breath of God .................................................... 15
Chapter 3: The Sword of the Spirit .............................................. 26
Chapter 4: The Pillar of Cloud and Fire ......................................... 40
Chapter 5: The Living Water ..................................................... 51
Chapter 6: The Anointing Oil .................................................... 59
Chapter 7: The Baptism with Fire ................................................ 69
Chapter 8: The Spirit of Wisdom ................................................. 79
Chapter 9: The Holy Spirit in the Book of Judges ................................ 89
Chapter 10: A Spirit-Filled Man ................................................. 99
Chapter 11: The Holy Spirit in the Lives of Saul and David ..................... 106
Chapter 12: The Holy Spirit in the Book of Proverbs ............................ 117
Chapter 13: The Still, Small Voice ............................................. 126
Chapter 14: The Pot of Oil ..................................................... 138
Chapter 15: The Valley of Ditches .............................................. 146
Chapter 16: The Spirit of Inspiration .......................................... 154
Chapter 17: The Holy Spirit in the Book of Joel ................................ 164
Chapter 18: The Holy Spirit in the Book of Isaiah .............................. 174
Chapter 19: The Holy Spirit in Life and Testimony of Jeremiah .................. 184
Chapter 20: The Holy Spirit in Ezekiel ......................................... 197
Chapter 21: The Spirit of the Resurrection -- Ezekiel 37: 8 .................... 207
Chapter 22: The River of Blessing .............................................. 215
Chapter 23: The Holy Spirit in the Days of the Restoration ..................... 224
Chapter 24: The Olive Trees and the Golden Lamps ............................... 234

Chapter 25: The Last Message of the Holy Ghost to the Old
  Dispensation .................................................................................. 244

**Volume 2:**

Chapter 1: The Holy Spirit in the Life of the Lord Jesus Christ ................. 252
Chapter 2: The Baptism with the Holy Ghost ............................................ 261
Chapter 3: The Wise and Foolish Virgins; or, The Holy Spirit and the Coming of the Lord ................................................................................................ 268
Chapter 4: The Parable of the Pounds; or, Power for Service .................... 275
Chapter 5: The Holy Ghost in the Gospel of John ...................................... 286
Chapter 6: The Comforter .......................................................................... 294
Chapter 7: Waiting for The Spirit .............................................................. 302
Chapter 8: Power from On High ................................................................ 311
Chapter 9: Filled with the Spirit ................................................................. 323
Chapter 10: The Holy Spirit in the Epistle to the Romans ......................... 332
Chapter 11: The Holy Spirit in the First Epistle to the Corinthians ........... 341
Chapter 12: The Holy Spirit in the Body of Christ ..................................... 350
Chapter 13: The Holy Spirit in Second Corinthians ................................... 356
Chapter 14: The Holy Spirit in Galatians ................................................... 363
Chapter 15: All the Blessings of the Spirit, or the Holy Ghost in Ephesians 372
Chapter 16: The Holy Spirit in Philippians ................................................ 383
Chapter 17: The Spirit of Love ................................................................... 392
Chapter 18: The Holy Spirit in Thessalonians ........................................... 400
Chapter 19: The Holy Spirit in the Epistles of Paul to Timothy ................ 408
Chapter 20: Regeneration and Renewal .................................................... 418
Chapter 21: The Holy Spirit in the Epistle to the Hebrews ....................... 426
Chapter 22: God's Jealous Love ................................................................. 435
Chapter 23: The Holy Spirit in the Epistles of Peter ................................. 445
Chapter 24: The Holy Spirit in the First Epistle of John ........................... 453

Chapter 25: The Holy Spirit in Jude ........................................................ 464
Chapter 26: The Sevenfold Holy Ghost .................................................. 474
Chapter 27: The Spirit's Last Message to the Churches ......................... 480
Chapter 28: The Holy Spirit's Last Message ........................................... 491

# Brief Biography

Albert Benjamin Simpson (1843 - 1919) was born on Prince Edward Island, Canada, of Scottish ancestry, where his father was a Presbyterian minister, shipbuilder, and businessman. The family moved to Ontario where young Albert accepted Christ as his Savior at age fifteen, and was shortly "called by God to preach" the Gospel.

He graduated from Knox College in Toronto in 1865, and accepted his first pastorate at Knox Church in Hamilton, the second largest church in Canada. The church had 1,200 members and added another 750 before he left 8 years later for a pastorate in Louisville, Kentucky.

He eventually became a highly respected minister in Canada and USA, a sought after speaker and pastor, founder of a major evangelical denomination; The Christian Missionary Alliance; published over 70 books, edited a weekly magazine for nearly 40 years, and wrote many gospel songs and poems.

A. W. Tozer wrote a biography of Simpson's life. William MacArthur, a friend and co-worker, said Simpson once told him: "I am no good unless I can get alone with God." MacArthur added: "His practice was to hush his spirit, and literally cease to think, then in the silence of his soul, he listened for the 'still small voice'".

Simpson had a compassion for the lost, and a desire to evangelize. Daniel Evearitt wrote a biographical article on Simpson and said; "those who knew him paint a picture of a dynamic but humble worker for God who inspired others to total commitment to God's service and Kingdom. They portray him as a loving, caring, patient man."

Simpson held a city-wide revival in Lewisville, KN, and "The city was moved to its depths and hundreds were converted. At the close of the campaign, large numbers were received in to the churches," said Tozer.

Simpson pastored in Kentucky through the Civil War, then felted called to New York City, to the Thirteenth Street Presbyterian Church in 1879. But one year later he resigned and became an independent preacher. One year later he built Gospel Tabernacle and began his missionary work. He helped to form and head up two evangelization organizations; The Christian Alliance and The Evangelical Missionary Alliance. Then in 1897, they were joined to become *The Christian and Missionary Alliance*. He continued his work there until his retirement in 1918, and died in 1919.

His final words were spoken in prayer for all the missionaries he had helped to send throughout the world.

# Chapter 1

# Like a Dove

The first emblem under which we see the Holy Spirit in the New Testament is the dove descending upon the head of Jesus at His baptism on the banks of the Jordan.

The first emblem under which the Holy Spirit is presented in the Old Testament is also a dove. In the story of creation, in the first chapter of Genesis, second verse, we read: "The earth was without form and void, and darkness brooded over the face of the deep, and the Spirit of God brooded upon the face of the waters." This is the figure of the mother dove brooding over her nest and cherishing her young. What a strange background for such a picture: chaos, desolation, the seething waters, the hissing flames, the wild abyss, the starless night, the reign of ruin, death, and desolation! This was the scene where the mother dove of eternal love and peace began to build her nest, and she rested not until out of that scene of wreck she had evolved a bright and happy world, and a smiling paradise, with its human family and its pure and heavenly happiness and hope.

We pass over seven chapters, and we come to another scene of desolation and wreck. The waters of the deluge are sweeping around the world. The work of twenty centuries is submerged beneath that awful flood, and the world's countless millions are lying in death beneath those waves. One solitary ship is riding above the storm with eight human beings within its walls, the sole survivors of all earth's population.

Once again we behold the figure of the dove. We read in Genesis 8: 6-12: "And it came to pass, at the end of forty days, that

Noah opened the window of the ark which he had made; and he sent forth a raven, which went forth to and fro, until the waters were dried up from off the earth. Also, he sent forth a dove from him, to see if the waters were abated from off the face of the ground; but the dove found no rest for the sole of her foot, and she returned unto him into the ark, for the waters were on the face of the whole earth; then he put forth his hand, and took her, and pulled her in unto him into the ark. And he stayed yet another seven days, and again he sent forth the dove out of the ark; and the dove came in to him in the evening; and, lo, in her mouth was an olive leaf, pluckt off; so Noah knew that the waters were abated from off the earth. "And he stayed yet another seven days, and sent forth the dove, which returned not again unto him any more."

Back of this dove there is another figure, the black-winged raven, the emblem of Satan, as the other is of the Holy Ghost.

And now we see three very remarkable stages in the sending forth of this dove, and they seem to speak of three dispensations of the Holy Spirit. First, we have the dove going forth from the ark, and finding no rest upon the wild and drifting waste of sin and judgment. This represents the Old Testament period, perhaps, when the Holy Ghost visited this sinful world, but could find no resting-place, and ever went back to the bosom of God. Next, we have the dove going forth and returning with the olive leaf in her mouth, a symbol and a pledge of peace and reconciliation, a sign that judgment had passed and peace was returning. Surely this may beautifully represent the next stage of the Holy Spirit's manifestation, the going forth in the ministry and resurrection of Jesus Christ, to proclaim reconciliation to a sinful world. But, as yet, He is not at liberty to reside in this sin-cursed earth. There is, therefore, a third stage, when, at, length, the dove goes forth from the ark and returns no more, but makes the world its home, and builds its nest amid the habitations of men. This is the third and present stage of the Holy Spirit's blessed work.

Thus He has now come forth, not to visit this sinful world, returning again to heaven, but to make it His abiding home. During the ministry of Christ on earth the Spirit dwelt in Him, and not in men. Jesus said He was with the disciples, but He adds, "He shall be in you." Like Noah's dove, still lingering in the ark, and going forth only to visit the earth, so the Holy Ghost dwelt in Jesus, and touched the hearts of men from time to time.

But now Jesus has sent Him forth, and His residence is no longer in heaven, but in the heart of the believer, and in the bosom of the Church. This earth is now His home; and here among sinful, suffering men, the same dove is building her nest and rearing her brood for the celestial realms, where they shall one day soar and sing in the light of God. Such is the symbolical unfolding of the Holy Spirit in these two first pictures of the Old Testament. Let its now gather out of the figure itself, some of its most pointed lessons and suggestions.

The first thought is motherhood. It is the figure of the mother dove. In one of the recent and most brilliant works of Mr. Drummond, he develops with great fullness the idea that the goal of nature is always motherhood. In the vegetable creation everything moves toward seed and fruit. The flower is but the cradle and the swaddling bands of the living germ. The plant lives simply to develop the life of another plant, to reproduce itself. Thus, in the natural world, the first appearance of love is not in the sexual, but in the maternal relations; and in like manner, the great thought in the heart of God is motherhood, and God Himself possesses in Himself that true nature which has been manifested in the creation.

There is in the divine Trinity a personality corresponding to human relationships. Human fatherhood expresses a need which is met in God the Father. Human motherhood has its origin in the Holy Ghost. Human brotherhood, and the higher, closer fellowship of the husband and the bridegroom, are met in Christ, the Son of God, our Brother and our Bridegroom. We cannot reason out the divine Trinity, but God can make it real to our spiritual instincts.

There are times when we need a father's strength and love, and our pressed spirits cry out, "Oh, if my father were only here, how quickly he would help me!" And God our Father answers that cry.

There are times when the orphaned spirit feels the need of a mother's more delicate and tender touch, and we think how mother once used to comfort and help us as no other friend could do. Then we need the mother heart of God. I envy not the man who has outgrown the weakness of needing a mother's love, and whose heart finds no response to such words as these:

> Who fed me from her gentle breast?
> Who taught me in her arms to rest?
> And on my lips sweet kisses pressed?
> My mother.
> Who ran to help me when I fell,
> And would some pretty story tell,
> Or kiss the place to make it well?
> My mother.

The Holy Ghost, the author of the mother's heart and the child's dependent love, is able to meet in us the deep need which has outgrown our infant years, and still looks up to God with its orphaned cry for love and sympathy.

Also there is in every human heart the memory of some brave, true brother, and a longing for a divine arm that can uphold us with a love "that sticketh closer than a brother." Yes, there is a deeper longing for a friendship more intimate and a fellowship more dear, which Jesus meets as the divine Husband, the Ishi of our heart.

All the representations which the Scriptures give us of the Holy Ghost are in harmony with this thought of divine motherhood. The regeneration of the soul is described as a new birth, and the Holy Ghost is the mother that gives us this birth. The guidance and nurture of the Spirit after our conversion are described in language borrowed from the nursery and the home. In the deeper needs of the soul, the comfort of the Holy Ghost is described to us under the very image of a mother's caresses and a mother's love. "As one whom his mother comforteth, so will I comfort you, and ye shall be comforted, saith the Lord."

In turn, as we are filled with the Holy Ghost, we ourselves have the mother-heart for others, and are able to reflect the blessing and dispense the comfort which we have received. Our prayers for others become maternal longings, travails, and soul-births, and we learn to say with the apostle, "My little children, of whom I travail in birth again, until Christ be formed in you," and to understand such language as this, "As soon as Zion travailed she brought forth."

The Holy Ghost in the consecrated heart often gives a yearning for others, and a prayer for the lost and the tempted, as intensely real as the pangs of maternal anguish and love; and people are born of us as truly as the children of our households, and are linked to us by bonds as real as our natural kindred.

The figure of the dove is suggestive of peace. The dove from the ark was the messenger of peace, and brought back an olive branch as the symbol of reconciliation. Thus is the Holy Spirit the messenger of peace with God through the Lord Jesus Christ. He leads the soul to understand and accept the message of mercy and to find the peace of God. He then brings the deeper "peace of God, which keeps the heart and mind through Christ Jesus." Wherever the Holy Spirit reigns there is peace.

Back of the picture of the dove is the raven, restlessly passing to and fro, to and fro, to and fro, a type of the troubled spirit of evil, that finds no rest even in the pleasures of sin, but is driven from excitement to excitement in the vain pursuit of rest, until at last it is thrown upon the wild billows of a lost eternity, the victim of everlasting disquietude and unrest.

But the spirit in which the Holy Ghost rules is at rest. It has a peace that nothing can offend, "the peace of God that passeth all understanding."

### THE DOVE IS THE SYMBOL OP PURITY

"Harmless as a dove," is Christ's interpretation of the beautiful emblem. The Spirit of God which is purity itself, cannot dwell in an unclean heart. He cannot abide in the natural mind. It was said of the anointing of old, "On man's flesh it shall not be poured." The purity which the Holy Spirit brings is like a white and spotless little plant which grows up out of a heap of manure, or out of black soil, without one grain of impurity adhering to its crystalline surface, spotless as an angel's wing. So the Holy Spirit gives a purity of heart which brings its own protection, for it is essentially unlike the evil things which grow around it. It may be surrounded on every side with evil, but it is uncontaminated and pure because its very nature is essentially holy and divine. It cannot be soiled, because like the plumage of the dove, which, protected by its oily covering, comes forth from the miry pool unstained and unsullied by the dark waters, it sheds off every defilement and is proof against the touch of every stain.

### THE DOVE IS THE SYMBOL OF GENTLENESS

The Comforter is gentle, tender, and full of patience and love. How gentle are God's dealings even with sinners! How patient His forbearance! How tender His discipline with His own erring children! How He led Jacob, Joseph, Israel, David, Elijah, and all His ancient servants, until they could truly say, "Thy gentleness hath made me great"! The heart in which the Holy Spirit dwells will al-ways be characterized by gentleness, lowliness, quietness, meekness, and forbearance. The rude, sarcastic spirit, the brusque manner, the sharp retort, the unkind cut — all these belong to the flesh. They have nothing in common with the gentle teaching of the Comforter. The Holy Dove shrinks from the noisy, tumultuous, excited, and vindictive spirit, and finds His home in the lowly breast of the peaceful soul. "The fruit of the Spirit is gentleness, meekness."

### THE HOLY SPIRIT IS THE SPIRIT OF LOVE

The dove is the special emblem of affection. The special object of the divine Comforter is to "shed abroad the love of God in our hearts," and to show that "the fruit of the Spirit is love." Wherever He dwells there is to be found a disposition of unselfishness, consideration for others, loving helpfulness, and kindness; and He wants love from us. He asks not so much our service as our communion. He has plenty to serve Him; but He wants us to love Him and to receive His tender love for us. He is longing for our affection and is disappointed when we give Him anything else.

A very sweet thought connected with the symbol of the dove, and true also of the Holy Spirit, is that we find in the Scriptures many allusions to the mourning of the dove. It is a bird of sorrow, and its plaintive notes have more of sadness in them than the voice of any other bird. Any one who has heard the cooing of the turtle dove will never forget the plaintive sadness of its tone.

How can this be true of the Holy Spirit? Simply because love is always sensitive to suffering. The more we love, the more we sorrow, especially when the loved one disappoints our expectations, or our affection. The lone dove coos for its lost mate, and mourns for its scattered brood. And so the Holy Spirit is represented as loving us even unto the extreme of sorrow. We do not read of the anger of the Holy Ghost, but of the grief of the Spirit. "They rebelled and vexed His Holy Spirit," and we are warned, "Grieve not the Holy Spirit whereby ye are sealed unto the day of redemption."

There is a beautiful passage in James which has been unhappily translated in our Revised Version: "The Spirit that dwelleth in us lusteth to envy." It ought to be, "The Spirit that dwelleth in us loveth us to jealousy." It is the figure of a love that suffers because of its intense regard for the loved object. The Holy Ghost is so anxious to accomplish in us and for us the highest will of God, and to receive from us the truest love for Christ, our divine Husband, that He becomes jealous when in any way we disappoint Him, or divide His love with others. Therefore, it is said in the preceding passage, "Ye adulterers and adulteresses, know ye not that the friendship of the world is enmity with God?"

Oh, shall we grieve so kind a Friend? Shall we disappoint so loving a Husband? Shall we provoke so tender and unselfish a jealousy? Shall we not meet the blessed Holy Spirit with the love He brings us, and give in return our undivided and unbounded affection? Strange, indeed, that God should have to plead with us for our love. Strange that He whom all Heaven adores should have a rival in the hearts of the children whom He has created, and the beings who owe everything they have to His infinite mercy! Strange that so gentle a Friend should have to plead so long and so tenderly for our affections! Let us turn to Him with penitential love, and cry:

> "Come Holy Spirit, Heavenly Dove,
>   With all Thy quickening powers;
>   Kindle a flame of sacred love
>   In these cold hearts of ours."

## Chapter 2

## The Breath of God

"And the Lord God formed man of the dust of the ground, and breathed into his nostrils the breath of life; and man became a living soul." Genesis 2: 7. "The wind bloweth where it listeth, and thou hearest the sound thereof, but canst not tell whence it cometh, and whither it goeth: so is everyone that is born of the Spirit." John 3: 8. "And when He had said this, He breathed on them, and said unto them, Receive ye the Holy Ghost." John 20: 22.

The first of these passages contains the second reference to the Holy Spirit in the Old Testament, and the other passages prolong the line, and fix the application of the beautiful picture in Genesis to the person and work of the Holy Spirit. The emblem under which the Spirit is here presented to us is the breath and the air, the atmosphere in which we live, and the act by which we inhale or exhale its vital properties and its vitalizing power.

The value and importance of the atmosphere is self-evident. We can live for days without food, and for a lifetime without sight or hearing, but we cannot live an hour without breath. To breathe is the most essential of all our physical functions and is in the Scriptures almost synonymous with life. Again and again we find such expressions as, "Every living thing that hath breath upon the earth." We cannot see it, we can scarcely feel it, and yet around us there is an ocean of air without which we could not exist, and without which almost all of our senses would be blind, deaf, and vain. Sound could not be communicated without air, the sweet hymns that we have sung could not have been uttered or heard, the voices of our friends would never reach us, and the harmonies of music would be silent and dead. Sight also is dependent upon the atmosphere. Yonder sun seems like a ball of fire in the midst of a pall of darkness, when we get beyond the earth's atmosphere. Like a fine, transparent lens, the atmosphere receiving the solar rays, diffuses them in floods of light for the organs of vision. Without the atmosphere heat would be unknown. In yonder upper spaces, although seeming to be nearer the sun, there is an everlasting frigid zone; and every drop of blood in our body would be frozen into ice in an instant, were we to pass beyond the tempering air which receives and distributes the solar heat.

Such is the striking and beautiful image under which the Spirit of God is represented. He brings to us the very breath of life for spirit, soul, and body, and creates the atmosphere in which we see the things of God, hear His voice, and dwell in the warmth and radiance of His love. The present passage unfolds the work of the Spirit in man's original creation, and also suggests the Spirit's work in the higher unfolding of His restoring and quickening grace.

The first thing we notice in this passage is the marked distinction that is made between the creation of man and that of all other animals. At the creative word, they sprang immediately into existence, and fell into their places in the great economy of nature, without further note or comment. But when man's creation is about to begin, everything is different. By a significant pause our attention is called to a most important crisis. Then, step by step, the great transaction is accomplished, and we see the first human being coming forth from his Creator's direct touch in all the completeness of his manifold nature, the wondrous handiwork of God.

We see even the Creator Himself appearing under a new name and in an entirely new aspect. The higher criticism has been fond of questioning the unity of the book of Genesis, because this second chapter gives an entirely new name to God. Because we here meet with Jehovah Elohim, the critics have worked up the astute hypothesis that this is a different God from the Elohim of the first chapter, and that this chapter, therefore, must have had a different author. They tell us also that this is another of the old fragments of Hebrew lore that have come down to us along with Babylonian and Egyptian scrolls and tablets, and that this distinctly proves that Moses could not have been the author of both these chapters. Ah, how much deeper is the thought of God! They used to tell us that the creation of the sun on the fourth day contradicted the statement that light was formed in the beginning. But science has lately discovered that light did exist before the sun, and still exists apart from it; and thus has this earlier wisdom fallen into a ruinous mound of folly.

Moreover, reverent and heaven-taught scholarship has found that there was an infinitely wise and beautiful reason for the change in the divine Name in the second chapter of Genesis. In the first chapter the writer is speaking about dead and soulless matter, and it is quite proper that he should thus speak of God as the Creator of matter. In the second chapter he comes to deal with God in direct relation to His children. It is the Father coming to His household. Man in his spiritual nature is now to be created and presented to us in all the tender spiritual relationships which he is to sustain to God, and to his own race. Therefore, it is as a Father that God comes down into human relations with man and reveals His name as Jehovah God, the God of infinite love and tenderness, the God who was about to send His Son, our Lord and Savior Jesus Christ. The very change of name is both a mark of the kindest design and the tenderest proof of love.

Next we see the formation of the human body out of the dust of the earth. Man's form was not created out of nothing. The elements of matter were made from nothing, but man was made out of elements already existing, made however, not by a process of evolution which gradually developed a human being of a higher order, but made immediately a complete human form. It was still lifeless, until God touched it with His divine breath, from His own lips; just as in the vision of Ezekiel, where the picture of the final resurrection shows the body first appearing reorganized in all its constituent parts, "bone to its bone, with flesh and skin to cover them above; but there is no breath in them." There is no evolution here, but the immediate act of creation, succeeded by another act of animation, inspiration, and the divine quickening of the soulless matter into immortal life.

We see here surely, the sacredness of the human body and the value and importance of life. It is the direct work of the Holy Spirit. Therefore, the life of a man is infinitely more precious than the life of a beast; and the crime of murder is recognized by God as a blow struck at God's own life, and one which He will most terribly avenge. The daring act of suicide, therefore, is a defiance of the Creator and a reckless destruction of His grandest work. It is one of the awful signs of our times that not only are men killing others, but that in our public press, one of the leaders of infidelity has been allowed publicly to discuss the question of suicide, and to point out the perfect right of every man to do what he chooses with his own life. It is no wonder that such discussions have been followed by an awful increase of suicides in our midst. Such men are desperate and dreadful criminals who pass red-handed in the very act and crime of rebellion into the presence and up to the judgment seat of God. No man has a right even for an instant to entertain such a thought. Life is God's gift and man's momentous trust, to be used for God and given back to Him at last in the great account.

We see here that human life comes through the human soul, not through the human body, and springs from the direct touch of the Creator and the inspiration of the Almighty. Man's life is not, like the life of the brute, a part of his physical organism. The human organs are complete before they receive the touch of life. Our life came not from the ground, nor from the physical forces and functions, but from the imparting of the human soul through God's direct in-breathing.

Man's life is so sacred, because it is the direct gift of God's love, and the very communication of God's own life. We see the Holy Spirit presented here as the author not only of life, but also of mind and soul. What a glory it gives to our conception of the Holy Ghost, to think of Him as having part in creation! Job says : "Thy Spirit hath garnished the heavens." The glowing stars, the beautiful firmament, the rainbow, the golden sun, the silvery moon, the sunset clouds in all their radiant glory, are but touches of His infinite wisdom and taste. The talents and endowments of the highest minds, the splendid genius of a Homer and a Milton, the refined taste of a Phidias and a Rembrandt, the sublime musical harmonies of a Haydn and a Beethoven, as well as the seraphic and lofty flights of an Isaiah and a John; all these likewise came originally from the Holy Spirit, and all must reflect the higher qualities of wisdom, grace, and glory which constitute His infinite attributes.

True, man has perverted these splendid gifts, and often made them become selfish, unholy, and even diabolical; but they are none the less splendid, and they were no less originally the gifts of the Spirit and the proofs of His wisdom and power. Is it not inspiring to think that this Holy Ghost who fills our heart, is no mere sentiment of spiritual ecstasy or emotional joy, but is the great Mind from which all minds come, the mighty Soul by Whom all souls were made, the Infinite Spirit from whom all being emanated? As we look at the rainbow as it spans the cloud, and the verdure as it crowns the mountain, the fragrant blossoms that hide in every nook, clothe every rock, and smile on every field, let us think that these are only some of His royal robes, revealing to us a little of what His own essential glory means, and making us think : "How beautiful, how glorious, how infinite is the blessed Holy Spirit!"

Brother, sister, He made thy soul, He gave you your mind, He created for Himself and His high purpose your talents and your powers of both brain and being. What are you doing with your trust? What will you say, when He will ask it back, and call upon you to give an account of your stewardship?

We see here the peculiar characteristic of man as originally created. "Man became a living soul." The predominant characteristic of natural man is expressed by this word, "soul," just as the predominant characteristic of the new man in the New Testament is expressed by the word, "spirit." The soul represents the intellectual and emotional elements that constitute man. The spirit represents the higher and the divine life which links us directly to God, and enables us to know and to come into relationship with divine things.

There is no doubt that man, as originally created, had also a higher and spiritual nature, because the true translation of this passage is, "The Lord God breathed into his nostrils the breath of life, and man became a living soul." His life was manifold. There was physical life, mental life, and spiritual life, but the controlling element was soul. So we read in Corinthians, "The first man Adam was made a living soul, the second man Adam was made a quickening Spirit."

It would seem as if, at his fall, man lost his spiritual life, or, at least, it became so utterly subordinated to his soulish nature that the natural man was not spiritual. He needed to be born from above by the Spirit of God, and to receive a new spiritual being, in order to be saved. Even in his highest estate Adam was distinctively a living soul, rather than a lofty spirit. His soul-life was predominant. It was sinless and loyal to God, but it was a lower life than that which redeemed men now enjoy.

It was, notwithstanding, a very glorious life, received as it was by a very significant and glorious touch from the Spirit of God. "The Lord God breathed into his nostrils the breath of life." The Great Artist fashioned his outward form from the finest clay, and perfected every feature and every function; and then, like a fond mother, kissed the cold lips with His own warm breath of life, flashing into the lifeless form the spark of His eternal life, and lo! the beautiful form sprang into His arms, and man became the living child of his loving Creator. It was only a touch of life, a touch of love, that forever separated and distinguished man above all other beings as the special object of God's infinite love and care.

"Lord, what is man? Extremes how wide
In his mysterious nature join;
His flesh to worms and dust allied,
His soul immortal and divine."

Such was the Spirit's work in the original creation of man. Our text suggests, what the New Testament so freely unfolds, the higher work of the Holy Spirit in the new creation. The Lord Jesus in His discourse respecting the new birth, in the third chapter of John, gives us a very significant hint of this work under the same figure which we find in our text. There He introduces the figure of the wind in its invisible, yet mighty energy and potency, in connection with the regeneration of the human soul by the Holy Ghost.

In His closing interviews with the disciples, in the twentieth chapter of John, "He breathed upon them, and said, 'Receive ye the Holy Ghost.'" That picture is so much like the picture of our text that the one seems the complement of the other. In the one case we see the Spirit breathe the old creation into life, and in the other the same Spirit breathes into the new creation the life of God and the power of a higher principle. The figure of the new creation runs through all the Epistles of Paul. "If any man be in Christ Jesus, he is a new creation." "Put on the new man, which after God is created in righteousness and true holiness." "After God" distinctly implies not only resemblance to God, but derivation from God.

Now, what is the work which the Holy Spirit performs in this new creation? Is it simply the restoration of the Adamic nature in perfection, or is it something higher and more divine? Most assuredly it is the latter. "The first man," the apostle tells us, "was of the earth earthy, the second Man was the Lord from heaven; the first man was made a living soul, the second Man a quickening Spirit." Then he adds, "As we have borne the image of the earthly, so shall we also bear the image of the heavenly."

The Adamic life at its best was only a human life. The Christ life is divine. Natural life is soul life. Divine life is Spirit life.

When the New Testament talks about the natural man it does not mean a gross, sordid, sensual, brutal wretch, groveling in swinish lusts; but it means a man with all the graces and gifts of the highest genius and the most refined culture. He may be a poet like Shakespeare, a composer like Mozart, a sculptor like Phidias, a painter like Raphael, an architect like Wren, an orator like Cicero, or a man with a face as beautiful as an angel and a life as virtuous and stainless as a marble statue, and yet be purely natural, earth-born, and merely a soulish man. When the apostle speaks of "the natural man who perceiveth not the things of God, nor can he know them, because they are spiritually discerned," he uses the word "psychical" man. Now everybody knows that Psyche was not the figure of sensualism, but of beauty, virtue, and moral purity.

The spiritual man is entirely distinct from all this. His life ever finds its center in God, and its delight in His will and fellowship. Its sphere of existence is not the earth, but the coming world, the heavenly kingdom. It does not belong here. Its very instincts turn higher. It has its natural affection and qualities; but they have been transformed by death into a higher life and have risen from the old to the new life, from transient to everlasting. It is true by the very nature of things that "they that are of the Spirit do mind the things of the Spirit." As the river runs to the sea, as the fire ascends to the sun,

> "So a soul that's born of God
> Pants to see His glorious face;
> Upward tends to His abode,
> To rest in His embrace."

Thus the chief characteristic of the spiritual man is to have his abode with the Heavenly Spirit. It is not so much the man, as the addition to the man, which constitutes his high character and heavenly power. A spiritual man is not so much a man possessing a strong spiritual character as a man filled with the Holy Spirit. So the apostle says, "Ye are not in the flesh, but in the Spirit, if so be that the Spirit of God dwelleth in you."

The glory of the new creation, then, is not only that it recreates the human spirit, but also that it fits it for the abode of God Himself, and makes it dependent upon Him for its life, just as the flower is dependent upon the sun, and the child upon the mother. The highest spirituality, therefore, is the most utter helplessness, the most entire dependence, and the most complete possession by the Holy Spirit. The beautiful act of Christ in breathing upon His disciples, and imparting to them from His own lips the very Spirit that was already in Him, expressed in the most vivid manner the crowning glory of the new creation. When the Holy Spirit thus possesses us, He fills every part of our being. Our spirit is His central throne, our soul is under His control, and even our body becomes "the temple of the Holy Ghost." We may be sanctified wholly, that is, in the whole man; and our whole "spirit, soul, and body preserved blameless unto the coming of Jesus Christ."

The final stage of this glorious indwelling will be reached when the vision of Ezekiel is fulfilled, and the Spirit shall breathe into the resurrection body the life of glorious immortality. "And we shall be like Him when we shall see Him as He is."

There are some lessons which we may learn from this picture and from the whole subject.

1. The lower is dependent upon the higher, and should be kept subordinate to it. Man's physical frame was lifeless until his higher nature, the soul, entered it; and then he lived. So, still, our life is dependent upon our higher being; and life and health come not from below, but from above and from within. This is the essential principle of divine healing, founded as it is on the great law of creation, and expressed by Christ Himself in His answer to the tempter, about His own physical life and ours, "Man shall

not live by bread alone, but by every word that passeth out of the mouth of God."

Our higher spiritual nature should control the soul. Just as the soul is superior to the body, so the spirit should be predominant to the soul. The fatal defect of natural life is that the soul is predominant, and the natural mind controls both spirit and body. The cultivated Athenian, therefore, is just as much in the flesh as the brutal African savage. The true life is where the body and the soul are under the control of the spirit, and the spirit is under the control of the Holy Ghost, the indwelling Spirit and Life of God.

2. The beautiful figure of the breath and the air teaches us some practical lessons about the receiving of the Holy Spirit. It is a simple law of nature, that air always comes in to fill a vacuum. You can produce a draft at any time, by heating the air until it ascends, and then letting the cold air rush in to supply its place. Thus we can always be filled with the Holy Spirit by providing a vacuum. This breath is dependent upon exhausting the previous breath before you can inhale a fresh one. We must in like manner empty our hearts of the last breath of the Holy Spirit that we have received; for it becomes impure the moment we have received it, and we need a new supply to prevent spiritual asphyxia.

We must learn the secret of breathing out, as well as breathing in. Now the breathing in will continue if the other part is rightly done. One of the best ways to make room for the Holy Spirit is to recognize that the needs that come into the life as vacuums are for Him to fill. We will find plenty of needs all around us to be filled; and, as we pour out our lives in holy service, He will pour His Life in, in full measure.

A board of trustees once put a heating apparatus into a church, and then put in a furnace, and announced the opening service. But the church was as cold as a barn. The hot air would not come in, although the ducts were open and the fire burning at its hottest. An expert was called in, who quietly told them that while they had made provision for letting in the fresh air, they had made none for letting out the old air in the building, and that no fresh air could come in until the old air was expelled. As a result the people sat there shivering.

Thus some of us are shivering and wondering why the Holy Spirit does not fill us. We have plenty coming in, but we do not give it out. Give out the blessing you have; start larger plans for service and blessing. You will soon find that the Holy Ghost is before you, and that He will present you with blessings for goodness and will give you all that He can trust you to give away to others.

There is a beautiful fact in nature which has its spiritual parallels. There is no music so heavenly as that of an Eolian harp. This harp is nothing but a set of musical cords arranged in harmony, and then left to be touched by the unseen fingers of the wandering winds. As the breath of heaven floats over the chords, it is said that notes almost divine float out upon the air, as if a choir of angels were wandering around and touching the strings.

It is possible to keep our hearts so open to the touch of the Holy Spirit that He can play upon them at will. As we quietly wait in the pathway of His service, again and again the touch of hands unseen will wake the echoes, and the heavenly song will spring within the depths of our being, and we shall wonder at our strange gladness. But it is still the Eolian harp of a heart wholly consecrated and attuned to God, and under the touch and breathing of the Holy Ghost.

This is what it means, "The Lord thy God in the midst of thee is mighty; He will save, He will rest in His love, He will joy over thee with singing."

## Chapter 3

## The Sword of the Spirit

"So He drove out the man; and He placed at the east of the Garden of Eden Cherubim, and a flaming sword which turned every way, to keep the way of the tree of life."—Genesis 3: 24. "And the Sword of the Spirit, which is the Word of God."—Eph. 6: 17. "For the Word of God is quick and powerful, and sharper than any two-edged sword, piercing even to the dividing asunder of soul and spirit, and of the joints and marrow, and is a discerner of the thoughts and intents of the heart."—Hebrews 4: 12.

We are accustomed to think of this scene at the gate of Eden as a picture of terror and judgment. Cowering under their awful curse, the fugitive pair stand in the front of the picture, hurrying forth from their happy Eden home, to return no more; while behind them, and above the gate that was closing upon them forever, a fiery sword flashes with angry severity, to keep the way of the tree of life from which they are henceforth to be debarred, as they go forth on their sorrowful journey to the grave.

But as we take a second look at that glorious symbol, it assumes a brighter phase; until, after a little while, we learn to behold it as a symbol of grace, and not of judgment. Doubtless it so became to them, and ere long, the very symbol of the divine presence that marked the place of worship where they came to meet with their covenant God at the gate of Eden.

The figure of the cherubim, which appears for the first time in this chapter, becomes in the later Scriptures the very signal of God's covenant love and manifested presence. We see it in the tabernacle of the wilderness above the mercy-seat. We see it in the visions of Isaiah and Ezekiel in connection with the throne of God. And it reappears in the Apocalypse in the vision of heavenly glory.

It was doubtless a type of the Lord Jesus Christ, or, at least, a symbol of His person and glory. The four faces of the lion, the ox, the eagle, and the man, represent His kingliness, His sacrifice, His humanity, and His Deity; and the four Gospels of Matthew, Mark, Luke, and John are just an unfolding of His person in these four glorious aspects.

As this figure appeared at the gate of their lost Eden, it became to our first parents the symbol of Him, the promised seed of the woman, in whom that lost inheritance was to be restored and that forfeited paradise regained. It did not mean that the tree of life was lost forever; but rather it pointed out the new way by which that tree could be restored again, restored by way of the cherubim, through the redeeming work of the Lord Jesus Christ.

BUT WHAT ABOUT THE SWORD?

The sword was the token and emblem of the Holy Spirit, even as the cherubim was the figure of Christ. The word in the Hebrew is, The Lord God Shekinah, the cherubim, the flaming sword. This was the same Shekinah that afterward appeared in the Holy of Holies. This flaming sword, therefore, was nothing else than the special symbol of God's immediate presence with the Holy Ghost.

It was the symbol, therefore, of grace rather than of judgment; and while it involved essentially the principle of the divine righteousness, which could no longer permit a sinful race to partake of the tree of life in the old way, yet it also pointed forward to the coming redemption and the provision through Jesus Christ which was to open those gates of mercy even to sinful men through the blood of Jesus and the renewing grace of the Holy Spirit.

The flaming sword at the gate of Eden was the embryo of the cross. It emphasized the great truth that judgment must come before mercy, that death must be the gate to life, and that the old natural life must fall before the piercing sword, ere we can enter through the gates of the new paradise, and partake of the tree of life, that life that is incorruptible and everlasting.

I.

It represents the slaying power of the Spirit. The sword is the symbol of death, and death is the deepest revelation of Christ's great salvation. The grave is forever the symbol of the Gospel, and the Cross means not only His death, but ours too. Therefore Satan hated it, and tried to make Peter reject it, as he cried, "Pity Thyself, Lord"; but Jesus refused it, and told him his thought was born of Satan.

The reason men try to get the Cross and the Blood out of their new Gospel is because they have a shrewd suspicion that as there was a cross for Him, so there must also be a cross for them; but in no other way can we enter into life everlasting. All that is born of the flesh is flesh, and under the curse. Every fragment and fibre of the natural life is evil. You may coax it, you may flatter it, and it will smile upon you; but some day, if you cross its will, it will spring upon you and strike you.

Therefore, the sentence of death has passed upon all the Adam race, and the fiery sword must destroy every vestige of the old humanity before the new life can enter in and partake of that life-giving tree which stands behind the glorious cherubim.

And this is the work of the Holy Spirit, to put to death the life of self and sin. We cannot do it, He alone can. We may try to crucify ourselves and mutilate ourselves with a thousand blows; but every time we will succeed in just missing a vital part, and the old 'I' will come through the process, all alive still. Only the flaming sword can smite to death the self-centered, self-destroying life of the natural man. We, therefore, read in the eighth of Romans, "If ye through the Spirit do mortify the deeds of the body, ye shall live."

We see this truth foreshadowed through the whole Old Testament. The destruction of the race by the flood was but a figure. The Apostle Peter says of the true baptism, "The like figure whereunto baptism doth also now save us, by the resurrection of Jesus Christ." Therefore, the apostle intimates that the eight souls who passed through the waters of the flood were saved by water, not from water.

The flood that destroyed and swept away the ungodly race that was engulfing everything in corruption, was God's merciful judgment, sending salvation through destruction. God Himself had said, "The end of all flesh is come before me." The deluge was just the death and burial of the great putrid carcase of corrupt flesh into which humanity had ripened.

The sacrifice on Mount Moriah was another foreshadowing of the life that comes through self-surrender. The sufferings of Joseph were the very pathway to his elevation and coronation. The passage through the Red Sea was Israel's baptism of death. The death of the first-born and the destruction of Egypt's host in the same flood emphasized and vivified the same picture. And the redemption of Israel's firstborn was God's own striking figure of the fact that the whole nation was accounted dead, and saved as from the dead.

Before Israel could enter Canaan, the old generation was left in Egypt to die, and a new race passed through the gates of Kadesh. The passage of the Jordan was but the type of deeper death. The death of Moses and the succession of Joshua who alone could bring them into the promised land, still further emphasized the death-side of their higher inheritance and ours.

The circumcision was the figure of God's death-stroke upon our natural life. All the types of the canonical law were touched by the death-mark. Through the blood of burnt offerings, sin offerings, and peace offerings, the Hebrew worshippers and the Aaronic priests entered into their place of privilege and acceptance.

The cleansing of the leper was accompanied by the touching figure of the death of the little bird and the sprinkling of its blood upon the wing of its companion. The two were the parable of God's cleansing of the sinful heart of man. Even the razor must cut off the last hair of his natural strength before he could pass in among the worshippers. And in the ordinance of the red heifer, not only the scarlet wool that was the figure of sin, but also the little hyssop which represented our natural life and the finest tendrils of its strength and beauty, must be consumed with the burning heifer.

Not only must "the grass wither, but the flower of the grass must perish, because the Spirit of the Lord bloweth upon it." The death sentence must be executed against the beauty and the blossom, as well as against the grossness and the sensuality of the natural life.

Even the very best things become a curse to us so long as we hold them with our natural hands and hearts and self-centered spirits. That sweet and innocent child whom God has taught you to love, can be only an idol until he ceases to be your child, and becomes God's child, and the death stroke passes upon your love, and you learn in the resurrection life to hold him for God, and love him not as a selfish pleasure but as a sacred trust.

Even the husband into whose strong hand God may have put your trusting little hand, may become but a substitute for your God, and a separating influence from Him, until you die to your own selfish affection, and learn to love him not for your own gratification, or his, but in God and unto God and for his own highest good.

Money cannot hurt you if you do not love it for its own sake. It is not your fortune that hurts you, but your clinging fondness for it; and so long as that fondness is alive, your little world of five hundred dollars a year is as much a hindrance to you as would be a millionaire's palaces and vast investments. It is not the size of your world that God sees, but the extent to which it fills your heart.

Even your Christian influence, your reputation as a worker for God, and your standing among your brethren, may be to you an idol that must die, before you can be free to live for Him alone.

If you have ever noticed the type on a printed page, you must have seen that the little "i" has always a dot over it, and that this dot elevates it above the other letters in the line.

Now, each of us is a little 'i'; and over every one of us there is a little dot of self-importance, self-will, self-interest, self-confidence, self-complacency, or something to which we cling and for which we contend, which just as surely reveals self-life as if it were a mountain of real importance.

This 'i' is a rival of Jesus Christ, an enemy of the Holy Ghost, and of our peace and life. Therefore, God has decreed its death, and the Holy Spirit, with His flaming sword, is waiting to destroy it, that we may be able to enter through the gates and come to the Tree of Life.

How can this be accomplished?

We must ourselves consent to it. We must recognize the true character of our self-life and the real quality of the evil thing. We must consent to its destruction, and we ourselves must take it as Abraham did Isaac, and lay it at the feet of God in willing sacrifice. This is a hard work for the natural heart; but the moment the will has been yielded and the choice has been made, that death is past; the agony is over, and we are astonished to find that the death is accomplished.

Usually the crisis of life in such cases hangs upon a single point. God does not need to strike us in a hundred places to inflict a death wound. There is one point that touches the heart, and that is the point God usually strikes, the dearest thing in our life, the decisive thing in our plans, the citadel of the will, the center of the heart. When we yield there, there is little left to yield anywhere else; and when we refuse to yield at this point, a spirit of evasion and compromise enters into all the rest of our life.

The man or woman who has honestly and entirely met God at the decisive point will always be found uncompromising and thorough at every other crisis; and the man or woman who has begun with a half-surrendered will always has a reservation up to the end of the chapter, unless he meets with God at some later point and begins where he ought to have begun before.

The cause of Saul's ruin was his unwillingness to obey God

and yield up Agag and Amalek to death. Saul carried out the divine commission through every chapter but one. He fought his battles bravely, he managed his campaigns skillfully, he subdued Amalek, he captured Agag, he left no point in the possession of the enemy; but he kept the best of the spoil and the life of the king for his own gratification, pretending that he did it for the worship of God.

This was the cause of his ruin. Old Samuel gave to the ages to come an object lesson of what God meant when he took his great broadsword and hewed Agag to pieces before the king, and told his cowardly master "that obedience is better than sacrifice, and to hearken than the fat of rams."

At one time when we talked with a dear friend who had been struggling for years to enter into a satisfactory spiritual experience, she told us how disappointed and unsatisfied her heart was. As we looked at her earnest face it seemed to us that there must be something in the way, and we asked her if there were not some reservation in her entire consecration. We did not need to wait for the answer for it bespoke itself. We then asked her if she would not be brave enough to let the last cord go, to give herself unreservedly to Christ at any cost, and especially to let go the thing that she shrank most at the thought of surrendering. She looked so sadly in our face, and answered, "I have not the courage."

Alas! it is the old and oft-repeated story; and yet those cowardly hearts who shrink from God's gentle sword will yet have to bear sufferings inconceivably more severe, and to be pierced with sorrows that make one's heart ache even to think of. The brave heart that dares to die once for all and forever is the wise heart, the happy heart, the heart that finds "the yoke easy and the burden light."

Beloved, will you dare to die, or rather to yield unto death that thing in your heart, your life, your will, which constitutes the strength of your natural life, and the axis around which all your being is enfolded?

Having yielded yourself unto death, you must next believe that God accepts you, and that the Holy Ghost undertakes the work, and really accomplishes it. The command of the Scriptures is very simple and explicit at this point, "Reckon yourselves dead indeed unto sin, but alive unto God, through Jesus Christ our Lord."

This act is purely a matter of faith. Faith and sight always differ to such an extent that, while to your senses it does not seem to be so, your faith must still reckon it as true. This is a very difficult attitude to hold, and only as we thoroughly believe God, can we thus reckon upon His Word and His Working. As we do so, however, faith will convert it into fact, and it will be even so.

These two words, "yield"and "reckon,"are passwords into the resurrection life. They are like the two edges of the "Sword of the Spirit" through which we enter into crucifixion with Christ.

This act of surrender and this reckoning of faith are recognized in the New Testament as marking a very definite crisis in the spiritual life. It does not mean that we are expected to be going through a continual dying, but that there should be one very definite act of dying, and then a constant habit of reckoning ourselves as dead and meeting everything from this standpoint.

In the sixth chapter of Romans, the apostle takes the position that we are to meet God as those that are alive from the dead, and thus enjoy the benefit of an accomplished act of crucifixion. Once for all we are to hand over our sin, our self, and all our belongings to the Holy Ghost; and henceforth, whatever comes up in us, we are to reckon it as no longer a part of ourselves, but to steadily refuse to recognize it, and count it simply as a temptation. Thus we shall have power to overcome it, and shall be able to maintain our consciousness of purity and victory unmoved.

As any evil comes up, and the consciousness of any unholy thing touches our inner senses, it is our privilege at once to hand it over to the Holy Ghost and to lay it upon Jesus, as something already crucified with Him; and as of old, in the case of the sin offering, it will be carried without the camp and burned to ashes.

There may be deep suffering, there may be protracted pain, it may be intensely real; but throughout all there will be a very sweet and sacred sense of God's presence, of intense purity in our whole spirit, and of our separation from the evil which is being consumed. Truly, it will be borne without the camp, so that even the smell of the burning will not defile the holy sanctuary of the consecrated heart; and we shall come out of the fire without even the smell of the flames upon our garments.

It is so blessed to have the Holy Spirit slay things. No sword but His can pass so perfectly between us and the evil, so that it consumes the sin without touching the spirit. Just as the skillful surgeon, with brave heart and keen instrument, can pass between the arteries and veins with such exquisite delicacy that no fibre is severed, and no injury done to a single organ, so the blessed Holy Spirit, and He alone, can separate the evil from the good, and "pierce even to the dividing asunder of soul and spirit, and of the joints and marrow."

II.

This brings us to the searching power of the Holy Spirit, for this fiery sword is a heart-searching weapon as well as a sin-destroying power. Undoubtedly the passage in the fourth chapter of Hebrews already quoted, refers to this ancient figure. "The Word of God is quick and powerful, and sharper than any two-edged sword, piercing even to the dividing asunder of soul and spirit, and of the joints and marrow, and is a discerner of the thoughts and intents of the heart; neither is there any creature that is not manifest in his sight."

There is a strong and subtle power in electric fire to search out and discriminate between substances and detect abnormal and unwholesome conditions. When the electric sponge passes over the human frame, it leaves no sensation in the healthful places; but if there is disease anywhere it will cling to the spot and seem to search it out and penetrate it with a subtle touch, often with the keenest pain.

In like manner the Holy Ghost passes through those portions of our being that are right and pure, without any sense of resistance, or, perhaps, without any sensation whatever. He has such free course that He just seems to blend with our own consciousness. But when He comes to anything wrong, there is immediate resistance; and as He presses His hand upon it, there is intense suffering. The sword of the Spirit is searching out the evil and compelling it to declare itself, just as the skirmishing companies in the advance guard of the army, by their firing and their feint attacks, bring out the foe and compel him to show his position. The greatest hindrance to our spiritual life and progress is found in the disguise of the enemy and the deception of our own nature. The evil cannot be crucified until it is recognized, diagnosed, brought into the light, and delivered over to death.

Self clothes itself in so many disguises that nothing but the piercing sword of the Holy Spirit and the Holy Scriptures can compel it to take its true place, and own its evil character. Some one has said that it is half the battle of life to call things by their true names. The Holy Spirit searches out our sins, and He finds sin in many places where our own self-complacency would never have suspected it. Not only does He detect and condemn the grosser forms of immorality and disobedience, which have to deal directly with the ten commandments and the law of righteousness; but He brings us face to face with the law of love, and shows us that even the unkindly thought is murder, the unforgiving spirit is an unpardonable sin, the habit of living to ourselves rebellion against God, and a selfish motive, even in the holiest act, a soul-defiling sin.

He brings us face to face with the law of faith, and shows us that to doubt God is a crime, to treasure an anxious care for the morrow is wickedness, to pray in unbelief is to take the name of God in vain, and, in short, that "whatever is not of faith is sin." He takes us through the realm of truth and error. He gives us the touchstone whereby we detect the false, and learn to answer even Satan's quotation of Scripture by Christ's own weapon, "It is written again."

He discriminates between the false peace and the true, the earthly and the incorruptible joy, the love that is purely a natural instinct and the charity that is Christ's love, which never fails, the zeal of Jehu, which is but a selfish passion, and the holy zeal that burns as strongly when no man approves, and stands as firmly when it costs us our very life as when it leads us to a throne. He discriminates between the false and the true worship, the prayer prompted by the Holy Spirit to the Father who seeth in secret, and the religious emotion which is kindled in the aesthetic nature by an eloquent sermon, a pathetic story, a sentimental appeal, or a sublime musical symphony which may bring tears to the eyes while the heart is as hard as adamant to God and our fellow-men.

He shows us the difference between true and false submission and the weakness that yields to sickness and Satan. On the other hand, He shows us the true patience that lovingly bows to the will of God, but refuses the weights that the adversary would put upon us.

He leads us to pray with the Psalmist, "Search me, O God, and know my heart; try me and know my thoughts; and see if there be any wicked way in me, and lead me in the way everlasting." He gives us that perfect abandonment of spirit which makes us willing to be searched and glad to be laid open to the eye of God, and to cry, "See if there be in me any way of grief," as the margin reads, or "any way of pain," as the new version renders it. It makes us glad to be sanctified from not only the wicked but also the earthly thing, and to be so separated from all self-life that every way of pain shall be prevented, and everything in us that could hurt us will be subdued. Thus shall we be enabled not only to lay aside the sin that so easily besets us, but every weight that would so lightly hold us back.

The blessed Holy Spirit, who possesses the consecrated heart, is intensely concerned for our highest life, and watches us with a sensitive, and even a jealous love. Very beautiful is the true translation of that ordinary passage in the Epistle of James, "The Spirit that dwelleth in us loveth us to jealousy." The heart of the Holy Ghost is intensely concerned in preserving us from every stain and blemish, and bringing us into the very highest possibilities of the will of God. The Heavenly Bridegroom would have His Church free not only from every spot, but also from "every wrinkle, or any such thing." The spot is the mark of sin, but the wrinkle is the sign of weakness, age, and decay. He wants no such defacing touch upon the holy features of His Beloved. Therefore, the Holy Ghost, who is the Executor of His will, and the divine Messenger whom He sends to call, separate, and bring home His Bride, is jealously concerned in fulfilling in us all the Master's will, and is ever searching us through and through, with more and more tenderness, and with the most earnest solicitude, to find out every hidden fault and every unsupplied lack, and to bring us up into the fullness of the stature of spiritual manhood and entire preparation for the marriage of the Lamb.

Will we welcome His loving scrutiny and His faithful care? Will we cry, "Search me, 0 God, search me and know my heart, Search me and try me in the hidden part; Cleanse me and make me holy as Thou art, and lead me in the way everlasting."

THE SUBDUING POWER OF THE HOLY SPIRIT.

The Holy Ghost is God's Executive not only for the salvation and sanctification of His people, but for the conviction of sinners and the judgment of wicked men, the destruction of the enemies of God, and the final punishment of the devil and his angels. This sword is God's weapon for slaying the proud and willful sinner and laying him at the feet of mercy. We can entertain and interest men, but only the Holy Ghost can convict them of sin, and pierce them to the heart with profound and soul-saving conviction. We are so glad that there is One who bears this mighty sword, and uses it through His Holy Word, when faithfully presented, to break the sinner's heart and bring him to the feet of Jesus.

But the Holy Spirit is also God's mighty hand to avenge His honor against the wicked, and punish those who disobey Him and harm His people. The same power that struck down Ananias and Sapphira in Pentecostal days is still in the church and the world; and wherever God's presence is, there, in a remarkable degree, His judgments are made known. It is a very solemn thing to presume against the Holy Ghost. He is the author of human life, and in a moment He can take it away. "If I whet my glittering sword, and my hand take hold on judgment," God Himself has said, "Who is he that can deliver out of my hand?" That is a true and awful word : "Vengeance is mine, I will repay, saith the Lord," and again, "Defraud not one another, for God is the avenger of all such." I would not like to have orphan children and widowed wives cry out against me to God. I would not like to have the little hand of wronged and innocent children pleading to heaven for my punishment. I would not like to have to meet that tremendous sentence, after a life of reckless evil-speaking against the servants of God, "Touch not mine anointed, and do my prophets no harm." I would rather play with the forked lightning, or take in my hands living wires with their fiery current, than speak a reckless word against any servant of Christ, or idly repeat the slanderous darts which thousands of Christians are hurling on others, to the hurt of their own souls and bodies.

You may often wonder, perhaps, why your sickness is not healed, your spirit filled with the joy of the Holy Ghost, or your life blessed and prosperous. It may be that some dart which you have flung with angry voice, or in an idle hour of thoughtless gossip, is pursuing you on its returning way, as it describes the circle which always brings back to the source from which it came every shaft of bitterness, and every idle and evil word. Let us remember that when we persecute or hurt the children of God, we are but persecuting Him, and hurting ourselves far more.

Finally, there is an hour coming, in which "the Lord with his sore and great and strong sword shall punish Leviathan, the piercing serpent, even leviathan, that crooked servant; and He shall slay the dragon that is in the sea." Then even Satan himself will feel the sharp and fiery force of that flaming sword, which he saw for the first time in its awful gleam, as he went out from Eden's gate with the fearful crime of man's destruction upon his head, and the tremendous curse which that fiery sword is yet to execute. That hour has not yet fully come; but even yet, thank

God, that Blessed Holy Spirit is here to resist and to overcome the power of the destroyer.

He was Christ's strength and defense in the conflict in the wilderness, and He Himself has said, "When the enemy cometh in like a flood, the Spirit of the Lord will lift up a standard against him."

There are some things that only God can wither; and it is very blessed that, in connection with the only miracle of judgment that Christ performed, the withering of the fig tree, He gave to us His strongest lesson touching upon human faith, and told us that we might claim such faith as would wither the barren fig tree, and destroy the powers of evil that were too strong for us.

It is blessed to have a God who knows how not only to cleanse and purify us, but to destroy our spiritual foes, and to deal even with our human adversaries. "Our God is a consuming fire, and the Lord shall judge His people." If we could only realize what those tremendous words mean, "Our God is a consuming fire," we should feel so sorry for the man who wrongs us, that we should wish him no evil, but would tremble at the thought of his judgment. We would get down upon our knees and plead with God to have mercy upon him.

Beloved, let us pass through this flaming sword without a reservation. Then we shall not only be fearless of its power to harm us, but it will be our mighty weapon against every adversary and every evil, and the power of our aggressive warfare for the service of men and the triumph of our Master's Kingdom.

## Chapter 4

## The Pillar of Cloud and Fire

"And the Lord went before them by day in a pillar of cloud, to lead them the way; and by night in a pillar of fire, to give them light; to go by day and night: he took not away the pillar of the cloud by day, nor the pillar of fire by night, from before the people." Exodus 13: 21, 22.

"And the Angel of God, which went before the camp of Israel, removed and went behind them; and the pillar of cloud went from before their face, and stood behind them: and it came between the camp of the Egyptians and the camp of Israel; and it was a cloud of darkness to them, but it gave light by night to these: so that the one came not near the other all night." Exodus 14: 19, 20.

"Then a cloud covered the tent of the congregation, and the glory of the Lord filled the tabernacle. And Moses was not able to enter into the tent of the congregation, because the cloud abode thereon, and the glory of the Lord filled the tabernacle. And when the cloud was taken up from over the tabernacle, the children of Israel went onward in all their journeys: but if the cloud were not taken up then they journeyed not till the day that it was taken up. For the cloud of the Lord was upon the tabernacle by day, and the fire was on it by night, in the sight of all the house of Israel, throughout all their journeys." Exodus 40: 34-38.

"And the cloud of the Lord was upon them by day, when they went out of the camp. And it came to pass, when the ark set forward, that Moses said, 'Rise up, Lord, and let Thine enemies be scattered, and let them that hate Thee flee before Thee.' And when it rested, he said, 'Return, 0 Lord, unto the many thousands of Israel.'" Numbers 10: 34, 36.

"Moreover, Moreover, brethren, I would not that ye should be ignorant, how that all our fathers were under the cloud, and all passed through the sea; and were all baptized unto Moses in the cloud and in the sea. " 1 Corinthians 10: 1, 2.

The application to the Holy Spirit of these beautiful passages, and of the sublime figure that runs through all of them, is rendered certain by the words of the prophet Isaiah, in the sixty-third chapter. "In all their affliction He was afflicted, and the angel of His presence saved them: in His love and in His pity He redeemed them: and He bare them, and carried them all the days of old. But they rebelled, and vexed His Holy Spirit: therefore He was turned to be their enemy, and He fought against them. Then He remembered the days of old, Moses, and his people, saying, Where is He that brought them up out of the sea with the shepherd of his flock? Where is He that put His Holy Spirit within him? That led them by the right hand of Moses with His glorious arm, dividing the water before them, to make Himself an everlasting name? That led them through the deep, as an horse in the wilderness, that they should not stumble? As a beast goeth down into the valley, the Spirit of the Lord caused him to rest: so didst Thou lead Thy people, to make Thyself a glorious name."

The prophet expressly recognizes the Holy Spirit as the presence who dwelt in the midst of Israel, and led them through the Red Sea and the wilderness. The figure under which He is represented in these passages is striking and sublime. It was customary for ancient armies, when marching through a foreign country, to be led, especially by night, by great illuminations of torches and beacons carried in front of the advancing host, and rising in the darkness with lurid smoke and flame. It would not, therefore, be altogether surprising for the host of Israel to see in front the majestic signal of the pillar of cloud and fire; and yet, this was no merely human beacon light. With a majesty unearthly and divine, it reared its fiery column to the sky, and marched, like a mighty sentinel, before the host, pausing when they were to rest, moving when they were to advance, separating them from their foes, and sometimes spreading its folds like the canopy of a great celestial tent about their heads, and sheltering them from the fiery heat of the desert, sun.

1. It was a supernatural symbol. They were to be guided henceforth by Jehovah Himself. This was their peculiar distinction, that "the Lord alone did lead them." This was the place where Moses was interceding for them with God. "Wherein shall we be distinct from all the other people of the earth, except Thou go with us," and His gracious answer was, "My presence shall go with you and I will give you rest." The pillar of cloud and fire did not represent even an angel's guidance and guardianship. It was the sign of God's own presence.

In the same way the Church of the living God has a supernatural leadership. The Christian has a divine guide. Our holy Christianity is not a collection of wise human opinions, and an organization combining the strongest forces of human wisdom and power. It is nothing, if it is not divine. Give us a supernatural religion, or none at all.

The church of the Apostles was a living miracle, and so should the church of the nineteenth century be. Anything less and anything else is a disappointment to God and to every true man. Not with such transcendent portents as in days of old does He now appear. But none the less real are His living presence and His mighty working in the hearts of His people and in the events of His providence. Why should God be less real and glorious today than in the days of Moses, the triumphs of Joshua, and the miracles of Pentecost? Let us send up to Him the heartfelt prayer, "Awake, O arm of the Lord, as in the days of old!" And let us hear in answer, His own summons to us: "Awake, awake, put on thy strength, O Zion, thy beautiful garments, O Jerusalem!"

2. The pillar of cloud and fire was a source of light, of truth and guidance to His people. Barbaric superstition delights in the wonderful, but divine power manifests itself in the practical and the useful. God wants not to play with us, as a magician with his

wondering audience, but to guide us as a shepherd would his flock. Because He wants to give us His life, His Word has little to say about subjects that appeal principally to our curiosity, but speaks mainly to the intelligence, the understanding, and the heart.

The Holy Ghost comes not to give us extraordinary manifestations, but to give us life and light. The nearer we come to Him, the more simple will His illumination and leading be. He comes to "guide us into all truth." He comes to shed light upon our own hearts, and to show us ourselves. He comes to reveal Christ, to give, and then to illumine the Holy Scriptures, and to make divine realities vivid and clear to our spiritual apprehension. He comes as a Spirit of wisdom and revelation in the knowledge of Christ, to "enlighten the eyes of our understanding, that we may know what is the hope of his calling, and what the riches of the glory of his inheritance in the saints, and what is the exceeding greatness of his power to us-ward who believe, according to the working of his mighty power."

Without Him there is no true light. These holy mysteries, these divine realities which to us are so dear, are incomprehensible to the most intelligent human minds. Two men sitting side by side hear the same truths, read the same words, live under the same religious influences. To the one they are uninteresting and unreal, while to the other they are his very life. As of old, when the same cloud was light to Israel, and darkness to the Egyptians, "so that they came not near each other all the night," so still it is true that "the natural man perceiveth not the things of the Spirit of God, neither indeed can he know them, for they are spiritually discerned; but he that is spiritual searcheth all things, yea, the deep things of God."

3. As it was a pillar of cloud as well as of light, so, as we have seen, the Holy Ghost is as dark to the unbeliever as He is light to the saint. The things of God are as dark to the world as they are beautiful and plain to the true disciple. And even to God's children there is an element of cloud, as well as luminousness.

There is a veiled light which is as necessary sometimes as the unclouded sun. The Holy Ghost is given to reveal many things to us, "but we cannot bear them now." He reserves His deeper teachings until we can stand them and understand them. We do not always see our way, and it is better that we do not. We must learn, as well as trust, even in the cloud. The very highest lessons on faith are taught by the veiled light, and the way we cannot understand. "I will lead them by the way they know not," is still His word to every trusting child; but He always adds, "These things will I do unto them, and not forsake them."

The presence of clouds upon your sky, and trials in your path, is the very best evidence that you are following the pillar of cloud, and walking in the presence of God. They had to enter the cloud before they could behold the glory of the transfiguration. A little later that same cloud became the chariot to receive the ascending Lord, and it is still waiting as the chariot that will bring His glorious appearing. Still it is true that while "clouds and darkness are round about His throne," mercy and truth are ever in their midst, and shall go before His face.

Perhaps the most beautiful and gracious use of the cloud was to shelter them from the fiery sun. Like a great umbrella, that majestic pillar spread its canopy above the camp, and became a shielding shadow from the burning heat in the treeless desert. No one who has never felt an oriental sun can fully appreciate how much this means, a shadow from the heat. So the Holy Spirit comes between us and the fiery, scorching rays of sorrow and temptation, and under His shadow we sit and sing:

"All my hope on Thee is stayed,
All my help from Thee I bring;
Cover my defenseless head
With the shadow of Thy wing."

4. It was a pillar of fire. Fire is more than light. It not only

illumines, it warms, it purifies, it destroys. It is the same Holy Ghost who baptizes with water and with fire, but it is not the same measure of the baptism. The baptism of fire is a baptism that penetrates the inmost fibers of our being, consuming the old life, cleansing and quickening our entire being, and enduing us with power from on high. God wants to bring every one of us to such a place, that we shall not fear the fire, because everything combustible will have been consumed.

5. The pillar went before them. They saw it first in front of them, far off, and far above them. It came to them first when they were in Egypt, and it led them out of the land of bondage.

And so the Holy Spirit comes to us even in our life of sin, and leads us out of the world to Christ, and to begin our pilgrimage toward our Promised Land. The presence of the Holy Ghost in His first manifestation is distant, and we shrink, perhaps, from His closer touch. We know Him as One that brings to us the knowledge of God, the message of Christ, and the hope of salvation, and guides us in our first steps into Christian life; but we have not yet come to know Him as our indwelling Guest and our everlasting Comforter.

6. The pillar of cloud came closer to them, passed through the camp, and baptized them in its very presence, and then passed and stood behind them. This was as they went through the waters of the Red Sea. When that hour of peril came, and they walked down by faith into what seemed a living death, then their glorious Guide came nearer to their trembling hearts, enfolded them in His very arms, and then stood behind them like a wall of defense against their foes. Thus when we step out in living faith, and cross the Red Sea which separates us from our past and sinful life, and we go down into the waters of death with Jesus, the Holy Spirit comes nigher and baptizes us with His very touch and presence.

The baptism of water, which is the type of death, is significant of the baptism of the Holy Ghost. When Jesus went down into the Jordan and received baptism at the hands of John, "He saw the heavens opened, and the Spirit, like a dove descending, and it abode upon Him." And the promise of the Spirit, in Acts was connected with baptism. "Repent and be baptized, every one of you in the name of Jesus Christ, for the remissions of sins, and ye shall receive the gift of the Holy Ghost." So we read that "they were all baptized unto Moses in the cloud and in the sea." As they stepped into the Red Sea, the heavenly cloud enwrapped its folds around them, and they were immersed in both baptisms. Probably at the moment when the cloud passed through the midst of the camp, they were less conscious of its presence than they had been when it stood in the front.

So when we pass into the cloud we are not conscious of it. All we are conscious of is mist and darkness, so that, frequently, when we receive the Holy Ghost we are not directly conscious of what is occurring. We are, perhaps, so plunged in darkness, so consumed with hunger and desire, and so constantly reaching out to God that we do not realize our own condition. All the better, should it be so. A friend said to me the other day, "I am so hungry. I so long for the baptism of the Holy Ghost." I asked him, "Who made you so hungry? Who gave you this longing? It was the very Holy Ghost. He is already with you in the shadow-side of the blessing, and He who gave the capacity for the appetite is Himself near to meet it and satisfy it."

7. The pillar stood behind them. The Holy Spirit is ever our rearguard. He takes our past and hides it from us. Behind them lay Egypt and the Egyptians, all the past with its sin and its shame, and all their adversaries. Thus the Holy Ghost shuts us off from all that we have been, and from all that can come against us. Oh, how blessed it is, to put Him between you and your sins, between you and your troubles, between you and your enemies, between you and your memories, and to have Him for your glorious rearward!

8. The pillar of cloud and fire, a little later, came and dwelt within them. There came a day — and it was an era in their history — when a very wonderful change occurred in the position of that pillar. It was the first day of the first month, in the second

year of their history. They had just completed the erection of the tabernacle, that simple and divinely planned little sanctuary, which was God's perfect pattern and type of the Church and the individual saint. Every board, tache, loop, and curtain had been finished and placed according to God's precise command. Every article of furniture was in its place, and they simply took their hands off, and gave it God, anointing it with oil, as the symbol of the Holy Spirit's receiving and accepting the offering. Immediately that majestic cloud which had crowned the mount with its fiery glory, and floated in the heavens in its lofty grandeur, stooped from the skies and entered that holy place; and there, in the Holy of Holies, between the wings of the cherubim and the mercy seat, it took its place as the glowing Shekinah, that mysterious light and awful flame, which henceforth became the supernatural sign of God's immediate presence, and which lit up the holy chamber with supernatural light and glory. God had moved into His consecrated and accepted abode, and henceforth He was no longer at a distance on a throne of glory, but within the midst of Israel, seated on the throne of grace.

And so in the opening verses of the very next chapter we read that God spoke unto Moses, not from the mountain, nor from the cloud, but from the tabernacle. Mystery of mysteries! Gift of gifts! Privilege unspeakable and divine! This is the promise which He has at length fulfilled to His Church and His people, and which every believer may now personally claim. "Know ye not that ye are the temple of God, and that the Spirit of God dwelleth in you?" "I will put my Spirit within you, and cause you to walk in my statutes, and ye shall keep my judgments, and do them." "I will dwell in them, and walk in them; and I will be their God, and they shall be my people."

"If any man will hear my voice, and open the door, I will come in unto him, and sup with him, and he with me." "He dwelleth with you, and shall be in you." "At that day ye shall know that I am in my Father, and ye in me, and I in you." "If a man love me, he will keep my words; and my Father will love him, and we will come unto him, and make our abode with him."

Where is thy God? Yonder on a throne of glory, in the heights of heaven, or here in the sanctuary of your heart, enthroned within you? Yes, this is the second great era of Christian life, the first day of the second year. The first year was the Passover, the sprinkled blood, the acceptance of Jesus as the Savior. That was the beginning of Israel's history, for God said it should be the beginning of months. But this is the second blessing, a crisis just as definite, an era just as marked, a moment just as eternally memorable. That was Calvary. This is Pentecost. It has its time, and there is a day, when Pentecost has fully come. No soul that has ever known it can mistake it or forget it. Beloved, has it come to you, or rather has He come to abide in you forever?

9. The pillar of cloud and fire continued to lead them thenceforward in all their journeys. When they were to march, it moved before them. When they were to rest, it paused and spread its covering wings above them, as the mother bird brooding over her young, as the mighty canopy of a heavenly tent under which they were gathered. And so the Holy Spirit is our Guide, our Leader and our Resting-place. There are times when He presses us forward into prayer, into service, into suffering, into new experiences, new duties, new claims of faith and hope and love; but there are times when He arrests us in our activity, and rests us under His overshadowing wing, and quiets us in the secret place of the Most High, teaching us some new lesson, breathing into us some deeper strength or fullness, and then leading us on again, at His bidding alone. He is the true guide of the saint, and the true leader of the Church, our wonderful Counselor, our unerring Friend. He who would deny the personal guidance of the Holy Ghost in order that he might honor the Word of God as our only guide, must dishonor that other word of promise, that His sheep shall know His voice, and that His hearkening and obedient children shall hear a Voice behind them saying, "This is the way, walk ye in it."

And now let us notice that the pillar of cloud which had entered the tabernacle did not linger there and cease to be visible externally; but it rose from the presence chamber where the Shekinah shone, and hovered above it, and then spread over the sky just as before, an external as well as an internal presence. The difference was this. In its first stage it was an external sign only; then it became an internal presence; and then, finally, it become both internal and external, the Shekinah within and the cloud above.

So in our earlier experiences we know the Holy Ghost only at a distance, in things that happen in a providential direction, or in the Word alone; but after awhile we receive Him as an inward Guest, and He dwells in our very midst, and He speaks to us in the innermost chambers of our being. The external working of His power does not cease, but it is increased and seems the more glorious. The Power that dwells within us works without us, answering prayer, healing sickness, overruling providence, "Doing exceeding abundantly above all that we ask or think, according to the Power that worketh in us." There is a double presence of the Lord for the consecrated believer. He is present in the heart, and He is mightily present in the events of life. He is the Christ in us, the Christ of all the days, with all power in heaven and earth.

As that pillar led them all the way, triumphing over their enemies, dividing the waters of the Jordan, and never leaving them until they entered the promised land, so the Holy Ghost is our Wonder-worker, our all sufficient God and Guardian. He is waiting in these days to work as mightily in the affairs of men as in the days of Moses, of Daniel, and of Paul.

10. It will be noticed, however, that after they entered the Land of Promise, all the external manifestations of God's presence disappeared, and the vision that came to Joshua in front of Jericho — the Son of God with a drawn sword in His hand — became henceforth a pledge of the same presence, protection, and power. Henceforth, the external sign was withdrawn, and their Leader was to be with them by faith and not by sight. In like manner, when we come into the fullness of Christ, we have fewer signs, we have less of the wonderful in form; but we have more of the working of faith and power.

God showed Himself to Joshua, not by the luminous cloud, but by the falling of the walls of Jericho, by the defeat of the Canaanites at Beth-horan, by the capture of Hebron, by the conquest of the Anakim, and by the subjugation of all the thirty-one kings of Canaan. These were the wonders of His power and the signals of His presence.

Thus God, as He leads us into a deeper life of faith and power, will show to us His mind, and manifest His presence by the things He does every day through us, by the salvation of souls around us, by the breaking of proud and sinful hearts, by the opening of heathen nations to the Gospel, by the working of His providence in the events of our time, by the evangelization of the world, by these mighty overturnings which are to bring the glorious advent of His Son.

But in all this, the blessing will be given to faith, and not to sight. We must learn to trust the Holy Ghost, even when we cannot perceive the signals of His presence.

In conclusion; have we kept pace with this advancing cloud? Have we followed Him from Egypt down into the depths of the Red Sea and the floods of the Jordan? Have we let Him lead us into the Promised Land? Has He come to be our holy Guest, our indwelling Presence? Have we proved His mighty works with us as well as in us, and has He led us out into victories of faith and service for which His own heart is longing, that He may glorify Jesus and hasten His return? Shall we not send up the prayer:

Holy Ghost I bid Thee welcome,
Come and be my holy Guest;
Heavenly Dove, within my bosom
  Make Thy home, and build Thy nest.

## Chapter 5

## The Living Water

"And all drink the same spiritual drink; for they drank of the spiritual Rock that followed them: and that Rock was Christ." 1 Cor. 10: 4. "Having therefore, brethren, boldness to enter into the holiest by the blood of Jesus, by a new and living way, which He hath consecrated for us, through the veil, that is to say, His flesh; and having a high priest over the house of God; let us draw near with a true heart, in full assurance of faith, having our hearts sprinkled from an evil conscience, and our bodies washed with pure water." Hebrews 10: 19-22.

There is no emblem of the Holy Spirit more frequently used in the Scriptures than water. Naturally suggestive of cleansing, refreshing, and fullness, it expresses most perfectly the most important offices of the Holy Ghost. It is not possible for us to refer to all the passages

and incidents which are based upon this figure; but we shall call attention to four remarkable passages which unfold in logical and chronological order the work of the Holy Spirit in our redemption and complete salvation.

1. The first of these passages, quoted above, refers to the first three of these unfoldings of the Holy Spirit. They are all connected with incidents in the journey of the Israelites through the wilderness. The first is the smiting of the rock in Horeb, of which we read in the seventeenth chapter of Exodus. They had come to the fountain at Meribah, but found it dry; and, as usual, instead of trusting and praying, they began to murmur and complain. Then God commanded Moses to lead them to the rock in Horeb, and

to smite it with the rod wherewith he had divided the Red Sea and performed the miracles of judgment in Egypt. The cleft rock gave forth a flood of water, and the people drank abundantly, and their cattle.

The smiting of the rock in Horeb was, of course, a type of the Lord Jesus Christ and the stroke of the Father's judgment on Calvary by which our guilt was expiated and the fountain of mercy was opened for sinful men. But the water which flowed from that rock was also a type of the Holy Spirit, purchased for us as the most precious gift of His redemption. Water is always a type of the Holy Ghost. Jesus, Himself, has explained the symbol in John 7:38-39, where, after speaking of the living water which was to flow from the believer, he added, "This He spake of the Holy Spirit, which they that believe on Him should receive."

The water from the rock in Horeb was the type of the outpouring of the Holy Spirit at Pentecost, in consequence of Christ's accomplished redemption. This is its dispensational meaning. So far as the successive eras of our Christian life are concerned, it prefigures our first experiences of the Holy Spirit after our conversion. There is a very real sense in which the Spirit of God is given to the believer as soon as he accepts the Lord Jesus Christ as his Savior. There is a deeper fullness which follows at a later stage. But let not that discredit nor displace the other real experience in which He comes to the believer, in so far as the heart is open to receive Him. This was the first promise to the infant church and the youngest believers of Pentecost, "Repent, and be baptized every one of you for the remission of sins, and ye shall receive the gift of the Holy Ghost; for the promise is unto you, and to your children, and to all that are afar off, as many as the Lord, our God, shall call." This is the only security for the establishing and standing of any believer; and no convert should be left until he has definitely received the Holy Spirit, and been sealed unto the day of redemption by the indwelling power and the presence of God.

2. In the twentieth chapter of Numbers we have a second incident very similar to the first and yet essentially different. Again

the people come to the place of extremity. They are without water and ready to perish from thirst. Once again, God interposes for their deliverance. Once again, He leads them to the rock and the waters flow in abundance for the supply of all their need, "and the people drink, and their cattle," and they are refreshed and satisfied. All this seems exactly like the other miracle, but when we look a little closer we find important differences. In the first place, it is forty years later in their history. The first miracle was at the beginning of their wilderness life. This is near its close, and is intended, therefore, to mark some advanced stage in their experience. It is at a different place — Kadesh. The word "Kadesh" means holiness, and we know that Kadesh was the gate to the Promised Land. This, therefore, would suggest that the outpouring of the Holy Spirit here set forth has reference to the more advanced stages of our Christian life.

There is an era in every complete Christian life; there is a Kadesh where God brings us into His holiness and gives to us the Spirit to dwell within us, and causes us to walk in His statutes and keep His judgments and do them; there is a promised land whose gateway lies at Kadesh, into which we enter by receiving the Holy Ghost in His fullness. There is a place where we either pass out of the wilderness into the "rest that remaineth for the people of God," or where we pass on to the ceaseless round of failure and disappointment in which so many are living.

There is an infinite difference between this reception of the Holy Spirit and His coming to us at our conversion. There He comes to witness to our acceptance and forgiveness; here He comes to accept our perfect offering of ourselves to Him, and to possess us fully for Himself, bringing us into personal union with Jesus, and keeping us henceforth in obedience and victory.

Again, it will be noticed that the manner of the miracle was entirely different. In the first instance, the rock was to be struck by the rod of the lawgiver, but in this case it was not to be struck. Moses was simply to speak to it, and its would give forth its waters at the quiet voice of faith and prayer. Moses disobeyed this command and vehemently struck the rock repeatedly. "Hear now, ye rebels, must we fetch water out of the rock?" God, displeased with his haste and unbelief, severely punished him by excluding him from the Promised Land; yet He honored His own promise by giving the water to the people, notwithstanding the failure of Moses.

All this action is exceedingly significant. The rock was not to be struck again, because it was already smitten and opened, and the waters were already flowing freely. All that was needed was to receive by faith what had already been secured by the great sacrifice. And so for us, the Holy Ghost is given, the sacrifice is finished, the price is paid, the conditions are fulfilled, the heavens are opened, and the Holy Ghost has come. Let us not crucify Christ afresh, or ignore the value of His death by trying to bring down the Spirit again from heaven. All we have to do is to simply receive Him and make room for His entrance. Our part is not to strike but to speak to the Rock, and, as we come in the simplicity of trust, quietly, expectantly claim His entering in; more willingly than a father would give good gifts to his children, will the Father on high bestow the Holy Spirit on them that ask Him. Not like the priests of Baal, with noisy clamor and unbelieving repetitions are we to ask for Him, but in unhesitating confidence and full assurance of faith are we to come and receive what He is waiting to bestow.

The bells within the innermost shrine of God's holy dwelling-place are very delicately hung, and a rude touch will jar the exquisite wires and break the delicate mechanism. All you need is the lightest touch. In the days of your childhood, you got access to a building by pounding on the door with a rude knocker; but now you come and softly touch a little button, and the electric current signals to the highest storey your approach. God's bells all move in answer to electric wires, and your rude, clumsy blows only hinder your petition.

The Holy Ghost is very sensitive, as love always is. You can conquer a wild beast by blows and chains, but you cannot conquer a woman's heart that way, or win the love of a sensitive nature. That must be wooed by the delicate touches of trust and affection. So the Holy Ghost has to be taken by a faith as delicate and sensitive as the gentle heart with whom it is coming in touch. One thought of unbelief, one expression of impatient distrust or fear, will instantly check the perfect freedom of His operations as much as a breath of frost would wither the petals of the most sensitive rose or lily.

Speak to the Rock, do not strike it. Believe in the Holy Ghost and treat Him with the tenderest confidence and the most unwavering trust, and He will meet you with instant response and equal confidence. Beloved, have you come to the rock in Kadesh? Have you opened all your being to the fullness of the Spirit? And then, with the confidence of the child to the mother, the bride to the husband, the flower to the sunshine, have you received by faith? And are you drinking of the fullness and dwelling in the innermost center of His blessed life?

3. We come to the third stage in the following chapter, Numbers 21. We have a very striking little picture: "And from thence they went to Beer: that is the well whereof the Lord spake unto Moses, Gather the people together, and I will give them water. Then Israel sang this song, Spring up, O well; sing ye unto it; The princes dug the well, the nobles of the people dug it, by the direction of the lawgiver, with their staves. And from the wilderness they went to Mattanah."

At first sight the meaning is a little obscure, but as we look more closely, we see a very striking picture. The people have passed on from Kadesh, and again the parched desert is all around them. There are no oases, rills, or flowing streams in sight, and they are famishing with thirst. Then comes the divine command: "Gather the people that I may give them water." "Where shall they be gathered? Gathered to the well of Beer. Oh! there is no well in sight." "Never mind, gather them all the same. Right there in the desert sand, bring them together."

Now the command is given to the nobles to bring out their pilgrim staves and to dig the well in the desert sand; and while they dig, the people are gathered around and are commanded to sing. And so they dig and sing, and sing and dig, and their song is given us in this simple refrain: "Spring up, O well; sing ye unto it." As they sang, the waters burst forth from the depths, and overflowed and ran like a river through the camp; and the people drank and sang and wondered.

This is the explanation of that strange expression in the text, "They drank of that rock that followed them." This is the way it followed them. The rock did not travel through the desert behind the camp, nor was it carried about with them in their caravan, like some fetish or car of Juggernaut; but the water of the rock followed them. It ran under the desert sands, a subterranean stream. They could not see it on the surface, but it was there all the same. All they needed to do was to gather above it, and with their staves dig the well and sing the song of faith and prayer, and lo! the waters flowed abundantly.

What a beautiful picture of the abiding life in the Spirit, and of the continuous sources of our spiritual life! When we receive the fullness of the Spirit, the same blessed promise of life and salvation continues to follow us through all our wilderness journey. Not always will we see the water, or be able to trace the channel of the river; but it is there beneath our feet, even under the fiery sun and burning sands of the hottest desert, and all we need to do is to dig the well of need with the staff of promise, then sing the song of trust, and the Holy Spirit will be found springing up, as ever, in His infinite supply for all our need.

Every promise in the Bible has some fitness to some need in our life. As we use the promise faithfully and meet its simple conditions, we shall find that the waters will spring and our wants will be supplied from the Fountain of Life. To dig is not always very pleasant work. There is a good deal of excavation, and room has to be made by scooping out the sand; and so the promises of God have their sharp edges as well as their gracious fullness. They empty us as well as fill us; but as we meet the conditions, we shall always find them faithful and full, "exceeding abundantly above all that we ask or think."

This striking figure of the desert well teaches us the secret of abiding in the Spirit. Our deeper life in Christ is not always apparent even to ourselves, for it is hid with Christ in God; but the fountain is always there, and we may ever drink from its hidden depths and find the supply of every need in Him.

4. There is another figure of the Holy Spirit suggested by the passage quoted from the Hebrews. There we see the worshiper entering into the Holy of Holies with his body washed with pure water. This suggests the ancient laver which stood at the entrance of the tabernacle, and was intended for the use of the priests who went within to wash their faces and their hands and cleanse their robes from every spot and stain whenever they entered the holy precincts. It was made out of the looking-glasses of the women of Israel, and it is probable that externally it was a great polished mirror in which they could see themselves and their defilements, Then in the water they could cleanse away the stains.

This laver was the type of the Holy Spirit as our fountain of cleansing and our way of approach to the holy place of Christ's immediate presence. Only as we are cleansed in that laver can we enter in as the priests of God and feed upon the Living Bread, dwelling in the light of the golden lamps, and breathing the sweet odor of the incense that fills the presence chamber with the atmosphere of heaven. At once it reveals and removes the defilements of our hearts and lives. There is a sense in which, once for all, the Holy Spirit cleanses us. This was what our Master meant when He said, "He that is washed needeth not save to wash his feet, but is clean every whit."

But there is a constant liability to contract at least the stains of earth, if not the taint of sin. The very atmosphere we breathe is so laden with the breath of evil that it is almost impossible to escape its touch and taint; but the blessed Holy Spirit stands ministering within the sacred temple of the heart, and is ready every moment to wash away the faintest touch of earth or evil, and to keep us spotless, undefiled, and perfectly accepted in His sight.

"If we walk in the light as he is in the light, we have fellowship one with the other, and the blood of Jesus Christ, his Son, cleanseth us from all sin." The laver speaks to us of the permanent and unceasing operations of the Holy Spirit. The rock in Horeb and Kadesh, and even the well in the wilderness, were but the transient types of these spiritual verities. But the laver was God's abiding symbol, and continued in the tabernacle through all their future national life. It speaks to us of that continual provision which He has made for our abiding life. Let us, therefore, receive Him and abide in Him; let us wait in the Holy Place; let us not only come for cleansing, but let us keep coming; and let us so dwell under the continual influences and in the very atmosphere of His love that we shall never be out of communion, and that we shall be kept cleansed from all sin.

We read, in the description of the tabernacle, not only of the laver but also of its foot. What was the intention of the foot of the laver? Perhaps it was a little outlet through which the waters could more easily flow within the reach of one who sought cleansing. The laver itself was too high to be easily reached, at least at its brim; but through this little pipe, which probably could be opened by a simple mechanism, the waters flowed to the ground and were always within the reach of even the littlest child, had it needed to come.

How truly this illustrates the blessed nearness of the Holy Ghost! Not in the highest heaven do we need to seek Him, not afar off do we have to cry to Him; but He is our Paraclete, One by our side, One very near and ever near to help in time of need. He is to us the presence of the Holy God, already given and ever present in the heart of His Church. He is as ready to enter the yielded and trusting heart as light is to flow into the open window and sunshine to meet the petals of the opening flower. Let us send up to Him the simple, whole-hearted prayer,

Blessed Holy Spirit
Welcome to my breast;
In my heart forever
Be my Holy Guest.

## Chapter 6

## The Anointing Oil

"Now He which stablisheth us with you in Christ, and hath anointed us, is God." 2 Cor. 1: 21.

The use of oil is more common in eastern lands than it is with us. The olive tree is one of the typical trees of Palestine. It is a wonderful tree. Its leaf is lustrous and seems always as if it had been bathed in the oil of its own olive tree, and the tree itself seems almost indestructible. It is usually crooked, gnarled, twisted, and almost torn to pieces. Nearly every tree is hollow, and often you see the larger part of the trunk apparently torn away, with perhaps a single root adhering to the soil; but above it rises a luxuriant mass of boughs and foliage seeming to be imbued with imperishable freshness. Some of the olives of Gethsemane must be at least a thousand years old; indeed the olive tree seems as if it could scarcely die.

It is a good type of the Holy Spirit and the soul anointed with His life and power. He may be exposed to all the trials of time; but, filled with the elixir of imperishable life, his leaf is always green, and he shall not cease from yielding fruit even in the parched land and the most inhospitable climate.

The ordinance of anointing with oil was one of the most common and significant ceremonials of the Old Testament. The leper was anointed, the tabernacle was anointed, the priests were anointed, the prophets were anointed, the kings were anointed, the guest was anointed, the sick were anointed. It was the special symbol of the Holy Ghost and the dedication of the person anointed to His service and possession.

## I. THE PREPARATION OF THE ANOINTING OIL

We have a full account of this in Exodus 30: 23-33. "Take thou unto thee principal spices, of pure myrrh five hundred shekels, and of sweet cinnamon half so much, even two hundred and fifty shekels, and of sweet calumus two hundred and fifty shekels, and of cassia five hundred shekels, after the shekel of the sanctuary, and of olive oil a hin: and thou shalt make it an oil of holy ointment, an ointment compound after the art of the apothecary: it shall be an holy anointing oil. And thou shalt anoint the tabernacle of the congregation therewith, and the ark of the testimony, and the table and all his vessels, and the candlestick and his vessels, and the altar of incense, and the altar of burnt offering with all his vessels, and the laver and his foot. And thou shalt sanctify them, that they may be most holy: whatsoever toucheth them shall be holy. And thou shalt anoint Aaron and his sons, and consecrate them, that they may minister unto me in the priest's office."

The method was particularly prescribed in every de-tail, and no counterfeit was allowed under the most severe penalties. It will be noticed:

1. That this oil was specially prepared. It was not ordinary olive oil; but other ingredients were added, chiefly perfumes, making it exquisitely fragrant, so that it not only was visible to the eye, but expressed to the sense of smell the sweetest suggestions of the divine presence, of which fragrance was always a peculiar sign.

The Holy Ghost has been prepared in like manner for His special work in us, just as the body of Jesus was prepared and His incarnation arranged for, so that He might come to us, not as the pure Deity alone, but as God manifest in the flesh. So the Holy Ghost has been prepared to dwell within us and to bring us into the presence of God in the way best adapted to our weak human nature.

The Holy Ghost who dwells in the believer is not the Deity who comes directly from the throne in the majesty of His Godhead. He is the Spirit that dwelt in the human Christ for three and a half years, the Spirit who wept in His tears, suffered in his agonies, spake in His words of wisdom and love, took the little children in His arms, healed the sick and raised the dead, allowed John to lean upon His bosom, and said to the sorrowing disciples, "Let not your heart be troubled." This is the Spirit, therefore, that comes to us, softened and humanized by His union with the blessed Jesus, and calling Himself the Spirit of Christ, so that in receiving Him we receive the heart of Jesus and the person of Jesus into our inmost being. How gracious of the Holy Ghost to come to us thus fitted to meet our frailty and our need and to satisfy the wants of all our being!

2. As the oil was fragrant and sweet, so the Holy Ghost brings to us the very sweetness of heaven. All these spices have, perhaps, some special significance. The myrrh used, as we know, for embalming the dead, suggests to us the comfort of the Holy Ghost; the cinnamon was sweet to the taste, and fitly expresses the delightful and joyful influences of the Spirit; and the cassia, a healing and wholesome ingredient, reminds us of the Holy Ghost as our Health Bringer and our Sanctifier.

3. The oil was not to be counterfeited or imitated. Neither can the Holy Ghost be imitated. Satan has always tried to simulate the Spirit of God, and to get us to worship him instead of Jehovah. Even in the days of Moses men sometimes brought strange fire; but they were met with fiery judgment from the jealous God, who will not suffer His holy things to be profaned or confounded with evil. Men are still constantly in danger of accepting the false for the true. Spiritualism, Christian Science, and Theosophy come with their unholy imitations, but no deep discernment is needed to detect their disguises. He would be a bold man who willingly would be mixed up with these sorceries and Satanic delusions which leave a blister and a scar wherever they touch the soul.

There are other counterfeits less glaring and daring. Intellectual brilliancy, eloquence, and pathos often presume to imitate the operations of the Spirit and produce the impression which only He can bring. Music attempts to thrill our esthetic nature with the emotions and feelings which many mistake for real devotion. Architecture and art are called into play to impress the imagination with the scenic effects of sensuous worship. But none of these do the work of the Holy Spirit. People can weep under entrancing music and heart-stirring eloquence, and yet as much as before go out and live lives of cruel selfishness and gross unrighteousness. People can bow with a kind of awe under the imposing arch and before the vivid painting, or the impressive pageant of ceremonial worship, and yet have no fear of God before their eyes. There is no substitute for the Holy Ghost. He alone can produce conviction, divine impression, true devotion, unselfish life, and reverent worship.

4. The oil must not be poured on man's flesh. It was to be used exclusively for the consecrated and separated ones. No stranger was to receive this anointing. It was the badge of separation to God. Thus the Holy Ghost comes upon the separated, dedicated, consecrated heart. You cannot receive it upon a carnal and fleshly soul. God will not dwell in a sinful spirit. You must separate yourself from evil, dedicate yourself to Him, and be crucified with Christ to self and sin before He will make your heart His abiding place. His promise is: "I will take away the stony heart out of your flesh, and a new spirit will I put within you." Then he adds, "I will put my Spirit within you and cause you to walk in my statutes, and ye shall keep my judgments and do them."

You cannot get power from God until you receive holiness. Simon Magus wanted this power from the Apostle Peter; but his wicked heart received only God's terrific rebuke and the awful words, "Thou art in the gall of bitterness and the bond of iniquity." Men are still trying to get power without holiness, but it can only bring disappointment and danger. In their search for power they will probably end where Simon Magus did, with the unholy power of the wicked one and the curse of a holy God. The Spirit's first work is to cleanse us, to separate us, to sanctify us, to dedicate us wholly to God. Then as the property of God, He takes possession of us for God and uses us for His service and glory alone.

## II. PARTICULAR CASES IN WHICH THE ANOINTING OIL WAS USED

1. The anointing of the leper is described in Leviticus 14. This represents the Holy Spirit's cleansing and consecrating work upon the sinner. This poor leper outside the camp represents our worst estate, and it is for such sinners that the Holy Ghost has come to bring all the fullness of Jesus.

First, the poor leper must be met and welcomed, and then brought by the priest inside the camp and under the cleansing water and sprinkled blood; then the anointing oil is applied, and he is touched over the blood-mark that has already been given, upon his right ear, his right thumb, and his right toe. This means the consecrating and the filling of all his powers of apprehension and reception represented by the ear, all his powers of appropriating faith and holy service represented by the hand, and all his steps and ways represented by his feet. All these are dedicated to God and taken possession of by the Holy Ghost.

The oil does not come first, but the blood. Then the oil is placed upon the blood. The Holy Ghost comes only to those who have received Jesus. There is no spiritual power apart from the cross and the Savior. Those higher revelations and deeper teachings which discard the blood of Calvary come from beneath. Like the ancient St. Francis, we can always know the true Christ by the print of the nails and the spear. However, we need the oil as much as the blood. Our ears, our hands, and our feet must be divinely quickened, possessed, and filled before we can rightly hear and understand for God, rightly appropriate the things we know, rightly work for Him, and walk in His holy ways.

But this is not all. This is but a drop of oil. We now read that the remnant of the oil was poured upon the head of him who was to be cleansed. This is a much larger filling. The very word "pour" means a fullness of blessing, and the remnant of oil means all the oil that was left, all that was in the priest's hand. We know that the priest is no one else than the Son of God, the Mighty One, who holds the ocean in the hollow of His hand,

and, therefore, the rest of the oil that the palm of His hand can hold is an ocean of infinite fullness. It means that all the oil, that Jesus himself had, is poured upon our head. The same anointing came upon Him that He also shares with us. All this for a poor leper!

Beloved, have you received the remnant of the oil?

2. The anointing of the priest is unfolded in Exodus 29: 7-21, and Leviticus 8:12, 30. Here we find a different application of the oil. It is applied to the priest with the object of fitting him for service in waiting upon the Lord and ministering in His presence. We also must receive the holy anointing, not only for cleansing but for service. We are not fit to represent God in the world or to do any spiritual work for Him until we receive the Holy Ghost.

You will notice a double operation here in connection with the oil. First, Aaron is anointed, and then afterwards his sons are anointed with him. Aaron is anointed alone, even as Christ received the baptism of the Holy Ghost first upon Himself on the banks of the Jordan; and then later He shed the same spirit upon His disciples. Even as He, we may receive this divine anointing. The oil that falls on Aaron's head goes down to the skirts of his garment. The Spirit that was upon Him He shed upon His followers. Standing in their midst, He breathes upon them and says unto them, "Receive ye the Holy Ghost," and then He explains the great enduement and the great commission by the strange and mighty words, "As my Father hath sent me, even so send I you."

This is our true preparation for the highest of all priestly ministries, for prayer, and for every other service in which we would represent God or bless men. Even the Master did not venture to go forth to fulfill His great commission until He could stand before the world and say, "The Spirit of the Lord is upon me; because he hath anointed me to preach the gospel to the poor; he hath sent me to heal the broken hearted, . . . . to set at liberty them that are bruised, to preach the acceptable year of the Lord." For any man to presume to represent the Son of God, to stand between the living and the dead, to acts as ambassador for

Christ, to bear salvation to dying men, to bring men from darkness to light and from the power of Satan unto God without the anointing of the Holy Ghost, is the most daring presumption and the most offensive impertinence to the God whom he misrepresents and to the men on whom he imposes.

3. The anointing of the tabernacle represents something higher than even cleansing or service; namely, the indwelling and abiding presence of God Himself in the believer, as His consecrated temple. We read the full account of it in Exodus 40: 9-16. As we have seen in a former chapter, it is a great day; it marks a special era in their national history. It was on the first day of the first month of the second year. It marked a new departure and a higher experience. The glory that had hitherto marched in front of them or shone above them in the cloud or on the mountain, was henceforth to be brought into their very midst in the Holy of Holies. But before that presence could come and dwell among them, that tabernacle, that was to be its shrine and home, must be completed according to the divine commandment in every part, and then presented to God in the solemn ordinance of anointing.

It was definitely laid at the feet of Jehovah, and the sacred oil was poured upon it, as a symbol that God Himself now took possession of the sacred edifice and was to make it henceforth His personal abode. Then the cloud descended and the tabernacle became the very throne of the divine presence.

And so, when we present our bodies "a living sacrifice, holy, acceptable unto God," we become the sacred abode of the Holy One. Be not conformed to this world, but be ye transfigured, is the apostle's inspiring message to such consecrated lives. Life henceforth becomes a transfiguration and we go forth shining like the Master, with the glory of the inward presence which the world cannot understand, but which the angels perceive, and which makes the consecrated heart the house of God and the very gate of heaven. Beloved, have we come to this also? Have we reached the glory of this mystery, which is "Christ in you, the hope of glory"?

Ancient minds in heathen lands dreamed of something like this, when they cut in marble their ideals of beauty and grace and then called them gods. It was the dream of the human heart, trying to bring God down in union with man. But Jesus has accomplished it through His incarnation in our image and the indwelling of the Holy Ghost in our hearts, the incarnation of the Father in Jesus and the incarnation of Jesus in us by the Holy Ghost.

This is the climax; this is the consummation; this is the crowning glory of redemption; and all that which is now being realized in the individual, shall yet, some glorious day, be gathered together into the whole number of glorified and transfigured ones. Then when the whole Church of Christ shall meet and the body shall be complete, and the building shall be crowned with the glorious headstone, then the universe shall look upon a spectacle for which all ages have been preparing, the infinite and eternal God, enshrined in glorified humanity. And the heavens shall cry, "Behold, the tabernacle of God is with men, and he will dwell with them, and they shall be His people, and God Himself shall be with them, and be their God."

There are three or four other instances of anointing, to which we shall briefly refer, inasmuch as they will be considered more fully in a later chapter.

4. The ancient prophets were anointed. Thus Elisha was called to his high office. And thus we are called and qualified by the Holy Ghost to present the will of God, to bear the Word of God to our fellow-men.

5. Kings were anointed, as David was set apart by the anointing oil to be God's chosen king. Likewise we are anointed kings and priests unto Him — a royal priesthood of love and victorious life, to bear upon our brow the majesty of the saints of God as the joint heirs with Christ in His coming kingdom.

6. The sick were anointed for healing. The Holy Ghost becomes to us the quickening and health-bringing power, who imparts the life of Jesus to our mortal frames, expelling disease and bringing us into the divine and resurrection life of the Son of God.

7. Guests were anointed. We read in the twenty-third Psalm the beautiful picture of the guest sitting at the table of the royal banquet and exclaiming, "Thou preparest a table before me in the presence of mine enemies: thou anointest my head with oil; my cup runneth over." We find Jesus complaining to the Pharisee, "My head with oil thou didst not anoint; but she hath anointed my feet." The ancient host received his guest with great courtesy and took him into the bathroom, where the stains of the wayside were washed away, where fresh garments were put upon him. Then sweet and fragrant oil was poured upon his head.

So the blessed Holy Ghost not only becomes our guest; but He turns around and makes us as guests, and then anoints us with the sweet, fragrant oil and feeds us with the heavenly banquet of His love.

A missionary of the Northwest tells us that once in a while he and his wife used to visit the Indians and have a little feast with them in their homes. The missionary's wife would tell the Indian mother on Sabbath at the little chapel to be ready for her on a certain day that week, and to prepare her best for dinner. The poor squaw perhaps would answer that she had nothing worthy of the missionary save a little fish. But the missionary would tell her to prepare what she had and to have everything clean and bright, and it would be all right. So on the appointed day the missionary would arrive, and she would take from her dog-sleigh bundle after bundle of things. There were tea and coffee, there were sugar and bread, there were potatoes, and perhaps butter and little delicacies that the poor savage never had seen before. When all was ready the missionary husband would arrive in another dog-sleigh from visiting the stations, and then the feast would begin, and they would dine together. The missionary and his wife were the real host and hostess, and the poor Indian family ate of things that day that they had never tasted before; and the missionaries found their joy in the joy which they brought.

Ah, that is the way that our precious Lord loves to do with us. We take Him into our humble home, and we give Him our best, although it is very poor at the best, and He condescends to accept it; and then He brings His best — all that heaven affords — and He feeds us out of His bounty, and it is true, as He promised, "I will sup with him and he will sup with me." He takes what we have to give, but He brings His richer gifts to us; and as we sit at His table and feast upon His love we say with the Psalmist, "Thou preparest a table before me in the presence of mine enemies ; thou anointest my head with oil; my cup runneth over."

## Chapter 7

## The Baptism with Fire

"He shall baptize you with the Holy Ghost, and with fire." Matthew 3: 11. "For our God is a consuming fire." Hebrews 12: 29.

Fire is one of the most powerful and striking elements of the material world. It has always been an object of importance and of superstitious regard in the religious ideas and customs of all nations. In ancient Greece and Rome the sacred fire was guarded by consecrated priests and vestal virgins, and was the center of the commonwealth and the home. When the fire went out, all executive and national affairs were suspended, and it had to be rekindled, either from the lightnings of the skies, from the concentrated rays of the sun, or by the process of friction and the rubbing together of two pieces of wood.

The foreign ambassador had to walk by the holy fire before he could be received in the Council of State. The Slavonic and Teutonic bride had to bow before the holy fire as she entered her new home. The Red Indian sachem walked thrice around the camp-fire before he would give his counsel or confer with his public visitor. The twelve Grecian tribes brought their twelve firebrands to Theseus, and were thus consolidated into the State, and their sacred fires were combined in the Oracle of Delphi. The Persian fire-worshipers looked upon the sun and the flame as sacred things, and it was an unpardonable profanity to spit in the fire or commit any impropriety in the presence of these holy elements. Fire was recognized as identical with life, and the Parsees of India today worship it with holy veneration.

God had always recognized it in His Word, not as an object of superstitious regard, but as the symbol of His own transcendent glory, and the power of His presence and His Holy Spirit.

As the discoveries of science and the progress of human knowledge increase, we learn to trace the deeper analogies and more significant lessons in this sacred symbolism. Fire is the most valuable physical force with which we are acquainted. In yonder sun it is the center of power in our whole planetary system. Stored up in our vast coal-mines, it is the power that drives the engines of commerce and the wheels of industry throughout the world. We see it in the tremendous forces of modern artillery, the torpedo, the bomb, the dynamite, the nitro-glycerine, and the death-dealing cannon. It is the prime factor in all the implements of modern warfare.

In the still higher forces of electricity, with their countless and ever-increasing adaptations, it is revolutionizing all the methods of modern business, and directing the whole course of trade and labor. Science is beginning to believe that the ultimate force of all nature is just electricity, and that the power that moves the planets in their orbits and the stars in their courses is but a form of electric fire. The truth is, that when they get to the end of their ultimatum they will find that God Himself is there, the personal source of all these forces, and by His own will directing this tremendous battery by which the universe is kept in motion. For "power belongeth unto God." and He is the "Consuming Fire" from whose bosom all other forces emanate.

The Holy Ghost Himself has taught us to recognize in this tremendous force His own appropriate symbol, "He shall baptize you with the Holy Ghost and with fire." There is something very striking in the analogy between the story of fire and the dispensational unfolding of the Holy Ghost. There was a time in the history of the natural world when yonder celestial fires were the objects of mystery, uncertainty, and almost dread. The lightnings of the skies were known to be real forces, but men knew not when they would strike, and dared not attempt to use or control them. But in these last days science has scaled the heavens, has caught the lightnings, and has brought the tremendous forces of electricity under the direction of such laws that the simplest child can use them at pleasure. They have become the instruments of our everyday life, ringing our front doorbells, driving our streetcars, lighting our chambers and our streets, moving our machinery, carrying on our business, and even conveying our messages on the phonographic and telegraphic wires over the world.

So, in like manner, there was a time when the Holy Ghost's heavenly fire was a mysterious force, flashing, like the lightning in the skies, we knew not why or whither; coming now upon a Moses, and again upon an Elijah; sometimes falling as at Carmel, in awful majesty upon the altar of sacrifice; sometimes striking, as in Israel's camp, in the destroying flame of God's anger; sometimes appearing, as in the burning bush at Horeb, as the strange, mysterious symbol of Jehovah's presence.

But since Christ's ascension the Holy Spirit has condescended to dwell amongst us under certain plainly revealed laws, and to place at our service and command all the forces and resources of His power, according to definite, simple and regular laws of operation, in accordance with which the simplest disciple can use Him for the needs of his life and work just as easily as we use the force of electricity for the business of life. He has even been pleased to call Himself "the law of the Spirit of life in Christ Jesus."

He has come down to the level of our common life, and is ready to meet us in every need of our being, and to become to us, not only the Author of our higher spiritual life, but the Director and power of our daily conduct, and of all our work here, whether in the secular or the spiritual sphere. Let us first look at some of the illustrations of this figure in the Scriptures, especially the use of fire in the Mosaic ritual.

At the very beginning of the Exodus we find God revealing Himself to Moses under the symbol of the burning bush, the tree that burned but was not consumed, thus making the emblem of fire the special symbol of His presence with Israel. The pillar of cloud and fire was but a grander manifestation of the same glorious emblem. As in the vision of Abraham, centuries before, the symbol of the divine presence that appeared in the night vision given to the patriarch, was a burning lamp and a smoking furnace, so all through the wilderness it was by fire that God manifested His presence. In Mount Sinai He descended in fire and spake to the people from the midst of the fire. The Shekinah glory in the midst of the Holy of Holies was probably a glowing flame of fire. It was by fire that He answered the prayer of Elijah on Mount Carmel, accepted the sacrifice of Samson's parents, and revealed His presence in times past to His servants.

In all the sacrifices and offerings fire was an important element. The paschal lamb was roasted in the fire and eaten by the people as a symbol of Christ's flesh prepared for us and ministered to us by the Holy Ghost as our Living Bread. The sin offering was carried without the camp and burned with fire, as a symbol of our sin laid upon Jesus and consumed by the Holy Ghost outside the pale of our consciousness, so that we have nothing more to do with it, but simply to lay it on the Lamb of God and leave it with Him. The burnt offering was consumed upon the altar by fire, the type of Christ, offered not for our sins, but for our acceptance with God, and the type of our true consecration as we yield ourselves up to God by the Holy Ghost.

As the fire was kept ever burning, so the Holy Ghost in the consecrated soul will make our whole life a living sacrifice, holy and acceptable unto God. The peace offering was also connected with the sacred fire. It was the type of our communion with God. In this sacrifice the fat and the inwards were given to God, and consumed upon the altar by the fire. This was the type of God's part in the communion of the believer. Then the shoulder and breast were given to the priest and eaten by him, a symbol of our part in this holy communion. But it is the Holy Ghost alone that can maintain the true fellowship of the peace offering, and enable us first to give to God the worship and homage due to Him, and then to take our part and feed upon Christ as our Living Bread.

Next, the meat offering was an offering by fire. It was fine flour baked in the fire, mingled with oil and frankincense, and free from leaven and honey. It was the type of Jesus Christ, our spiritual sustenance, nourishing and feeding us with His own life by the fire of the Holy Ghost.

It is one thing to feed upon the truth; it is another thing to feed upon Christ. Only the Spirit of God can make even the life of Christ our Living Bread. The difference is just the same as if you should attempt to feed upon raw wheat instead of prepared bread. It is the work of the Holy Spirit to prepare for us the Bread of Life, and to minister it to us as the Living Christ.

One of the most beautiful of all the offerings was the incense presented in the holy place. This also was an offering by fire. The sweet spices were ground and mixed, some of them beaten very small; and then they were burned in the golden censer, and their sweet fragrance went up in clouds of incense before the Lord, filling all the holy place with fragrance, and breathing out the very spirit of worship continually. This is the type of Christ's priesthood first, and then of our true ministry of prayer. Like the incense beaten small, it may have to do with the most trifling things. Like the spices, whose very names we do not now understand, and whose nature is unknown, except the frankincense, so in all prayer there is much of mystery, and much that even the praying heart does not fully comprehend. And yet, like the frankincense, which was well known, there are ingredients and elements in prayer of which we do know, and things for which we ask of which we are definitely aware, and for which we may definitely believe.

But above all, the fire which consumed the incense is the type of the Holy Ghost, without whom all our prayers must stop short of heaven, and through whom alone our desires can reach the throne and become effectual with God. There is no deeper experience in the Christian life than this ministry of prayer in the Spirit. "For we know not what to pray for as we ought, but the Spirit maketh intercession for us with groanings that cannot be uttered. And he that searcheth the heart knoweth what is the mind of the Spirit, because he maketh intercession for the saints according to the will of God."

Again, we see the use of the fire in the ordinance of the red heifer. This type was especially for God's people in their wilderness life. The red heifer represented Christ our Sacrifice, slain and consumed for us on the altar of God. But in the burning of the heifer there come the scarlet wool, the cedar and the hyssop leaves, representing something which is to be consumed, along with the death of Christ. The scarlet wool represents our sins, the cedar our strength, and the hyssop our weakness and the clinging element in our nature. All these things are to be crucified with Christ, and this can be done only through the power of the Holy Ghost. We are not equal to the task of self-crucifixion, but we can hand over anything and everything to Him, and consent that it shall die. Then by the power of His Holy Spirit He will put it to death and make the crucifixion real.

Even after the death of the heifer the fire was to be preserved and made perpetual by the preservation of the ashes. You know ashes are a kind of preserved fire. By pouring water upon these ashes you create lye, a very acrid, pungent, burning substance. Now, these ashes were preserved and water poured upon them, and used as a water of separation or purification when any one had contracted any sin or defilement whatsoever. It was the type of the work of the Holy Spirit in constantly cleansing us from defilement or pollution contracted from earthly things and absorbed from the atmosphere in which we live. This cleansing is not always pleasant. It is sometimes like the touch of lye, a consuming fire; but it is a wholesome thing, like the burning away of proud flesh by caustic, to have our very nature purified for us from self and sin. It is blessed to be able thus to come in every moment of defilement, and to walk in the constant cleansing of the Holy Spirit, knowing that we are not only cleansed but kept clean, ever acceptable to God through Jesus Christ, and ready for constant fellowship and holy service as He may require.

We find the fire manifested in a very remarkable way in connection with Elijah's history. On Mt. Carmel the fire came from heaven as a special sign of God's acceptance of the sacrifice and the manifestation of His power to His returning people. As it fell upon the altar it not only consumed the sacrifice, but it licked up the water in trenches. To complete the faith of the people in Jehovah, He made the miracle as difficult as possible by covering the altar and filling the trenches round about with floods of water, so that deception was impossible. God met the faith of His servant, and wrought a work so glorious and divine that it was manifest to every eye that it was the finger of God; and the great multitude sent up the cry, "Jehovah, He is God! Jehovah, He is God!"

The Holy Ghost is thus the power of God in our work, the fire that all the devil's floods cannot extinguish, the fire that delights in the hardest places and the most difficult undertakings. We need not fear to claim this power for even the impossible, but may boldly bring to God the mightiest difficulties, and glorify Him all the more in the face of Satan's fiercest and most formidable opposition.

Once more, we see the fire as the emblem of destruction. When the presuming priests dared to offer strange fire before the Lord, then God's consuming fire fell upon them and destroyed them. And so the Holy Ghost is still present as God's avenging power. He that struck down Ananias and Sapphira in their presumption and hypocrisy, is still present in the Church as the Executive of Jehovah, and the "consuming fire," to whom we can safely leave all our enemies and all the hate of earth and hell.

There are several lessons which we may learn from the figure itself. Fire is a cleansing element. It differs from water in this, that, while water cleanses externally, fire purifies internally and intrinsically, penetrating to the very substance of things, and filling every fibre and particle of matter with its own element. The baptism of John represented the cleansing of our life and conduct, the reformation of our character, and the work of the law and the truth upon human hearts. But Christ's baptism was by fire, and went to the roots of conduct. The purity He required included motives, aims, and "the thoughts and intents of the heart." He not only requires but He gives the purity that springs from the depths of our being. Like the flame that consumes the dross and leaves the molten metal pure and unalloyed, so the Holy Ghost separates us from our old sinfulness and self-life and burns into us the nature and the life of Christ.

Again, fire quickens and gives life. The returning spring and the solar heat call into life the buried seeds of field and garden, and all nature springs into beauty and fruitfulness. The heated greenhouse germinates the seeds and plants of the gardener and pushes them forward into rapid and luxuriant growth. The process of heat incubates the little birdling in its shell and nurses it into life. So the Holy Ghost is the quickener of life. We are born again by the Spirit, nursed into spiritual being, and cherished into growth and maturity, by the Spirit of God.

Again, the Holy Spirit warms and quickens the heart into love. Like the change from the cold winter to the vernal sunshine of the spring is the transition which He brings into the heart. It is His mission to break the fetters of fear and sorrow, and to kindle in the heart the love of Christ and the joy of heaven, warming every affection of the new nature, and shedding abroad the love of God in the soul until it becomes a summer-land of love.

And, finally, fire is an energizing force. It gives power. So the Holy Ghost is the source of power. Surely, if He has been able to give to the forces of nature their tremendous power; to give to the sun the force that can hold the planets in their course, and quicken and warm the earth into life and luxuriance; if He has stored up in the lightnings, and the coal-mines, and the atmosphere, the yet only half-revealed dynamics which propel the industries of the human race, He Himself is able to accomplish more than any of His agencies or works.

How blind are they who are trying to do the work of God without His power! How we would laugh at the man who today would try to turn the great driving-wheel of a factory by a treadmill, with a dozen men turning it with their weight, as they still do in China! And yet thousands of Christians are trying to carry on their Lord's work by their own puny hands.

Science has grown wise enough to turn on the forces of steam and electricity. Oh, let faith turn on the dynamo of heaven and the power of the Holy Ghost! This is the secret, of victory over temptation and sin and all our spiritual enemies. Archimedes of old was said to have consumed the vessels of the enemies of his country by setting fire to them in the harbor of Syracuse by a burning-glass, by which he attracted the solar rays in a focus upon the hostile fleet; and they went up in a blaze of destruction. So let us consume our enemies and His by the fire of the Holy Ghost.

When the little camp on the vast prairie finds that a wave of fire is sweeping over the plain, and that in and hour or two they will be engulfed in flame and destroyed by the resistless element, they are wise enough to clear an open space around them and then start another fire from their own camp and send it out to meet the approaching wave. As it rolls across the open plain, destroying every combustible thing that is in the way at length it meets the advancing fire; and the two leap up to heaven in one wild outburst of fury and then expire for the want of fuel, The travelers are left in safety on the prairie, where there is nothing to feed the fire.

So let us meet the fire of evil with the fire of the Holy Ghost. We have divine resources. Why should we stoop to the human? We have God to fight our battles for us. Why should we do it ourselves?

In ancient Rome when the fire went out all state business had to cease. They dared not do a thing without the sacred fire. So all true work ceases when the Holy Ghost is withdrawn from the Church of God and from the midst of the work. God does not accept anything that is not done in the power of the Spirit. In ancient Rome the fire had to be rekindled either from the lightnings of the sky, or from the sun, or from the friction of two pieces of wood. So sometimes God sends us the lightnings of his power to rekindle the flame. Although this is often a very dangerous thing, He has sometimes to strike with a stroke of judgment before His people awake to their need. We can always draw the fire by the burning-glass of faith from the Son of Righteousness. And God has yet another way of increasing our spiritual fire, and that is by friction. The other day, in one of our cities, I was asked to notice the factory where the electric force was generated for the trolley engines. I found it was generated entirely by friction. Great wheels were constantly revolving and producing the electric force by rubbing together.

So God in like manner often quickens our lives and deepens our spiritual force by the tests and trials which throw us upon Him, and compel us to take more of His life and strength. Then let us, instead of quarreling with our circumstances and mourning over our trials, use everything that comes to bring us more of God, and strengthen us for higher service and mightier usefulness, through the power of the Holy Ghost.

## Chapter 8

## The Spirit of Wisdom

"God hath . . . given us the Spirit . . . of a sound mind." 2 Tim. 1: 7. "Thou gavest also Thy good Spirit to instruct them." Nehemiah 9: 20.

The latter passage suggests the work of the Holy Sprit as the teacher and guide of God's people through their history in the wilderness. The previous verses connect the passage with the history of Israel during the forty years of their wandering, and identifies the pillar of cloud and fire which led them through the wilderness as the Holy Spirit who is our Leader and Guide. The other passage from the Epistle to Timothy presents to us the Holy Spirit as the Spirit of wisdom and of a sound mind.

It is interesting and instructive to trace the revelation of the divine Spirit in the Old Testament, as the Spirit of wisdom and guidance. Let us look at a few special examples.

1. The first is the case of Joseph, referred to in Genesis 41: 38-40. "And Pharaoh said unto his servants, 'Can we find such a one as this, a man in whom the Spirit of God is?' And Pharaoh said unto Joseph, 'Forasmuch as God has shewed thee all this, there is none so discreet and wise as thou art: thou shalt be over my house, and according to thy word shall all my people be ruled; only in the throne will I be greater than thou.'" Here we get a glimpse of the secret that lay back of Joseph's extraordinary life; it was the Spirit of God. Perhaps there never was a life that touched more closely the common life of suffering humanity. We see in him a true and noble nature exposed to the discipline of the keenest suffering; separated from home and friends; carried

into captivity in a foreign land; misunderstood, traduced, unjustly condemned, and cast into a prison under the deepest and most unjust opprobrium and disgrace; and yet, so heroically standing true to God and righteousness, and so steadfastly trusting in the divine faithfulness and love, that he triumphed at length over all his difficulties, rose from the prison to a princedom of honor and influence, and from the very lowest place found a pathway to the highest position that it was possible for a mortal to attain. Was there ever a more extraordinary transformation, was there ever a more striking object lesson of the power of high and holy character?

But the passage we have quoted reveals the secret of it all. It was not the triumph of human character, but the result of a divine direction that led him through all his steps and lifted him above all his trials. It was a beautiful illustration of the work of the Holy Spirit in the practical affairs of human life, and the commonplace sphere through which the largest part of our existence here has to pass. The most beautiful fact about it all was, that even Pharaoh himself, the proud and ungodly king of Egypt, was the first to recognize this divine presence in Joseph's life. Joseph did not have to advertise himself as one possessed of the Holy Spirit; but as the men of the world watched him, they themselves were compelled to say, "Can we find such a one as this in whom the Spirit of God is?"

It is so beautiful when even ungodly men are compelled to see and glorify God in our lives. There is no greater triumph of holy character than to compel the testimony of the men of the world to the power of God in us. This was the glory of Daniel's life, that even his worst enemies had to say, "We can find nothing against this man, except it be as concerning the law of his God"; and the grandest testimony ever given to Jesus Christ by human lips was that of His judge, Pontius Pilate, when he was forced to say, "I bring Him forth to you that ye may know that I find no fault in Him."

O, men of the world, O, young men, looking out upon the future and wanting to know the secret of the highest success, would that you might know that the same Spirit that guided Joseph's steps, and led him through his painful pathway until from the dungeon of Pharaoh and the kitchen of Potiphar he reached the premiership of all Egypt, and indeed of all the world, is ready to be your Guide, your Teacher, your Wisdom, and the Source of all your strength, success, and happiness.

2. The next example is the case of Moses and Aaron: Exodus 4: 10-16. In this passage we have an account of God's call to Moses to undertake the leadership of Israel from Egypt to Canaan, and the special task of going to Pharaoh to demand the release of God's people from their bondage. We find Moses shrinking from the task because he was slow of speech and asking God to send somebody else. God answers Moses by saying, "Who hath made man's mouth, or who maketh the dumb, or deaf, or the seeing, or the blind? Have not I, the Lord? Now therefore go, and I will be with thy mouth, and teach thee what thou shalt say." Still Moses was unsatisfied and unwilling, and then God became displeased with him and bade him call his brother, Aaron. "And thou shalt speak unto him, and put words in his mouth: and I will be with thy mouth, and with his mouth, and will teach you what ye shall do. And he shall be thy spokesman unto the people: and he shall be, even he shall be to thee instead of a mouth, and thou shalt be to him instead of God."

Here we see God offering to be to Moses not only the wisdom to know what he ought to say, but the power of utterance to say it rightly. The faith of Moses, however, was not quite equal to the mighty promise. God, therefore, indulged him in his timidity and unbelief by sharing the commission with another, and giving him Aaron to be a voice and an utterance for him.

In accepting this compromise, Moses lost a great deal, for the same God that gave Aaron the power of utterance could just as well have given it to him. It was all of God from beginning to end, and Moses might just as well have had the whole blessing as the half. Indeed, as the sequel proved, the partnership of Aaron was perhaps a doubtful blessing, because the day came when this same Aaron became the tempter of Israel and the snare of Moses. It was he who made for the children of Israel the golden calf which they worshiped in idolatrous wickedness at the foot of Mt. Sinai, thereby bringing down upon their heads the anger and judgment of an offended God. So that, instead of being altogether a help to him, the prop that he leaned upon broke under his weight and pierced his own hand and heart.

The lesson is a very practical one for us. The same Spirit that called and commissioned Moses for his great undertaking is promised to us as our enduement of power for the service to which He sends us. He is able to be to us a "mouth and wisdom, which all our adversaries shall not be able to gainsay or resist." But if we look to our own strength or weakness, or lean upon the strength and wisdom of others, we, like Moses, shall find that our earthly reliance will become a snare, and we shall be taught by painful experience the wretchedness of "the man who trusteth in man and maketh flesh his arm," and the safety and happiness of depending only upon God for all our resources of wisdom and strength for the work for which He sends us.

3. The next example of the Spirit of wisdom we find in Numbers 6: 11-17, and also verses 24-29. This passage is similar to the last in its general significance. We find Moses feeling the heavy pressure of the responsibility that rested upon him as the leader of the people. Their unbelief and rebellion were continually grieving and breaking his heart, and at last he breaks out with a discouraged and petulant complaint against God, "Wherefore hast Thou afflicted Thy servant? . . . that Thou layest the burden of all this people upon me? . . . I am not able to bear all this people alone, because it is too heavy for me." God took him up immediately, as He is always ready to take us at our word.

It is a very serious thing to speak hasty words to God and words of discouragement and distrust. It is a very sad and solemn thing to ask God to relieve us of any trust that He has put upon our shoulders. It is very easy to miss our crown and our life service by petulance and unbelief. "And the Lord said unto Moses, 'Gather unto me seventy men of the elders of Israel, . . . and I will come down and talk with thee there: and I will take of the

Spirit which is upon thee, and will put it upon them; and they shall bear the burden of the people with thee, that thou bearest not thyself alone.'" And a little later it is added, "The Lord came down in a cloud, and spake unto him, and took of the Spirit that was upon him, and gave it unto the seventy elders: and it came to pass, that, when the Spirit rested upon them, they prophesied, and did not cease."

Now, at the first sight, all this looks like a very great increase of help and power to Moses; instead of bearing the burdens of the people alone he gets seventy men to help him, men of wisdom and experience, men possessing the same Spirit which was upon him. But when we look more closely at it we notice that these men did not receive any additional power whatever, but only a portion of the same Spirit which was already upon Moses. In other words, God took a little of the power that Moses already had and distributed it among a number of persons, so that instead of one person having the power, seventy-one persons now had it; but there was no more power among the seventy-one than there had been upon the one. All the wisdom of God and all the strength of God had been given to Moses personally, and God had no more to give to the seventy elders. It was spread out a little more and over a wider surface. Nay, before the story was ended, these seventy elders became as great a trial to the heart of Moses as Aaron, his brother. Indeed, they were the beginning of the famous Council of Seventy, who afterwards were called the Sanhedrin or Council of the Seventy Elders, the very Council of Seventy who afterwards condemned to death and became guilty of the crucifixion of the Son of God Himself. These, the seventy elders for whom Moses in his unbelief asked, instead of being a real help, became, perhaps, a hindrance.

What is the lesson for us? That the Spirit of God is our All-Sufficiency for every work to which He sends us, and that He is able to work as well by few as by many, by one as by one thousand. Our trust should not be in numbers or in human wisdom, but in the strength of God Himself, whether that strength is given without human instrumentalities, or through the sympathy and help of multitudes. Men may help us in the work of God, but only as God sends them and fills them with His own power.

A little later in this narrative we have the account of two of the elders, namely, Eldad and Medad, verses 26-29, who were found prophesying beyond the limits of their special appointment. Moses' friends were disposed to rebuke them and restrain them, but Moses in his large-hearted wisdom recognized the fact that God's gifts often overrun all ordinary channels and that the Holy Spirit cannot be confined by our ideas of propriety. He let them alone, as we should do with our brethren when we see them working for God and witnessing for the truth, even outside the pale of our conventional forms and organizations. God's power is greater than our petty programs, and if a man is but honoring Christ and witnessing for Him in the power of the Holy Spirit, let us not try to bring him into our particular set or make him pronounce our petty Shibboleth.

4. The next example of this divine enduement is Joshua, Numbers 27: 18. "And the Lord said unto Moses, Take unto thee Joshua the son of Nun, a man in whom is the Spirit, and lay thine hand upon him; and set him before Eleazar the priest, and before all the congregation; and give him a charge in their sight."

In this passage we see Joshua already possessing the Spirit before Moses ordains him to a special charge, showing that personal preparation must always come before public ordination. It is not the act of ordination that gives a man the Spirit, but it is the possession of the Spirit that entitles a man to public ordination. God must make a minister first by his own direct enabling. When God has given him the Spirit, it is the part of man to recognize what God has done and to set apart the truly consecrated instrument for special service.

There is another passage, Deuteronomy 34: 9, which shows how the act or ordination may be followed in a truly consecrated person by added blessing and deeper fullness of the Spirit. "And Joshua the son of Nun was full of the Spirit of wisdom; for Moses had laid his hands upon him." Here we see that after Moses laid his hands upon Joshua there was added fullness of blessing.

There are two stages, therefore, in Joshua's spiritual history: first, he has the Spirit before he was called to his great trust; and then, his call to the trust brought him a higher fullness of the Spirit. Would we be honored with special service for God? Let us be filled with the Spirit continually, and ready at His hand for whatever ministry He needs us, and we shall be more likely to be called. Have we been called to special service? Then let us throw ourselves upon Him for larger measures of His grace and, like Joshua, be filled with the Spirit.

This was the secret of Joshua's wondrous life. While Moses was divinely endued for his great task by the Spirit of wisdom, and Joseph was fitted for his practical life by the Spirit of righteousness, discretion, and courage, Joshua needed just as distinct and divine an enabling for his mighty undertaking. He was to be the military leader of Israel's great campaign, the warrior captain of the Lord's triumphant host, and he needed peculiar equipment for his mighty task. He was sent against the mightiest nations of antiquity, the powerful Hittite kings, who, as we learn from the records of the post, were the rivals of the Egyptians themselves in military prowess. He was sent with an army of undisciplined men to attack the mightiest strongholds of powerful nations. Before his victorious legions in a few short years their mightiest citadels fell, and no less than thirty-one powerful sovereigns were brought into subjection.

No grander military campaign was ever fought, and the very highest qualities of wisdom, strategy, courage, faith, and perseverance were needed for this mighty undertaking. All these were given by the Holy Spirit; and all these the Holy Spirit can still give to the soldier of Christ and the servant of God for conflict, leadership, service in the grander undertakings of these last days when Christ is marshaling His hosts for the conflict of the ages and the coming of the King.

5. We have yet one more example of the practical gifts of the Holy Spirit. In some respects it is the most remarkable and encouraging of all. We find the record in Exodus 35: 30-35. It is the story of Bezaleel and Aholiab, who were specially skilled as me-

chanics and artisans to prepare the skilled work for the erection of the tabernacle in the wilderness. And Moses said unto the children of Israel, "See, the Lord hath called by name Bezaleel . . . and hath filled him with the Spirit of God in wisdom, in understanding, and in knowledge, and in all manner of workmanship; and to devise curious works, to work in gold, and in silver, in brass, and in the cutting of stones to set them, and in the carving of wood, to make any manner of cunning work. And He hath put in his heart that he may teach, both he and Aholiab . . . Them hath He filled with wisdom of heart, to work all manner of work of the engraver, and of the cunning workman, and the embroiderer, in blue, and in purple, in scarlet, and in fine linen, and of the weaver, even of them that do any work, and of those that devise cunning work."

Here we have a list of almost all kinds of mechanical and artistic work. It is work of the most practical kind and of the very highest style of decorative art, the work of the jeweler, the carver, the embroiderer, the sculptor. All this is the result not of education, nor of careful training, but of direct divine inspiration. Here were people who had come from the brickfields of Egypt, a race of slaves without the advantages of culture, and yet God divinely enabled them in the hour of need, to devise and execute the most elaborate and ornamental designs for the most perfect and beautiful edifice which ever was constructed by the hands of man.

What a lesson for the toiling artisan, for the hard-working Christian, for the man of business, in the practical affairs of our work-a-day life. Here we have the divine Presence revealed as not only for the pulpit, the prayer meeting and the closet of prayer, but just as available for the factory, for the workshop, for the business office, for the schoolroom, and even for the kitchen. Here is a Holy Spirit who is just as much at home amid the toiling hours and heavy pressures of Monday and Saturday, as in the holy worship and the religious occupations of the Sabbath. Here is a divine sufficiency, not only for our spiritual experiences and our religious duties, so-called, but for everything that fills up our common life.

Oh, how it helps and comforts us in the plod of life to know that we have a Christ who spent the first thirty years of His life in the carpenter shop at Nazareth, swinging the hammer, covered with sweat and grimy dust, physically weary as we often are, and able to understand all our experiences of drudgery and labor, One who still loves to share our common tasks and equip us for our difficult undertakings of hand and brain!

Yes, humble sister, He will help you at the washboard and the kitchen sink as gladly as at the hour of prayer. Yes, busy mechanic, He will go with you and help you to swing the hammer, or handle the saw, or hold the plow in the toil of life; and you shall be a better mechanic, a more skillful workman, and a more successful man, because you take His wisdom for the common affairs of life. The God we serve is not only the God of the Sabbath, and of the world of sentiment and feeling; but He is the God of Providence, the God of Nature, the Author and Director of the whole mechanism of human life. There is no place nor time where He is not able and willing to walk by our side, to work through our hands and brains, and to unite Himself in loving and all-sufficient partnership with all our needs and tasks and trials, and to prove Himself our all-sufficiency for all things.

Such then is the Old Testament picture of the Holy Ghost as the Spirit of wisdom and of a sound mind. In Joseph we see Him in the trials of human life. In Moses we see Him qualifying a great leader for his high commission, and able to sustain him through the most trying emergencies and pressures. In Joshua we see Him able to equip a mighty warrior for his conflicts and campaigns and to crown his career with splendid victory, and in Bezaleel and Aholiab we see Him coming down to the level of our secular callings and our commonplace duties, and fitting us for all the tasks and toils of life.

Blessed Holy Spirit—our Wisdom and our Guide! Let us enlarge the sphere of His operations, let us take Him into partnership in all the length and breadth of our human life, and let us prove to the world that,

"We need not bid for cloistered cell,
 Our neighbor and our work farewell.
 The daily round, the common task,
 Will furnish all we need to ask.
 Room to deny ourselves a road
 To bring us daily more of God."

## Chapter 9
## The Holy Spirit in the Book of Judges

"But God hath chosen the foolish things of the world, to confound the wise; and God hath chosen the weak things of the world, to confound the things which are mighty; and base things of the world, and things which are despised, hath God chosen, and things which are not, to bring to nought things that are; that no flesh should glory in his presence. 1 Cor. 1:27, 28, 29.

The book of Judges marks the deepest depression and declension in the Old Testament records, just as the book of Joshua which precedes it, marks the most glorious triumph of Israel's history. That triumph stands between the story of the wilderness on the one side, with its forty years of wandering, and the story of the Judges on the other, with its four hundred years of declension.

The dark cloud that followed the conquest of Canaan was far deeper and denser than the one that preceded it, and it lasted through four and a half centuries, until the time of the Reformation under Samuel and David. But God loves to use the darkest clouds as His background for the rainbows of His most gracious manifestations. The brightest exhibitions of God's grace have always been in the face of the adversary's most fierce assaults.

The ministry of Elijah came in the dark hour of Jezebel's idolatrous rule. The story of Jeremiah stands over against the sorrowful scenes of Judah's captivity and Jerusalem's fall; and the book of Judges, with its four and a half centuries of idolatry and sin, have given us the beautiful incidents of Othniel and

Deborah, Gideon and Barak, Jephthah and Samson. Each of these is an object lesson of the grace and power of the Holy Spirit, in calling and using His own agents and messengers for the great work for which He needs them.

1. Othniel represents the Spirit of courage, Judges 3: 10: "And the Spirit of the Lord came upon him, and he judged Israel, and went out to war: and the Lord delivered Cushan-rishathaim king of Mesopotamia into his hand." Othniel was the first of Israel's judges, and by the power of the Holy Spirit he conquered the mighty monarch of Mesopotamia, and secured for his country nearly half a century of peace.

All this is directly attributed to the Spirit. The same power that fitted Moses for his legislative work, and prepared Joshua for his military career, called and qualified Othniel for his successful presidency over the affairs of his nation, and gave him the lion-hearted courage that enabled him to defy the mightiest potentate of the world.

But as every distinguished career has an earlier chapter behind it, so there was an hour in the story of Othniel of which all his subsequent career was but the sequel. The earlier chapter is given to us in Joshua 15: 16, 17. It is the little incident connected with the capture of one of the strongholds of Canaan. After Caleb had conquered Hebron, he found an adjacent city, Kirjath-sepher, which was the literary capital of the Canaanites. It means "The City of Books." To the brave warrior who should conquer it he offered the hand of his fair daughter Achsah. Othniel was the hero who accepted the challenge and won the double prize.

When we see some public character accomplishing distinguished service before the eyes of the world, and leaping apparently from obscurity to fame in a moment, we are apt to forget that back of that brilliant success there lies some little incident that happened, perhaps long years before, but which really struck the keynote of that life, and prepared that individual for the public service which the future held in store.

God is always preparing His workers in advance; and when the hour is ripe He brings them upon the stage, and men look with wonder upon a career of startling triumph, which God has been preparing for a lifetime. That was a wonderful day in Israel, when, in a moment, the chambers of the dead heard the voice of God, and the first human spirit came back from the world beyond to the tenement of clay, and her living son was placed in the arms of a Hebrew mother at the word of the prophet Elijah. But if we look back a few years, we find the key to all this in a little incident that happened one day in that Hebrew home. The old prophet was passing by when he met that mother and asked of her a mighty sacrifice, even that she should take the last morsel in her famine-stricken home, prepare it for him, and leave her child to die of want along with herself. But she shrank not from the test. Without a moment's hesitation she obeyed the prophet's command, and from that hour she and her little son lived in that home on the bread of heaven. When the test came that required a faith that would bring back her child even from the dead, she was ready for the hour.

God is preparing His heroes still, so that when the opportunity comes He can fit them into their places in a moment while the world wonders where they came from. Let the Holy Ghost prepare you, dear friend, by all the discipline of life, that when the last finishing touch has been given to the marble, it will be easy for God to put it on the pedestal, and fit it into the niche. There is a day coming when, like Othniel, we, too, shall judge the nations, and rule and reign with Christ on the millennial earth. But ere that glorious day can be, we must let God prepare us as He did Othniel at Kirjath-sepher, amid the trials of our present life, and in the daily victories, the significance of which, perhaps, we little dream. At least, let us be sure of this, that if the Holy Ghost has got an Othniel ready, the Lord of heaven and earth has a throne prepared for him.

2. Deborah shows forth the ministry of woman, Judges 4. Deborah is the first example of a woman called to public service by the Holy Ghost. True, Miriam had already been known as the leader of sacred song in Israel, but this was the first time that a woman had been called to exercise the public functions of a leader.

What a glorious multitude of noble women have followed in her train ! The great ministry of the Church today is being done by holy women. It is less than half a century since women began to go to the foreign mission field, and already more that half the foreign missionaries in the world are women. They are the most potent spiritual and moral forces of our age. Deborah's name means "a bee," and her little beehive under the palm tree of Mount Ephraim has swarmed and spread over all ages and lands until the hearts of millions have tasted of the honey, and every form of evil has felt the wholesome sting; but Deborah, like every true woman, had a good deal more honey than sting.

It is too late in the day to question the public ministry of woman. The facts of God's providence, and the fruits of God's Spirit, are stronger than all our theological fancies. The Holy Spirit has distinctly recognized woman's place in the Church, not only to love, to suffer, and to intercede, but to prophesy, to teach, and to minister in every proper way to the bodies and the souls of men. And yet, when we have said this, all this, there yet remains a restriction which every true woman will be willing to recognize. There is a difference between the ministry of woman and of man. God Himself has said that the head of every woman is the man, and the head of every man is Christ, and the head of Christ is God. "I suffer not a woman to teach, nor to usurp authority over the man." After all that can be said on both sides of this question, it seems to remain, as the practical conclusion of the whole matter, that woman is called without restriction to teach, to witness, to work in every department of the Church of Christ, but she is not called to rule in the ecclesiastical government of the Church of Christ, or to exercise the official ministry which the Holy Ghost has committed to the elders or bishops of His Church; and whenever she steps out of her modest sphere into the place of public leadership and executive government, she weakens her true power and loses her peculiar charm.

Deborah herself, the first public woman of the ages, was wise enough to call Barak to stand in the front, while she stood behind him, modestly directing his work, and proving in the end to be the true leader. It is no disparagement of woman's ministry to place her there. Who will say that the ministry of Moses as he stood that day on the mountain, with his hands up-lifted to God, while Joshua led the hosts in the plain below, was a lower ministry than that of Joshua? He was the true leader and the real power behind the hosts of Israel, although he was unseen by the eyes of men. This was Deborah's high honor, and no one was more ready than Barak himself to acknowledge her pre-eminence. May God more and more mightily direct and use the high and holy ministry of woman, in these last days, for the preparation of her Master's coming!

3. Gideon, or the Holy Ghost, used the weak things of the world to confound the mighty. There is something dramatic and almost ludicrous in the calling of Gideon. When hiding behind his barn for fear of the Midianites, the angel of the Lord appeared to him and called, "The Lord is with thee, thou mighty man of valor." Gideon was taken by surprise with the strange greeting, and seems himself to have felt as if the angel were laughing at him, for he was anything but a mighty man of valor; indeed, at that very moment, he was hiding from his enemies in abject fear. His answer to the angel seems to express this feeling, but God meets him with the reassuring word, "Go, in this thy might, and thou shalt deliver Israel from the Midianites." The new might which God had pledged him was His own great might, the power of the Holy Ghost. Accordingly, every step of his way from that hour was but an illustration of the principle of our text, "that God hath chosen the weak things of this world to confound the things that are mighty."

Next, we see the same principle in Gideon's workers. God could not use the great army that gathered to his standard. They were too many to afford an opportunity for God to work and, therefore, He had to sift them, and then resift them, until from over thirty thousand they were reduced to only three hundred. It is beautiful to notice how the Holy Spirit sifted them. He allowed them to do it themselves, by a natural process of reduction. First, all the timid ones were allowed to go home, and this thinned out two-thirds of the crowd. Next, all the rash and reckless ones were tested by giving them the opportunity of drinking at the brook that lay across their line of march; and, as Gideon watched, it was not difficult to find out, by the way they drank, the character of the men. The reckless ones just got down on their hands and knees and drank, without even stopping to think of their danger or their enemies. The prudent ones, on the contrary, looked carefully around, and keeping guard against a surprise from their foes, drank with prudent care, dipping up the water with their hands, and looking carefully around with their watchful eyes; thus were the wary ones chosen, and the others dismissed.

God wants not only brave men, but prudent men, for His work and warfare; and every day we live we are passing judgment on ourselves, and electing ourselves either to places of honor and service, or to be left at home, because of our unfitness. God wants fit men for His work, and He lets every man prove his fitness or unfitness by the practical tests of his daily life. We little dream, sometimes, what a hasty word, a thoughtless speech, an imprudent act, or a confession of unbelief may do to hinder our highest usefulness, or to turn it aside from some great opportunity which God was preparing for us.

Although the Holy Ghost uses weak men, He does not want them to be weak after He chooses and calls them. Although He uses the foolish things to confound the wise, He does not want us to be foolish after He comes to give us His wisdom and grace. He uses the foolishness of preaching, but not, necessarily, the foolishness of preachers. Like the electric current, which can supply the strength of a thousand men, it is necessary that it should have a proper conductor, and a very small wire is better than a very big rope. God wants fit instruments for His power, wills surrendered, hearts trusting, lives consistent, and lips obedient to His will; and then He can use the weakest weapons, and make them "mighty through God to the pulling down of strongholds."

Again, we see the Holy Spirit using the weak things of this world in the weapons of Gideon's warfare. They were very simple — lamps, pitchers and trumpets. That was all. The lamps, or torches, were expressive of the light and fire of the Holy Ghost; the pitchers suggested the broken vessels of our surrendered bodies and lives; and the trumpets signified the Word of God and the message of the Gospel that we are sent to proclaim. These are sufficient to defeat and destroy the hosts of Midian; and these are the weapons of our warfare, which are still mighty through God to the pulling down of strongholds.

A single officer of the court, with the proclamation of the president behind him, is stronger than a mob of a thousand men; and the humblest servant of the Lord Jesus Christ, armed with the Holy Ghost and the Word of God, stands with the whole power of heaven behind him. Men reject His message at their peril; for Christ has said, "He that receiveth you receiveth me, and he that rejecteth you rejecteth me." The true secret of all power with God and men is to stand behind our message and our Master, and, like Gideon's pitchers, to be so broken ourselves, that the light of our heavenly torches can flash through the broken vessels through which the message comes.

4. Jephthah, or the Holy Spirit, used "the things that are despised." Jephthah, through no fault of his own, was the child of dishonor. He had the bar sinister on his breast, and was an outlaw from his father's house. But God loves to use the things that man dispises. The stone which the builders disallowed has often become the head of the corner. It was Isaac, not Ishmael, the first-born; it was Jacob, and not Esau, the father's favorite; it was Joseph, the persecuted, wronged and outcast son; it was Moses, the son of a race of slaves, and the foundling child of the Nile; it was David, the shepherd lad of Bethlehem, and the despised one of Jesse's house; these were they whom God chose for the high place that each received in the story of His chosen people. Accordingly the outcast and the outlaw of Gilead, poor Jephthah, was chosen of the Lord to deliver his people from the Ammonites. The call of Jephthah is expressly ascribed to the Holy Spirit. "Then the Spirit of the Lord came upon Jephthah, and he passed over . . . unto the children of Ammon . . . and the Lord delivered them into his hand." 11: 29.

The Lord still is using the things that are despised. The very names of 'Nazarene' and 'Christian' were once epithets of contempt. No man can have God's highest thought and be popular with his immediate generation. The most abused men are often the most used. The devil's growl and the world's sneer are God's marks of highest honor. There is no need that we should bring upon ourselves by folly or wrong the reproaches of men; but if we do well, and suffer for it, fear not, but, "let Shimei curse, the Lord will requite us good for his cursing this day."

There are far greater calamities than to be unpopular and misunderstood. There are far worse things than to be found in the minority. Many of God's greatest blessings are lying behind the devil's scarecrows of prejudice and misrepresentation. The Holy Ghost is not ashamed to use unpopular people. And if He uses them, what need they care for men?

There was once a captain in the British army, promoted for merit, but despised by his aristocratic companions. One day the colonel found it out, and determined to stop it. So he quietly called on the young officer, and walked arm and arm with him up and down the parade ground, the captains meanwhile being obliged to salute both him and his companion every time they passed. That settled the new captain's standing. After that there were no cuts nor sneers. It was enough that the commanding officer had walked by his side.

Oh, let us but have His recognition and man's notice will count for little, and He will give us all we need of human help and praise. Let us make no compromise to please men. Let us only seek His will, His glory, His approval. Let us go for Him on the hardest errands and do the most menial tasks. It is honor enough that He uses us and sends us. Let us not fear in this day to follow Him outside the camp, bearing His reproach, and bye-and-bye He will own our worthless name before the myriads of earth and sky.

5. Samson in whom the Holy Ghost is the source of physical strength. There is no more remarkable figure in the Bible than the sturdy giant of Timnath-serah, who represented in his own

body, as no other man has ever done, the connection between physical strength and the presence and power of the Holy Ghost. The strength of Samson was not the result of physical culture and unusual size and vigor of bone, muscle, or members, but was entirely due to the presence and power of the Holy Spirit dwelling in him and working through him. The secret of his great strength is given very simply and plainly in such passages as these: Judges 13: 25; 14: 6, 19; 15: 14. In all these cases it will be noticed that it was the Spirit of the Lord that moved upon Samson and gave him his superhuman strength of body. It was not the strength of muscle or frame which comes from food or stimulants; but it was the direct power of God Himself working through his being. This was connected entirely with his separation to God and his obedience to his Nazarite vow. The strength of Samson, therefore, was divine strength given through spiritual conditions and entirely dependent upon his righteousness of life and obedience to God.

This is the very principle of divine healing, as God is teaching it to us in these last days. It is not the self-constituted strength of physical organism; but it is the supernatural force of a divine presence, filling our frame and quickening our vital system when we are wholly separated from earthly and forbidden things and living in touch with the Holy Spirit. It may be enjoyed even in the fullest measure by a feeble constitution and a man or woman naturally frail. It is not our life, but the life of Jesus manifested in our mortal flesh. It is a very sacred life, for it keeps us constantly separated from the world and unto God, and is a wholesome check upon the purity and obedience of our lives.

Samson lost his strength the moment he touched the forbidden world and the lap of Delilah. For us, too, the secret of strength is this: "If thou wilt diligently hearken to the voice of the Lord thy God, and wilt do that which is right in his sight, and wilt give ear to his commandments, and keep all his statutes, I will put none of these diseases upon thee, which I have brought upon the Egyptians: for I am the Lord that healeth thee." This is the blessed ministry of the Holy Ghost; first, to give us this practical righteousness and keep us in the perfect will of God, and then to give us the physical life and quickening promised in connection with obedience. His own promise is, "If the Spirit of Him which raised up Jesus from the dead dwell in you, He that raised up Christ from the dead shall also quicken your mortal body by His Spirit that dwelleth in you."

Such, then, is the blessed fullness of the Holy Spirit as unfolded in this ancient book of Judges. How much more rich and full the grace we may expect from Him today!

Shall we take Him with Othniel as the Spirit of courage; with Deborah, for woman's high and glorious ministry; with Gideon and Jepthah, to use the weak things of this world to confound the mighty, and the things which are despised, yea, and the things which are not, to bring to naught the things which are; and shall we, like Samson, "out of weakness be made strong, wax valiant in fight and turn to flight the armies of the aliens"?

# Chapter 10

# A Spirit-Filled Man

"But there is a spirit in man: and the inspiration of the Almighty giveth them understanding." Job 32: 8. "The Spirit of God hath made me, and the breath of the Almighty hath given me life." Job 33: 4.

The book of Job is the oldest poem in the world. It has come down to us from a period somewhere between the time of Abraham and Joshua. It is a profoundly interesting drama, unfolding some of the most important principles of the divine government, and revealing God's personal dealings with His people through the Holy Spirit.

First, Job himself appears upon the scene as the type of a high and noble character, a man of perfect uprightness, one who represents the very highest ideal of human character. Next, we see God testing this man, revealing to him the depths of self and sin which lie concealed in every human soul, until, at length, Job appears under the searchlight of the Holy Ghost a pitiful spectacle, not only of disease and suffering, but of self-righteousness, self-vindication, and rebellion against God Himself. One by one various characters appear upon the scene, representing the wisdom and comfort and friendship of the world — in fact, all that the world can do to help us in our trouble. We have Bildad and Eliphaz and Zophar representing, perhaps, the wisdom, the wealth, and the pleasure of the world, but all failing to bring to Job the comfort, the instruction, and the discipline that he needs.

Finally, Elihu appears upon the stage; and, for the first time, he brings the message and the help of God. His very name signifies God Himself, and his words are in keeping with the source from which his message comes. Let us look at him as one of the oldest examples of the indwelling, inworking, and outflowing of the Holy Spirit. First, we have the man. Secondly, we will consider his message. And then we will notice the effect of his message in its influence upon Job, the object of attention in the whole drama of this wonderful book.

First, he tells us himself that he was a young man. "I am young," he says, "and ye are very old; wherefore I was afraid, and durst not shew you my opinion." God can speak to and through even the youngest of His disciples. But notice the modesty of Elihu. He was sensitive, shrinking, and full of that modest diffidence which is always the criterion of true worth. The more God uses us, the more should we shrink out of self-consciousness and human observation. Then, we see not only his modesty, but his respect for others and his beautiful disposition to wait and to show the utmost deference to those who are naturally his superiors. There is no reason why we should thrust ourselves forward because we have the Holy Spirit and are trusted with His messages. The Spirit-filled man will always be filled with deference and consideration for others. In speaking to the New Testament assemblies, the apostle tells them particularly to guard against this very thing, for He says, "The spirits of the prophets are subject to the prophets." When God gives us a message He can afford to have us wait. So Elihu waited till the others were through, and then he spoke with effect.

But while Elihu is respectful and modest, he is at the same time perfectly independent of the opinions of people, and is bold and fearless in obeying the voice of God, which he has heard in the depths of his own soul. "Let me not, I pray you, accept any man's person; neither let me give flattering titles unto man. For I know not to give flattering titles; in so doing my Maker would soon take me away." And so the Spirit-filled man is free from all men. He does not try to copy any man, but listens directly to the voice of God through His Word and His Spirit. So many of us are parrots, catching the opinion and the ideas of others. God wants individual characters and individual messages, and every one of us to be himself filled and taught of the Holy Ghost.

We see in Elihu a man so filled with the Holy Ghost that he cannot keep back his words. He says, "The Spirit within me constraineth me. Behold, my belly is as wine which hath no vent; it is ready to burst like new bottles." This is the way the apostle felt, "We cannot but speak the things which we have seen and heard." We need this volcanic power to give force and propelling power to the message with which God trusts us.

Again, we see in Elihu a man supremely anxious to glorify God, and grieved because Job's friends have not answered his questions and vindicated God. His one desire is to glorify his Maker and his Master. Such a man always will be taught and used of His Master. The Holy Spirit is waiting for such men and women.

II. THE MESSAGE OF ELIHU

It is a very wonderful message. It unfolds the deepest principles of God's moral government, and rises to the loftiest height of inspired eloquence. There is no profounder discussion of God's dealings with His children. God is always speaking to His people. "God speaketh once, yea, twice, yet man perceiveth it not," is heedless, or blind and deaf, failing therefore, to understand his Father's voice.

Then God has to speak again through sickness and physical suffering; and so we have the picture in the thirty-third chapter, from the nineteenth to the twenty-second verses. It is the picture of a poor sufferer chastened with pain, sinking day by day into emaciation and exhaustion, until he is ready to drop into the grave. This, however, is not God's last voice; there is another message, but oh, how rarely and how seldom the true messenger is found! "One among a thousand." What a blessed message He brings! He shows man His uprightness, the loving kindness of His chastening, leading him to repentance, and then He unfolds the blessed message of the great atonement, and cries, "Deliver him from going down to the pit; I have found a ransom." What is the effect of this? "His flesh shall be fresher than a child's; he shall return to the days of his youth."

This is the blessed Gospel of the Atonement — atonement for sickness as well as sin; this is the blessed Gospel of Healing — healing for body as well as soul. It was God's ancient thought, and it is still unchanged — His will for all who will simply believe and receive. This is God's uniform principle of dealing with His children. "These things worketh God oftentimes with man, to bring back his soul from the pit, to be enlightened with the light of the living." God's chastenings are not the zigzag lightnings of the sky, that strike we know not where or when, but the intelligent, intelligible, loving dealings of a Father, who will let us understand why He afflicts us. He Himself has told us in the New Testament, "If we would judge ourselves, we should not be judged. But when we are judged, we are chastened of the Lord, that we should not be condemned with the world." This is God's object in dealing with His children, to bring them out of some position that is wrong into His higher will; and as soon as we learn our lesson, He is glad to remove the pressure, and to bring us into the full manifestation of His favor and blessing for both soul and body. Can we find anywhere a wiser, broader, truer unfolding of God's gracious providence and His loving, faithful dealings with His children than in the old message of Elihu, more than three thousand years ago.

Then He passes on to a more sublime discourse, in which He sweeps the whole circle of the heavens and the whole field of nature, and unfolds the glory and majesty of God in all His works. At length, as He reaches His loftiest height, God interrupts Him, and closes His sublime oration with a yet grander peroration, as He speaks through the whirlwind to Job with a voice that he can no longer answer nor gainsay.

### III. THE EFFECT OF THE MESSAGE

This brings us to the effect of the message upon Job himself. This is the great central thought of the whole book and the entire drama. Job meets us as the central figure and the type of ourselves. He represents man at his best, just as Elihu at the close represents man at God's best.

We see in Job an upright man, the best man of his time, the best that man can be by the help of divine grace, until he dies to himself altogether and enters into union with God Himself.

The first picture of Job is a favorable one, both to himself and to everybody else. He seems to be all right, until God brings the searchlight and the surgical probe to bear upon him, when, like everything else that is human, he breaks completely down, and shows himself in all the weakness and worthlessness of our lost humanity. The worst thing that we find in Job is Job himself. God was not trying to convince him of any glaring sin, but of his self-sufficiency, self-righteousness, and self-confidence. The thing that we have to deny is self. The hardest thing to see and to crucify is our own self-confidence and self-will; and we have to pass through many a painful incident and many a humiliating failure before we find it out and fully recognize it.

Accordingly we find Job, under the divine searchlight, signally failing, revealing his unbelief, vindicating himself, and even blaming God for unjustly afflicting him. One by one his various friends appear upon the scene representing the wisdom, wealth, and pleasure of the world; but Job sees through the fallacy of all their arguments, and refuses their messages, until, at length, Elihu comes with the inspired message of God. God follows it by directly revealing Himself to Job, and speaking from the whirlwind with a voice that he can no longer resist. Job, in the light of God, at length wakes up to his own worthlessness and nothingness, and falling silent at Jehovah's feet, he cries, "I have heard of Thee by the hearing of the ear: but now mine eye seeth thee. Wherefore I abhor myself, and repent in dust and ashes." This is, at last, the death of self; and now God is ready to pick up His servant, to forgive his errors and faults, and even to vindicate him in the face of his friends.

Then, for the first time, we hear God approving Job and saying to his unwise friends, "Ye have not spoken of me the thing which is right, as my servant Job hath." What was the thing which Job had spoken of Him that was right? It was his language of self-condemnation, humiliation, renunciation. Job had now ended and God was ready to begin. God immediately responds to him not only with His favor and blessing, but with all the prosperity and blessing which he had lost; and Job rises to a new place in every way.

This is the resurrection life unfolded in the ancient type. This is the resurrection life into which the Holy Ghost is waiting to bring all who are willing, like Job, to die to the life of self. God was not looking in Job for any open sin or flagrant wrong; but He was searching for the subtle self-life which lies concealed behind a thousand disguises in us all, and which is so slow and so unwilling to die. God has often to bring us not only into the place of suffering, and to the bed of sickness and pain, but also into the place where our righteousness breaks down, and our character falls to pieces, in order to humble us in the dust and to show us the need of entire crucifixion to all our natural life. Then, at the feet of Jesus we are ready to receive Him, to abide in Him, to depend upon Him alone, and to draw all our life and strength each moment from Him, our Living Head.

It was thus that Peter was saved by his very fall. He had to die to Peter that he might live more perfectly to Christ.

Have we thus died, and have we thus renounced the strength of our own self-confidence? Happy, indeed, are we if this be so; for we shall have Christ and all His resources of strength. Then He can afford to give to us, as he did to Job, all the riches of His goodness and all the gifts of His providence that we need in our secular and temporal life. We begin life with the natural, next we come into the spiritual; then, when we have truly received the Kingdom of God and His righteousness, the natural is added to the spiritual, and we are able to receive the gifts of His providence and the blessings of life without becoming centered in them or allowing them to separate us from Him.

This is the sweet lesson of the life of Job. This is the bright and happy sequel to all his sorrow. This is the ripening of the seed of death and pain. This is the blessed fruition of all his affliction. This is but a little type of that richer resurrection life which the New Testament reveals.

The blessed Holy Spirit is waiting to lead us all into the path of life through the gates of death. Some one tells of a gentleman who called upon an old friend and was invited by the proprietor to go with him to survey his splendid new warehouse. As they started to go to the upper floor, the visitor began immediately to climb the stair. "Oh,"said his friend, "this way,"and opened a little side door and led him down a few steps to a platform where a door opened into an elevator. "This is the way we go up now"; and then they mounted by that elevator to the very top of the building, eight or ten stories high, and came down from floor to floor without the slightest effort. As they returned to the office the gentleman said: "I have just been thinking that this is God's new way of ascension. He leads us down first, and then He puts us into His elevator and lifts us up to Himself."

This is the story of Job. This is the story of Jesus. This is the story of every true life. "Except a corn of wheat fall into the ground and die, it abideth alone; but if it die, it bringeth forth much fruit." God help us to die. Fear not the pain, the sacrifice, the surrender. "Though I walk through the valley of the shadow of death, I fear no evil: for thou art with me."And on the other side you shall say, "Thou anointest my head with oil; my cup runneth over. Surely goodness and mercy shall follow me all the days of my life; and I will dwell in the house of the Lord forever."

Oh, how sweet it is to die with Jesus,
To the world and self and sin!
Oh, how sweet it is to live with Jesus,
As He lives and reigns within!

## Chapter 11

## The Holy Spirit in the Lives of Saul and David

"Create in me a clean heart, O God; and renew a right spirit within me. Cast me not away from thy presence; and take not thy holy Spirit from me. Restore unto me the joy of thy salvation; and uphold me with thy free Spirit." Psalm 5: 10-12.

These words express the prayer of David at an important era in his life, and suggest to us his relation to the Holy Spirit in his deepest experience. Back of this picture there lies in dim outline another picture, that of a life that had also possessed the Holy Spirit but had lost His blessing; and it was, perhaps, in reference to this dark, sad background that David cried, "Take not Thy Holy Spirit from me." The other picture is that of Saul. These two lives stand side by side as companion pictures illustrating the dealings of the Holy Spirit with two opposite characters, and leading to entirely opposite results. It is a very solemn contrast and a very instructive lesson.

1. First, in the story of Saul we find that he, too, had the Holy Spirit. We have a very distinct account of his call and enduement by the Spirit. We find the story in the tenth chapter of First Samuel. Here we see the Spirit coming upon a man almost unsought, and apparently without any spiritual preparation. It was the Spirit of God coming for service, giving him power to prophesy, to conquer, to rule, the enduement for service rather than for personal experience.

There is always real danger just at this point. It is a very serious thing to want the Holy Ghost simply to give us power to work for God. It is much more important that we should receive the Holy Spirit for personal character and personal holiness. Perhaps the deep secret of Saul's failure was that, like Balaam, he had power to witness and to work rather than to live and obey.

God's graces are higher than God's gifts, and one grain of love is worth a thousand lightning flashes of prophetic fire.

Again, we see, perhaps, another secret of Saul's failure, in the fact that the power came upon him largely from others. It was when he was in company with the prophets that the spirit of prophecy came upon him.

There is always the danger of absorbing much from the atmosphere around us, and being too little self-contained and directly centered in God. "Cursed is the man that trusteth in man, and maketh flesh his arm, and whose heart is departed from the Lord." The difference between Saul and David was that David knew God for himself, and knew Him from a deep personal experience of the indwelling life of the Spirit, and the outflowing life of habitual obedience, while Saul knew Him only as a supernatural impulse for his public life.

But notwithstanding these drawbacks, the enduement of Saul with the Spirit of God was very deep and very important. It marked a complete crisis in his life, and his heart was changed into another heart, and he became another man.

It is very remarkable how fully God can possess a human soul. We read of demoniac possession through which the entire being of a man becomes so controlled by evil spirits that they are able to add tenfold intensity and force to his life. Why may not a man be just as much God-possessed as he can be Satan-possessed, so that every faculty and power of his being shall be filled with the power of the Holy Ghost, and his energy and capability shall be redoubled?

This was the case with Saul, and it may be true of us. Look again, how all-sufficient His divine presence was for every emergency. "When this is come upon thee," Samuel said, "thou shalt do as occasion serve thee; for God is with thee."

We do not need to have elaborate plans or depend upon our own wisdom; for we have a Guide and a Friend that will direct us as need shall require, and, if we will acknowledge Him in all our ways, He will direct our paths.

So Saul started in his career. No man ever had a more promising beginning, supported by splendid personnel, an enthusiastic people, a clear call of God and a manifestly divine enduement for his great work. Surely he had every opportunity to accomplish the grandest results for God and man.

But, alas! he ended in disappointment and failure. His kingdom ere long was rent from him by the hand of God, and his sun went down in darkness and blood. What were the causes of his failure, and what are the lessons of this strange career?

We find the test coming to him very soon. Samuel sent him on a high commission, and told him to wait a certain time until he should arrive. He bade him tarry seven days, promising him to come and offer sacrifices to God before marching against their enemies. Saul waited until the seven days had expired, and then, becoming impatient and anxious, he rashly offered the sacrifice himself. No sooner was the sacrifice accomplished than Samuel arrived and told him that, by his disobedience, he had forfeited the approval of God and the permanence of his kingdom.

It may seem a little thing, but little things are always deciding the issues of life because they are the best tests of real principle and character. It was but a little thing that wrecked the human race. One trifling act of disobedience, one minute detail of God's commandments in which our first parents dared to take their own way and began the career of rebellion and independence which has brought upon the human race all their sorrow.

This act indicated the true spirit of Saul. One word expresses that better than any other, self-will.

Although God had appointed him to be His king, Saul insisted upon being his own master, thereby proving himself unfit for his trust.

It was not long before the second test came. God gave Saul another chance, He sent him on an expedition against the Amalekites, Israel's ancient foes, types of the flesh and the world, and the enemies of the true life of God in the soul. His instructions were implicit and peremptory. He was to destroy Amalek utterly. Because God went with him in his expedition and crowned him with success, Saul returned victorious, having subdued Amalek and laid waste all their cities; but he brought back with him the best of the spoil and Agag, their king, to grace his triumph.

Samuel arrived just as he was congratulating himself on his splendid success, and his faithful fulfillment of his great commission. Saul met him with confidence, but Samuel responded with a stern rebuke. "I have obeyed the commandment of the Lord,"says the king. Then followed those terrible words of divine denunciation, which ended at last in the withdrawal of Samuel. As Saul clung to him in despair, the prophet's garment parted in the hands of the king, and Samuel declared that it was the pledge of the broken covenant and the loss of his kingdom.

Saul betrayed the real earthliness of his heart by his last appeal. "Honor me," he cried, "at least before the people," and God granted him the little gratification which for the time satisfied his poor shallow heart. Out of this dark and dreadful scene there comes one sentence which is the keynote of true obedience and true success. "Obedience is better than sacrifice and to hearken than the fat of the rams." This was the secret of Saul's failure; he lacked the true hearkening spirit and the obedient will.

He was quite willing to go half way with God as long as it did not cross his personal preferences; but when there came a test and a sacrifice, his obedience failed, and he pleased himself rather than God. This was the essential difference between Saul and David. It was this that made David a man after God's heart. He wanted to obey God, and the real purpose of his heart was to please Jehovah.

Saul was a man after his own heart, and he wanted to please and glorify poor Saul. He was the type of a man that had power without grace, and gifts without holiness.

His desire to spare Agag was but a sample of his whole spirit. He wanted to spare himself. Agag is the type of the self-life and the whole story illustrates the great lesson of self-crucifixion, which lies at the threshold of all spiritual blessing. Amalek and the flesh must die. Saul was not willing that they should die, and, therefore, Saul had to die. He that would save his life must lose it, and he that is willing to lose his earth-life will keep it unto the life that is not of earth but eternal.

This was the turning point in Saul's career. From this time the Spirit of God left him, and "an evil spirit from God" possessed him. It was the spirit of Satan, but it was by divine permission.

We touch a very awful theme here, but one that we dare not evade. We are taught in many places in the Holy Scripture that when men refuse the leading of the Holy Ghost, and choose their own way and the ways of Satan, the Lord lets them be filled with their own devices and gives them over to the power of evil.

Oh, let us not trifle with the sacred things of God! Let us not talk lightly of the perseverance of the saints when we are presumptuously disobeying God. Like the little child who keeps her hoop steady in its movement by touching it first on the one side then upon the other, so God speaks to us His promises and His threatenings as we are ready to receive them. To the disobedient and careless disciple He says with great solemnity, "Let him that thinketh he standeth take heed lest he fall." But to the poor trembling heart, sinking in its own discouragement, He cries, "I will never leave thee nor forsake thee"; "My sheep hear my voice, and I know them, and they follow me: and I give unto them eternal life; and they shall never perish, neither shall any man pluck them out of my hand."

Like the pilgrim in Bunyan's dream, let us both hope and fear. Let us guard against the first step backward. We never know where it is going to end. The apostle hints that it may be unto perdition, and he pleads with us, "Cast not, therefore, away your confidence." "If any man draw back, my soul shall have no pleasure in him. But we are not of them who draw back unto perdition, but of them who believe to the saving of the soul."

2. David, likewise, has his experience of the Holy Ghost.

In the same paragraph that tells us of the Holy Spirit's departing from Saul, we read these simple words, "Then Samuel took the horn of oil, and anointed him in the midst of his brethren: and the Spirit of the Lord came upon David from that day forward." (1 Samuel 16: 13).

The first effect of the Holy Spirit upon David is shown in the next reference, in the eighteenth chapter of first Samuel and the fifth verse, where we read that "David went out whithersoever Saul sent him, and he behaved himself wisely."

This was not only an anointing with power, but an anointing also of wisdom and grace, enabling him to live a true life and to commend himself to this master and to all men.

The subsequent story of David's life is but an unfolding of the power of the Holy Spirit. In the book of Psalms we have the inner life of David, and in the historical books we have the outer story that corresponded to this.

We find David himself attributing his military exploits and his physical power, as well as the success of His whole kingdom, to the power of the God upon whom he depended. There is no finer illustration of this than the eighteenth Psalm, in which he himself tells us the secret of his strength.

"He teacheth my hands to war, so that a bow of steel is broken by mine arms."

"Thou hast also given me the shield of thy salvation: and thy right hand hath holden me up, and thy gentleness hath made me great." Yet the warrior king recognized in his body the same power which gives us strength today in the name of the Lord Jesus Christ, and attributed all his victories to the power of the Holy Ghost.

In the story of his campaigns we have some vivid illustrations of his constant dependence upon the presence of God and the leadership of His Spirit. Even when he wandered as a fugitive among his enemies, we find him constantly inquiring of the Lord about all his movements. When, as he ascended the throne, the

Philistines came up against him, we see him at once appealing to Jehovah, and asking, "Shall I go up to the Philistines? Wilt thou deliver them into my hand? Not until the answer came and the order was given to move, did he presume to go forward.

It is needless to say that his movements were crowned with victory. A year later when the same enemy returned in force, David did not go against them as before. He again went to God for direct guidance, but he received an entirely different direction.

"Thou shalt not go up; but fetch a compass behind them, and come upon them over against the mulberry trees. And let it be, when thou hearest the sound of a going in the tops of the mulberry trees, that then thou shalt bestir thyself: for then shall the Lord go out before thee, to smite the host of the Philistines." Surely this was a divine plan of battle and a divine victory.

Thus he fought his battles, thus he won his crown; thus he ruled and organized his people; thus he planned the glorious temple; and thus he lived his wondrous life in the power of the same Holy Spirit which comes to us in the fuller light of the New Testament Dispensation.

We have in the Psalms some delightful revelations of the relation of the Holy Spirit to his inner life. We find in one of the most profoundly spiritual of them this prayer, "Thy Spirit is good; lead me into the land of uprightness." We see in some of them the unfoldings of a deeper life which makes them lighthouses for us upon the voyage of our higher Christian experience.

Nowhere else can we find a profounder conception of faith than in some of these Psalms. The thirty-seventh Psalm is not unlike the beatitudes of the Lord Jesus Christ Himself.

There we see two pictures, one corresponding to the story of Saul and the other to the spirit of David. There we see a man who is plotting against God's servant and seeking to slay him; and there we see the spirit of trust, fretting not because of evildoers, but trusting in the Lord with holy obedience, committing his way unto the Lord, and waiting patiently for Him, resting in the Lord and delighting himself in Him, and receiving from Him the desires of his heart.

Surely the man who could write this must have drunk deeply of the fountain of the Holy Spirit.

In the passage which we have quoted as our text we have a most definite unfolding of the Holy Spirit in David's personal experience. He is represented here in a threefold aspect, and under three distinct names. First, as the right spirit, "Renew a right spirit within me"; second, as the Holy Spirit, "Take not thy holy Spirit from me"; third, as the free spirit, which literally means the princely spirit, the lofty, noble spirit, the spirit which communicates life and liberty. "Uphold with thy free spirit."

These are not repetitions. First, there is the right spirit. This is connected with the clean heart. It is it work of creation. It is the spirit of the newborn soul. It is the heart that has been purified. It is not so much the indwelling person of the Spirit as the effect of His work in producing rightness of heart toward God and toward man.

Secondly, we have the Holy Spirit. This is the person of the Holy Ghost Himself, which will come into the heart that has been made right, and dwell within us in His power and holiness.

It is the Holy Spirit, the spirit which brings holiness; and holiness just means wholeness, completeness, entire conformity to the will of God. David here intimates the possibility of losing this Holy Spirit, as Saul had done; but he cries, "take not thy holy Spirit from me."

David's trust is very beautiful. He had come to a great crisis. He had forfeited his kingdom and his place of deeper blessing. Had it not been for his confidence in God, he would have been driven to despair. He had fallen and fallen so far that his whole moral nature was stunned, and his spiritual sensibilities were so paralyzed that he was left for four long years without the consciousness of his very fall. When he awoke from his dream to the dreadful consciousness of his sin, the realization of his iniquity was fearful.

He beheld himself in the light of the Holy Ghost, and cried again, "Against thee, thee only, have I sinned." Yet, in the face of this dark and dreadful vision, he saw the grace of God as perhaps no one ever saw it before; and he was able to rise from the depths of sin to the heights of mercy, and cry, "I shall be whiter than snow." Judas had a similar vision of his sin, but without the vision of mercy, and he sank to rise no more. But God in His infinite mercy gave David the faith to realize the divine love, so he rose from the abyss of sin to the heights of salvation. We have a similar incident in the story of the woman of Canaan, to whom Jesus gave the fearful words, "It is not meet to take the children's bread and to cast it to the dogs." That expression, "dogs," meant the very depths of sin and unnatural crime. She did not deny it; she accepted it with lowly heart. Then she leaped from the depths of her unworthiness and penitence to the highest place in His love, and claimed, even as a dog, a crumb of her Master's bread. Jesus looked upon her with wonder, because she had been able to see her own unworthiness and yet to accept His mercy and grace.

This was the spirit that enabled David to trust God even in the darkest hour, and doubtless it brought David nearer to God than he had ever been before.

There is a third designation of the Holy Spirit here, "Uphold me with thy free spirit." There was danger that, in coming back to God from such an awful state, he should come in the spirit of servile fear.

And so he asks that God would give him the spirit of love and holy liberty. David is the prodigal coming back to take the highest place, to wear the best robe, the royal ring, and to sit at the heavenly banquet. God wants us all to have this spirit. It is the spirit of sonship; it is the spirit of confidence; it is the newborn spirit; it is the princely spirit.

God takes us in Jesus Christ "even as He." He has made us accepted in the Beloved, and we cannot honor Him so much in any other way as by accepting the place He gives us and counting ourselves the objects of His perfect complacency and infinite love through Jesus Christ our Lord.

This is the spirit of power, the spirit of love, the spirit that has spring in it and force in it, and leads us out to self-sacrifice and unselfish love. And so He adds, "Then will I teach transgressors thy ways; and sinners shall be converted unto thee . . . and my tongue shall sing aloud of thy righteousness."

Was it with reference to this experience that he wrote the wondrous twenty-third Psalm? Surely we find here the same progression of thought and experience. First we see the restored sheep under the Shepherd's care, rejoicing in the green pastures and lying down by the waters of rest. Next we see a different picture. It is t he wandering sheep, but the wandering sheep is not remembered except in the song of restoration. He restoreth my soul, He maketh me to walk in the right paths, for His name's sake.

It is here that the crisis comes, "The valley of the shadow of death." This is not literal death, but that deeper death to self and sin through which every true life must pass, and through which, perhaps, David passed after the tragedy of Uriah and Bathsheba.

Although it is a very dark valley, there is one bright thing through it all — the presence of the Lord. "Thou art with me; thy rod and thy staff they comfort me"; "I will fear no evil."

You will notice that here He speaks of the second person. It is no longer He but Thou. God is now by his side and in his very heart. Now, how all has changed! Instead of the Shepherd, it is the Father; and instead of the fold, it is the banqueting house and the home circle. Instead of the painful returning of the prodigal, it is the table spread in the presence of his enemies, the head anointed with oil, and the overflowing cup. This is "THE FREE SPIRIT." This is the blessing that there is not room enough to receive. Before him all is brighter still. As he looks out into the coming vista he cries, "Surely goodness and mercy shall follow me all the days of my life; and I will dwell in the house of the Lord forever."

Beloved, these are "the sure mercies of David." The Lord is waiting to give the same right spirit, the same Holy Spirit, the same free spirit, the same fullness of blessing for spirit, soul, and body. Oh, it may be that some of us, like David, have sunk with him into sin and despair! Do not yield to discouragement, but recognize the hand of mercy in the fall. Perhaps it was divine love, showing you that you were not strong enough to stand alone, and bringing you back, not to the old place of blessing, but to a place where He is able to keep you from stumbling, and to present you faultless before the presence of His glory with exceeding joy.

That blessed Holy Spirit is ready to come to you and to "cause you to walk in his statutes, so that you shall keep his judgments and do them." That "Free Spirit" is longing so to fill you that "the water that he shall give you shall be in you a well of water, springing up into everlasting life"; nay, more, that drinking of His fullness you shall not be able to hold the blessing, and out of your inmost being shall go forth to others rivers of living water; and your blessing shall reach its consummation in David's closing song, "Then will I teach transgressors thy way; and sinners shall be converted unto thee." "O Lord, open thou my lips; and my mouth shall shew forth thy praise."

## Chapter 12

## The Holy Spirit in the Book of Proverbs

"Wisdom crieth without; she uttereth her voice in the streets; "She crieth in the chief place of concourse, in the openings of the gates: in the city she uttereth her words, saying, "How long, ye simple ones, will ye love simplicity? and the scorners delight in their scorning, and fools hate knowledge? "Turn you at my reproof: behold, I will pour out my Spirit unto you, I will make known my words unto you. " Prov. 1: 20, 21, 22, 23.

There is a beautiful incident in the early history of Solomon which reveals the secret of his extraordinary life. Just after his accession to the throne of his father, David, the Lord appeared to him in Gibeon, and gave him the right to choose any blessing he desired. Instead of choosing wealth, power, long life, and the lives of his enemies, he simply asked for wisdom; and God was so pleased with him for his simple single choice that He gave him not only wisdom, but all these other blessings also. Solomon became renowned for superhuman wisdom, and, in this book of Proverbs, we have some of the utterances of that wisdom, crystalized in the form of these short, sententious words, which have been well called "pearls at random strung."

It, is said that the people of Scotland are accustomed to carry in their vest pockets a small copy of the book of Proverbs, as a sort of "vade mecum," a kind of manual of practical wisdom, for the guidance of their everyday life.

This book reveals to us a phase of life that is extremely practical and important, and shows us the teachings and workings of the Holy Ghost as they affect our everyday life. The keyword to this whole book is the word Wisdom. It occurs scores of times.

It is a peculiar Hebrew word, and in these pages it becomes personified until it is really a proper name. It is very much like another term applied to our Lord Jesus Christ in the New Testament; namely, the Word, or Logos, introduced to us in the first chapter of the Gospel of John. Indeed, the Word in John and Wisdom in Proverbs are really the same Person, the Lord Jesus Christ Himself, revealed in these ancient pages in His primeval glory. But the Lord Jesus Christ always stands connected with the Holy Spirit, who reveals Him, and who filled Him, and spake and wrought through Him during His earthly ministry; so that Wisdom in the book of Proverbs is not only the personification of Jesus Christ but also of the blessed Holy Ghost.

Let us look at some of the pictures of this blessed Person in these ancient pages.

I. First, we see Him in His personal and primeval glory. This is unfolded in the sublime vision of the eighth chapter of Proverbs. "The Lord possessed me in the beginning of his way, before his works of old." This blessed Person is older than the creation. "I was set up from everlasting, from the beginning, or ever the earth was. When there were no depths, I was brought forth; when there were no fountains abounding with water. Before the mountains were settled, before the hills was I brought forth: while as yet he had not made the earth, nor the fields, nor the highest part of the dust of the world."

Next, we see Him taking part in the work of creation. "When he prepared the heavens, I was there: when he set a compass upon the face of the depth; when he established the clouds above; when he strengthened the fountains of the deep; when he gave to the sea his decree, that the waters should not pass his commandment; when he appointed the foundations of the earth: then I was by him, as one brought up with him; and I was daily his delight, rejoicing always before him."

Oh, what depths of light these strange illuminated verses pour upon the fellowship of the Father, the Son, and the Holy

Ghost, in the remote eternal ages! And, oh, what love to our poor human race these words reveal, "Rejoicing in the habitable part of his earth; and my delights were with the sons of men"!

This blessed Christ, this blessed Comforter, who seeks your love, is no less than the second and third Persons of the Eternal Godhead. By them these heavens were made and this earth was formed. All the majesty of nature is their handiwork. All the wisdom of the ages has come from their eternal mind. Not only do they represent the wisdom and power of God, but they represent a love that has thought of us from the very beginning, and will love us to the end.

When this world was made, when the mountains were settled and the fountains and the rivers were opened, God was thinking of us, the Holy Ghost was planning for our happiness and welfare.

The whole material universe, the whole structure of nature, the whole economy of the ages was planned with a view to our creation, our redemption, our eternal glory. Redemption is no afterthought of God; but when He made this earth, and settled the stars in their orbits, He did it with a view to man's creation and future destiny. Oh, surely we can trust Him with our future when we think of His eternal past ! Oh, surely we need not hesitate to commit our destiny to those Almighty hands, that have spanned these heavens and laid the foundations of the earth, and to that heart of eternal love that loved us from the first of time, and loves us to the last!

But not only do we see His part in creation, but also in providence. "By me," he says, "kings reign, and princes decree justice. By me princes rule, and nobles, even all the judges of the earth." His is the wisdom that has inspired every high and mighty thought of man; His is the fire that has kindled every touch of human genius. He is the foundation of all life, and truth, and wisdom, and power; and He offers to be at once our wisdom, our guide, our power, and our all-sufficiency.

Surely we may well heed His gentle voice, as He calls to us in the light of all this record of glory: "Now, therefore, hearken unto me, ye children; for blessed are they that keep my ways. Hear instruction, and be wise, and refuse it not; for whoso findeth me findeth life, and shall obtain the favor of the Lord, but he that sinneth against me wrongeth his own soul; all they that hate me love death."

II. The next chapter reveals to us this divine Wisdom building her house, hewing out her seven pillars, killing her sacrifices, spreading her table, inviting her guests, and calling her friends to the banquet of her bounty and grace. This, also, is a picture of the Holy Ghost. The house that she is building is the Church of Christ. The seven pillars that stand in the front are truth, righteousness, life, faith, love, power, and hope. The sacrifice is that of Christ, our great atonement; and the banquet prepared is the feast of His love, the Living Bread which He Himself provides, and the wine of joy and blessing that comes from the indwelling of His Holy Spirit. Into this blessed house of mercy and unto this table of every heavenly blessing, the Holy Spirit is inviting a starving world.

In contrast with this blessed woman, who stands in the front of the picture, there is another woman revealed in the closing verses. It is the woman that so often appears in the pictures of Proverbs, that evil woman who sits in the highway of life calling to the passers-by to

partake of her unhallowed joy, inviting the foolish and the simple to partake of her forbidden pleasures, saying to them, "Stolen waters are sweet, and bread eaten in secret is pleasant." But, alas! there is an awful skeleton behind that door, and a fearful cry that comes from that house of folly and sin, for the prophet tells us "that the dead are there; and her guests are in the depths of hell."

So the two houses stand face to face on the highway of life; the heavenly house, with the Holy Ghost standing at its door and inviting in the children of sin and sorrow, and saying, "Ho, every one that thirsteth, ... come ye, buy and eat; yea, come, buy wine and milk without money, and without price. Wherefore do ye spend your money for that which is not bread? and your labor for that which satisfieth not?" And right across the way, with the multitude surging by and pressing in the house of pleasure, the house of shame, the house of sin, whose steps are hard by the gates of hell.

III. We turn back to the first chapter of Proverbs, and we have another picture of Wisdom as an impersonation of the Holy Ghost. She is standing now in the streets of the great city, in the entering in of the gates, in the places of public concourse, and calling to the passing crowd as they go heedlessly by, "How long, ye simple ones, will ye love simplicity? and the scorners delight in their scorning, and fools hate knowledge. Turn you at my reproof: behold, I will pour out my spirit unto you, I will make known my words unto you. "This is the Holy Ghost pleading with a lost, perishing world. This is the Spirit of God, in the messengers of the Gospel, inviting men to turn to God. This is the vision of divine mercy trying to save men through the message of the Gospel.

Notice that she does not stand behind a pulpit railing and inside upon the marble steps of a splendid cathedral. This was the way that Isaiah prophesied, that Jonah preached, that Jesus preached, and that Paul often proclaimed the Gospel.

We cannot wait for a sinful world to come to our doors. We must go out quickly, and constrain them to come in; and if we are filled with the Holy Ghost, our cry, like Wisdom's, will still be heard in the streets, and amid the concourse of crowds, and at the entering in of the gates. It is the same old cry, "Repent"; "Turn you at my reproof." It is the call to men to turn from sin and turn to God; and the promise comes with it that God will give His Spirit to the returning sinner, and enable him to repent, believe, and obey.

Oh, is there any sinful soul listening to this message or reading these lines? He calls to thee, "Turn you at my reproof," and He will pour out His Spirit upon you as you put yourself in the place of blessing, and He will make known His words unto you, and lead you into all truth as you follow on and obey the light that He has already given you. But there is the same solemn warning to those that refuse to repent and believe. Oh, how sad and solemn is this warning cry, "Because I have called, and ye refused; I have stretched out my hand, and no man regarded; but ye have set at nought all my counsel, and would have none of my reproof; I also will laugh at your calamity; I will mock when your fear cometh as desolation, and your destruction cometh as a whirlwind; when distress and anguish cometh upon you." Oh, how dark the angry cloud!

And then there comes a strange and awful change in the structure of the sentence; from the second person it changes to the third person. It is no longer you, but they; for God has now gotten so far away that He is speaking to the poor lost soul no more, but only speaking about it. "Then shall they call upon me, but I will not answer; they shall seek me early, but they shall not find me: for that they hated knowledge, and did not choose the fear of the Lord: they would none of my counsel; they despised all my reproof: therefore shall they eat of the fruit of their own way, and be filled with their own devices." This is still the Holy Spirit's solemn voice to all who reject His message and refuse the Gospel of His grace.

But as the storm cloud sweeps away, the rainbow rises upon its last dark shadow, a rainbow of promise to those who have heeded His warning and have hearkened to His voice. God grant, brother, that it may be His word to you, and thou even yet shall turn at His reproof. "Whoso hearkeneth unto me shall dwell safely, and shall be quiet from the fear of evil." Blessed promise; saved from all evil, saved even from its shadow and from its touch.

IV. How shall we find the truth? How shall we receive this heavenly wisdom? The answer is given in the second chapter of Proverbs and the first nine verses. "If thou will receive my words, and hide my commandments with thee; so that thou incline thine ear unto wisdom, and apply thine heart to understanding; yea, if thou criest after knowledge, and liftest up thy voice for understanding; if thou seekest her as silver, and searchest for her as for hid treasures, then shalt thou understand the fear of the Lord, and find the knowledge of God." Here is the secret of divine teaching, deep earnestness and singleness of purpose, and perseverance of pursuit; the ears, the heart, the whole being must be yielded up. We must desire God above everything, and seek Him as men search for treasures and mines, for silver and for gold.

God has hidden every precious thing in such a way that it is a reward to the diligent, a prize to the earnest, and a disappointment to the slothful soul. All nature is arrayed against the lounger and the idler. The nut is hidden in its thorny case; the pearl is buried beneath the ocean wave; the gold is imprisoned in the rocky bosom of the mountain; the gem is found only after you crush the rock that encloses it; the very soil gives its harvests as the reward of industry to the laboring husbandman. So truth and God must be earnestly sought. "They that seek shall find; to him that knocketh it shall be opened."

The Holy Ghost is given in His fullest measure to deep earnestness and singleness of purpose and desire. You cannot have the higher things of God without the sacrifice of everything else. "I have suffered the loss of all things, and do count them but dung," "for the excellency of the knowledge of Christ Jesus my Lord." This is the true Spirit of divine attainment. The prize is not for all. All run, but one receiveth the prize. God give us the diligence, the singleness, the self-sacrifice, the concentration of desire, purpose, and every power upon the one thing which really means all things, and we, too, shall find that God is waiting to reward the true heart with Himself. It is as true as ever, "ye shall seek me, and find me, when ye shall search for me with all your heart."

V. The message of wisdom to the seeker and searcher after treasure is found in Proverb 3: 13-18, "Happy is the man that findeth wisdom, and the man that getteth understanding: for the merchandise of it is better than the merchandise of silver, and the gain thereof than fine gold. She is more precious than rubies: and all the things thou canst desire are not to be compared unto her. Length of days is in her right hand; and in her left hand riches and honor. Her ways are ways of pleasantness, and all her paths are peace. She is a tree of life to them that lay hold upon her; and happy is every one that retaineth her."

Then again, in chapter 8: 10, 11 we find: "Receive my instruction, and not silver; and knowledge rather than choice gold. For wisdom is better than rubies; and all the things that may be desired are not to be compared to it."

And in verses 18-21 we read: "Riches and honor are with me; yea, durable riches and righteousness. My fruit is better than gold, . . . and my revenue than choice silver. I lead in the way of righteousness, in the midst of the paths of judgment; that I may cause them that love me to inherit substance; and I will fill their treasures."

These are some of the treasures which this heavenly wisdom has to bestow upon those who truly seek her.

The keynote of the whole lesson was given in Solomon's own life. He had the wisdom to choose wisdom and wisdom only, and God added to him all the things he did not choose. It is still true for us that, if we will choose the Holy Ghost, He will become to us the sum and substance of all good things.

He will be to us peace and happiness, joy and rest, health and strength, providence and protection, guidanceand provision, freedom from fear and care, and all the gifts and blessings which God can bestow upon a trusting heart.

Like the widow's pot of oil, the Holy Spirit in us will be the equivalent of everything that heart can desire or life can need. God help us to make the wise and happy choice, and have all in Him and Him in all; and, as we seek the Kingdom of God and His righteousness, all things shall be added unto us.

This was where Solomon began his illustrious career. Happy would it have been for him if he had ended where he began. Alas! God's very blessing became a snare. His heart turned away from the source of all his blessings to the blessing themselves. His affections were set on the things that surrounded him, his wives, his friends, his treasures, perhaps his own wisdom; and he sank from the Creator to the creature, from the height of wisdom to the depths of folly, shame, and sorrow.

Alas! Moses had to fail to show that the law made nothing perfect, and Solomon had to fail to show that the highest wisdom of man is insufficient for the child of God. Thank God, "a greater than Solomon is here," the Lord Jesus Christ; not wisdom but Himself, the wise One; not holiness but Himself the Holy One, not our best but Himself within us to be His best.

Let us receive Christ, the wisdom of God, and let it be true of us, that "of him are ye in Christ Jesus, who of God is made unto us wisdom, and righteousness, and sanctification, and redemption."

The blessed Holy Ghost is waiting to bring Him into our hearts, and to reveal Him and unfold Him in our life, the Wonderful, Counselor, the Mighty God, the Everlasting Father, the Prince of Peace, the Light of the World; and "He that followeth him shall not walk in darkness, but shall have the light of life."

## Chapter 13

## The Still, Small Voice

"And he said, Go forth, and stand upon the mount before the Lord. And behold, the Lord passed by, and a great and strong wind rent the mountains, and brake in pieces the rocks before the Lord; but the Lord was not in the wind: and after the wind an earthquake; but the Lord was not in the earthquake: and after the earthquake a fire; but the Lord was not in the fire: and after the fire a still, small voice. And it was so, when Elijah heard it, that he wrapped his face in his mantle, and went out, and stood in the entering in of the cave. And, behold, there came a voice unto him, and said, What doest thou here, Elijah?" 1 Kings 19: 11-13.

This beautiful expression, "A still, small voice," has almost come to be recognized as one of the names of the Holy Spirit. The whole scene is a fine illustration of the Spirit's working not only in the ages and dispensations, but in the experience of every individual heart.

The scene is a most dramatic one. Elijah had just reached the climax of his marvelous ministry. In that magnificent scene on Carmel we behold him in the very zenith of his career. God has answered his faith and prayer by the descending fire. The whole nation has been swayed at his will, and the very king is helpless as a child at his bidding; while the prophets of Baal, unable to resist the storm of popular enthusiasm, have been swept away by a stroke of judgment. Even the very heavens that have been closed for years have opened the floodgates at the prophet's command, and, like a commander-in-chief of the armies of earth and heaven, Elijah has led the victorious procession to the very gates of the capital. But now another scene occurs as dramatic as the first.

There is one other heart in Israel as thoroughly possessed of the devil as Elijah was possessed of the Holy Ghost. She hears the startling tidings without the quiver of a muscle or a nerve, and with a face of flint and a heart of steel, she speaks but one sentence, of fierce, defiant threatening, "So let the gods do to me, and more also, if I make not thy life as the life of one of them by tomorrow about this time." It was a well directed shot from the batteries of the pit. In a moment it had done its fearful work, and the prophet of fire was broken like a child. There is something almost ludicrous in the graphic description of his flight, "Elijah arose and went for his life"; nor did he stop till he had reached the utmost confines of the land, away down at Beersheba. Nor even there did he linger, but, leaving his servant, he hastened on across the desert, until, exhausted with hunger and fatigue, he sank on the sand, and lay down beneath a juniper tree with one gasp of hopeless despair, "Lord, take away my life; for I am no better than my fathers."

God tenderly nursed and cherished His weary child, put him to sleep, then awoke him and fed him by angel hands, until he was strong enough for his farther journey. Then He sent him on to Horeb, the Mount of God.

There, on some mountain crag and at the entrance of a cave, he waited for the message of his Lord. His spirit was all agitated and chafed. He felt his life was a failure, and he longed for power to accomplish the things for which he felt unable. Perhaps he even thought that if he could rule the world for a little how different things would be. He was just in that mood where he wanted something to happen. Anything was better than this silence, and the very war of the elements would seem to such a spirit a luxury of rest.

It was not long before his thought was fulfilled, and God began to speak to him through the voice of nature. First came the mighty earthquake, heaving the solid ground, tearing the rocks asunder and making the desert's bosom heave like the billows of the ocean, till it seemed that he himself must be torn from his resting place, or engulfed in the awful chasms that were opening round him on every side. But he looked upon the whole scene unmoved. There was nothing in it to touch his spirit; the earthquake came and went, and he felt hat "the Lord was not in the earthquake."

Next came the wild tornado, filling the air with clouds of sand, sweeping through the mountains, and tearing the solid rocks from their base and hurling the forests into Hie abysses below, while the air reverberated with the crashing thunder, and quivered with the awful lightning. His ears were stunned with the tempest's awful roar; but through all the wild confusion the prophet stood unmoved . Perhaps his fiery spirit was even rested by the elemental war. There was nothing in it that spoke to his deeper heart. The whirlwind passed; but "the Lord was not in the whirlwind."

Then came the fire. Perhaps it was the thunderbolt of the sky; perhaps it was some flame caused by the lightning stroke, kindling the forests and sweeping over the mountains, with fiery blaze; or, perhaps, it was some supernatural and awful flame, falling from the skies, quivering before his gaze like the fire that came dawn on Sinai ages before, when Moses received the law. But even this did not blanch his cheek nor move his heart; he gazed upon it with his spirit still unbroken, and his heart chafing as before. And then, like the hush that comes before the storm, or like the emphatic pause in some musical strain, there came an awful stillness, and there fell upon his ear a strange and "still, small voice," or as the New Version expresses it, "A sound of gentle stillness,"softer than evening bells, sweeter than a mother's tones, gentler than music's tenderest notes. Perhaps it spoke as much to the senses of his soul as to his outward ear; but there was something in it so deep, so tender, so penetrating that it thrilled his inmost being. It broke his whole spirit into tenderness and awe, and, gathering his mantle about him, he crept into the cave, and fell upon his face at the feet of God to listen to His message. The fiery heart at length is subdued, the mighty will is broken, the stern prophet is like a little child.

What is the meaning of all this wondrous drama?

I. ELIJAH'S LESSON.

In the first place, it has a meaning for Elijah himself. He needed to be quiet, he needed to find that the forces that he was longing for were not the highest forces at God's command, and that even his own stern, strong nature needed to be subdued and taught the deepest power of gentleness and love.

II. ELIJAH AND ELISHA.

Secondly, it had a yet higher meaning: it was a sort of picture of the two ministries of Elijah and Elisha. His was but a temporary dispensation; he came as the winter before the spring, as the plow before the sower, as the storm before the shower. His was the ministry of judgment and destruction. But the sunshine of spring is stronger than the storms of winter, and the little seed that drops into the soil is mightier than the plowshare that digs the furrow or the dynamite that blasts the rocks. So the gentle ministry of Elisha which was to follow was more mighty and more fruitful than all the destructive miracles of the great Elijah. He had his place; but the earthquake, the whirlwind and the fire of his awful judgments had to pass away, and "the still, small voice" of Elisha's gentler teachings and miracles of grace had to come instead.

III. THE NEW DISPENSATION.

All this was prophetic of a yet higher era and a grander transaction. For Elijah and his ministry were typical of the law and the dispensation of Moses, while Elisha, was the type of the Lord Jesus Christ and the gospel of His grace. And so the scene on Horeb is a representation of the difference between Law and Grace, Judgment and Mercy, the Old Dispensation and the new.

God had already proved how much, or rather how little discipline can do to perfect human character and lead to lasting righteousness.

All that suffering and chastening can accomplish to purify a people was done for ancient Israel. What can ever surpass the pathetic story of Israel's fall, Judah's captivity, and Jerusalem's doom? But alas! how transitory the effect upon the character of the nation! They wept, they suffered, they died, they left the awful record burned into the very heart of the nation; but the next generation went on repeating the sins and follies of their fathers, and God could only cry, "Why should ye be stricken any more? Ye will revolt more and more. The whole head is sick, and the whole heart is faint. From the sole of the foot even unto the head there is no soundness in it; but wounds, and bruises, and putrefying sores."

Thank God, there is a better way. The Gospel of His grace, the gentleness of His love, and the power of His Holy Spirit, have accomplished what law and terror never could while they wrought alone. "The still, small voice" of Jesus' love is mightier than all the thunder of Mount Sinai's law, or Assyrian or Chaldean armies. The law made nothing perfect, but the bringing in of a better hope did. "The earthquake, the whirlwind, and the fire" have gone, but "the still, small voice" of Calvary and Pentecost is speaking to the hearts of millions, and speaking them back to God and righteousness and heaven.

IV. THE EXPERIENCE OF THE INDIVIDUAL SOUL.

The scene at Horeb is often repeated in our individual life. We, too, have to pass through the earthquake, the whirlwind, and the fire in our vain search for God; and, at last, we find Him as the still, small voice in the depths of our soul. Perhaps the experience comes through great trial, outward or inward sufferings, tests that rend our very heart and crush our spirit. But the suffering has no saving power. The human heart can be torn to pieces, and yet every single piece be as full of pride and rebellion as the whole.

It needs the quiet divine influence of the Holy Spirit to change the heart and sanctify the soul. Suffering without the Holy Ghost is the saddest thing on earth. Trials unsanctified are like the lightning strokes that blight but cannot bless.

Sometimes it is not so much external suffering as a struggle within the secret soul itself to find God and peace. Oh, how we labor and long and try! But the best result of all our struggles is to show their own fruitlessness and to lay us helpless and silent before the feet of Christ; and then we awake in the arms of His love and power. And as we awake, we find that there is so little in the new experience that is tangible or strongly marked. In fact, the most frequent experience is to find that we really have come into nothingness. The stillness is so quiet that there is often the absence of all self-consciousness and feeling, and even the presence of God is "a still, small voice" so quiet that we have to hush every other sound before we can hear it.

Indeed, the first experience is often one of great emptiness, bareness, and nothingness, and one is apt to be disappointed, and to say, "Is this all that is meant by the rest of faith?" But we soon find that the nothingness of self is but the beginning of God's all-sufficiency, and as we are willing to rest in our nothingness and the all-sufficiency, we soon begin to know the sweetness and the power of that voice.

V. THE HOLY SPIRIT AS THE VOICE OF GOD.

The keynote of all this wondrous story is THE VOICE. The earthquake had a sound, but it had no voice. The tempest and whirlwind could make a mighty noise, but there was no voice. The fire could speak through the sense of vision, and fill the soul with awe, but it had no voice to speak to the heart. But "the still, small voice" had behind it an intelligent mind, a living personality, a loving heart, and it was mightier than all the lifeless forces which had gone before.

Oh, the power of a voice! How it lingers in our memory! How certain tones arrest our attention and wake up all the old chords of the past! How that voice speaks to us of the difference between nature and revelation, between the language of the earth and sky, and the language of God's precious Word! God hath spoken once in the voice of creation, but it is only like the inarticulate language of the earthquake, the whirlwind, and the fire. God hath spoken a second time, in the voice of His Holy Word and His blessed Son, and this is the message that brings light and life and salvation to man.

A voice is more than a message, more than a printed page, more than even an inspired book. A voice means the presence of the person who speaks, and his personal and living words to us. And so God speaks to us, not only in the Bible, but by His own personal voice. His sheep know His voice, and "a stranger will they not follow, but will flee from him: for they know not the voice of strangers."

There is more in the Bible and in the revelation of Christ than merely a message of truth. It is also a personal message of love. He has a special voice for every one of His children, and it is our privilege to know His voice.

Oh, how that voice can speak to us! It is not an audible voice; it does not reach our outward senses; it would not be possible to explain to a stranger how it makes itself understood in the heart; but, as we kneel in prayer and ask His counsel, as we come with our heavy-laden hearts and throw ourselves upon His bosom for comfort; as we bring our petitions and wait for the whispered answer, how it speaks to us, how it satisfies us, how it identifies itself to us, and makes us know "it is the Lord!" How it gives its approval to the plans that He commends! How it seals the promise that is suggested to the mind, and lets it fall upon the heart like balm upon the bleeding wound! How it brings home the words that fall from the speaker's lips, and makes them God's living messages to our hearts! How it emphasizes every word we read, and how its sweet and heavenly whisper fills all our inmost being with peace and joy and life, until our glad and grateful heart can only say, "I will hear what God the Lord will speak; for he will speak peace to his people and to his saints"!

VI. THE POWER OF GENTLENESS.

The New Version translates this phrase, "The sound of a gentle stillness." It speaks of God's gentleness. Gentleness is always an attribute of the highest natures. The bravest soldier, the loftiest character, is always the most child-like, simple and tender.

Jesus Christ was the incarnation of meekness, lowliness, and gentleness.

The apostle used this as his strongest plea when he besought His disciples "by the meekness and gentleness of Christ." "I am meek and lowly in heart" was the Master's own highest claim. And this was but the ancient prophetic picture. "He shall not strive nor cry, nor cause his voice to be heard in the streets; a bruised reed shall he not break, and the smoking flax shall he not quench."

Is there a more sublime spectacle, is there a more heart-moving sight in all history, than that patient Sufferer standing in the judgment hall or hanging upon the Cross and allowing His murderers to do their worst, answering not a word, "led like a lamb to the slaughter, and as a sheep before the shearers is dumb, so he openeth not his mouth"? The Holy Ghost, the Representative of Christ, also is gentleness itself. He came upon Jesus as the Dove, and He dwells in us as a Monitor so kind, a Comforter so tender, that we can only "grieve" and "vex" Him, but we cannot make Him angry. He appeals to our obedience by His sensitiveness to the hurt that we can give Him. Oh, let us be gentle as He; let us treat Him with the consideration that His sensitiveness should claim!

He will not force an entrance to our heart. He will not do violence to the freedom of our will. He will not compel us to do what we do not choose, nor to surrender what we want to keep. He appeals to the finest motives of our being, to the will that springs from our deepest heart, and to the obedience which we are only too glad to give.

Let us imitate His gentleness; let us ask Him to translate it into all our beings until we shall be simple, sensitive, considerate, yielded, lowly, meek and childlike, "even as He." Our faces, our manners, our tones, and the whole complexion of our life shall be the blending of the spirit of the Lamb and the Dove.

## VII. THE POWER OF STILLNESS.

It was "a still, small voice," or "the sound of a gentle stillness." Is there any note of music in all the chorus as mighty as the emphatic pause? Is there any word in all the Psalter more eloquent than that one word, "Selah, (Pause) "? Is there anything more thrilling and awful than the hush that comes before the bursting of the tempest or the strange quiet that seems to fall upon all nature before some preternatural phenomenon or convulsion? Is there anything that can so touch our hearts as the power of stillness?

The sweetest blessing that Christ brings us is the Sabbath rest of the soul, of which the Sabbath of creation was the type; the Land of Promise, God's great object lesson. There is for the heart that will cease from itself "the peace of God that passeth all understanding"; "a quietness and confidence" which is the source of all strength; a sweet peace which "nothing can offend"; a deep rest which "the world can neither give nor take away." There is, in the deepest center of the soul, a chamber of peace where God dwells, and where, if we will only enter in and hush every other sound, we can hear His still, small voice.

There is, in the swiftest wheel that revolves upon its axis, a place in the very center where there is no movement at all; and so in the busiest life there may be a place where we dwell alone with God in eternal stillness.

This is the only way to know God. "Be still, and know that I am God." "God is in his holy temple; let all the earth keep silence before him."

A score of years ago a friend placed in my hand a little book which became one of the turning points of my life. It was called "True Peace." It was an old mediaeval message with but one thought, which was this, that God was waiting in the depths of my being to talk to me if I would only get still enough to hear His voice.

I thought this would be a very easy matter, and so I began to get still. But I had no sooner commenced than a perfect pandemonium of voices reached my ears, a thousand clamoring notes from without and within, until I could hear nothing but their noise and din. Some of them were my own voice, some of them were my own questions, some of them were my own cares, and some of them were my very prayers. Others were suggestions of the tempter and voices from the world's turmoil. Never before did there seem so many things to be done, to be said, to be thought; and in every direction I was pushed, and pulled, and greeted with noisy acclamations and unspeakable unrest. It seemed necessary for me to listen to some of them, and to answer some of them, but God said, "Be still, and know that I am God." Then came the conflict of thoughts for the morrow, and its duties and cares, but God said, "Be still." And then there came the very prayers which my restless heart wanted to press upon Him, but God said, "Be still." And as I listened and slowly learned to obey and shut my ears to every sound, I found after awhile that when the other voices ceased, or I ceased to hear them, there was a still, small voice in the depths of my being that began to speak with an inexpressible tenderness, power and comfort. As I listened it became to me the voice of prayer, and the voice of wisdom, and the voice of duty. I did not need to think so hard, or pray so hard, or trust so hard, but that "still, small voice" of the Holy Spirit in my heart was God's prayer in my secret soul, was God's answer to all my questions, was God's life and strength for soul and body, and became the substance of all knowledge, and all prayer, and all blessing; for it was the living God Himself as my Life and my All.

Beloved, this is our spirit's deepest need. It is thus that we learn to know God; it is thus that we receive spiritual refreshing and nutriment; it is thus that our heart is nourished and fed; it is thus that we receive the Living Bread; it is thus that our very bodies are healed, and our spirit drinks in the life of our risen Lord, and we go forth to life's conflicts and duties like the flower that has drunk in, through the shades of night, the cool and crystal drops of dew. But as the dew never falls on a stormy night, so the dews of His grace never come to the restless soul.

We cannot go through life strong and fresh on express trains, with ten minutes for lunch. We must have quiet hours, secret places of the Most High, times of waiting upon the Lord, when we renew our strength and learn to mount up on wings as eagles, and then come back, to run and not be weary, and to walk and not faint.

The best thing about this stillness is that it gives God a chance to work. "He that is entered into his rest, he also hath ceased from his own works, as God did from his"; and when we cease from our works, God works in us; and when we cease from our thoughts, God's thoughts come into us; when we get still from our restless activity, God worketh in us both to will and do of His good pleasure, and we have but to work it out.

Beloved, let us take His stillness, let us dwell in "the secret place of the Most High," let us enter into God and His eternal rest, let us silence the other sounds, and then we can hear "the still, small voice."

There is another kind of stillness, the stillness that lets God work for us, and hold our peace; the stillness that ceases from its contriving, and its self-vindication, and its expedients of wisdom and forethought, and lets God provide, and answer the unkind word and the cruel blow in His own unfailing, faithful love. How often we lose God's interposition by taking up our own cause and striking for our own defense.

Never shall I forget a little scene which happened not long ago. A quiet Christian girl was sitting at table among a party of friends, who were discussing a Christian work in which she was deeply interested. Some of the criticisms were very severe, and, as she thought, unjust and unfair. She said a few simple words to correct the statements; but then, as the criticism, more and more severe, went on, she simply held her peace. I saw the mantling brow and the tear just springing to her eyes, and I thought how easy it would have been for her to give the quick reply, and answer just as sharply as she might have done. But the grace of God had become ascendant in that young heart; the Holy Ghost was on the Throne. She sat in silence, and simply suffered and waited. After a few moments I saw she could stand the struggle no longer, and she gently and lovingly rose and left the table and went to her room to lay her burden upon the bosom for her Savior.

In a moment it all flashed upon the other person, who loved her very tenderly. He saw how he had wounded her; he knew how she would have answered months before. The sweetness and gentleness of her spirit cut him to the very heart, and taught him a lesson that he was manly and noble enough fully to acknowledge. Never again will his lips utter those hasty words, and never will he forget that spectacle of gentleness and silence.

It was her best vindication, and it made up for her, besides, a jewel of unfading lustre in the crown above.

There is no spectacle in all the Bible so sublime as the silent Savior answering not a word to the men that were maligning Him, and whom He could have laid prostrate at His feet by one look of divine power or one word of fiery rebuke. But He let them say and do their worst, and He stood in the power of stillness — God's holy, silent Lamb.

God give to us this silent power, this mighty self-surrender, this conquered spirit which will make us "more than conquerors through Him that loved us." Let our voice and our life speak like "the still, small voice" of Horeb and as "the sound of a gentle stillness." And after the heat and strife of earth are over, men will remember us as we remember the morning dew, the gentle light and sunshine, the evening breeze, the Lamb of Calvary, and the gentle, Holy, Heavenly Dove.

## Chapter 14

## The Pot of Oil

"Tell me: what hast thou in the house? And she said, Thine handmaid hath not anything in the house, save a pot of oil. Then he said, Go, borrow thee vessels abroad of all thy neighbors, even empty vessels; borrow not a few. And when thou art come in, thou shalt shut the door upon thee and upon thy sons, and shalt pour out into all those vessels, and thou shalt set aside all that which is full. So she went from him, and shut the door upon her and upon her sons, who brought the vessels to her; and she poured out. And it came to pass, when the vessels were full, that she said into her son, Bring me yet a vessel: and he said unto her, there is not a vessel more. And the oil stayed. Then she came and told the man of God: and he said, Go, sell the oil, and pay thy debt, and live thou and thy children upon the rest." 2Kings 4: 2-7.

The events of Elisha's life are more like those of the life of Christ than are any others in the Old Testament. Just as Elijah represented the Spirit of the Lord and the ministry of John the Baptist, a ministry of judgment and fire, so Elisha represented the ministry of Jesus Christ in its gentleness, benignity and grace; and very many of his beautiful miracles are distinctly parallel to the miracles of our Lord, while they preach the same lesson and breathe the same spirit of love and graciousness.

The passage before us is a striking object lesson of the Holy Ghost in His all-sufficiency for the supplying it every source of need.

1. HER NEED. First, we have, in the case of this poor widow, an example of great need. Her situation was one of debt, danger, distress, and of complete helplessness. She had no one to go to but God, and, unless delivered by Him, her situation must have become one of the greatest extremity. It represents the very worst and most helpless state in which a child of God can be found. But such a situation is often the greatest blessing that can come to us, because it throws us upon God, and compels us to trust in the all-sufficiency of His grace.

Nearly all the great examples of faith and victorious grace which we find in the Scriptures came out of situations of extremity and distress. God loves hard places, and faith is usually born of danger and extremity.

It was thus that Jacob was transformed from Jacob to Israel in the conflict at Peniel. It was thus that Israel was awakened to claim the great redemption from the bondage of Egypt, by the doubling of the tale of brick and by the heated furnace of iron. It was thus that David learned to know his God, and was able to testify, "Thou hast known my soul in adversity." Let us not be discouraged by difficulties, nor regard them as always misfortunes; but rather let us receive them as challenges to our faith and opportunities given to us by our God to show that there is nothing too hard for Him.

2. HER RESOURCES. Was there, then, nothing left for her? Was she entirely without resources? "Tell me, what hast thou in the house?" And she answered, "Thy servant hath nothing, save a pot of oil." To her that seemed nothing, and yet it contained the supply of all her need. God loves to utilize and economize all the resources which He has already given to us. Just as a master workman can do a great deal of excellent work with very common tools, so God can work with very simple instruments; but He wants us to utilize what He has already given. It was very little that Moses had, but that little rod was sufficient to divide the Red Sea and to break the power of Pharaoh. It was very little that the lad on the Galilean shore had that day; but his five

loaves and two small fish were sufficient to feed the five thousand, when they were given to Jesus and placed at His service. Our least is enough for God, if we allow Him complete control.

But that little pot of oil was not a little thing. It represented the power of the Holy Ghost, the infinite attribute of God Himself.

We need not stop to prove that oil is the Scriptural symbol of the Holy Spirit. This little vessel of oil represented the presence and the power of the Spirit, which every believer may have, and in some measure does have, and which, if we only know how to use Him, is equal to every possible situation and need of our Christian life. But in how many cases is this an unrealized power and an unemployed force?

There is a grim story told of a poor Scotchwoman who went to her pastor in her extremity, and told him of her poverty. He kindly asked her if she had no friend nor member of her family who could support or help her. She said she had a son, a bonny lad, but he was in India, in the service of the government. "But does he not write to you?" "Oh, yes; he often writes me, and sends the kindest letters, and such pretty pictures in them. But I am too proud to tell him how poor I am, and, of course, I have not expected him to send me money." "Would you mind showing me some of the pictures?" said the minister. And so Janet went to her Bible, and brought out from between the leaves a great number of Bank of England notes, laid away with the greatest care. "These," she said, "are the pictures." The minister smiled, and said, "Janet, you are richer than I am. These are bank notes; and every one of them might have been turned into money, and you might have had all your needs supplied. You have had a fortune in your Bible without knowing it."

Alas, beloved, many of us have fortunes in our Bibles without knowing it, or without using our infinite resources. The Holy Spirit is given to us to be used for every sort of need; and yet, with all the power of heaven at our call, many of us are going about in starvation, simply because we do not know our treasure, and do not use our redemption rights. "Know ye not," the apostle asks us, "that your body is the temple of the Holy Ghost?" If we but use the power that is given within our breast, behind the name of Jesus and the promises of God, we would fail no more, we would fear no more, we would no more be a reflection upon our Savior and a dishonor to His name, as well as a discouragement to the world, but we would rise up into victory, and cry, "Thanks be to God, who always causeth us to triumph, in Christ."

What is the difference between Japan and China today? It is this: while Japan has learned the secrets of modern progress, and is using them in still victorious warfare, China does not know what other races have learned. What is the difference between our age and the age of our grandfather? It is simply that we have learned from nature. We are using the great secrets of steam, electricity, and the various appliances of practical science in all our industrial life, so that one man can do today what it took twenty to do in the days of our fathers. The business man can sit in his office and annihilate both space and time as he talks through his telephone to the most distant parts of the land, and through his phonograph into the ears of the coming generation.

What was the matter with Hagar in her bitter sorrow? Nothing but this; she could not see the fountain that lay so near, she and her child were perishing with thirst. There was no need that the angel should create a fountain; he needed only to open Hagar's eyes and let her see it and drink of it.

There was no need that God should make a spring of sweetness at Marah's waters; all that was needed was to show to Moses the branch of healing that was already there. As he plunged it into the waters the people were healed.

There was no need that an army of angels should come to the help of Elisha on the mountainside. The angels were already there; all that was needed was that the eyes of Elisha's servant might be opened to the heavenly army that surrounded and defended them. In like manner the fountain of life is waiting for us to drink; the waters and the branch of healing are at hand, the angelic army are all around us. All we need is to see them, to know that they are there, to realize our redemption rights, and then to claim them and triumph in His name. God is saying to us, "Arise, shine; for thy light is come." Christ has appeared, the Holy Ghost has come, and all that we need to do is to know and receive and use the great divine commission.

3. THE CONDITIONS OF RECEIVING AND REALIZING DIVINE HELP. First, she, the woman, was directed to make room. She must get vessels, empty vessels, to hold the supply which was about to be revealed. Our greatest need is to make room for God. Indeed, God has to make room for Himself by creating new vessels of need. Every trial that comes to us is but a need for Him to fill and an opportunity for Him to show what He can be to us and do for us. But it is not enough to have need; we must also have empties. We must realize our needs, and we must realize that He alone can supply them. We must be emptied of self-consciousness and dependence upon man; and as we lie fully at His feet, He will prove "How wise, how strong His hand."

Again, there must be faith to count upon God and go forward expecting Him to meet our needs. This woman did not wait till the oil was running over from her little pot; but providing the vessels in advance, she acted as though she had an unbounded supply. So it was that the disciples had to go forward to feed the multitude with their five loaves and two fish, and had to count upon the supply which had not yet appeared. We must anticipate God's fulfillment and trust Him sufficiently to pay in advance; then He will make good our expectations in His glorious and ever-flowing grace.

Again, we must have not only faith, but unselfish love. These were borrowed vessels. The needs were not all her own; and, no doubt, as the vessels went home they did not go home empty. God loves to give to us when we are, like God, receiving that we may give to others.

The most blessed thing about the blessed God must be this, that He has no needs of His own; but that He is always giving, always blessing, and always seeking some new channel through which to bless and to pour out the fullness of His life. If we would receive that fullness, we, God-like, must be great givers. The secret of joy is to want nothing for ourselves, to be rich in dispensing His grace and blessing, to live for others, and to be ever filling the vessels of need from the world around us with the overflowing of His heart and of ours. The beauty of the parable of the friend at midnight lies chiefly in this, that he wanted the loaves from his friend that he might give them to another that was in need. Likewise, when we come for grace and help to the helpless, we shall find that God will open the windows of heaven and pour us out a blessing until there shall not be room to receive it.

Again, the woman's faith was necessary. She must show it by beginning to pour out the contents of the little pot into the larger vessel. As she poured, the oil continued to flow and overflow until every vessel was filled, and it might have been flowing still if there had been room enough to hold its multiplying stream.

So faith must go forward and act out its confidence and risk itself by doing something and putting itself into the place where God must meet it with actual help. It was when the water at Cana was poured out that it became wine. It was when the man stretched out his hand that it was healed. It was as the lepers went on their way that they were made whole. It was as the father went back to his home that the messenger was sent to tell him that his son was alive.

There is a beautiful expression in Hebrews, to the effect that the ancient fathers were persuaded of the promises and "embraced them," or rather as the new version translates it "ran to meet them." Let us run to meet the promises of God. Let us measure up to them. Let us act our confidence, and God will meet us more than halfway with His faithfulness and grace.

There is yet another lesson, the most important of all: "Go, sell the oil, . . . and live thou and thy children of the rest." The oil was but the representative value, and was convertible into everything that she could need. It, was equivalent to currency, food, houses, clothes, lands, anything and everything that possessed value and could meet her need. Thus is the Holy Ghost convertible into everything that we can require.

There are parallel passages in the Gospels of Matthew and Luke which teach a great lesson. In the one passage it reads, "if ye then being evil, know how to give good gifts unto your children; how much more shall your heavenly Father give the Holy Spirit to them that ask him?" In the parallel passage in the other Gospel, instead of the Holy Spirit, it reads, "Give good things to them that ask him." That is to say, the Holy Ghost gives all good things, and He is equivalent to anything and everything that we need. Do we need salvation? He will lead us to Christ, and bring us to witness of our acceptance. Do we need peace? He will bring into our hearts the peace of God. Do we need purity? He will sanctify us and "cause us to walk in His statutes, and keep His judgments to do them." Do we need strength? He is the Spirit of power. Do we need light? He is the Teacher and Counselor and Guide. Do we need faith? He is the Spirit of faith. Or love? By Him "the love of God is shed abroad in our hearts." Would we pray and have our prayer answered? "The Spirit itself maketh intercession within us with groanings which cannot be uttered." Do we need health? He will quicken our mortal bodies by the Spirit that dwelleth in us. Do we need courage? He will give us faith, faith that shall claim the supply of all our needs by believing prayer. Do we need circumstances changed by the mighty workings of God's providence? He is the Spirit of power. The hearts of men are in His hands and He can turn them as the rivers of water, and make all things work together for good to them that love God.

He is the Almighty Spirit, the Great Executive of the Godhead, and with Him in our hearts, God can do exceeding abundantly for us "according to the power that worketh in us."

Oh, let us use the Holy Ghost, not merely for spells of emotional feeling or what we call spiritual experience, but in the whole circle of our life as the Executor of God, the all-sufficient Leader of our victorious faith!

There is yet another lesson taught us here; namely, that we may increase and multiply the effectiveness of the Spirit of God in our lives, by wisely using the power and grace He gives us.

The idea of trading with our spiritual gifts is brought out more fully in the New Testament in the great parable of the pounds, where the one pound that represented, no doubt, the gift of the Holy Ghost, is increased to ten by wise and profitable use. So we can take the Holy Ghost, and as we obey Him and learn to use Him, and become subject to the great laws which regulate His operations, we shall find that there is scarcely a limit to the extent of His working and the sufficiency of His power. All that is needed is room, opportunity, vessels of need, and faith to go forward in dependence upon Him.

The oil did not stop until the woman stopped; God was still working when her faith reached its limit. The same God is working still, and our faith will stop long before His willingness and His resources are exhausted. Shall we trust more boldly? Shall we recognize every difficulty, every situation which conveys an opportunity of proving Him yet more gloriously; and shall we go on from strength to strength until every adversary has been subjected and compelled to help us, till every mountain of difficulty has become a mountain of praise, and every hard place in life a vessel into which God may pour the overflowing fullness of His all-sufficiency?

Beloved, as we step out into the future, shall we forget the experiences we have had and press on to higher and greater? Shall we leave the vessels that have been satisfied, and bring new vessels for him to fill? Shall we forget the blessings we have had from the Holy Ghost, and think rather of those we have not yet had? And shall we go on to prove His mighty promise, "I will open the windows of heaven and pour you out a blessing until there shall not be room enough to receive it"?

## Chapter 15

## The Valley of Ditches

"Thus saith the Lord, Make this valley full of ditches. For thus saith the Lord, Ye shall not see wind, neither shall ye see rain; yet that valley shall be filled with water, that ye may drink, both ye, and your cattle, and your beasts. And this is but a light thing in the sight of the Lord: He will deliver the Moabites also into your hand." 2 Kings 3: 16-18.

This is another of Elisha's parabolic miracles; for it was both a parable of divine teaching and a miracle of divine working. It is full of practical lessons about the Holy Spirit in our lives.

1. A GREAT EMERGENCY. First, we see a great emergency. The king of Israel and the king of Judah had united in a campaign against the Moabites, and in marching through the wilderness they had come into great straits. Their water supply was cut off, and they were in danger of perishing of thirst. This may represent any hard places in our lives. Such an emergency is God's opportunity of blessing, and is the only way by which many of us can ever be brought to realize the fullness of divine grace.

There was a peculiarity, however, in this trying situation to one of the party at least. To Jehoshaphat, the king of Judah, it was a trouble that he had brought upon himself, and he had no one else to blame for his ill fortune. Because he had hastily and generously formed an unholy alliance with a wicked king, he was suffering on account of his forbidden act. As God has warned us to have no fellowship with wicked men, we never can disobey this commandment, either by mixed marriages or by business partnerships, without suffering in consequence.

We see at once the difference between a wicked man and a child of God. In his extremity the wicked king of Israel gave up in despair, and never once thought of turning to God for help. He uttered a hopeless cry, and said practically, "God has brought us here to destroy us." That is the way ungodly men look at their troubles.

In contrast with him, Jehoshaphat at once thought of God and called for His servant and His message. No matter how trying our situation, no matter how much to blame we ourselves are for it, let us always go at once with it to God, and seek his direction and deliverance ; and we shall never seek in vain.

Jehoshaphat called at once for the prophet of the Lord. It was a prophet he wanted. He was willing to hear God's message and to take God's way of deliverance. It is so beautiful to find that the prophet was there. Elisha was the beautiful type of the Holy Ghost and the ever present Christ. Unlike Elijah, who was the prophet of judgment and represented the law, Elisha was always among the people, helping the poor widow in her poverty, the students on the banks of the Jordan when the axe went off the handle, and even the army of his country when on this laborious and dangerous expedition. He represented that God who is always within our call and a God at hand. The very meaning of the word Paraclete or Advocate is, One near by, One we can call to our side and call upon in every time of need. Let us bring Him all our burdens; let us cast upon Him all our care; let us use Him for every emergency, and prove His all-sufficiency in every time of need.

2. PREPARATION. We next see the preparation for God's deliverance. First, Elisha called for a minstrel. You know that this minstrel represented the spirit of praise. Our prayers, too, should always begin with praise. If our difficulty and dangers be met with a song of believing triumph, we shall find God ready to echo it back with the song of deliverance. When we cannot pray, it is a good time to praise.

Next came the divine message, "Thus saith the Lord." God must be heard in this matter, His voice must be listened to, His message received, and His way adopted. When trouble comes we usually run in every other direction first, get everybody else's advice and help, and then at last think of appealing to heaven.

The first thing in trouble is to hearken and ask, "What saith the Lord?" What lesson is He teaching? What rebuke is He sending? What direction is He giving? What way of escape would He have us take? God has always one way out of every difficulty, and only one.

Next, they must make room for the coming blessing. "Make this valley full of ditches." One would have supposed that the valley was deep enough without the ditches. But the valley was there anyhow; the ditches must be made on purpose. It is possible to have need of God and not have room for God. These ditches represent special preparation and the opening of the channels of faith to receive the blessing.

What is a ditch? It is a great, ugly opening in the ground. There is nothing ornamental nor beautiful about it; it is just a void and empty space, a place to hold water. How shall we open the ditches for God to fill? By bringing to Him our needs, our failures, the great rents and voids and broken up places in our lives. It is a good time at the commencement of another year to think of the places where we have come short, and the needs in our hearts that have not yet been supplied. Let us bring them to Him, and like the widow's vessels, He is able to fill them all.

The answer must be claimed by simple faith. "Ye shall not see wind, neither shall ye see rain," said the prophet, "yet that valley shall be filled with water." There was to be no outward demonstration, but it was to come quietly and without observation. This is the way God loves to bless us, and this is the way that faith must always receive the blessing. This is not, however, the way that unbelieving man likes to have it come. He would like to see wind and rain, and have great display of outward circumstances; then he would be able to believe in the coming of the water. "Except ye see signs and wonders, ye will not believe," was the Master's reproof in His own day; and it is as pertinent today as ever.

Faith, however, is "the substance of things hoped for, the evidence of things not seen," and it loves to claim the promise and rest in the Promiser, allowing Him to bring the answer in His own way and time, and counting upon it as though it were already a present fact. Shall we thus trust our God and learn to walk by faith and not by sight?

3. THE DIVINE ANSWER. The divine answer was not long in coming. With the morning light, lo! the ditches had disappeared and the valley was filled with water, reflecting the crimson hills of Edom from its glassy bosom, and looking to the Moabites as pools of blood.

It was water that came, and only water. That was all they wanted. Water was the symbol of the Holy Ghost, and the Holy Ghost is all we want in our extremity and need. He will be to us answered prayer, temporal provision, spiritual supply, and all things pertaining to life and godliness.

Notice again that when the water came, the ditches disappeared from view. Likewise, when the Holy Ghost comes, our needs will be supplied, and the very remembrance of our sorrow and distress will leave us. So long as you are looking at the ditches and thinking of your desperate need, you are not filled with water. God wants so to fill you that He will even obliterate the remembrance of your sin and sorrow, and, as Job beautifully expressed it, you will remember your misery as waters that pass away.

Again, when the water came there was enough, not only for them to drink but also for their cattle and their beasts; so when God fills your life with the Holy Spirit, the blessing overflows not only to every person around you, but the very beasts that serve you will be the better for your blessing. That truck-man was not far astray when he said that his horse and his dog knew that he had been converted. Oh, the groans of the irrational creation around us that are ever going up to God, because of man's sin.

Oh, the blessing that will come to the whole universe when man receives his Savior and becomes prepared to be the lord of this lower creation!

There is a very remarkable expression used respecting this glorious miracle of divine grace and bounty. "This is but a light thing in the sight of the Lord." This wonderful blessing was not, in God's estimation, anything extraordinary nor at all hard for him to do. Nor is it a great or difficult thing for Him to baptize you and me with the Holy Ghost till all our wants are supplied and all our being is filled with His blessing. We are constantly thinking of it as though it cost Him some great effort. Thousands of Christians are looking forward to it at a great distance as the culminating point of life. On the contrary, it is but a light thing for God to do, and is intended to mark rather the beginning than the close of a career of usefulness.

The great purpose of Christ's coming was "that we, being delivered out of the hand of our enemies might serve him without fear, in righteousness and holiness before him," — not the last days, but "all the days of our life." It is not our preparation for heaven but our preparation for life.

4. THE GREATER BLESSING. Next comes God's deliverance and the greater blessing which He has for them. "This is but a light thing in the sight of the Lord: he will deliver the Moabites also into your hand." This was the great purpose of their campaign and the design of God in delivering them in their peril, that they might go forward and conquer their enemy and His. This also is God's purpose in our sanctification.

He does not give us the Holy Ghost that we should receive a clean heart merely, and then spend our lives complacently looking at it and telling people about it, but that we should go forth in the power of His Spirit and His indwelling life, to conquer this world for Him. We, too, have a great foe to face and a great trust to fulfill. We are sent to conquer the world, the flesh, and the devil, and to give the Gospel to the whole inhabited earth. It is a shame that thousands of Christians should spend their lives without even claiming this baptism; and it is a far greater shame that thousands more should be occupied all their days in getting a satisfactory interest in Christ and an experience of sanctification.

What would you think of the gardener who, after spending five years in planting an orange grove in Florida, in watering, pruning, and cultivating it, should then find that he has to spend a quarter of a century more keeping the plants in a healthy condition, without any return of fruit? You would certainly think it a poor investment. It is all right to spend a while in getting your orchard ready; but you expect this to end some day, and the trees will begin to do something better than grow, even to reward your labors with the abundant harvest.

What would you think of the manufacturer who took all the trouble to set up a water wheel, and a lot of machinery, and then simply amused himself with having the wheel turn round, without driving any machinery, or doing any practical work? God must get very tired of everlastingly keeping us in repair. Surely he has a right to expect that the time of fruit will come. God help us, beloved, to get at things and to stay at them. Keep your engine out of the repair shop. Get it in working order as quickly as you can, and then ask God to put an express train behind it, and let it run and carry its precious freight on the great highway of His holy will.

It is very miserable work to be always getting sanctified, and it is very unworthy of God's infinite grace and power. Let us get into conflict and victory and aggressive work for God and this lost world, and He will surely deliver our enemies into our hand, and make us more than conquerors through Him that loved us. And then we shall find that the using of our blessing is the best way to keep it, and the running of the wheel is the surest means of keeping it from falling.

5. THOROUGH AND FINISHED WORK. They were commanded, as soon as they had conquered the Moabites, to do thorough work, to smite every fenced city, to spread stones upon every fertile piece of land, and to fill up every well of water, leav-

ing the land desolate and worthless. It was simply an illustration of thorough and completed work.

When God begins to work for us, it is time for us to work for Him, and our work should be as thorough as His. It is all folly for us to sit down and fold our arms, and say, "God will do it." We must work out our own salvation, all the more because it is God that worketh in us.

When David heard "a sound of going in the tops of the mulberry trees," it was the very time for him to bestir himself and do His best, for God had gone out before him to deliver his enemies into his hand. When we see the almighty working of our God, it is the very time for us to stir ourselves up to faithful cooperation and thorough work.

It was the failure of Israel to do thorough work that lost them the blessing which Joshua's conquest secured. They left some of their enemies in the land, and in due time this remnant became their masters. It is very foolish for us to leave a vestige or a trace of evil behind us. Let us do thorough work in our repentance, in our obedience, in our sanctification, in our divine healing, in our service for God.

How foolish it is for the builder to rear the costly walls and leave them unroofed; the elements will soon crumble the unprotected masonry to a heap of worthless ruins. Let us finish our work day by day. Let everything we say and do be as thorough and complete as the finished measure of the musical melody and harmony, without which the rest of the note would be thrown away. So let us live from day to day, that, when the close shall come, we shall have nothing to do but to go to our reward and say with our departing Master, "Father, I have glorified thee upon the earth, I have finished the work which thou gayest me to do."

Beloved, it is a time of God's mighty working in the world and among the nations. Let it stimulate us to arouse ourselves to holy action, and to cooperate with Him in His mighty purpose of preparing the world for the speedy return of His dear Son, our blessed Lord and Savior Jesus Christ.

There is "a sound of going in the mulberry trees," and the Lord has gone up before us. Let us bestir ourselves, and haste the day of our Master's coming and the cry of victory around the world and from the ranks above, "Alleluia; for the Lord God omnipotent reigneth."

As Dr. Chalmers has so wisely said, "Let us trust as if all depended upon God, but let us work as if all depended upon ourselves."

## Chapter 16

## The Spirit of Inspiration

"No prophecy of the scripture is of any private interpretation. For the prophecy came not in old time by the will of man: but holy men of God spake as they were moved by the Holy Ghost." 2 Peter 1: 20, 21.

This passage directs our attention to the inspiration of the ancient prophets, and to the work of the Holy Ghost as revealing the will of God to His chosen messengers. God at sundry times and divers manners spake to our fathers by the prophets.

Divine revelation began in Eden, and God has never ceased to maintain communication with His devoted subjects. In the antediluvian and patriarchal dispensations He spake at intervals to particular men, revealing His will to them; but from the time that He called Moses to lead the chosen people out of Egypt, He has had a special class of messengers through whom He has revealed His will to His people. These have been called the prophets of the Lord. Moses was, perhaps, the first of them.

In the fourth chapter of Exodus, God distinctly calls him to this special ministry. "Now, therefore, go," He says, "and I will be with thy mouth, and teach thee what thou shalt say." When afterwards He appointed Aaron to be His spokesman, He added, "Thou shalt speak unto him, and put words in his mouth: and I will be with thy mouth, and with his mouth, and will teach you what ye shall do. And he shall be thy spokesman unto the people: and he shall be, even he shall be to thee instead of a mouth, and thou shalt be to him instead of God."

Moses recognized himself as a prophet, and said of his Antitype, "A prophet shall the Lord your God raise up unto you, of your brethren, like unto me; him shall ye hear."

The next great prophet was Samuel. Like Moses he also appeared at a special crisis in the history of his people. They had been for centuries in the deepest declension and distress. Like Luther, God's instrument in the Reformation of our own time, God sent him to call Israel back to Himself. The call of Samuel was most marked and his ministry most important. In 1 Samuel 3: 19-21, we read concerning him, "The Lord was with him, and did let none of his words fall to the ground. And all Israel . . . knew that Samuel was established to a prophet of the Lord. And the Lord appeared again in Shiloh: for the Lord revealed himself to Samuel in Shiloh by the word of the Lord."

Indeed, Samuel was really the founder of the prophetic institutions and the schools of the prophets which from his time we find in Israel. No nobler race of men ever lived than the prophets of Israel. They were the only class that was true to God. The kings, with a few exceptions, were disastrous failures; and even the priesthood became subservient to a corrupt throne and a godless populace. But the prophets were God's true representatives and witnesses, and stood for righteousness and godliness in the darkest ages of God's ancient people.

When Saul failed to meet the purpose of his high calling, Samuel was still true to Jehovah. When David sank in his double crime, Nathan was there to reprove him and to bring him the message of Jehovah. When Solomon allowed his heart to be turned away from God, the prophet Abijah was there to bear God's message of warning, and to tell Jeroboam what God was about to do in rending the kingdom asunder. When Rehoboam succeeded his father and was about to ruin his kingdom in presumptuous recklessness, the prophet Shemaiah was ready to carry God's message to him and arrest him in his reckless purpose. When Jeroboam had ascended the throne of Israel and reared his idolatrous altars at Dan, there was a prophet of the Lord ready to stand before him and to warn him of God's judgment because of his idolatry. When the wicked Baasha, king of Israel, had filled his cup of sin, God had His servant, Jehu the prophet, ready to utter His message of warning and judgment against the wicked king. When Shishak, king of Egypt, came up against Rehoboam, then Shemaiah the prophet was there to call the nation to repentance, and to promise them deliverance from the hand of the enemy.

When King Asa summoned his people to meet the common enemy, and to trust in the arm of Jehovah, then God sent Azariah the prophet to bear to him the message of encouragement and covenant promise; and when, later in his reign, Asa became willful and self-reliant, and turned from God to the arm of flesh, God sent Hanani the prophet to tell him of the divine displeasure and of the judgment which he was about to bring upon himself. When Jehoshaphat stood face to face, with the Ammonites and Moabites in the valley of Berachah in great peril and humiliation, then God sent the prophet Jeheziel to announce the victory of faith that was to come with the morrow.

When Joash, king of Judah, turned away from God, then Zechariah, the prophet of the Lord, stood up to reprove him for his sin, and suffered martyrdom at the hands of the king and people, the first of that band of witnesses who sealed their testimony with their blood. When Ahab and Jezebel reigned in Samaria, and all Israel was given up to the worship of Baal, then Elijah appeared as God's messenger of fire to warn the people and to lead them back to their allegiance to heaven. When Elijah's ministry was completed, Elisha, coming as the messenger of peace, for half a century guided and counseled the king and the people in the name of Jehovah, the glorious type of the coming Christ.

The brightest light of the good Hezekiah's reign was Isaiah, the prophet of the Lord. Even when Jerusalem fell, and Judah passed into captivity, Jeremiah, like a guardian angel, hovered over its dark midnight, and sought by his warning and pleading to avert its cruel fate; and then, when he could do no more, like the Master Himself, he wept over the city that he had loved. The last days of Israel were linked with the prophetic ministry of Hosea, the prophet of love. The exile of Judah was lighted up by the prophetic ministry of Ezekiel by the river Chebar, and of Daniel in far off Babylon. The days of Restoration were less dependent upon the leadership of Zerubabel than upon the prophetic ministrations of Haggai and Zechariah; and, finally, the Old Testament Dispensation was closed by Malachi, the messenger of Jehovah and the prophet of the coming age.

The very names of these prophetic messengers are beautifully significant. "Isaiah" and "Hosea" mean that God is the Savior; "Jeremiah,"God is high; "Ezekiel," God is strong; "Daniel," God is judge; "Joel," Jehovah is God; "Elijah," God is Jehovah; "Elisha,"God is our Savior. "Jonah," who stands first among the prophets whose writings are recorded, means "the Dove," and suggests the Holy Ghost in His gentle grace. "Nahum," who wrote amid the sorrows of Israel's ruin, signifies "the Comforter," and "Malachi," who was the messenger of the new dispensation, means "My messenger." Thus were their very names and lives consistent with their high character and their divine commission.

The prophets of Israel may be divided into two classes; first, those whose lives alone are recorded; and, secondly, those whose writings have come down to us. The latter company may again be divided into six classes.

First, we have Jonah, standing alone as the pioneer and the earliest of the prophets whose writings are recorded. Next, we have the prophets who were connected with Israel's last days; namely, Hosea, Amos, and Nahum. Thirdly, we have the prophets connected with Judah from the reign of Hezekiah for about two generations and about a century before the fall of Judah. These were Joel, Micah, and Isaiah. They lived in the palmy days of Judah's kingdom, and were sent to hold the nation back from the captivity to which they were hastening. Through their ministry the catastrophe that came to Israel was averted from Judah for more than a century. It came at last, however, and we have a fourth group of prophets, who cluster around the sinking fortunes of the kingdom of Judah and fall of Jerusalem. They are Jeremiah, Obadiah, Zephaniah, and Habakkuk.

We have a fifth class a little later, who may be called the prophets of the exile. They prophesied in captivity. They are Ezekiel and Daniel, the one in the country, the other in the capital of Babylon.

Finally, we have the prophets of the Restoration, the men who counseled and comforted the returning bands who went back to rebuild the temple and city of Jerusalem. They were Haggai, Zechariah, and Malachi. These sixteen names constitute the glorious company of the prophets whose writings have come to us. They are commonly divided into the major and minor prophets, Isaiah, Jeremiah and Ezekiel belonging to the former, and all the others to the latter class. They all claimed to be the special messengers of Jehovah, and they were all accredited by His signal presence and power. They belong to that class of whom our text says they "spake as they were moved by the Holy Ghost." The same language might yet more emphatically be applied to the prophets and writers of the New Testament.

And so we come to the great subject of the inspiration of the Holy Scriptures and the messengers of God's will in the various dispensations. Let us briefly consider; first, the nature of inspiration; secondly, its evidences; and, thirdly, the responsibility that it lays upon us.

1. As to the nature of inspiration what do we mean by the inspired prophets and the inspired Scriptures?

The Scripture writers themselves settle this question. There is no doubt that they claim for themselves, and the Lord Jesus Himself recognizes the claim, that they are the special messengers of God and bring to man the expression of His will. It may not be easy for us to explain the precise nature of their inspiration. All we need to know is its practical extent and value, and that it was a divine influence which so possessed them that it preserved them from all error and enabled them to give to men a correct and infallible record of the facts they intended to represent, and the message which God intended they should bear. It was such a superintendence by the Holy Ghost as made their message absolutely inerrant and infallible. It was not always necessary that they should receive a revelation of all the facts in the case, because they may already have been familiar with many of them or even all of them. What they needed was such a divine guidance and control as would enable them to state these facts accurately and as fully as God required.

This divine control did not make them necessarily passive and mechanical. They were not writing as a phonograph would speak, or as a typewriter would obey the touch of the performer. While in many instances they may have been unconscious, in others they undoubtedly wrote and spoke in the free possession of all their faculties and in the exercise of their own intelligence. We know that they acted with perfect individuality, and that each man's message was colored by the complexion of his own mind, so that we know the writings of Isaiah from those of Jeremiah; we know the voice of Elijah from that of Elisha; we know the style of John from that of Paul. The Book of God is like a beautiful garden, where all the flowers grow upon the same soil and are watered from the same heaven, but each has its own unique colors, forms, fragrance and individuality. This is a harp of nearly a hundred strings; but all are in perfect harmony, and every measure is resolved into one glorious refrain, JESUS, REDEMPTION, "Glory to God in the highest; on earth peace, goodwill to men." It is not necessary for us to believe that the Holy Ghost inspired the wicked words which the Bible records, the ungodly speeches and the foolish utterances contained in the Book of Job, and many such things. All that was necessary was that it should give a correct record of what Job's wife and Job's friends really said, and even of the devil's wicked speeches. The speeches were inspired by the devil, but the record of them was inspired by the Holy Ghost.

The Apostle Paul records the nature and fullness of inspiration very explicitly when he says, in 1 Cor. 2: 12, 13, "Now we have received, not the spirit of the world, but the Spirit which is of God, that we might know the things that are freely given to us of God. Which things also we speak, not in the words which man's wisdom teacheth, but which the Holy Ghost teacheth. "We, therefore, know that these records are divine, that these messages are from the throne, and that this blessed book is the very Word of the living and everlasting God.

2. The Lord Jesus Christ bears witness to the inspiration of the Scriptures. Again and again He quotes from the Old Testament books, and He tells us that it was the Word of the Lord and the Word of the Spirit through the prophet.

The New Testament bears witness to the Old, and the Holy Spirit, through His later messengers, confirms His messages through former oracles.

The message brings its own evidence, and bears to every true heart the conviction of its divinity and its truth.

The best evidence of the Holy Scriptures is the response which they find in the consciences of men. Listening to the great Teacher, we are compelled to say, "He told me all that ever I did." "Is not this the Christ?"

To the child of God the divinest testimony to the Holy Scriptures is the blessing which they have brought to his own soul, the witness of the Holy Ghost within him, and the effect that this book has produced upon his heart and life.

Its miracles of grace are its divinest credentials. It has changed the sin-possessed soul into a saint of God, and has made the wilderness of evil and misery to blossom as the rose.

But it has also divine and supernatural credentials. Side by side with God's inspired Word have always marched the twin witnesses of miracles and prophecy. These mighty words have moved the heavens and shaken the earth. In response to their command the dead have been raised, the living have been transformed, and all the powers of nature have witnessed to the supreme authority of God's inspired commands.

This book is the panorama of the ages, and history has kept time to all its paragraphs. Here we find, centuries in advance, God's inspired prophecies of coming events, which have all been fulfilled so literally as to read more like history than prophecy. When Babylon was in its glory, Daniel dared to say that it would fall and be superseded by the Persian Empire. He lived to see the prophecy fulfilled.

When Cyrus was flushed with universal conquest, again Daniel looked through the horoscope of prophecy and saw the coming of Grecian and Roman conquerors. Again all the events of later times and history have literally fulfilled the visions of Daniel, and are fulfilling them today.

What but a divine mind could have given these predictions? What but an inspired book could contain such records?

Even in the minutest particulars we see the traces of divine wisdom and omniscience. The ancient prophet declared in one place that Zedekiah, the last king of Judah, should be carried to Babylon, and in another place he declared that Zedekiah should never see Babylon. It looked like a discrepancy at first, but history literally fulfilled it. Zedekiah, blinded by Nebuchadnezzar before He reached the city, entered it a captive, but never saw it with his sightless eyes. Thus has God been confirming His Word as the ages have come and gone.

One of the greatest mosques of the Mohammedan world has recently been destroyed by fire in the city of Damascus. It was an ancient Christian temple, on whose facade was cut in stone this inscription, "Thy kingdom, O Christ is an everlasting kingdom, and Thy word endureth to all generations." When the Moslems captured Damascus, and took possession of the old Christian church, they obliterated the inscription on the front by plastering it over and emblazoning in gold a verse from the Koran above it.

As ages went by, that archway spake only the message of the false prophet. But by-and-by time wore off the plaster, so that within the past two years the old Christian inscription has come out again, and God's word stands forth through all the wreck of time. When a few weeks ago the old church was burned down, strangely enough, the tower was left standing with the inscription untouched by the destroying elements; and there it stands today, declaring to the world, "Thy word, O Christ, endureth to all generations."

3. We have our responsibility for God's Holy Word. If this is the inspired Word of God, how solemn and supreme its claims! Let us believe it implicitly; let us believe it without compromise or questioning.

Let us not try to eliminate the supernatural and bring it down to the plane of our own reason and knowledge; but let us bow submissively before the throne of Him who speaks from heaven, and say with every fibre of our being, "It means just what it says."

But let us also obey. Believe means to "live by." Our faith has two sides; one is faith, the other is faithfulness. One is trust, the other is trustworthiness. They are the two wings that bear us above the dark abyss; they are the two oars that carry us through the dangerous rapids; they are the two hands that grasp and hold fast forever the eternal covenant.

Obedience is always the condition of faith. Only as we live by this blessed book can we fully claim its promises and rest upon its words of grace.

Let us live up to the fullness of our Bible. Let us translate every word of it into our lives. Let each of us be a new edition and a new version of the Scriptures, translated into flesh and blood, words and acts, holiness and service.

God has spoken to the successive generations, expecting each age to correspond to the message given; but to our generation He has given the largest measure of His truth and the fullness of His revelation. He expects from us a deeper, fuller, larger life. Let us live out the whole Bible in this dispensation.

There is a day coming when we shall have larger revelations of truth and an eternity in which to live them out: but in this life let us measure up to the Word of God without abatement, and, like the Master Himself, fulfill every word of Scripture before we shall have run our course.

Have we lived out all the Bible? Have we proved its every promise? Have we illustrated its every command? Have we translated it into the living characters our own record? God help us, not only to have a Bible, but each of us to be a Bible.

Finally, if this is God's inspired Word, it can be understood only by inspired men. There are two senses in which inspiration can be received and understood. The inspiration of the apostles and the prophets was to write the Bible, but we need an inspiration just as real to read it and to understand it. It was not written for the cold intelligence of natural man, but for the spiritual eyes of the heart. And so no man knoweth the things of God, save the Spirit of God which is in him. We must have "the mind of Christ" and the Holy Ghost before we can rightly and fully understand the Holy Scriptures.

Shall we receive His blessed Spirit to understand His blessed Word? Shall we read the Bible, not as a book of history and biography, but as the love letter of a Friend, the personal message of our Bridegroom and our Lord? Then shall we understand it, love it, and know its blessed meaning and heavenly power.

A poor blind girl was dying. Her cold fingers had ceased to feel. She called for her dear old Bible, and tried to read the raised letters once more, but all sense having gone from her hands, she turned away with sorrow, and clasping it to her bosom, and pressing it to her lips, she said, "My dear Bible, I cannot read you longer, but; I love you still." At that very moment she found that as her lips touched the characters they could still feel and read them. She gave a great cry of joy, and as she passed her lips from line to line the words still spake to her intelligence and to her heart.

Beloved, let us take the Bible a little closer, and we shall understand it better, and it will speak from the heart of God to our inmost heart as the living message of His love.

## Chapter 17

## The Holy Spirit in the Book of Joel

"And it shall some to pass afterward, that I will pour out my spirit upon all flesh; and your sons and your daughters shall prophesy, your old men shall dream dreams, your young men shall see visions." Joel 2: 28.

Joel was the oldest of the prophets of Judah whose writings have come down to us. His little book contains the substance and the text of the deeper and larger unfoldings of Isaiah, Jeremiah, and the later prophets, and is the keynote of the Day of Pentecost and the Christian Dispensation.

It is the text of all the volumes that have been written about the Holy Ghost, and the germ of all the manifestations of His power and grace throughout the ages that have followed this ancient message.

Just as God gave to Habakkuk, in one little verse, the text of the whole Gospel of salvation, so He gave to Joel the text of the whole doctrine of the Spirit. Like a rainbow upon the storm cloud, like a gleam of sunshine out of a dark sky, like a blossom amid the regions of eternal snow, so Joel's beautiful vision comes out of a dark calamity, a great national catastrophe.

It opens with the picture of an invasion of locusts, one of the most frightful scourges of the East. But beyond this little picture there is evidently some greater trial suggested, and some more formidable enemy foreshadowed. Perhaps the locust plague was but the type of the invading armies of the Chaldeans, and of the more dreadful judgments that are yet to come to Israel.

In the midst of this great national trial the prophet was sent to utter the trumpet call to the people to come together in fasting, penitence, humiliation, and prayer, and to seek the interposition and deliverance of their covenant God. Nor did they call upon Him in vain. He sent the gracious answer; and, as He always does, He gave more than they asked, even the promise of His own personal coming to dwell among them, and the outpouring of the Holy Spirit in the fullness of Pentecostal times, and the brighter promise of the glory which is to follow through the advent and reign of the Son of God Himself.

The whole vision is a kind of ground plan of the Dispensations, and especially of the Christian Dispensation and the times of the Spirit. It is also a sort of outlined sketch of God's dealings with the Church still in the manifestation of His presence and the outpouring of His Spirit; and not only with the Church, but with every individual soul.

I. THE MINISTRY OF REPENTANCE. Before the promise of the Spirit could be fulfilled, there must come the dispensation of repentance, humiliation, and earnest prayer. There came, therefore, the call to national penitence. "Blow the trumpet in Zion, sanctify a fast, call a solemn assembly: gather the people, sanctify the congregation." It was to be a general and deeply earnest movement, including all classes. "Gather the children and those that suck the breasts: let the bridegroom go forth of his chamber, and the bride of her closet. Let the priests, the ministers of the Lord, weep between the porch and the altar, and let them say, `Spare Thy people, O Lord, and give not thine heritage to reproach.'"

Such a dispensation of repentance must precede at every season of spiritual blessing. Its great type is John the Baptist and his ministry of warning and reformation. Doubtless it is prefigured by the vision of the prophet, and it preceded the coming of the Lord Jesus Christ and the outpouring of the Holy Ghost. So, still, before any church or people can receive the showers of heavenly blessing, they must humble themselves before God;

turn from sin, worldliness, and disobedience; publicly recognize God as the Author of their blessing; and wait upon Him in definite acknowledgment of their dependence. Then there will come to them the same gracious answer which the Prophet Joel was sent to bear to God's ancient people: "Fear not, O land; be glad and rejoice: for the Lord will do great things. . . . Be glad then, ye children of Zion, and rejoice in the Lord your God: for He hath given you the former rain moderately, and will cause to come down for you the rain, the former rain, and the latter rain."

II. THE COMING OF CHRIST. Next, there came the personal presence of the Lord Himself. "Ye shall know that I am in the midst of Israel, and that I am the Lord your God, and none else: and my people shall never be ashamed." This personal manifestation of the Lord in the midst of Israel was fulfilled in its most emphatic manner by the coming of Jesus, and His incarnation and ministry on earth after the preparatory ministry of John the Baptist. So Jesus must come personally before we can receive the full baptism of the Holy Ghost. Jesus does come to the penitent heart, the surrendered heart, the humble heart, and makes it His abode. "But to this man will I look, even to him that is poor and of a contrite spirit, and trembleth at my word."

Jesus is the giver of the Holy Ghost, "He that baptizeth with the Holy Ghost;" and we must receive Christ before we can receive the Spirit. The sinner's first act is not to receive the Holy Ghost, but to receive Jesus, turning to penitence from all sin, and opening his heart to the Savior. "As many as received him, to them gave the power to become the sons of God." And then He gives the heart in which He dwells the same Spirit which dwelt in Him.

IV. THE COMING OF THE HOLY SPIRIT. "And it shall come to pass afterward, that I will pour out my Spirit upon all flesh; and your sons and your daughters shall prophesy, your old men shall dream dreams, your young men shall see visions: and also upon the servants and upon the handmaids in those days will I pour out my Spirit. And I will shew wonders in the heavens and in the earth, blood, and fire, and pillars of smoke. The sun shall be turned into darkness, and the moon into blood, before the great and the terrible day of the Lord come. And it shall come to pass, that whosoever shall call upon the name of the Lord shall be delivered." This is the very promise the Apostle Peter quoted on the day of Pentecost as the explanation of that extraordinary manifestation of the presence of God.

1. First, we will notice that it is a personal coming of the Spirit. It is not, "I will pour out of my Spirit," but "I will pour out my Spirit." It is the Spirit Himself who comes.

The Third Person of the glorious Trinity removed His residence from heaven to earth, just as literally as the Second Person, the Lord Jesus Christ, removed His residence from heaven to earth when He became incarnate and dwelt for thirty-three and a half years in Galilee and Judea.

This world is now the home of the Holy Ghost, a real personal Being, with affections, intelligence, and will like our own. The very Spirit that dwelt in Jesus during His earthly ministry is now residing among us, and is willing to dwell within every consecrated heart.

2. The abundance of the outpouring is very strongly expressed. The Hebrew word "pour" means a very large effusion, a boundless filling of the Spirit. God does not give some of the Spirit, but gives the Spirit in all His infinite fullness. There is no limit whatsoever. He gives the Spirit "without measure" unto Jesus, and Jesus gives us all that He has of the Spirit's fullness.

We have not yet begun to realize the illimitable power and resources which God places at the call of His people's faith and obedience.

3. The extent of the outpouring is universal "upon all flesh." Hitherto the Spirit's manifestations had been confined to individuals and to a single nation. Now there was to be no distinction of race or nation. It was to be a universal blessing for Jews and Gentiles, and equally open to all the human race.

There is, perhaps, an intimation of the physical aspect of the blessing. The Holy Ghost makes our flesh His home and our body His temple.

4. There was to be no distinction of age. The promise was to "the young men and to the old men," to "the sons and daughters" as well as to the sire. Henceforth even experience, age, and natural advantages were not to count; but the Holy Ghost was to be the wisdom and power of all that trusted Him. He would use the youngest; as well as the oldest, and "out of the mouths of babes and sucklings" would "ordain strength" and "perfect praise."

As we reach nearer to the climax of the age, the fullness of the Spirit, and the coming of the Lord, we find God choosing the young as well as the old, and making them the special instruments of His power. Many of the saintliest lives of today are those of young men heroes and young women heroines of the mission field, the holy ones whose consecration is more marked because it is not expected so much from them, amid the attractions and allurements of their youth and their worldly surroundings. Oh, that the young might know that the blessed Holy Ghost is willing and able to possess them in all the enthusiasm of their nature, in all the freshness of their love, in all the glow of their ambition, and not only to fill and satisfy their own hearts, but to use them as "burning and shining lights"!

The saintliest man that ever lived in Scotland was young McCheyne, whose spirit still lives in the present generation. The most influential lives that have ever adorned the mission field have been those of the young men and the young women who have given up their life as a sacrifice for Christ. Yes, and the very Leader whom we love to follow was Himself a young man, and never will be old. He will put His young heart, and His glorious Spirit, into the youngest as well as the oldest, and will accept the bright and beautiful offering of a consecrated youth, and give to it the glory that the world can never bestow. Let us receive Him, and give Him our brightest and best.

5. All social classes and conditions without distinction had the promise. "The servants and the handmaids," mentioned in the next verse, literally mean the slaves, for the servants in an-

cient families were bond-slaves, and the absolute property of their masters. Upon this class the especial gifts of the Holy Ghost were to descend under the Christian Dispensation.

There is no record of a slave's having been called specially into service and divine enduement in the Old Dispensation; but under the New, the poorest, the lowliest, and most unlikely classes were to be elevated and to receive the enduement of power from on high, and the honor of special service in the kingdom of God. So we find in the New Testament, Onesimus, the slave, recognized as the friend of Paul, and commended to the affection of Philemon, his former master. In his epistles the Apostle Paul enjoins the servants to accept their position as service for Jesus, and promises them an equal recompense in the kingdom of the Lord, when all social positions maybe reversed and they may win the crown of highest service in the millennial age.

Indeed, the outpouring of the Holy Ghost upon the servants and handmaids is specially emphasized in this verse. The two little words, "and also," are meant to designate this class as the particular objects of the divine care and blessing. Surely it has been true that the outcast classes of society have been raised up under the Gospel to be the vessels of God's richest mercy, and many of them the instruments of His noblest work.

N o man is so low nor so pressed down by natural hindrances as to prevent his taking the highest place in the kingdom of Christ. Let the young, let the lowly, let even the illiterate know that the Holy Ghost is willing to choose them as the vessels of His grace, and is able to train them for the highest spiritual culture and the most honored service for that blessed Master, with whom is no respect of persons.

6. Special gifts and manifestations of the Holy Spirit were to be bestowed. "Your sons and your daughters shalt prophesy, your old men shall dream dreams, your young men shall see visions." These various expressions have reference to the peculiar gifts of the Spirit in the revelation of His will to man, and the high service for which He fits us.

Prophesying is speaking the divine message in the power of the Spirit. Dreams and visions refer to the special illuminations which He is pleased to give to His consecrated servants.

Of course, it includes the peculiar ministry of inspiration of which we have formerly spoken, and which is not continued in the Church. But there is a sense in which God still opens the inner ear to hear His voice, and illuminates the "eyes of the heart" to behold the visions of His glory and His Word.

It would seem as if to the aged it came in dreams and to the young in visions. To the old, the faculties of nature being somewhat suspended, the voice of God has to be more direct. In the young the spiritual and mental powers are still in vigorous activity, and they are illuminated and quickened to catch the heavenly vision.

We do not encourage such an interpretation of these words as would give liberty for the extravagant and dangerous spiritualistic manifestations of the trance and medium, the pretended revelation, and other illusions and vagaries of our times. But after we have made necessary provision for holy caution, and the sober regulation of all spiritual manifestations, there is ample room for the quickening of the spiritual mind, the illuminating of the spiritual eye, and the unfolding of the mind of the Spirit to the humble, holy, and listening ear. God does give His visions still, especially to the young. He gave them to Joseph, He gave them to Timothy. He gave them to Paul. He gave them in the hour of consecration, in the season of waiting upon God, in the retirement of the closet, in the time when the nearest heart looks out upon a world of sin, and upon the vision of prophecy and inspired truth. God does make real to us His purpose for our lives, His purpose for the world, and the great prophetic plan which He is pleased to unfold through the Holy Ghost to the humble heart. He will "show us things to come." He will give to us inspirations, illuminations, aspirations, hopes, assurances, which become to our faith and hope like the little glimpse of sunlight which comes to the mariner on the pathless ocean, when for a moment the clouds divide, and a single observation can be taken of the sun in the blue heavens; and then the clouds return and the ship sails by that little glimpse of sunlight for the days to come.

God does give the holy heart its visions. Let us be sure they are the voices and the visions of God; then let us cherish them, let us live by them, let them lift up, and lead us on to all the heights of His love and will. "Thine eyes shall see the King in his beauty: they shall behold the land that is very far off." "I am the light of the world: he that followeth me shall not walk in darkness, but shall have the light of life."

7. The coming of the Holy Ghost will bring salvation to all who are willing to receive it. Not only does He endue the few with power for special service, but he opens the doors of mercy to all who are willing to believe and receive the Savior.

In the day of His coming it shall come to pass that "whosoever shall call upon the name of the Lord shall be saved." And so the Day of Pentecost is not only a day of blessing to the disciples, but a day of salvation to the multitude, and when He comes to us, "he will convict the world of sin, of righteousness, and of judgment."

How easy it is to lead souls to Christ when we are filled with the Holy Ghost! How the whole atmosphere charged with heavenly power when God's waiting people are baptized with the fullness of His Spirit! Then the consciences of men are stricken sometimes without a single word, and hearts are led to seek the Savior through an influence that they cannot understand.

Doubtless, as the days go by and the coming of the Lord draweth nigh, there shall be great revivals, times of wonderful awakening, seasons of special blessing, when multitudes shall seek the Lord, both at home and abroad, and there shall be great ingatherings from among the unsaved.

Our own generation has witnessed some examples of these great movements; and we may be encouraged to look for them still, as we go forth in the power of the Spirit, and give the Gospel in its fullness and simplicity to men.

8. This promise also includes the supernatural manifestation of divine power. "I will shew wonders in the heavens above, and signs in the earth beneath."

The Holy Ghost came at Pentecost with supernatural power; and He still operates through the faith of His people in His healing and wonder-working might, as a testimony to His word and a witness to an unbelieving world that He is still the living and the present God.

These wonders also include the manifestations of His providence in answering prayer, in removing difficulties, in breaking down barriers, in providing means for the carrying on of His cause, and in all those wonders of providence and grace of which so many examples have been given in our own time.

The Holy Ghost, who dwells in the Church, is the omnipotent Executive of the Godhead, and is able to control the hearts of men, the elements of nature, and the events of providence, and to work together with His people, not only in the ordinary operations of His grace, but in the extraordinary manifestations of divine power which may best bear witness to His word and work.

We may trust Him for all the power we need for the carrying on of His work, and for the accomplishment of His will. If He dwells within us, He will work without us. If He is pregnant in our hearts, He will show His dominion in the whole empire of His Divine power, both in the things that are in heaven, and the things that are on earth, and the things that are under the earth.

9. Once more we see the coming of the Holy Ghost leading up to the coming of the Lord Jesus Christ. The vision of the wonder-working Spirit leads right up to the events that preceded and ushered in the advent of Christ. The next chapter is the picture and prophecy of His coming. It is full of profound prophetic interest.

Among its pictures are the restoration of Israel from their long captivity, the final conflict of the ungodly nations with Christ and His people, the great battle of Armageddon, the coming of the Lord Jesus Christ, and the establishment of His blessed kingdom.

Just as the coming of Jesus brought the Holy Ghost, now the coming of the Holy Ghost in the fullness of His power will bring the second coming of Jesus; and as that advent approaches, His power will be more gloriously manifested, and His people will better understand His great purpose and His infinite resources. Oh, let us understand His special business, which is to gather out of the nations a people for Christ, to finish the work of the Gospel, to sanctify and prepare the Bride for her coming Lord, then to present her to Jesus, and hand over to Him the government of the millennial world.

The Holy Ghost is longing for Christ's coming, and longing for a people that can understand Him and can cooperate with Him in bringing it about.

Just as the coming of the Holy Ghost in His fullness will bring the millennial Advent, so there is a sense in which His coming to each heart will bring a millennial blessing to that heart.

There is a millennium for the soul as well as for the Church. There is a kingdom of peace and righteousness and glory into which, in a limited sense, we can enter with Him here. There is a Kingdom of God which in within us, which is righteousness and peace and joy in the Holy Ghost. Come, blessed Comforter, and usher it into every willing heart.

## Chapter 18

## The Holy Spirit in the Book of Isaiah

"Well spake the Holy Ghost by Esaias the prophet unto our fathers." Acts 28 : 25.

The name "Isaiah" means the "Salvation of Jehovah." Isaiah is the prophet of salvation, and the revealer of the Lord Jesus Christ and the Holy Ghost, the divine agent in the work of salvation.

1. ISAIAH'S CONSECRATION. Isaiah's revelation of the Holy Ghost begins with his own call and consecration. We have the account of this remarkable experience in the sixth chapter of Isaiah. It began with a vision of the glory of God, which the Apostle John tells us, was the vision of Christ in His primeval glory.

The immediate effect of it was the revelation of his own sinfulness and unworthiness, and he threw himself upon his face, crying, "Woe is me! for I am undone; because I am a man of unclean lips, . . . for mine eyes have seen the King, the Lord of hosts."

Every true baptism of the Holy Ghost must begin with the revelation of our sin, and this must come from the revelation of God's holiness and glory. As soon as we get undone, God is willing to begin to do exceeding abundantly above all that we ask or think.

Isaiah took the place of death, and then came the touch of life. A living coal from the heavenly altar was brought by one of the seraphim and laid upon his lips. What an angel's fingers could not endure, the lips of mortals can receive. This was the baptism of fire, and its effect was to cleanse his lips and purge away his iniquity, that he might be fitted for his great commission.

No man is fit to represent God and be the instrument of the Holy Ghost until he first receives the cleansing power of God. It is not the baptism of power we first receive, but the baptism of purity, of fire that consumes and cleanses intrinsically and utterly.

Like the baptism of Pentecost, which was a tongue of fire, so it came to Isaiah's lips and so it must come to ours. The effect was consecration for service. Then he could hear the voice of God. Then he could see the great purpose of Jehovah, desiring to fill the earth with His glory. Then he could hear the heavenly cry, "Whom shall I send, and who will go for us?" And then he could answer unreservedly and unconditionally, "Here am I; send me."

God wants to send His workers, but He will send only volunteers. There must be perfect partnership. We must be willing to go, and then we must be sent.

But how was Isaiah sent? He was sent to do the hardest work. He was sent to a people that would not receive him. He was sent knowing that his message would be rejected. He was sent to a place of failure and persecution, and, at last, to a martyr's death. He was sent to know that his words would come back as echoes in his own lifetime, and that not until later generations would they be fully received and the glorious harvest gathered.

This knowledge, however, made no difference to Isaiah. Enough that God had sent him, and that he was carrying out the divine commission. Some would receive it; but it would be a tenth, a remnant, a little flock, who would hearken to his voice and become the seed, the holy seed, of a future harvest.

So God sends us, when we receive the baptism of fire. Often there is hard, uncongenial, unrequited service. Let us go, like Isaiah, as the witnesses even of unpopular truth and a misunderstood ministry. So long as the Master is honored and pleased, what are men?

We are talking through the telephone of the ages. Some day the answer will come, and the Lord will say, "Well done!"

2. THE HOLY SPIRIT IN THE LORD JESUS CHRIST. Isaiah's next unfolding of the Holy Ghost is in connection with the person and work of the Lord Jesus Christ. He gives us three pictures of the baptism of Jesus with the Spirit.

The first is in the eleventh chapter, from the second to the fourth verse: "And the Spirit of the Lord shall rest upon him, the spirit of wisdom and understanding, the spirit of counsel and might, the spirit of knowledge and of the fear of the Lord; and shall make him of quick understanding in the fear of the Lord: and he shall not judge after the sight of his eyes, neither reprove after the hearing of his ears: but with righteousness shall he judge the poor, and reprove with equity for the meek of the earth: and he shall smite the earth with the rod of his mouth, and with the breath of his lips shall he slay the wicked."

Here we have three sets of qualities which the Holy Ghost was to bring Christ. First are His intellectual enduements, "The spirit of wisdom and understanding."

Wisdom is the power to apply knowledge, understanding knowledge. Both are necessary to real practical wisdom. One may know much, and yet not know how to use it to advantage.

The Holy Ghost gives not only knowledge, but practical wisdom. So He rested upon the Lord Jesus, as He will rest upon those in whom Jesus still abides, unfolding the will of God, the mind of Christ, the meaning of the Scriptures, their particular messages to us, and the lessons of our lives and our times.

In the second class of qualities bestowed on Christ is executive power, the spirit of counsel and might. Counsel is the power to plan rightly, and might the power to execute our plan.

Without a good plan the most earnest work is often a failure, and without executive ability the best plans often come to nought. In human affairs, these are usually divided; one has the conceiving mind, and another the executive right arm. But the Holy Ghost is both, and He gave both to the Lord Jesus Christ, making Him the Wonderful Counselor, and, at the same time, the Mighty God, whose counsel shall stand and who will do all His pleasure.

The third class of attributes represents the moral and spiritual: "The spirit of understanding, and the fear of the Lord." And this is still further amplified by the words, "He shall make him of quick understanding (or quick smell) in the fear of the Lord." These are highest attributes of character. These the Lord Jesus possessed in an infinite measure.

The Scotch have a phrase which is very expressive. They talk of "sensing" things. To sense a thing is not to reason it out or know it by information, but it is to know it by instinct and intuition. It is somewhat like the sense of smell, or the instinct of the bird that knows the poison berry by the flash of intuition, while the scientist must analyze it and detect the poison by a chemical search.

Jesus had this intuition of right and wrong, this instinctive intuition of His Father's mind and will, this holy fear of evil, and this holy intuition of good; and this the sanctified soul has in proportion as it knows the Lord Jesus and is filled with the Holy Ghost.

It may seem strange to talk about Jesus, the Son of God, having the fear of His Father. But the more intimate we are with the truest lives, the more respect and veneration we have for them. Love is not opposed to fear in this high, sweet sense, for the more we love and trust a friend, the more we will dread to displease him, fear to offend him, and sensitively seek to please him.

This is the fear of the Lord, which is the beginning of wisdom, which the Holy Spirit is willing to give to every true and sanctified heart. Beloved, let us receive this indwelling Christ and the baptism of the Holy Ghost, which He brings in wisdom, executive power, and the quick sense of right and wrong.

The second picture of the baptism of Jesus with the Spirit is in the first four verses of the forty-second chapter of Isaiah: "Behold my servant, whom I uphold, mine elect, in whom my soul delighteth; I have put my Spirit upon him; he shall bring forth judgment to the Gentiles. He shall not cry, nor lift up, nor cause his voice to be heard in the street. A bruised reed shall he not break, and the smoking flax shall he not quench: he shall bring forth judgment unto truth. He shall not fail nor be discouraged till he have set judgment in the earth: and the isles shall wait for his law."

Here we have a beautiful blending of gentleness and power in the character of the Lord Jesus Christ. "He shall not cry, nor lift up, nor cause his voice to be heard in the street. A bruised reed shall he not break, and the smoking flax shall he not quench; he shall bring forth judgment unto truth. He shall not fail nor be discouraged till he have set judgment in the earth: and the isles shall wait for his law."

Every truly great character is simple and gentle. Jesus is the perfect combination of the lion and the lamb, of the dove and the eagle; and He will so fill us that we shall be crowned with the glory of meekness and the strength of love.

There is a third picture of the baptism of the Lord Jesus Christ with the Holy Ghost. It is found in the first four verses of the sixty-first chapter: "The Spirit of the Lord God is upon me; because the Lord hath anointed me to preach good tidings unto the meek: he hath sent me to bind up the brokenhearted, to proclaim liberty to the captives, and the opening of the prison to them that are bound; to proclaim the acceptable year of the Lord, and the day of vengeance of our God; to comfort all that mourn; to appoint unto them that mourn in Zion, to give unto them beauty for ashes, the oil of joy for mourning, the garment of praise for the spirit of heaviness; that they might be called trees of righteousness, the planting of the Lord, that he might he glorified. And they shall build the old wastes, they shall raise up the former desolations, and they shall repair the waste cities, the desolations of many generations."

This well known passage was directly applied to Himself by the Lord Jesus Christ in His public address at Nazareth. Here we see the Holy Spirit anointing the Lord Jesus; first, for the ministry of the Gospel of salvation to the poor; secondly, with the ministry of healing; thirdly, the ministry of deliverance for the captives of sin; fourthly, the ministry of teaching, the recovery of sight to the blind; fifthly, with the message of His coming, to proclaim the acceptable year of the Lord and the day of vengeance of our God; and, finally, the message of comfort and consolation to all that mourn.

This was Christ's ministry, and He fulfilled it in the power of the Holy Ghost. He did not presume to preach the Gospel until He had received this enduement; neither should we. And, as we receive the same Spirit, ours will be a ministry of salvation, a ministry of healing, a ministry of sanctification, a ministry of teaching, a ministry of hope, a ministry of consolation, joy and gladness.

There is a very striking order in these three passages respecting Christ's baptism. First, it is promised in the second chapter, by the prophet. Next, it is proclaimed in the forty-second chapter by the Father to the Son. Here, it is confessed by the Savior, and claimed by Himself, as He goes forth to exercise the ministry and claim the power.

Only thus can we receive the baptism of the Spirit. It is promised to us as well as to Him, and there must come a moment when it is really given by the Word of God and our act of consecration. Then there must come a third step when we ourselves confess it, accept it, and step forward to realize it in the actual exercise of the gift we have claimed, by proving our faith in our obedience. As we, like Jesus, go forth with the Gospel of salvation in dependence on the power of the Spirit, we, too, shall find, like Him, that we are endued with power from on high.

3. THE HOLY SPIRIT ON ISRAEL AS A NATION. We have a beautiful picture of this outpouring of the Spirit upon Israel in Isaiah 27: 15-18: "Until the Spirit be poured upon us from

on high, and the wilderness be a fruitful field, and the fruitful field be counted for a forest. Then judgment shall dwell in the wilderness, and righteousness remain the fruitful field. And the work of righteousness shall be peace; and the effect of righteousness, quietness and assurance forever. And my people shall dwell in a peaceable habitation, and in sure dwellings, and in quiet resting places."

This follows a long season of national depression and sorrow. It brings a complete and blessed revolution, turning the nation to righteousness and God, and changing every sorrow into prosperity, blessing, and peace. The first droppings of this blessed rain are already beginning to come, and the remnant of Israel is turning to God, as well as many to their ancient fatherland.

The Holy Ghost is beginning to visit the seed of Abraham, and soon the wilderness of Palestine shall rejoice and blossom as the rose. Let us pray for Israel, and its restoration will be to the Gentiles and to the world as life from the dead.

There is another picture of the same national blessing in Isaiah 59: 19-21. The Apostle Paul, in his letter to the Romans, quoted from this passage with direct reference to the coming of Christ and the return of Israel. This is to be accompanied by a wide effusion of the Spirit from on high, which is to be a permanent and everlasting presence.

The Holy Ghost is not going to leave this world when Jesus comes back, but, as of old He dwelt in Christ in the days of His suffering and humiliation, so He shall dwell in Him again as He comes to reign in glory.

All that we know of His comfort, joy, love quickening life, and effectual power, is but the merest foretaste of the glory with which He will fill us in those coming ages. Then we shall know not only the fullness of Jesus, but we shall receive the residue of the Spirit, and it shall be true of Israel and of the Church of Christ, "My Spirit that is upon thee, . . . shall not depart out of thy mouth, nor out of the mouth of thy seed, nor out of the mouth of thy seed's seed, saith the Lord, from henceforth and forever."

IV. THE HOLY SPIRIT FOR EACH OF US AS INDIVIDUALS. There is another and a greater promise of the Holy Ghost in Isaiah which each of us may claim for ourselves. It is found in the forty-fourth chapter, verses three to five. "For I will pour water upon him that is thirsty, and floods upon the dry ground; I will pour my Spirit upon thy seed, and my blessing upon thy offspring; and they shall spring up as among the grass, as willows by the watercourses. One shall say, I am the Lord's; and another shall call himself by the name of Jacob; and another shall subscribe with his hand unto the Lord, and surname himself by the name of Israel." The only limitation of this promise is our fitness and capacity to receive it. We have here a beautiful picture of the field, the flood, and the fruit.

First, the field is "the thirsty and the dry ground." In nature as well as in grace there must be a preparation of the soil for the seed and the harvest. The same seed on one field comes to nothing, and on another it produces one hundredfold; so the Holy Ghost is affected by the personal qualities of the heart in which He dwells, and the capacity of the soul for spiritual life, power and blessing. Some seem to be vessels prepared unto glory, and others only for sin and evil.

Two men sit down at the same table. To one it is a feast, to another it is a famine, simply because the one is hungry and the other satisfied. The very best dish on our dinner table is a good appetite. So God's spiritual preparation for the coming of His Spirit is a deep hunger and thirst. Let us thank Him as He gives it to us, and show more need than fullness, more want than blessing; for "blessed are they which do hunger and thirst after righteousness: for they shall be filled."

Our best preparation for the Holy Spirit is emptiness, a sense of need, and a real spiritual capacity. Sometimes God has to bring this about by our very failures, and a revelation to us as to our nothingness and worthlessness.

Next, we find that on such a soil He will pour out "floods." It is not merely a few drops of rain, but the abundant rain, the ample, boundless overflow of His Holy Spirit. Oh, that we might prove the richer fullness of this promise, and let Him pour out a blessing until there should not be room to receive it!

Finally, there is a threefold fruition. First, there is the salvation of individuals. "One shall say, I am the Lord's." Next, there must be the public confession of those who are saved. "Another shall call himself by the name of Jacob." And, thirdly, there is the deeper consecration of God's people. "Another shall subscribe with his hand unto the Lord, and call himself by the name of Israel." This describes a higher spiritual life.

This is a covenant voluntarily signed between the soul and the Lord, in which there is a perfect and entire surrender, and a complete claim of all His blessing and fullness.

Then comes the new surname, which, as with the patriarch Jacob of old, marked a crisis in his history, and a new departure of power and blessing. Israel means "a Prince with God," the conquering soul, the life that has entered into the divine fullness.

This is the work of the Holy Ghost, to lead us on to all these things; first, to accept the Lord, then to unite with His people and to acknowledge Him publicly, and then to go on into all the fullness of His grace and blessing.

As we receive the Holy Ghost, we must go on, and only as we go on, can we continue to receive His increasing and satisfying fullness. Beloved, have we taken all the steps? Have we signed the personal covenant? Have we special relations with God? Is He to us what He is to no one else? Have we received the eternal surname, and are we written in heaven in characters which no one knoweth, save Him that gave the name and the soul on whom He has inscribed it?

Such, then, is Isaiah's vision of the Holy Ghost, the Spirit that came first upon him and enabled him to reveal it to others in his yet more glorious ministry, in the person of the Lord Jesus, in the future glory of the Jewish nation, and in the soul that receives His fullness.

All this has come to pass in the ages since Isaiah's time. We are living in the noontide light and glory of the Holy Ghost. Have these ancient promises and prophesies been fulfilled to us? Has the vision been translated into our life? Have we proved this part of God's holy Scriptures?

Let us come to Him as did Isaiah, in deep spiritual hunger, self-renunciation, and consecration. Let us receive the living seal which the hand of Jesus is ready to put upon our lips and leave upon the altar of our hearts; then let us go forth like Isaiah, in the power of the Spirit to proclaim His grace and fullness, and to become spiritual conductors, passing the blessing on to the souls that are hungering and perishing around us; let our lives, like Isaiah's signify "the Salvation of Jehovah."

# Chapter 19

# The Holy Spirit in the Life and Testimony of Jeremiah

JEREMIAH, although occupying in comparison with Isaiah the second place in our Old Testament canons, really occupied the highest place in the mind of his people, and in the estimation of the rabbis and religious leaders of the Jews. So supremely was he regarded as the guardian spirit of Judah and Jerusalem that they expected him to come back from the dead and to usher in some new bright era of national hope and prosperity. Therefore, when Jesus of Nazareth was performing His wondrous miracles upon earth, and was attracting the attention of all the people, we find that many of them supposed that He was no other than Jeremiah who had risen from the dead.

The life of Jeremiah is inseparably linked with the last days of ancient Judaism and the fall of Jerusalem. The period of his ministry, occupying as it did about forty years, was singularly parallel to the forty years of the ministry of Moses in the beginning of Israel's history. It was parallel, also, to the forty years of trial and probation which preceded the fall of Jerusalem in later centuries, after the testimony of Christ and His apostles had been at length rejected.

These three periods of forty years were all times of probation, and, alas! of provocation, on the part of Israel. Just as Moses was the divine messenger under the first, so Jeremiah stood under the second with loving loyalty to his country and supreme fidelity to His God. He strove to avert the awful catastrophe which he saw so swiftly and surely coming upon his people. When at last he could not prevent it, he shared it with his people; and finally, it seems probable, perished at their cruel hands.

The story of his life and the record of his testimony are full of the most touching and beautiful manifestations of the divine character and love and of the working of the Holy Ghost.

The New Testament has borne most distinct witness to his inspired messages, and recognized his words as the messages of the Holy Ghost. We shall glance first, at his personal call; next, at the relation of his life and ministry to his own people and times; and, finally, at his messages for later ages and for us through the Spirit.

1. JEREMIAH'S CALL AND COMMISSION. Jeremiah has given an account of his call and commission in the first chapter of his prophetic book. It is not unlike the story of Isaiah's consecration in the sixth chapter of his prophecy. God came to him and announced to him before his birth he had been called to be a prophet unto the nations.

His commission is a very glorious one. "I have this day set thee," He says, "over the nations, and over the kingdoms, to root out, and to pull down, . . . and to plant." Not only did his commission extend to his own people, but at his prophetic word the mightiest nations of his time rose and fell. The mighty armies that traversed the whole earth and made the nations to tremble, moved at the word of Jeremiah through the Holy Ghost. Alone in his quiet home at Anathoth, or suffering in his lone dungeon in Jerusalem, he was really the mightiest force of his time. It was his prophetic word that decided the fate of dynasties and kingdoms.

There is nothing more sublime than the simple power which the Holy Ghost gives to the humblest saint; and the ministry of prayer which He enables the lowliest child of God to exercise. Is there a spectacle more glorious than the picture given us nearly a century later of that mighty sovereign of the east, the all victorious Cyrus, after he had subdued the nations, after proud Babylon had fallen beneath his feet, after the whole world had become his empire, compelled by an influence that he could not understand, to fulfill the very words of Jeremiah's prophecy?

His was a peculiar prophetic ministry, no doubt; but God will give a similar power to every true saint who is willing in the name of Lord Jesus to accept the high commission and the holy ministry of prayer, and to grasp the scepter of faith through which He can touch the world with the power and blessing of the eternal God.

The commission of Jeremiah was a very remarkable one. Naturally he seemed wholly unfitted for it. Everything is his nature recoiled from the task to which he was called. He was sensitive, shrinking and loving. It was a fearful sacrifice of all his feelings to be compelled to stand in constant antagonism and to utter God's rebukes against the people that he loved, against princes, priests, and prophets.

Far sweeter would it have been for him to weep for Israel's sorrows and even to suffer for her sins; but God called that gentle nature to be the messenger of His most fearful warnings and judgments, and to pass through an ordeal of suffering from which the bravest heart might shrink. He did shrink. "I am a child," he said, but God would not allow him to plead his weakness. It was not Jeremiah's strength that was to prevail, but God's mighty enduement of power from on high. So the hand of God stretched out and touched his lips. The power of God was communicated to his shrinking weakness, and he was commanded to stand forth without a doubt or a fear, and to speak the words that God should inspire, and to be like a wall of adamant and a fortress of fire against the priests, the princes, the prophets, and the people of the land.

In like manner God often calls us to ministries for which we are naturally unfitted; but if He calls and enables, what need have we to fear? Indeed, the only thing we have cause to fear is the spirit of fear; and when we step forth at the divine command to fulfill such sacred trusts, we must stand in fearless courage and absolute obedience. Yes, we might almost say, audacity is the only safe position. "Be not dismayed at their faces, lest I confound thee before them" is still as true for us as it was for Jeremiah of old.

2. JEREMIAH'S RELATION TO HIS OWN PEOPLE AND TIMES. Jeremiah lived and testified through the reign of four of Judah's kings. He was called to his ministry early in the reign of young Josiah, who, having inherited a corrupt throne, found himself, while yet but a child, the sovereign of a people who had been stereotyped in idolatry and sin. The long reign of Manassah, which covered half a century, was paralleled only by the days of Ahab and Jezebel; and, although the last days of his life led him, through divine judgment, to sincere repentance, yet they were too short to undo the fearful crimes of a long reign. After the short reign of a son as wicked as himself, Josiah ascended the throne.

He was destined to be one of the best of Judah's kings, and to take his place beside Jehoshaphat and Hezekiah among the true successors of David. Beginning early to struggle against evil, he labored courageously and consistently till the close of his reign for the reformation of his kingdom. In these efforts he was seconded by the faithful Jeremiah. Indeed, there is no doubt that the reformation was due, under God, chiefly to the labors of Jeremiah himself.

Day by day he stood in the streets of Jerusalem, uttering his tender and solemn messages. His earlier addresses have been preserved to us in the beginning of his prophecy. Reminding the people of God's ancient covenant and their former faithfulness and blessing, he appealed with tender solemn pathos to their hearts. "Thus saith the Lord," he would cry, "I remember thee, the kindness of thy youth, the love of thy espousals, when thou wentest after me in the wilderness." And that he would renew the appeal, and cry, "Have I been a wilderness unto Israel? a land of darkness?" "My people have committed two evils. They have forsaken me the fountain of living waters, and hewed them out cisterns, broken cisterns, that can hold no water."

Then as he saw, perhaps, their cold indifference or scornful unbelief, there would follow some solemn message, the vision of coming calamity, the dramatic picture of the invader and the besieging army from the north and the impending fall of Jerusalem. Or sometimes his heart would break out in a wail of despair and anguish, "Oh, that mine head were waters, and mine eyes a fountain of tears, that I might weep day and night for the slain of the daughter of my people!" "Is there no balm in Gilead? Is there no physician there? Why then is not the health of the daughter of my people recovered?" "The harvest is past, the summer is ended, and we are not saved."

Thus he preached and pleaded and warned and waited, year after year. Gradually some improvement appeared, until after a while it seemed as though the clouds were passing, and the nation were returning to their God.

At this time a strange and important incident occurred. It was the finding of a lost copy of the law amid the rubbish of the temple. The house of God had become like a filthy stable, and had been given up to the rites of idolatry for generations. But, as they were cleansing it at the commandment of Josiah, they found amid the wreck and debris an old copy of the law of Moses. Perhaps it was the book of Deuteronomy; perhaps it was a larger scroll containing the entire law. It made the deepest impression upon the prophet and the king.

It was like the finding of Luther's Bible in the sixteenth century. It was solemnly brought to the king, and then the priests and the people were gathered together in public convocation and the sacred book was read. As thy listened to the voice of God, and learned His precepts and commandments, which for ages they had neglected and disobeyed, there began to fall upon them something like the spirit of a true humiliation and reformation.

Following up the movement, Josiah summoned the whole nation to Jerusalem, and sent out a universal call for a great Passover. They came from north and south and east and west; and some even of the remnant of Israel gathered with them; and there they kept the Passover as it had not been kept for generations.

One would have thought that all this must have filled the heart of Jeremiah with joy and confidence. Doubtless he did appreciate fully even the transient awakening. But it brought to him one of those crises which are most trying to a faithful minister. He saw the shallowness of the movement. He saw the deep insincerity on the part of the leaders. He saw that the heart of the people was wedded to idolatry and sin, and that all this was but superficial and would soon pass away. They were willing to go so far; but a radical revival that would separate them from all idolatry and sin, and from the gross vices and unrighteousness which pervaded the whole national life, for this they were unwilling. He saw with the vision of divine discernment that nothing short of this revival would avert the impending stroke.

So he pleaded more solemnly that ever. He summoned the princes, the priests, the prophets, and the people to righteousness and holiness; to circumcise their hearts and not merely rest in a ceremonial worship or an outward reformation.

But his messages found little response. The transient reformation passed by; the hearts of the people were still unsanctified; the prophet was sure that the day of judgment for Judah was only delayed but not averted.

It was not long before clouds began to gather more dark and hopeless than before. In an evil hour Josiah was led into a foolish and hasty campaign against the king of Egypt. Neglecting the warning which God sent to him through the lips of that heathen king, he rashly ventured into the forbidden conflict, and left his life upon the bloody field of Megiddo.

With Josiah's death the last hope of Judah died, and Jeremiah uttered over him a lamentation which wasthe very cry of despair. Then began that chain of crimes and ccalamities which culminated in the fall of Jerusalem and the captivity of Judah.

Jehoiakim, the immediate successor of Josiah, was a counterpart of Ahab and Jeroboam in the worst days of Israel. He set at naught all the counsels and warnings of the prophet. When, at last, Jeremiah had Barak to read to him from his prophetic scroll the solemn judgment which God had pronounced against him, instead of the least show of repentance, he took his penknife, cut the objectionable words out of the scroll, and threw them into the fire.

The prophet returned to his house, rewrote the threatenings of Jehovah with many terrible additions, and read them back to the king. Again and again was Jehoiakim warned of his impending ruin; but his heart seemed given up to an utter infatuation of willfulness and wickedness, until, at last, after an infamous reign of eleven years, he was slain in a night attack by the Babylonian army upon Jerusalem, and his lifeless body was exposed in the open fields. Men said in after ages that on the withered forehead could be read in awful characters the name of the evil spirit whom he had followed all his life.

Jeremiah had predicted long before that the wicked king should be, "buried with the burial of an ass," and his wretched life ended in shame and ruin. His reputation was so desperate that he was not even buried in the sepulchres of the kings.

He was followed by Jehoiachin, who was really the puppet and creature of the Babylonian monarch. After a short and uneventful reign, he in turn was succeeded by Zedekiah, the last of Judah's kings.

Zedekiah was weak and irresolute rather than obstinately wicked. His whole reign was marked by vacillation and cowardice. He had a certain measure of respect for the messages of Jeremiah, sometimes sending for him, and seeming to listen to his counsels and to desire to carry them out; but he feared the princes and the people, and had not the courage to obey his own convictions.

Again and again did Jeremiah assure him that, if he would but obey the voice of God, even yet he and his kingdom would be spared; but as surely as he persisted in the counsels of the people and the princes, and depended upon the alliances of the neighboring nations, both he and his kingdom should perish.

Many were the vicissitudes and trials of the faithful prophet during these last years. Again and again was he exposed to the charge of disloyalty and treated as an enemy of his country. Again and again did the false prophets testify against him and try to bolster up the hopes of the people by deceiving visions of coming prosperity. Sometimes he was pursued for his life. Often he was exposed to imprisonment and the severest hardships, and left even for days to sink in the mire of his dungeon, and was saved from death only by the interposition of compassionate strangers.

And so the years rolled by, until at last the cup of iniquity was full and the divine judgment could wait no longer. The Babylonians invaded the land. The cordon of destruction tightened around Jerusalem, and, at last, the walls were broken up and the Chaldeans entered. Zedekiah sought for safety in cowardly flight, and succeeded in reaching the plains of Jericho with a tartan retinue; but he was pursued by the Babylonians and captured. He and his sons were taken into the presence of Nebuchadnezzar. His sons were murdered before his eyes; and, as if to stereotype this last and hideous vision forever on his memory, his eyes were then cruelly put out, and he was taken in blindness and bondage to Babylon, and left to end his days as a royal captive.

What was the fate of Jeremiah? He had been true to God, and God had not failed him in this dark and dreadful hour. The Babylonian king having heard of his high and heroic character, gave orders to his officers that Jeremiah should be carefully sought out and guarded from all harm. Not a hair of his head was touched, but he was treated with honor and every consideration. He was given his choice of going to Babylon, with liberty and ample provision for his every need, or of remaining among his own people. Of course, he chose the latter. He had lived for them, and he was ready to die with them; and so he remained among the remnant that were left after the deportation of most of the leading citizens of Jerusalem as captives to Babylon.

It is said that he went down with those who went to Egypt and dwelt among them, still counseling them and teaching them the messages of God; but they refused his warnings and counsels, and ultimately, tradition has reported, they even took the prophet's life. He became one of the glorious list of martyrs of truth who sealed their testimony with their blood.

Humanly speaking, his life was not a success; but when the books shall be opened and the rewards shall be given, it will be found that Jeremiah's life outweighed the most successful and brilliant career. His was the high honor of remaining true to God and faithful to his trust, even in the fact of seeming failure and the martyr's death.

This is true success, and this was the glorious testimony of Jeremiah's life.

3. HIS MESSAGE TO OUR TIMES. Let us look finally at his message to us in later ages. His prophetic writings are full of messages for future times. The very failure of the kingdom of Judah was but a background for the vision of the true kingdom which the future was to bring.

He saw, as no other had ever seen, how powerless was the highest teaching or the severest suffering to lead to virtue and faithfulness. Alas! the secret of failure was found in the wretched material of poor, fallen human nature and the need of a strength higher than human purpose, or even the light of truth and example. He looked forward with deep longing to the bright day of the New Testament, the coming Savior, and the Holy Ghost.

As a result, Jeremiah has given to us out of the darkness and failure of his own time, the inspired vision of the new covenant, the Gospel, and the work of the Spirit. The writer of the epistle to the Hebrews has repeatedly quoted from this ancient prophet the most comprehensive statement of the new covenant which has ever been given to the Church of God.

It is found in the thirty-first chapter of Jeremiah, from the thirty-first verse to the thirty-fourth. "Behold the days come, saith the Lord, that I will make a new covenant with the house of Israel and with the house of Judah; Not according to the covenant that I made with their fathers, in the day that I took them by the hand, to bring them out of the land of Egypt; which my covenant they brake, although I was an husband unto them, saith the Lord; But this shall be the covenant that I shall make with the house of Israel; After these days, saith the Lord, I will put my law in their inward parts, and write it in their hearts; and will be their God, and they shall be my people. And they shall teach no more every man his neighbor, and every man his brother, saying, Know the Lord; for they shall all know me, from the least of them unto the greatest of them, saith the Lord: for I will forgive their iniquity and I will remember their sin no more."

The distinguishing feature of this new covenant which Jeremiah announced lies in the fact that God promises to write His law upon our hearts, and to "put it in our inward parts." The old covenant gave light and law, but it did not give the power and disposition to obey it. But the new covenant writes it in our inmost being; makes it part of our very nature; incorporates it into our will, our choice, our desires, our very intuitions, so that it becomes second nature to us, our spontaneous desire, and our deepest life.

This is the work of the Holy Ghost. This is the meaning of sanctification. This is the great purpose of Christ's redemption and His indwelling in the heart of the believer through the Spirit.

It is God who undertakes to keep this covenant. It is not dependent upon what we do; but He becomes our God first and makes us His people. He undertakes to teach us and to reveal to us by the Holy Spirit the meaning of His will, the nature of His covenant, and the purposes of His grace and love.

We are not dependent upon outward instruction merely; but each of us has access to Him, and may enjoy the personal teaching of the Holy Ghost.

It will be noticed that the forgiveness of sins is not the primary promise of this chapter. It is secondary, and follows as a matter of course; but the primary feature of the great promise is the power of divine grace to keep from sin, and to lead us into righteousness and holiness.

This is the glorious Gospel which Jesus has come to bring in its fullness, and of which the Holy Ghost is at once the Revealer and the Enabler. It brings not merely the message of repentance and forgiveness with the dreary prospect of continued sin. It comes not only to forgive the past, but to assure us of a power that will keep us for the future, and put into us a nature that is in its tendency holy and divine, and that leads us to choose the will of God and the life of holy obedience.

Beloved, have we learned this blessed message of the Holy Ghost through Jeremiah? Have we come into this new covenant? Have we proved the fullness of salvation through the indwelling of the Holy Ghost, and the law written upon our inmost hearts?

Another message which Jeremiah has left for later times is the lesson of faith which he has given in the thirty-second chapter of his prophecy. It was a very striking object lesson. In the days when the future was as dark as calamity could make it, when the whole land was in the possession of the Chaldeans, and the city was about to fall; at a time when real estate in Judah was practically worthless, Jeremiah was commanded to invest his means in his patrimonial estate in the village of Anathoth. It would seem like throwing money away; but instead of hesitating, he immediately obeyed the divine command, and, publicly, before all the people, completed the purchase, subscribed the papers, had the transaction duly attested and sealed, and put his little fortune into the piece of property which he knew for two generations would be under the blight of the long captivity of Judah.

What did it all mean? It was a practical expression of his faith in the future of his country, and of the fact that a day was coming when that inheritance would be worth all its cost, when that estate would come back to his family again, and when his own glorious promise of Israel's restoration would be fulfilled.

It was stepping out in the dark hour and committing himself to the promise of God. It was counting upon the things that are not as though they were. It was the faith that anticipates the future, and in the midnight hour lifts up its song of praise, and puts its foot upon the seeming void "and finds the rock beneath."

This is the spirit of true faith in every age. We too, like Jeremiah, must count upon God's Word when there is nothing else to count upon, and must exercise that faith that is "the substance of things hoped for, and the evidence of things not seen." We must step out, in the dark and empty void, and know that God is underneath us, and that the vision of faith and the promise of the future are as certain and real as His eternal throne.

There is yet another message for future times which Jeremiah has left us, and on which for a moment we linger. It is found in the eighteenth chapter of his prophecy. It is the figure of the potter and his vessel. The prophet, having gone down to the potter's house, saw him working a vessel upon a wheel; but, through some cause, the vessel was marred in the hand of the Potter. Perhaps the clay did not yield to his touch, and would not lie plastic in his hands. He had to throw it aside, and it seemed as if his work had failed, and that even the material was rejected. Oh, how solemnly it speaks to us of our past failures! Perhaps God took us in hand, and began to work out in our life some gracious purpose; but we shrank from the ordeal; we refused to submit to His will. We asked an easier way, we held back from the cross; and God seeming unable to accomplish His high and holy purpose, had to put us aside and let His gracious plan seem, for the time, to fail. Oh, how sad and solemn the wrecks that lie behind us through our willfulness, our unbelief, and our unwillingness to trust our Father's wisdom and love in the testing hour!

But there is a beautiful sequel to Jeremiah's parable. The clay was not thrown away; but the potter took it up again and fashioned it again, another vessel, "as it pleased the potter to make it." There was a time when I think I interpreted this vision wrongly, and thought it meant that God took up our broken lives and made the best of them that He could; but that it was not all that He had at first intended. I believe that the grace of God loves to triumph even over our self-will, and I cannot but think that even in the very terms of Jeremiah's object lesson, there are lines of hope and divine encouragement, and that we may dare to believe that the vessel which the potter made the second time was even a better vessel than he had tried to make before, because, we are told, "He made it again another vessel, as it seemed good to the potter to make it." This time it was not our pleasure but His that was accomplished. Perhaps he gave us grace to yield our stubborn will and to submit with confidence to his hand. Perhaps, in His wondrous and over-ruling mercy, He brought us to full surrender and subdued our willfulness. At least, His mighty love triumphed over all hindrances, His will was accomplished, and His high purpose was fulfilled. Yes, the grace of God is able, not only for Satan and for sin, but for self too, and strong enough to overcome the opposition of our weak and willful hearts.

Thank God for One whose sovereign grace saved us when we were dead in sin, and whose all-sufficient power is able to save us to the uttermost, to bring us to the place, where, some day, we shall say, "Not unto us, O God, not unto us, but unto Thy name be all the glory."

"Grace all the work shall crown,
To everlasting days,
It lays in heaven that topmost stone
And well deserves the praise."

## Chapter 20

## The Holy Spirit in Ezekiel

"The word of the Lord came expressly unto Ezekiel the priest, the son of Buzi, in the land of the Chaldeans by the river Chebar; and the hand of the Lord was there upon him." Ezekiel 1:3.

The ministry of Ezekiel was dramatic and pathetic. Like Jeremiah's, it was connected with the fall of Judah, but it differed in this, that while Jeremiah was present amid the scenes of sorrow connected with that awful tragedy. Ezekiel was far removed and saw it in vision only, from the distant banks of the river Chebar. God showed it all to him, and day by day the painful panorama passed before his eyes and was reproduced to his countrymen around him in his inspired visions; so that, the very day the city fell, he knew it in his spirit, although the tidings did not reach him until years afterward.

Indeed, in his own personal life he became a sort of object lesson of the events which he described, and in which he was so deeply interested as a prophet and a patriot. In his own person he suffered in type and figure what his country and people were enduring. He went through the days of famine, eating unclean food, and setting forth in his own sufferings the horrors of the approaching calamities.

The day that Jerusalem fell, his own wife died, and he knew that she was made in God's mysterious providence an awful picture of the blow that had fallen upon Jerusalem. Thus he both lived and taught the lessons of his time, and left the wondrous record for the instruction of later ages.

The events that were transpiring around him formed a fitting framework for the message of faith and hope which he was sent to unveil for the future. Through the wreck of Israel's national history, he was able to see, as through the broken walls of a ruined building, the light of the coming dispensation and the promise of a better hope.

His pages shine with the light of the Gospel, unfolding with a clearness, that even Isaiah does not surpass, the times of the Messiah, and especially the person and work of the blessed Holy Spirit. Nowhere are there more sublime heights of holy vision, and nowhere more clear, spiritual and practical unfoldings of truth revealing the spiritual life and the dispensation of the Holy Ghost. Let us look at three remarkable visions of his prophecy.

1. THE VISION OF THE GLORY. The prophecy opened with an extraordinary vision of peculiar sublimity and majesty, revealing the glory of the Lord in the mighty working of His Spirit and providence.

First, he saw a whirlwind coming from the north, the direction from which the enemies of Israel came, and where the great world empires had their seat. In the midst of this whirlwind there was a fire enfolding itself; a sort of whirlwind fire, turning upon its own axis, and sweeping on in majesty and glory. The whirlwind and the fire have already been made familiar as the symbols of God and His manifested presence and glory.

Next, he beheld in the midst of the fiery whirlwind four living creatures. These were the cherubim. We have already seen them at the gate of Eden and in the Tabernacle and the Temple, and they reappear in the vision of the Apocalypse.

They are special symbols of the Lord Jesus Christ, and God's infinite attributes and mighty workings through Him. The faces of the lion, the ox, the eagle, and the man represent the sovereignty, the power, the intelligence, and the love which guide all the government of God and the whole plan of redemption which He is working out through the Lord Jesus Christ.

These cherub forms were robed in fire, and they moved like the lightning and the living flame. As in the other representations of the cherubic figures, they had six wings, denoting the swiftness and celerity of their movements. To still heighten the figure, there were, next, four mighty wheels, so vast in the sweep of their circumference that, to the prophet's eye, they seemed terrible in their majesty. Their tires were full of eyes, all around their vast circumference.

These wheels kept time to the movement of the wings of the cherubim, and bore the cherubic forms wherever the Spirit directed: for "the Spirit of the living creatures was in the wheels."

This wonderful vision represented the majesty, the grandeur, the power, and the celerity of the operations of God's mighty Spirit and universal providence. It was the sublime figure of the omnipresence and infinite activity of the living God and the Holy Spirit, who, as the divine Executive, is ever carrying out His purposes and plans.

All this sublime imagery was but the foundation for something still grander. For the prophet next beheld, above the cherubim, the wings, and the wheels, a mighty firmament, shining in its transparent brightness like the terrible crystal; and on this firmament a glorious throne like a flaming jasper; on this throne, as the centre of the whole vision and the sublime climax of the whole picture, was "the likeness as the appearance of a man above upon it."

This was the glorious mediatorial throne of the Lord Jesus Christ, and around about it was the rainbow of covenant promise, softening all the awful brightness,and proclaiming to His people that He was their covenant King.

What a majestic vision of the glory of God, of the Son of Man, and of the Holy Spirit, through whom He works out His mighty plans, and whose swiftness, strength, omnipresence and omniscience are so majestically represented in the consuming fire, the gleaming lightning, the awful whirlwind, the cherub forms, the manifold wings, the living wheels full of eyes around their whole circumference, the crystal firmament, the sapphire throne, the Son of man; above it all, the rainbow of covenant promise, and the Holy Spirit working out all the purposes of God's infinite love and grace!

Such was the vision with which Ezekiel's ministry began. Such was the mighty One whose messenger he was called to be. Soon after, the personal call came, God commanded him to take the roll containing his message and eat it; and, as he did so, it became as honey in his mouth and in his bowels. Then the vision returned once more, and the glory again appeared before his sight, and God sent him forth to repeat the message, and to be a watchman unto His people, and to warn them from Him; and he went forth to his lifework, armed with the consciousness of that glorious presence, in view of which the power and the persecutions of his enemies were as naught.

To us, beloved, may not come the majestic vision which Ezekiel saw; but faith can clothe the gentle Presence that whispers to our hearts with all the majesty of those ancient garments. We can know that He who speaks to us so gently and works so patiently in our lives is the same majestic Presence that filled the heavens with His glory, whose mighty wheels of providence sweep with the celerity of the lightning around the vast circumference of the universe.

The vision has passed away, but the glory still remains. Though that glory is veiled today, yet it is nonetheless real; and some day we shall behold it, too, as Ezekiel saw it of old by the river Chebar.

2. THE DEPARTING VISION. This glorious vision which Ezekiel saw was yet in the midst of Israel. It was the Presence which had led them through all their history. It was the same God who had marched before them and hovered above them in the pillar of cloud and flame, dividing the Red Sea and the Jordan, conquering the Canaanites, establishing the throne of David, exalting Solomon to all his glory, and manifesting Himself in the miracles of Elijah and Elisha, and in the wonders of divine love and power through all the centuries of Israel's history. Now,

however, the incorrigible sins of the nation had worn out His patience and almost grieved Him away.

That glorious Presence was about to leave the temple that He had loved. Judah was ready to fall, desolate and forsaken, into the hands of her cruel foe.

There is nothing more tender and sublime than the vision of this departing glory. Like a mother bird, it seems to hover, unwilling to depart, lingering with fluttering wings above the cherubim and above the threshold of the house, and last upon the brow of Olivet, before it can bear to take its long, sad flight, and leave their house unto them desolate.

In the third verse of the ninth chapter, we see it beginning to depart, "The glory of the God of Israel was gone up from the cherub, whereupon he was, to the threshold of the house." Again, in the fourth verse of the tenth chapter it would seem that He had gone back and once more poised His wings and attempted the same flight. "The glory of the Lord went up from the cherub, and stood over the threshold of the house; and the house was filled with the cloud, and the court was full of the brightness of the Lord's glory. And the sound of the cherubim's wings was heard, as the voice of the Almighty God when He speaketh."

Then again, in the eighteenth verse of the tenth chapter we see His flight begun. "Then the glory of the Lord departed from off the threshold of the house, and stood over the cherubim, and the cherubim lifted up their wings, and mounted up from the earth in my sight; when they went out, the wheels also were beside them; and every one stood at the door of the east gate of the Lord's house."

But not yet did the vision take its final flight, for, in the twenty-second verse of the eleventh chapter, we see the glory lingering yet on Mount Olivet. "Then did the cherubim lift up their wings, and the wheels beside them; and the glory of the God of Israel was over them above. And the glory of the Lord went up from the midst of the city, and stood upon the mountain which is on the east side of the city."

Still God's patience waited and pleaded, and His judgment sought to awaken and change their stubborn hearts of sin; but all in vain. At length we hear the mournful conclusion, "Son of man, say unto her, Thou art the land that is not cleansed, nor rained upon in the day of indignation. . . . Her priests have violated my law, and profaned mine holy things. Her princes in the midst thereof are like wolves ravening the prey, to shed blood, and to destroy souls, and to get dishonest gain. And her prophets have daubed them with untempered mortar, seeing vanity, and divining unto them, saying, Thus saith the Lord, when the Lord hath not spoken. The people of the land have used oppression, and exercised robbery, and have vexed the poor and needy. . . . And I sought for a man among them that should make up the hedge, and stand in the gap before me for the land, that I should not destroy it, but I found none. Therefore, have I poured out mine indignation upon them; I have consumed them with the fire of my wrath: their own way have I recompensed upon their heads."

It was like that later vision, when the same Son of man stood upon the same Olivet, looking down upon the city that had refused His warnings and miracle of love, and said: "How often would I have gathered thy children together, as a hen doth gather her brood under her wings, and ye would not. Behold, your house is left unto you desolate: . . . ye shall not see me, until the time cometh when ye shall say, Blessed is He that cometh in the name of the Lord."

So the Spirit left them, and the next chapter begins the vision of judgment and destruction. Beloved, the same story has often been reenacted. It was reenacted when Jesus left the temple. The Roman legions followed, and Jerusalem fell again. It was reenacted when the Church of the Holy Apostles became corrupt and sank to medieval darkness because the Holy Spirit was grieved away.

The same calamity is threatening the Church again. The blessed Spirit is being grieved from her sanctuary and from her altars by compromises with worldliness and sin, and He is seeking a home in humble hearts and lowly missions and little companies of those who will obey Him and fully trust Him. It may be enacted in your life; for you, too, can vex the Holy Ghost and grieve Him away. The temple of your heart may be left desolate and forsaken, and your life become exposed to the judgments of God and the calamities of sorrow.

Many a sad life and many a sad death is but the story of Israel repeated once more. Oh, let us not grieve Him! Oh, let us not permit Him to pass away! Oh, let us cherish Him, honor Him, obey Him, make our heart His home, and Him our Holy Guest!

3. THE PROMISE OF THE SPIRIT'S RETURN. "Then will I sprinkle clean water upon you, and ye shall be clean; from all your filthiness and all your idols will I cleanse you. A new heart also will I give you, and a new spirit will I put within you; and I will take away the stony heart out of your flesh, and I will give you an heart of flesh. And I will put my spirit within you, and cause you to walk in my statutes, and ye shall keep my judgments, and do them. And ye shall dwell in the land that I gave to your fathers; and ye shall be my people, and I will be your God. I also will save you from all your uncleannesses; and I will call for the corn, and will increase it, and lay no famine upon you. And I will multiply the fruit of the tree, and the increase of the field, that ye shall receive no more reproach of famine among the heathen. Then shall ye remember your own evil ways, and your doings that were not good, and shall loathe yourselves in your own sight, for your iniquities, and for your abominations. Not for your sakes do I this, saith the Lord God, be it known unto you: be ashamed and confounded for your own ways, O house of Israel. Thus saith the Lord God, In the day that I shall have cleansed you from all your iniquities, I will also cause you to dwell in the cities, and the wastes shall be builded. And the desolate land shall be tilled, whereas it lay desolate in the sight of all that passed by. And they shall say, This land that was desolate is become like the Garden of Eden; and the waste and desolate and ruined cities are become fenced, and are inhabited. Then the heathen, that are left round about you, shall know that I the Lord

build the ruined places, and plant that that was desolate: I the Lord have spoken it, and I will do it." (Ezek. 36:25-36).

Of course this promise has a primary reference to Israel as a nation, and will yet be graciously fulfilled in their restoration from the captivity of ages and in the outpouring of the Holy Spirit upon the nation; but it has also a distinct reference to the New Testament times, and shines with the light of the Gospel of full and free salvation through the Lord Jesus Christ.

There are three very distinct stages in the promised blessing. The first includes forgiveness and conversion; that is the sprinkling of the clean water upon them, the forgiveness of their sins, and the taking away of the hard and stony heart, and the giving of the heart of flesh, the work of justification and regeneration.

There is no need to say more respecting these earlier verses. The teaching is as simple and clear as the third chapter of the Gospel of John or the epistles of St. Paul. But there is a second stage of blessing which is distinct and important. It is the indwelling of the Holy Spirit and the incoming of His cleansing and sanctifying power in the heart of the believer.

"I will put my Spirit within you, and cause you to walk in my statutes, and ye shall keep my judgments, and do them." This is something different from the new spirit and the new heart. It is God Himself coming to dwell in the new spirit by His Holy Spirit, and bringing a constraining and efficient power that causes the soul to walk in holiness and enables him to keep His commandments.

Could we put on canvas the picture it would be something like this; first, we would paint the natural heart black and sinful; then, second, in the centre of this black heart we would place a little white heart, denoting the regenerated spirit, the new heart that comes at conversion, but which is still in the midst of darkness and sin, and has to maintain a painful and often unequal struggle with the surrounding and encompassing evil.

In the third place, we would paint a ray of heavenly light, or a living coal of celestial fire, which we would put in the center of this new heart; and from it the effulgent rays of life and light would reach out into all the darkness round about, filling the new heart and the old, until the darkness and sin are crowded out, and God Himself possesses the whole being, enabled it to think and feel, to trust and love, to obey and persevere, even as Christ Himself would walk.

This is the Spirit that sanctifies; this is the cleansing power that our poor weak heart needs. This Is the efficient strength which the Holy Ghost wants to give to every heart that will surrender fully to His prower and receive Him in His all-sufficiency. Beloved, have we done so? Have we received not only the new Spirit but the divine Spirit, and learned to know the mystery which is "Christ in you, the hope of glory"?

There is still another stage in the promised blessing to be found in the outworking of this indwelling Spirit and the influence of the sanctified and victorious life upon our circumstances and external life. "Ye shall dwell in the land that I gave to your fathers." We become established, and get settled in God's will and blessing. "I will call for the corn, and will increase it and lay no famine upon you." We become nourished, joyful, happy Christians, and every one beholds in us the satisfied and benignant rest and glory of a victorious life.

"I will multiply the fruit of the tree and the increase of the field." Our work is blessed, our fruit abundant, and our blessing extends even to "the heathen." This is contemporaneous with our spiritual blessing. "In the day that I shall have cleansed you from all your iniquities, I will also cause you to dwell in the cities, and the wastes shall be builded." The barren wastes of life shall blossom as the rose. The things that have been sad and fruitless will become blessed and beautiful. The years that have been lost will be restored, and all we do shall prosper.

Nay, He says, "The desolate land shall be tilled, . . . and they shall say, This land that was desolate is become like the Garden of Eden; and the waste and desolate and ruined cities are become fenced and are inhabited. Then the heathen that are left round about" it shall know that God has done it.

Of course, this is yet to be fulfilled to Israel as a people. Already we begin to see the foretokening of that Millennial spring that is opening for the long downtrodden land and people. But it has a beautiful meaning to each individual Christian life. For God is "able to do for us exceeding abundantly above all that we ask or think, according to the power that worketh in us."

The soul that receives the Holy Spirit in all His fullness will find the providence of God keeping pace with His inward blessing, and the grace that we have experienced in our heart will reflect itself in all our outward life. The King that reigns supreme upon the throne of the heart will sway His scepter around the whole circle of our life, and bring into subjection everything that hurts or hinders us.

He will heal our bodies; He will answer our prayers; He will bless our homes; He will prosper our business; He will remove our difficulties; He will open our way; He will "cause the desert to rejoice and blossom as the rose," and "instead of the thorn shall come up the fir tree, and instead of the brier, shall come up the myrtle tree: and it shall be to the Lord for a name, for an everlasting sign that shall not be cut off."

The blessings of God's providence are inseparably connected with the indwelling of His Spirit and the experience of His sanctifying grace. It is only to those "who love God and are the called according to His purpose" that "all things work together for good."

They know that they work together for good. It is not a struggle to believe it. It is not a desperate effort to count it. When we walk with Him in holy trust and obedience, the inmost consciousness of our spiritual being bears witness to the promise, and we know without doubt or fear that all things are ours, for we are Christ's and Christ is God's.

## Chapter 21

## The Spirit of the Resurrection; Ezekiel 37:8

"For the law of the Spirit of life in Christ Jesus hath made me free from the law of sin and death." Rom. 8: 2. "But if the Spirit of him that raised up Jesus from the dead dwell in you, he that hath raised up Christ from the dead shall also quicken your mortal bodies by his Spirit that dwelleth in you." Rom. 8 : 11.

The thirty-seventh chapter of Ezekiel is one of the most remarkable exhibitions of the work of the Holy Spirit in the Old Testament, because it introduces with great clearness and definiteness the doctrine of the resurrection.

This truth, beyond all others, is characteristic of the system of redemption. It might be called the patent sign of the Gospel. Far more than the Cross, the symbol of baptism expresses the fundamental idea of the Christian religion; for, while the Cross speaks only of death, baptism tells also of resurrection and life.

This truth, foreshadowed in many Old Testament passages, and doubtless underlying the teaching of all the prophets, is brought out here with great distinctness, and makes the passage one of the marked ones of Old Testament revelation.

1. THE VALLEY OF DRY BONES.

First, we have the vision in the valley of dry bones. This is not a vision of the resurrection proper, but rather of a special resurrection. The prophet is taken in the spirit into the valley of dry bones. It is the scene of some ancient battle, where he beholds around him the skeletons of the fallen army, and, lo! they are very many, and, lo! they are very dry.

A generation has passed since they fell. The flesh has long ago withered from the skeletons, and the bones lie bleached and withered under the open sun. Suddenly the question comes to him, "Can these bones live?" And his wise answer is "Lord Thou knowest." Then there comes to him; first, the command to prophesy unto the bones, proclaiming to them the Word of the Lord, and announcing to them that they shall live. And, lo! there comes a noise and a shaking; and bone cleaves to his bone, and they assume the forms of men; but still there is no breath in them.

Then a second time the Word of the Lord comes to him, commanding him to prophesy unto the breath of life to come from the four winds and breathe upon these slain that they may live; and, lo! as he prophesies and commands, the spirit of life to come into these lifeless forms, there is a quivering moment, as the life passes into every frame, and they spring to their feet and stand before him a mass of living men, an exceeding great army.

2. THE APPLICATION OF THIS TO ISRAEL AS A NATION.

God does not leave the prophet in doubt as to the meaning of the vision. Its first and immediate application is to his people. They were mourning over their national ruin and saying, "Our bones are dried, and our hope is lost; we are cut off for our parts." But he tells them that the voice of God is yet to come to them; that the power of His Spirit is yet to breathe upon them; that even shattered and hopeless Israel shall revive; and that the nation shall spring to life once more and return to their own land to resume their place in God's great plan, while their divisions and disunions shall cease forever, and God shall dwell among them and restore His ancient sanctuary and renew His covenant with them forevermore.

There could scarcely be a more appropriate figure of Israel's depressed condition than the vision of the dry bones. For eighteen centuries their hope has been dead in a far more terrible sense than was true even under the Babylonian captivity. It is not a century ago since the children of Israel were disfranchised outcasts of every nation. Even in Great Britain itself the voice of the pulpit and of the whole Christian press was raised against the first proposal to give the right of franchise to Hebrew citizens and to allow the children of Abraham a place and a name among the Gentiles.

For centuries they have been truly "outcasts of earth and reprobates of heaven," and the idea of their restoration to their own land, and to their ancient blessing, might well be deemed the most hopeless prospect that language could express. But, lo! already the vision of the prophet begins to be fulfilled. The Word of God respecting Israel has been recovered and reissued. God's people have begun to understand His purpose concerning Israel and have begun to preach the Gospel, even to the unbelieving sons of Abraham, and to proclaim to them, like the ancient prophet, the word of hope and promise, and to call them from their graves to their true Messiah and their only hope. And, lo! already there is a noise and a shaking; and bone is beginning to come to his bone, and a national revival of Judaism is one of the most marked signs of the day.

A spirit of reunion and reorganization is everywhere abroad among them. National societies are being formed. The rich and the poor are coming together. Great leaders of the nation are lending their financial strength to the cause of the helpless and the outcast. While as yet it is not a spiritual movement, but merely a reorganization of national life and hope, it is just what the prophet predicted would first come to pass; and he must be blind indeed, who does not see the ancient vision being fulfilled today among the children of Israel in every nation under heaven.

But there is a deeper spiritual movement. The Holy Ghost is also beginning His saving work. The deeper heart of the nation is beginning to be touched; and some of her sons are recognizing their long rejected Messiah, and beginning to accept Him as their Savior and their King.

These are but precursors of that latter rain which is to fall, when the Spirit of grace and of supplication shall be poured out upon the house of David and the inhabitants of Jerusalem, and they shall look upon Him whom they pierced and shall mourn for Him as one that mourneth for an only son. And then shall a fountain be opened for the house of David and the inhabitants of Jerusalem, for sin and uncleanness, and all the blessed promises for Israel shall receive their spiritual fulfillment.

Then shall Israel and Judah be united. Then shall the severances of ages be forever healed. Then shall they be cleansed from their defilements and uncleanness and idolatries, to sin no more. Then shall they take the place of God's chosen people; and, as the Queen of nations and the special witnesses of Jesus, the sons of Abraham shall fulfill their high calling, and their restoration shall be complete.

Then shall God's sanctuary be among them once more. Neither shall He hide His face from them any more, but they shall dwell forever in His covenant love, the Light of the world, and the Leader of the nations.

3. THE APPLICATION OF THE VISION TO THE SPIRITUAL LIFE OF THE SOUL AND THE CHURCH.

There is something worse than the death of a nation, something worse than the death of the body. It is the spiritual death of those who lie sunk in trespasses and sins. The condition of human souls is like the bones in the valley of vision, very many and very dry. There is no human probability of restoration or life. But there is hope in God and in resurrection life.

There is the same twofold agency which we see in the nation. First is the Word of God. This is the divine instrument in the conversion of souls and the quickening of the spiritually dead. "Being born again not of corruptible seed, but of incorruptible, by the Word of God, which liveth and abideth forever."

Although souls are lost and dead, God commands us to proclaim to them the Word of God, and to tell them that He has sent them life, and is waiting to quicken them and bring them out of their graves.

<u>This very word </u>which they are unable to understand or feel or believe is the power through which they are to be awakened

and brought to life. There is a strange potency in the Gospel to awaken the human conscience and to quicken the human spirit by the power of the Holy Ghost.

But the Word of God alone can bring about only an outward reformation like the baptism of John, which changed the lives of men and the forms and habits of their conversation; but it cannot put breath in them. And so the first effect is the abandonment of sin, the reformation of life, the assuming of the forms of righteousness, but there is no breath in them. The great agent in the real and vital transfiguration is the Spirit of the Living God, "the breath of life from the four winds of heaven."

There is something very significant about the way in which the prophet was commanded to address the Spirit. It was not the language of entreaty, but of command. Just as he was commanded to prophesy to the dry bones and to bid them live, so he is commanded to prophesy unto the Holy Ghost and to bid the Spirit come and quicken those lifeless stones.

Is there not for us the significant suggestion and a solemn lesson that we are to speak the Gospel to men in the authority of God, and with the expectation of its power, and that we are to claim the Holy Ghost to accompany the words and to give efficacy to our testimony and work with the same authority? That we are not only to ask Him and invoke Him, but to command Him and to use Him, and fully to expect His almighty efficiency to accomplish the work for which He sent us?

Just as the laws of electricity, when properly understood, place at our command the forces of electricity, so, when we yield to the laws of the Spirit's operation, we may command the Spirit's operation and fully count upon His almighty working and infinite power. Is not this the real meaning of faith and the real province of Prayer in the ministry of the Gospel? Is not this the secret of many of our failures? Do we command Him as we might? Do we use these infinite forces which God has placed at our service for the accomplishment of the work for which He has sent us?

The effect of the Holy Spirit's work is not a mere reformation, but a transformation. The forms of life are quickened into real life, and the men spring to their feet, and stand before him, "an exceeding great army." They do not now need to be carried. They are themselves self-supporting; nay, they become an army of mighty power, and go forth in aggressive conflict to fight against the enemies of God and to impart to others the blessing which they themselves have received.

This mighty Holy Spirit is recognized as present in the world. The four winds indicate the four quarters of the earth, and they suggest the omnipresence and the ever-presence of that blessed Spirit who is with the Church, through the Christian dispensation, as the enduement of power for every commission on which the Master has sent her. Shall we claim our high and divine resources? Shall we utilize the infinite and all-sufficient supplies which our Master has committed to us? And shall we, with a simpler, bolder confidence, give forth the authoritative Word, and call down the Almighty Spirit to quicken the dry bones of a lifeless Church and to awaken the spiritually dead, that Christ may give them life?

4. THE FUTURE RESURRECTION.

While this passage is not a literal vision of the resurrection from the dead, at the same time it assumes it and takes it for granted. That glorious doctrine is more fully unfolded and differentiated in the teachings of the New Testament. We see it first in its great pledge and first fruit, the resurrection of the Lord Jesus Christ. We see it next in the resurrection of His people at His coming, and we see the vision of it in its final and glorious age at the consummation of all faith.

In every instance it will be, in some measure, at least, the work of the Holy Spirit. He who is working out the spiritual resurrection now, will accomplish it at the glorious appearing of our Lord, and will change the body of our humiliation, that it may be fashioned like unto the body of His glory, according to the working whereby He is able to subdue all things unto Himself.

We shall not dwell on this glorious doctrine now. It will be much more fully unfolded in later Scriptures. It is our blessed hope, and already we have its divine pattern and pledge in the first begotten from the dead, the glorious Prince of Life, the Lord Jesus Christ.

5. THE APPLICATION OF THE VISION TO THE WHOLE REALM OF FAITH AND SPIRITUAL POWER.

There is a greater truth presented than even the literal resurrection. The thought lying back of the prophet's vision, and the profound truth which it throws forward upon the prospective of faith is that the resurrection is t he pattern and the guarantee of all that God is able and willing to do in response to the faith of His people.

Expressed in a single sentence, the thought is that we have a resurrection God, and we ought to have a resurrection faith. Is not this the sublime thought which the Apostle Paul has presented in the magnificent climax of the first chapter of the Epistle to the Ephesians, where he prays that the "eyes of your understanding being enlightened; that ye may know what is the hope of his calling and what the riches of the glory of His inheritance in the saints, and what is the exceeding greatness of his power to usward who believe!"

Now comes the measure and standard of that power, "According to the working of his mighty power, which he wrought in Christ, when he raised him from the dead, and set him at his own right hand in the heavenly places, far above all principality, and power, and might, and dominion, and every name that is named, not only in this world, but also in that which is to come." Henceforth, the standard of faith and the measure of God's working for His people is the resurrection of the Lord Jesus Christ.

When any trying situation presents itself, when any hard question is asked, and unbelief seems to say, "Can these bones live?" we have the simple answer, "It is Christ that died, yea rather, that is risen again, who is even at the right hand of God."

There are things that are darker than the grave and sadder than death. There are spiritual situations; there are family troubles; there are business difficulties; there are catastrophes and calamities; there are needs and trials compared with which the tears of bereavement are sweet, and the darkness of the sepulchre is bright indeed. But, thank God, we can meet these difficulties, these trials, these situations, these seeming impossibilities, and say, "Our trust is not in ourselves, but in God, who raiseth the dead. Who delivered us from so great a death, who doth deliver, in whom we trust that He will yet deliver us." This is our hope for the hour of fierce temptation, for the time of sorrow and trial, for the conflict with sickness and pain, for the desperate campaign with the powers of the darkness as we go forth to save men and evangelize the world and bring the coming of our Lord.

All these are situations too hard for us; but, thank God, we can meet them every one with the God of the resurrection, with the hope of the resurrection, with the faith of the resurrection, with the life of the resurrection, with the pledge of the resurrection, and say, "Yes, it is all true. With men it is impossible — BUT GOD — who raiseth the dead."

> Break from your fears, ye saints, and tell
> How high your great Deliverer reigns;
> Sing how He spoiled the hosts of hell,
> And led the monster Death in chains.
> Say, "Live forever, Wondrous King,
> Born to redeem and strong to save;"
> Then ask the Monster, "Where's thy sting,
> And where's thy victory, boasting grave?"

## Chapter 22

## The River of Blessing

"Afterward he brought me again unto the door of the house; and, behold, waters issued out from under the threshold of the house eastward: for the forefront of the house stood toward the east, and the waters came down from under, from the right side of the house, at the south side of the altar. Then brought he me out of the way of the gate northward, and led me about the way without unto the outer gate by the way that looketh eastward; and, behold, there ran out the waters on the right side. And when the man that had the line in his hand went forth eastward, he measured a thousand cubits, and He brought me through the waters; the waters were to the ankles. Again he measured a thousand, and brought me through the waters; the waters were to the knees. Again he measured a thousand, and brought me through; the waters were to the loins.

"Afterward he measured a thousand; and it was a river that I could not pass over: for the waters were risen, waters to swim in, a river that could not be passed over. And he said unto me, Son of man, hast thou seen this? Then he brought me, and caused me to return to the brink of the river. Now when I had returned, behold, at the bank of the river were very many trees on the one side and on the other. Then said he unto me, These waters issue out toward the east country, and go down into the desert, and go into the sea: which being brought forth into the sea, the waters shall be healed. And it shall come to pass, that every thing that liveth, which moveth, whithersoever the rivers shall come, shall live: and there shall be a very great multitude of fish, because these waters shall come thither: for they shall be healed; and every thing shall live whither the river cometh. And it shall come to pass, that the fishers shall stand upon it from En-gedi even unto En-eglaim: they shall be a place to spread forth nets; their fish shall be according to their kinds as the fish of the great sea, exceeding many. But the miry places thereof and the marshes thereof shall not be healed; they shall be given to salt. And by the river upon the bank thereof, on this side and on that side, shall grow all trees for meat, whose leaf shall not fade, neither shall the fruit thereof be consumed: it shall bring forth new fruit according to his months, because their waters they issued out of the sanctuary; and the fruit thereof shall be for meat, and the leaf thereof for medicine." Ezekiel 47: 1-12.

This magnificent prophetic vision is doubtless a picture of the literal restoration of Israel's temple and Israel's race in the future days of millennial promise. Conceding this, it is quite legitimate for us to apply it also to the present working of the Holy Spirit in the hearts of His people, and in the midst of His Church, which is the temple of the living God.

Our Lord Jesus has Himself identified the living water in His beautiful words in the seventh chapter of the Gospel of John. There, amid the sacred solemnities of that ancient temple and the Feast of Tabernacles, He applied to Himself the beautiful figure of the water that was being poured out before their eyes, and cried and said, "If any man thirst, let him come unto me, and drink. He that believeth on me, as the Scripture hath said, out of His inmost being shall flow rivers of living water. (But this spake he of the Spirit, which they that believe on Him should receive: for the Holy Ghost was not yet given, because Jesus was not yet glorified)."

This is an exact paraphrase of the meaning of the vision of Ezekiel. It represents the Holy Spirit as a river of water flowing from the inmost being of a consecrated heart, and becoming rivers of blessing to others.

There is something about the entire imagery of this picture so oriental, so sublime, so rich, that, like a beautiful flower, we cannot analyze it too much without destroying some of its symmetry and sweetness. It speaks of something as glorious as the rich symbolism of the picture.

It speaks of the crystal stream and the deepening, broadening rivers flowing through desert lands, and transforming them into gardens of luxuriant beauty and verdure. It speaks of perennial fruits and leaves of healing and even the Dead Sea itself reclaimed by its healing waters, until it becomes a place of fishermen who stand upon its shores from end to end gathering their shoals of fishes. Finally, the Temple itself becomes the abode of God, and is named "Jehovah Shammah," the Lord is there.

There is something about such figures that cannot be analyzed. There is a freedom, a glow, a vague but real splendor, a something which is unutterable and full of glory, which truly describes a certain elevated phrase of our spiritual experience. There are things in our Christian life which, if you translate into coarse speech, become like the petals of a dissected flower, withered and dead; but let them alone, and they are full of life and joy. You cannot translate them, you cannot always understand them. It is the voice of the Spirit within you crying with unutterable groanings or unutterable joy. It is as full as the magnificent river, as pure as the crystal water, as fresh as the morning dew, as healing as the leaves of the tree of life, and as full of power and blessing as that river that made everything live where it came.

> Our hymnology is not exaggerated when we sing:
> "I am dwelling on the mountain,
> Where the golden sunlight gleams,
> O'er a land whose fadeless beauty
> Far exceeds my fondest dreams.
> Where the air is pure, ethereal,
> Laden with breath of flowers.

They are blooming on the mountain,
'Neath the amaranthine bowers."

But let us, notwithstanding, interpret as much as we may the rich and suggestive imagery of the picture. The first thing that strikes a thoughtful reader is the direction of this river. We know it represents the Holy Spirit, the blessed Person whose ministry is to cleanse, satisfy, comfort, help, and heal the disciples of Christ. But why is it flowing out and not in? Are we not always trying to get this river to run into us? Are we not always seeking a blessing and a baptism? But here the sanctuary seems to have only one business, to give out the water; and this river only one thing to do, to go forth on its ministry of unselfish mercy. That is the true life of the Holy Ghost. The true purpose of the Spirit in coming to us is to make us workers together with God, whose one business is ever loving, ever blessing, ever giving.

It was not after this river became deep and full that it began to flow out; but from the first little trickling drop it was at the same business. The Temple might have said, when the first two or three droplets began to ooze from beneath the threshold, "I can never spare you; you must remain in my reservoir." But no; it simply sent them forth, and away they went on their ministry of love; and so on to the end it was ever flowing, and, when it reached the Dead Sea, its living power was so great that the sea became transformed into life and freshness.

The real secret of the Dead Sea was that it had no outlet; it was just a great reservoir through the ages. But as it begins to overflow, it lives. Beloved, this is the secret of spiritual weakness and disappointment. You want a blessing for yourself. Begin to live for God and others, and He will give it back tenfold to you again.

The second thing we learn about this river is that it flows from a sanctuary. What is a sanctuary? It is a sacred, separated, holy, and divine place. First, it must be separated from sinful and common uses. Secondly, it must be dedicated to God and belong exclusively to Him. Thirdly, it must be occupied by God and be filled with Him as its Possessor, its Guest, and the Object of its worship.

In this sense the truly consecrated believer is God's sanctuary when he separates himself from all evil unto God, dedicates himself to be the property of the Most Holy, and receives the Holy Ghost to dwell in him, and to represent the Trinity as the occupant and owner of his heart and life. This is the sanctuary. This is holiness. This is the true Christian life, and from such a soul as this the river will always flow.

But you cannot be a blessing to others beyond your personal experience. You cannot give what you have not got. You cannot bring pure water out of an unclean fountain. Why are we not greater blessings? Because our hearts are not sanctuaries. We try to do a little for God and then find the whole hindered by a thousand forbidden uses; and God will have no partnership with evil, and will accept no service which is mixed or compromised.

Beloved, let us consecrate ourselves. Let Him sanctify us, fill us, and then flow from us in all the fullness of the Holy Ghost.

The third thing about this river is that it flowed from under the threshold of the sanctuary. It did not come from the roof, or from some hill behind it, or from the fountain in the holy court; but it came from the lowest place, from under the stairs, where people trod as they passed by. And so the Holy Ghost comes from the lowly heart, consecrates the humble spirit, uses the man who is most dead and who has become so lost to himself and all his graces that God can have all the glory, and can fill him without measure.

The fourth thing about the river is its direction. It is flowing toward the east. It is the river of the morning, not the river of the night. It does not represent the old life, whose sun is going down; but it represents the new life which has risen with the resurrection of Christ, and is looking out into the everlasting morning. It is a new and resurrection life, and it flows ever toward the rising sun.

This river begins in a few little trickling drops. It is scarcely a rivulet for the first half mile. It is so small that it just oozes from under the threshold, a few drops of moisture, but it becomes a mighty stream before it reaches the sea. So the Holy Ghost loves to begin in "the day of small things." He loves to speak to us in "the still, small voice," to show us that we are not very far off. If He shouted in our ear, it would be an intimation that He was at a great distance or that we were very stupid. There is no sweeter expression of confidence than a whispered secret. The blessed Holy Ghost comes to us with the faintest touches of His breath; and if we do not recognize Him in these small beginnings, we shall not see their growth and development, and we shall wonder all our days why we did not get the blessing. We are looking for wind and rain, for a cyclone of power, for electric storms, when the air is full of divine electric fire. We have only to make the connection, to take it as we need it, and to turn it on to all the machinery of our life.

Beloved, if you will recognize the first touches of God, the faintest whispers of His answering voice, the little finger of His touch, behind which stands all His omnipotence, He will prove to you that it is not by might nor by power, but by the Spirit of the Lord of Hosts.

The first stage of the river's course was about half a mile from the source. There the prophet was halted by his attendant and caused to pass over the little brook, and, lo! it had increased until it was "water to the ankles." The Hebrew word is much more expressive. It means literally water to the soles of the feet.

There was very little water there, perhaps not quarter of an inch deep, and if the prophet had despised it, he would have been kept out of all the glory of the vision. But he put his feet in the little water that he found. There was enough for the soles of his feet, and that was enough for him.

Is not this just what is said to us, "Every place the soles of your feet shall tread upon, that have I given you"?

What shall we call this putting down of our feet in the waters? Is it, perhaps, the act of stepping out on God's Spirit, of venturing on Him, of standing on His promises, of counting upon Him, of putting our weight upon Him, of trusting Him for everything, and publicly recognizing and confessing Him as our life and strength? Or does it mean obedience? Do the feet represent the steppings of duty? Is this not also one of the earliest stages of the Spirit's work? He comes to teach us faith and obedience, and He always requires us to do something very early in our spiritual career, something that often costs sacrifice, something that proves the sincerity of our motive, something that means everything to us; but as we obey Him and go on, we find Him coming to us in fuller measure, and giving us deeper revelations and leading us on to a larger fullness.

Beloved, shall we take both steps, and put our feet in the flood, and walk in the Spirit, and accept boldly and lovingly all the good and acceptable and perfect will of God?

"Waters to the knees." This is the ministry of prayer in the Spirit that follows a life of obedience and faithfulness to God. He will take us into the secret place of the Most High, and will permit us to bear the burdens of others and to share with Him the priesthood which He ever fulfills before the throne. This is more than our words and works. This is a place of real power, but it must be baptized in the Spirit or it will be fruitless and vain.

Next, we have "the waters to the loins."This is the girding of power, the baptism of the Spirit for service. The girding of the loins is the symbol of service and strength. God gives power to His servants to speak in His name with effectiveness and to accomplish the glorious results for which He has commissioned them.Without this power we have no business to attempt any service for God. Jesus did not begin His ministry until he received the baptism of the Holy Ghost, and it is presumption for us to dare to do so.

Next, we have the waters overhead, "a river to swim in." The waters had grown so deep now that the prophet is himself powerless even to cross them. His own movements are impossible, and all he can do is to lie upon the bosom of the current and let it carry him.

This speaks of a time where we come to the end of our own effort and fall into the fullness of God. Henceforth our work is God working in us, and we are just like the swimmer on the bosom of the river carried by the tide, but far stronger than if he were fording it, for he has all the strength of the river on his side. Of course, there had to be a surrender of his own work.

There must, of course, be a surrender of our own life before we can fall into the strength of God. Then shall we inherit all the fullness of the divine omnipotence; so far as we are in union with God's help, we shall have God's power. This power is spontaneous. Without a struggle, it springs from a source beyond ourselves, and it flows like the ever changing river.

Next, we notice the fruits upon the bank of this glorious river. There are fruits for the food of the saints, perennial fruits, fruits of infinite variety; all the trees of paradise are restored, renewing their harvest every month; each joy is a new joy, fresh as the fruits and flowers of paradise. Even the very leaves are for healing. They are not the most important part of the tree, but they have their place; and so the Lord's healing through the Holy Ghost is one of the ministries of the Spirit, but not His highest ministry, corresponding to the leaf of the tree while the fruit corresponds to the deeper spiritual life.

Then there are other fruits, especially the fruit of precious souls. The fishermen are standing on the shores of the Dead Sea gathering in their precious souls.

What a solemn picture the Dead Sea was, hard by Jerusalem's gate, continually reminding the world of the hell that lies near the gate of heaven! Yonder was Zion and the Temple, but yonder also was the sea of death and the gate of hell.

Ah, still it is ever so! While we are rejoicing in the blessed fullness of the Spirit, hard by our gates are the masses of wretchedness and sin, the depths of danger and sorrow that crowd our mighty and sinful city and our poor lost world. But as we are filled with the power of the Spirit, we, too, shall go forth as fishers of men to gather precious souls for Christ in the power of the

Spirit, and to turn the deserts of life into places of blessing, so that "everything wherever the river comes shall live."

There is one more picture. It is in the last chapter of the book. "The name of the city from that day shall be called Jehovah Shammah, the Lord is there."

This blessed river brings the Lord. This blessed Holy Spirit brings the abiding presence of God, and He is better than all His gifts, graces, and operations. He is seeking a home in some of our hearts. The Holy Spirit is knocking at the door to find entrance for the king of Glory. If we will let Him in, He will make it His palace and His home and dwell with us forever. To be the dwelling place of God, is the highest and sublimest glory of the Spirit's indwelling in the saint.

Like the ancient architect, who, when asked to build a temple for the sun, after others had constructed their beautiful models of granite and polished marble and resplendent gold, brought a design made of simple transparent glass, and said, "This is the true temple for the sun, for the sun himself can dwell within it and pass out and in without restraint."

God is wanting temples for Himself as transparent as the colorless glass, reflecting not their own glory but His; receiving Him without the necessity of opening a single door, but with every channel and capacity of ours so free, so open, and so in touch, that we live and move and have our being in Him, and He can find in us that congenial abode for which He searches the mighty universe and the highest heaven in vain; for are not we also "the fullness of Him who filleth all in all"?

## Chapter 23

## The Holy Spirit in the Days of the Restoration

"Not by might, nor by power, but by my Spirit, saith the Lord of hosts." Zechariah 4: 6.

The restoration was a period of Jewish history as distinctly marked as the Patriarchal or the Mosaic age, the times of the Judges, or the Kingdoms of Judah and Israel. It followed the captivity, and was intended to prepare the way for a yet greater event, the coming of the Lord Jesus Christ.

It was one of the most marked periods of divine working in the Old Testament, and it is full of the manifestations of the Holy Spirit. This little message which Zechariah gave to his people as the motto of that Restoration, more fitly than any other word expresses its entire history. It was a movement, not of human power, but of the Holy Ghost.

It was unaccompanied by the miraculous signs which attended almost every other important period of Old Testament history; but its providential miracles and its manifestations of the power of the Holy Spirit were even more signal and wonderful than the miracles of the wilderness and the land of promise.

Let us trace the workings of the Holy Spirit through this wonderful period.

1. The first stage might be described as the ministry of prayer. We have an account of it in the ninth chapter of the Book of Daniel. "In the first year of Darius, the son of Ahasuerus, of the seed of the Medes, which was made king over the realm of the Chaldeans; in the first year of his reign, I, Daniel, understood by the books the number of the years, whereof the word of the Lord

came to Jeremiah the prophet, that he would accomplish seventy years in the desolations of Jerusalem. And I set my face upon the Lord God, to seek by prayer and supplications, with fasting, and sackcloth, and ashes."

When God is about to work out any great purpose, He usually lays it as a burden of prayer upon the heart of some of His saints whom He can fully trust. So He called Daniel, His tried servant in Babylon, to this high ministry of prayer.

We cannot fail to notice the connection of Daniel's prayer with Jeremiah's prophecy. Seventy years before, the prophet of God had announced, not only the fact, but the duration of Judah's captivity; and Daniel had been carefully studying the sacred scroll and marked the period of his people's affliction. Now that the time seemed to have run its course, he was encouraged to go to God in intercessions and plead for the fulfillment of His promise and the accomplishment of the inspired prophecy.

Some would have said that, because God was going to do it, they should not be troubled about it. Why not wait and let Him work out His own counsel? But to true faith the promise of God is a direct incentive to prayer.

True faith always finds its warrant in the Word of God, and because it has pleased Him to commit Himself to us in the Word of Promise, we feel encouraged to present our petition, and to believe for its answer.

Not lightly did Daniel pray, but for three full weeks he humbled himself in fasting and prayer before his God. He was not praying for himself. He was not borne down by the weight of his own trial and care. His prayer was wholly disinterested and altogether for his country and his people and the glory of his God.

This is true prayer, and this is divine partnership with God Himself. This is the highest and holiest ministry given to mortal, and brings us into direct fellowship with our ascended and interceding Lord.

Not in vain did Daniel thus cry to heaven. In due time a messenger came to him from the sky, and directly announced to him;

first, that he was greatly beloved; and, next, that his prayer was heard and answered, and that from the very first day that he had set himself to ask it of God, God had recorded the answer in the decrees of the throne, and had set in motion all the forces of His power to accomplish it.

Indeed, this mighty angel had been three weeks on his way, hindered by the powers of darkness, and the principalities that rule over the governments of this world.

What a vision this gives us of the living forces of the world unseen, and of the power of prayer to press through all those labyrinths of evil to reach the heart and hand of God and the scepter of the universe!

Dear saint of God, you may be humble and unknown, you may have little talent and little wealth; but alone in your closet, you can touch the confines of the world, and set in motion forces which will influence the destiny of nations.

Yonder in Babylon we see a lowly suppliant on his face before God, in sackcloth and ashes and deep earnestness of heart. It looks to us like a spectacle of impotence. But wait; look a little further. Stretch your vision to the far circumference of yonder circle, and you shall see a mighty conqueror pausing in his career of triumph, issuing a decree from his throne, recognizing the power of Jehovah, and bringing all the forces of his government to carry out the prayer of that saint of God.

You shall see a long train of captives hastening from their exile to their distant home, and centuries on centuries of national prosperity reaching away down to Messianic times, and far beyond to millennial ages, all is the result of the prayer of Daniel, the beloved of the Lord.

The angel that came to him told him of the years that should intervene until the close of the Old Testament dispensation. He told him of the coming of the great Messiah. He told Him of His sacrifice and its blessed efficacy. He told him of the trials and troubles that should come to his people afterwards, and he reached out to the most distant ages, down even to the coming of the Lord Jesus Christ in His glory. O friends, when you talk to God and rise out of your own troubles, and stand with Him in the high and holy ministry of prayer, you get a much larger answer than you expect. God not only gives you what you ask, but He gives you an eternity beyond. "Lord, teach us to pray."

2. The next stage of the working of the Holy Spirit is seen in the providential movements which introduce the Restoration.

The first and most remarkable of these was the career of Cyrus. More than a century before, the prophet Isaiah had described this extraordinary man. He had even called him by his name and pointed him out as the special instrument of the divine purpose in the restoration of Israel. "Thus saith the Lord to his anointed, to Cyrus, whose right hand I have holden, to subdue nations before him; and I will loose the loins of kings, to open before him two-leaved gates; and the gates shall not be shut: I will go before thee, and make the crooked places straight; I will break in pieces the gates of brass, and cut in sunder the bars of iron: and I will give thee treasures of darkness, and hidden riches of secret places, that thou mayest know that I, the Lord, which call thee by thy name, am the God of Israel. For Jacob my servant's sake, and Israel, mine elect, I have even called thee by thy name; I have surnamed thee, though thou hast not known me."

What a wonderful picture! What marvelous prophecy, and how literally it was fulfilled in the romantic story of Cyrus, his rapid career of conquest, his capture of Babylon, the establishment of his universal empire, and then his remarkable part in the restoration of Israel and the rebuilding of the temple!

The next chapter in this extraordinary series of events is the proclamation of Cyrus in the first verses of the book of Ezra. "Now in the first year of Cyrus, king of Persia, that the word of the Lord by the mouth of Jeremiah might be fulfilled, the Lord stirred up the spirit of Cyrus king of Persia, that he made a proclamation throughout all his kingdom, and put it also in writing, saying, Thus saith Cyrus king of Persia, the Lord God of heaven hath given me all the kingdoms of the earth; and he hath charged me to build him an house in Jerusalem, which is in Judah. Who is there among you of all his people? His God be with him, and let him go up to Jerusalem, which is in Judah, and build the house of the Lord God of Israel (He is the God) which is in Jerusalem. And whosoever remaineth in any place where he sojourneth, let the men of his place help him with silver, and with gold, and with goods, and with beasts, besides the free will offering for the house of God that is in Jerusalem. Then rose up the chief of the fathers of Judah and Benjamin, and the priests, and the Levites, with all them whose spirit God had raised, to go up to build the house of the Lord which is in Jerusalem. Also Cyrus the king, brought forth the vessels of the house of the Lord, which Nebuchadnezzar had brought forth out of Jerusalem, and had put them in the house of his gods; even those did Cyrus bring forth by the hand of Mithredath the treasurer."

Here we see the conqueror of the world, in the very flush of his renown, turned aside by a divine impulse, and constrained to carry out the very purpose and will of God.

Oh, how wonderful the power of the Holy Ghost! He is able to deal with the hearts and minds of men, the highest as well as the lowest, and to overrule even their selfish ambitions and plans for the carrying out of His own purposes and the building up of His own kingdom.

He who has sent us His ambassadors to the nations has declared, "All power is given unto me, in heaven and in earth." "The king's heart is in the hand of the Lord, as the rivers of water; He turneth it withersoever he will."

Could we but believe more definitely in the power and providence of God, how much larger would our plans of service be, and how much less would we fear the oppositions of men!

We are living in the days when we may especially claim the overruling providence of God in the affairs of men, and when we may call upon the Holy Ghost to cooperate with the Church of Christ in sending the Gospel to the world, and hastening the coming of the Lord Jesus Christ.

In the history of missions there have been some very wonderful instances of God's interposing power through the affairs of nations.

The story of Japan, the story of Siam, the story of Madagascar, the Indian Mutiny, and the history of China for half a century are full of romances of providence as significant as the story of Cyrus. God has many such things in store for the hearts that can trust Him.

Oh, let us understand the immensity of our God and the far-reaching scope of His providence and His power, and enter into partnership with Him in His great design to give the Kingdom to His Son. The Ancient of Days has come, and is judging among the nations, to give the Son of Man His Kingdom, dominion, and glory. Let us recognize His Presence, and let us claim, as in the days old, the operation of His mighty power.

How sublime and solemn the spectacle upon which the eyes of the Church are gazing today! The mighty Colossus of China, so long opposed to foreign influence and the Gospel of Christ, is being broken to pieces like a potter's vessel, and plowed up as with the plowshare of God to prepare the way of the Lord. Doubtless it is in answer to some prayer of faith. Doubtless it is preparatory to some glorious aggressive movement of faith and evangelistic zeal. God help us to understand our times and to understand our God, and to be worthy of our high calling as workers together with Him!

Another extraordinary providential working of the Holy Ghost during these days is found in the story of Esther. It was another miracle of Providence, although on a different plane, and in a simpler sphere. This time a nation was to be delivered from extermination. The very race of Israel was to be preserved so as to form a line through which Christ could come. The devil had determined to blot out their existence, but God raised up a little maiden to be His instrument for their deliverance.

He had given Esther a beautiful face and a fair and attractive form; and these were trusts which He meant her to use for Him. He gave her favor in the eyes of the king, and He introduced her to his palace and his throne. Dear young friend, your face, your form, your place in society, these are mighty trusts to use for God. Take heed how you use them. There came a time when Esther must stand forth and fulfill her high commission, and even risk her life for the sake of her country. She hesitated; and had she faltered it would have involved, perhaps, not only the ruin of her people, but the destruction of herself and her father's house. God gave her grace to be true, and through her true, brave stand, her people were delivered.

The enemies of God were caught in the snare which they had prepared. So God today is working through individuals as well as nations. May He enable us, like Esther of old, to understand His solemn message, "Who knoweth whether thou art come to the kingdom for such a time as this?"

Quite as remarkable is the story of Zerubbabel, Ezra, Nehemiah, and the returning captives. It was no small undertaking to conduct a band of 50,000 unarmed men and women and children across that vast desert, but Ezra so fully trusted God that he would not even ask an escort. How touching his language! "Then I proclaimed a fast there, at the river of Ahava, that we might afflict ourselves before our God, to seek of him a right way for us, and for our little ones, and for all of our substance. For I was ashamed to require of the king a band of soldiers and horsemen to help us against the enemy in the way: because we had spoken unto the king, saying, the hand of our God is upon all of them for good that seek him: but his power and his wrath is against all that forsake him. So we fasted, and besought our God for this; and he was entreated of us." (Ezra 8:21). "Then we departed from the river of Ahava, on the twelfth day of the first month, to go unto Jerusalem ; and the hand of our God was upon us, and he delivered us from the hand of the enemy, and of such as lay in wait by the way. And we came to Jerusalem."

This was the work of the Holy Spirit, and thus He loves to guard and guide those who trust in Him. Their task was a most difficult one. First, they attempted to build the temple without restoring the walls. Their primary object was to set up the worship of their God, and they trusted Him to be a wall of fire round about and the glory in the midst.

They were surrounded by jealous foes who tried in every way to defeat their plan, and sometimes succeeded in delaying their work; but through innumerable vicissitudes and deliverances God safely brought them, until the temple was renewed, and the walls arose under Nehemiah, and the social and political foundations of their national life were once more restored.

This is the true secret of success in every work for God. This is the true meaning of the Church of Christ today. God is her Living Head, and the Holy Ghost is her all-sufficient Defender, her All-sufficiency and Guide; and those who fully trust Him never fail to find Him true and equal to all their exigencies and needs.

3. THE HOLY SPIRIT IN THE MESSAGES OF HIS INSPIRED SERVANTS. While God raised up Cyrus, Zerubbabel, Joshua, Esther, Ezra, and Nehemiah to lead this great restoration, He also sent His prophetic messenger to aid them by his counsel. By their divine messages, there were three special prophets connected with the work of the restoration, Haggai, Zechariah, and Malachi. Malachi's work belongs properly to a later period, and closes the Old Testament dispensation. Haggai and Zechariah were contemporaries. The one was an old man, the other was a young man. God has need of both classes in the ministry of His Church. We have time at present to refer to Haggai's messages only.

There were several. The first was one of stern rebuke. The people had begun to forget their great trust, and, instead of rebuilding the house of God in Jerusalem, were erecting for themselves costly homes and becoming absorbed in selfish comfort and ambition. The prophet comes with a very solemn rebuke. "Is it time for you, O ye, to dwell in ceiled houses, and this house lie waste?" His heart-searching cry is, "Go up to the mountain, and bring wood, and build the house; and I will take pleasure in it, and I will be glorified, saith the Lord."

His message was not in vain. The officers and the people rose up and went to work with fidelity and zeal.

Seven weeks later Haggai is authorized to deliver to the people a very different message full of divine encouragement and glorious promise, "Yet now be strong, O Zerubabel, saith the Lord; and be strong, O Joshua, the son of Josedech, the high priest; and be strong, all ye people of the land, saith the Lord, and work: for I am with you, saith the Lord of hosts: according to the word that I covenanted with you when ye came out of Egypt, so my Spirit remaineth among you: fear ye not."

The Holy Spirit was to be their guide and strength. Again and again the phrase is repeated, "Saith the Lord." It was the word of God, the presence of God, the Spirit of God, that was to be their dependence and their divine resource through all this great undertaking. And then the promise reaches out into all the grandeur of a millennial vision.

"For thus saith the Lord of hosts, Yet once, it is a little while, and I will shake the heavens, and the earth, and the sea, and the dry land; and I will shake all nations and the desire of all nations shall come: and I will fill this house with glory, saith the Lord of hosts.

"The silver is mine, and the gold is mine, saith the Lord of hosts. The glory of this latter house shall be greater than of the former, saith the Lord of hosts: and in this place will I give peace saith the Lord of hosts."

They were building a house that was to be visited in the coming centuries by the Son of God Himself, and that was to be glorified by His miracles of love and words of grace. Little did they realize the glory, the latter glory for which they were laying foundations. In a still later vision the prophet looks forward to the overthrow of nations and kingdoms, and the coming of the Lord Jesus Himself, and the recompense which then will await Zerubabel and his faithful laborers when the Lord shall make them like a signet of glory and honor.

This may be the glory of our work. This is the glory of all work done in the power of the Spirit. It is done for the coming of the Lord, and it will receive its recompense in that day of manifestations. Oh, let this be our high ambition!

Perhaps the house we build for Him will yet be trodden by the feet of the Son of man. The souls we bring to Him shall be presented in that day as our crown of rejoicing and His. The world that we win for Him shall be our kingdom as well as His in the day of His millennial reign. Yes, if we may but haste that coming and prepare the way by the evangelization of the nations, it may be our blessed hope and transcendent privilege, ourselves to live to meet Him in His glorious advent, and to welcome Him back to the world for which He died, then to share with Him the days, the ages of blessing and glory, which fill the vision of the prophetic age.

Oh, let our work take hold upon His coming, and be dignified and glorified by the same promise that cheered the heart of the restoration workers, "The glory of this latter house shall be greater than of the former, and in this place will I give peace, saith the Lord of hosts."

The prophetic messages of Zechariah were still more rich and full, but we must defer to another chapter the unfolding of his sublime and instructive images of the Holy Ghost.

## Chapter 24

## The Olive Trees and the Golden Lamps

"Not by might, nor by power, but by My Spirit, saith the Lord of hosts." Zech. 4: 6.

We have already looked at these words in connection with the history of the Restoration and the mighty movements of God's providence in bringing about that glorious result. We also referred to the prophetic ministry of Haggai, the elder of the two prophets who were God's messengers of counsel and encouragement to the leaders and people at this crisis.

Still more remarkable was the ministry of Zechariah, the younger prophet. His wondrous visions were all calculated to meet some special need and trial in their situation at this time.

The first vision was that of the man among the mulberry trees. The prophet saw in a vision a great plain of low, flat land covered with mulberry trees, and among them were horses moving to and fro. This represented the lowly condition of God's people; and the horses, God's ministers of power, who were moving in the midst of His people's trials and working for their deliverance. This was followed by a message of special encouragement, announcing that these low and desolate regions should yet be filled with multitudes of people, that the cities, through prosperity, should yet be spread abroad; and that the Lord should comfort Zion, and would choose Jerusalem.

Next came the vision of the horns and the carpenters. Four horns appeared before the prophet's view, representing the enemies that were scattering Judah and pushing to the wall God's suffering people. But, coming up behind them, were four carpenters, sent to fray the piercing horns of the enemy, and blunt their points, so that they would not be able to touch or harm God's suffering children. There were just as many carpenters as there were horns, and God's people in every age may know that wherever there is a foe to strike there is a force to counteract for those who trust Him.

Next came the vision of the man with the measuring line, going forth to measure the walls of Jerusalem, its length and its breadth, and proclaiming: "Jerusalem shall yet be inhabited as towns without walls for the multitudes of men and cattle therein." This was intended to encourage them amid the paucity of the population. A little handful of returned captives, they were trying to occupy the desolate land, and they seemed so few and contemptible that their enemies turned them to ridicule; but God declared that they would yet spread abroad and cover all the land. And as they looked at their unwalled city and the defenseless temple they were rearing in its midst, and thought of their exposure to all the surrounding enemies, God reassured them, through the prophet, with the precious promise, "I will be unto her a wall of fire round about, and will be the glory in the midst of her."

Next there came a still more encouraging vision. All the power of their enemies outside could not hurt them half so much as their own weakness and unworthiness within. They were conscious of their sinfulness, and they knew that they had already suffered for their fathers' unfaithfulness. They might fear that they, too, should forfeit the blessing of Jehovah. And so the prophet was sent with another vision. He beheld Joshua, the high priest, representing the people, standing before the Lord clothed with filthy garments, suggesting their guilt and sin, and Satan standing at his right hand, to resist him.

But as he gazed, lo! the command is given from the throne, "Take away the filthy garments from him, .. .and I will clothe him with a change of raiment, . . . and set a fair miter on his head," and, turning to the accuser, Jehovah answered all his reproaches, and said: "The Lord rebuke thee, O Satan; even the

Lord that hath chosen Jerusalem rebuke thee; is not this a brand plucked out of the fire?"

Then the vision was followed by a gracious promise of cleansing and blessing summed up in the glorious promise, "I will remove the iniquity of that land in one day." God stood not only between them and their enemies, but also between them and themselves, and all their own unworthiness and sinfulness. He thus stands between us and our guilt, our shield from the accusing of our conscience and the charges of our cruel adversary, so that we can cry, "Who is he that condemneth? It is Christ that died, yea, rather, that is risen again, who is even at the right hand of God, who also maketh intercession for us."

But now we come to the vision of our text, the most beautiful and significant of all, and unequaled by any other portion of the Holy Scriptures for delicacy and depth of sacred meaning.

It was intended to reveal to them the sources of their strength. They were weak, and their foes were strong. At this very time, through the intrigues of their enemies, a decree had come from the king of Persia, arresting for a time the progress of the work. We are told by Ezra that an army came and "with force and power" caused the work to cease. But, like the echo of man's impotent rage answering back from the throne, God sends Zechariah to say in the very same phrase turned back again, "Not by force, nor by power, but by my Spirit, saith the Lord of hosts."

Man had sent his force and power, his army and his might; but he had left God out of his calculations, and this work and this conflict was "not by might, nor by power, but by my Spirit, saith the Lord of hosts. Who art thou, O great mountain? before Zerubabel thou shalt become a plain: and he shall bring forth the headstone thereof with shouting, crying, Grace, grace, unto it!"

The vision itself was a very beautiful one. As he awakened out of sleep with all his powers quickened to take in its meaning, he saw before him a golden candlestick like that which stood in the holy place, with its seven branches of polished gold, surmounted by a vessel of oil and a glowing flame. Then above this candlestick there was a large bowl or reservoir connected by pipes with all the lamps, and containing the supply of oil. But how was this reservoir filled?

Look again at the wondrous and exquisite mechanism. There were no oil cans, no ministering hands, no clumsy machinery of human attendants or conveying tubes, but two living olive trees ripening their fruit continually and pouring it in through two olive branches into the reservoir, from which it flowed down into each of the lamps. How simple, how beautiful, how perfect, and how full of holy meaning ! What is its profound spiritual meaning?

I. THE CANDLESTICK. The golden candlestick represents the Church of God and the people of God. "Ye are the light of the world." "Let your light so shine before men that they shall see your good works and glorify your Father which is in heaven."

Israel of old was to that generation what the Church is meant to be today, the depository of divine truth and life and light, the true light of the world. As the candlestick was all of gold, so the true Church of Christ consists only of those who are partakers of the divine nature. Gold is the type of the divine, and only as we are restored to the image of God and filled with His light and presence can we be light-bearers for the world.

The candlestick was the only light of the temple. It had no windows. All its light came from God. And the world has no light apart from the Church of God. This holy book, illuminated by the Spirit, contains all that we know of God, redemption, and the future life.

He is a foolish man who tries to deceive himself and his people by the torchlight of his own eloquence, philosophy, and sensationalism.

The candlestick was one, yet manifold; and so the Church of God has infinite variety, and yet but one light and one body. God does not level every soul down to the same pattern, but He lets Isaiah and James and John to be each himself; and yet He fills all with God, and makes their life divine, yet perfectly natural, simple, free, and human.

Every part of our nature has to pass through the new creation, but every part is preserved, sanctified, and filled with God. So the whole spirit and soul and body is preserved blameless unto the coming of the Lord Jesus Christ.

The candlestick was not luminous. It was simply a light-bearer. It could make no light. It could reflect light from its polished and brilliant surface, but the light must come from another source. So we have no light in ourselves; we can simply receive the light and hold it. We are not ourselves the light of the world, but we are to so shine that men shall see our good works and glorify our Father which is in heaven.

We are to reveal not our goodness and our grace, but Christ in us. Let all men see how helpless and insufficient we are in ourselves, but what an all-sufficient and mighty Savior we have, and One available for them as well as for us. This is the light that the world needs, that the Holy Ghost and the person and grace of Jesus be held forth for their darkness and misery and sin.

The business of the candlestick was not to hoard the oil, but to consume it, to use it up, and to keep it ever burning in those glowing tongues of flame. If the lamps and pipes had tried to absorb and retain the oil, they would have lost it. They gave it up, they used it up. They consumed it in ceaseless burning. Men sometimes say to us: "Don't expend all your vitality; don't use all your strength; save yourself." Ah, that is the way to lose yourself. Only that which we give we have. That which we keep we lose.

Try to hold on to one of God's gifts, and it will go. Try to economize and keep for yourself your blessing, and it will disappear. Pass it on and it will burn forever. As those lamps exhausted the oil in their little cups, the residue of the oil poured in from above; and they were always full, and always fresh, and always burning, and always shining.

So let us be "burning and shining lights," and, as we give out what He has given, He will replenish the supply, and we shall have enough and to spare; and we, too, shall "shine in the midst of a crooked and perverse generation."

II. THE OIL IS THE EMBLEM OF THE HOLY GHOST. It is He who gives us all our light and life. It is He who produces in us all our graces, and works through us all our service for God and men.

Beloved, this is the test, and this is the difference between man and God. Five of the virgins were wise and five were foolish. They that were foolish took their vessels, but they took no oil in their vessels with their lamps; but they that were wise took oil in their vessels with their lamps, and when the Bridegroom came this was the point of separation.

The foolish virgins were virgins, too. They were pure; they were waiting and longing for the coming of the Bridegroom; they had a little light, and they had oil enough to light the lamp and keep it burning for a time; but they had not the residue of the oil, they had not the fullness of the Spirit, they had not the indwelling of the personal Holy Ghost. And so their lamps went out in their hour of need. They were unable to go in with the marriage procession.

The one point which settled the happy fate of the others was simply this, that they had "oil in their vessels with their lamps." They had the Holy Ghost personally indwelling. They had the source of grace within their hearts. They did not need to go and replenish. They were always ready.

Beloved, let a word be sufficient for the wise, and, oh! let us be filled with the Spirit, so that we shall be found of Him in peace.

III. THE SOURCES OF THE OIL. We come to the most beautiful and significant part of the picture, the sources of the oil. These were not the same human mechanism of ministering priests and great reservoirs from which the oil was carried and replenished day by day, but two living trees whose ripening fruit was continually pressed out by hands unseen, and flowed through two olive branches and two golden pipes, down into the reservoir and into the lamps. It was all perfectly spontaneous, simple, silent, and divine. The oil was always flowing; the reservoir was always full; the lamps were always burning.

This is the source of our divine supply. Who were these two olive trees? Certainly they can represent nothing human, but the divine source of our life in Christ. They represent the Lord Jesus Christ and the blessed Holy Ghost; the one on the divine side, the other on the earthly side of our spiritual life. Both are called by the same name. The apostle John speaks of Jesus as our Advocate or Paraclete with the Father, and he speaks of the Holy Ghost as our Paraclete from the Father. The one is the Advocate yonder, the other is the Advocate within.

One is on each side of us, and between two such Advocates how can a child of God be lost? From these two blessed Persons of the Godhead, distinct in their personality, yet one in their nature, we draw our spiritual life. We draw it as the olive trees gave forth their oil, spontaneously, silently, constantly, instinctively, just as we breathe the air in which we live, just as the blood circulates through our system, so quietly, so naturally, so simply, that we are unconscious of the process.

Thus we may abide in Him and live upon Him, and draw our strength from God alone. Beloved, have we learned the secret of the olive trees, the secret of abiding in Him?

But, what are these two olive branches that connect the olive trees with the reservoir and run into two golden pipes?

These are "the two anointed ones, or, the two sons of oil, that stand before the Lord of the whole earth." Ah! this is the ministry of believing and united prayer. This is the highest service given to saints on earth, a counterpart of the priestly service of Jesus Himself upon the throne.

Beloved, if we will let Him, God will teach us this high and holy service. First, these branches must come out of the trees and be so closely in touch with them that they can communicate directly and draw their very life; and so he that ministers at the altar of prayer must be in perfect touch with God on the heaven-side. But on the other side, he must be in perfect touch with man. The branches must run into the reservoir and connect with the lamps.

So if we would know this ministry of prayer, we must be sensitive to the needs of others. We must be lost to our selfishness. We must be in touch with our fellow-men. We must have a heart full of sympathy and love, and readiness to suffer for others and for God.

God give us this glorious ministry and teach us to know the meaning of that mighty promise, "If two of you shall agree on earth as touching anything that they shall ask, it shall be done for them of my Father which is in heaven."

VI. 1. The effects of the Holy Spirit's working will appear first in the overturning of obstacles. "Who art thou, O great mountain?" There is always a mountain of difficulty in the way of faith. The best evidence of God's presence and power is the activity of the adversary. Faith does not fear the highest mountain when the Holy Ghost is in charge, but trustingly and quietly stands, and says, "Who art thou, O great mountain? Be a plain." The Holy Ghost will give the faith as well as remove the mountains. One cannot but be struck with the similarity of this passage to our Savior's wonderful teaching regarding faith, where He says, that if we have faith as a grain of mustard seed, we shall say to the mountain, "Be thou removed, and be thou cast into the sea"; it shall be done.

Faith does not ask the mountain to be removed. Faith does not even climb the mountain; but it simply commands it to disappear, and uses the authority and power of God. This is the way the Holy Spirit works in the hearts of those who trust and obey Him and are led by the Spirit of God.

2. The work of the Holy Ghost gives all the glory to God. "He shall bring forth the headstone with shouting, crying, 'Grace, grace unto it!" Man's work reflects its honor upon man; but when we become possessed of God, and recognize His all-sufficiency, we can speak of His work without consciousness of

ourselves, and say with the apostle, "Not I, but the grace of Christ in me."

3. The work of the Holy Ghost is a finished work. He does not leave the broken column and the unroofed walls; but He accomplishes His purpose, and He leads us to see our expectation and finish our work. The hands of Zerubabel have laid the foundation of this house; his hands also shall finish it, and "Thou shalt know that the Lord of hosts hath sent me unto you." The work of human ambition and impulse is weak, unstable, and spasmodic; but the work that God inspires is carried through.

4. The work of the Holy Ghost is straight work, and perfectly plumb. "They shall rejoice, and shall see the plummet in the hand of Zerubbabel." The plummet is the symbol of righteousness. A plumb wall is a straight wall, a perpendicular wall; and so the work that God has is a straight work, pure work, and right work. The work that He inspires and carries forward has no compromises about it, and does not need to try to please men; but it rises on Scriptural foundations, and its walls are righteousness, and its gates, praise.

5. Finally, the work of the Holy Ghost is accomplished through feeble instrumentalities. "Who hath despised the day of small things?" This is the way it begins. "God hath chosen the weak things of the world to confound the things which are mighty, and base things of the world, and things which are despised, hath God chosen, yea, and the things which are not, to bring to nought things that are: that no flesh should glory in His presence."

I never read this text without remembering a cold November afternoon, in the year 1881, when a little company of seven persons met in an upper room in this city to confer and pray about giving the Gospel in its fullness to the neglected and churchless people of this great city. We were all poor, and there were but a few of us at that. We had come together in answer to a public call for a meeting of all who were interested in this subject.

As we sat down in the cheerless hall and gathered round the fire to keep ourselves from freezing, we looked at each other;

and, certainly, it was the day of small things. Then we asked God to speak to us. As we opened our Bible that afternoon, the leaves parted at the fourth chapter of Zechariah, and, without thinking, our eye feel on this very verse, "This is the word of the Lord unto Zerubbabel, saying, Not by might, nor by power, but by My Spirit, saith the Lord of hosts . . . . For who hath despised the day of small things?"

Never, perhaps, did a message come to human hearts with more strange and thrilling power than that message that afternoon. Kneeling down together, we let God pray His own prayer in our hearts; and the years that have followed have brought the blessed answer.

Do not be afraid of small beginnings. We may well fear large and pretentious resources, but God added to seven ciphers will amount to millions every time.

## Chapter 25

## The Last Message of the Holy Ghost to the Old Dispensation

"But who may abide the day of his coming, and who shall stand when he appeareth, for he is like a refiner's fire, and like fullers' soap: and he shall sit as a refiner and purifier of silver; and he shall purify the sons of Levi, and purge them as gold and silver, that they may offer unto the Lord an offering in righteousness." Mal. 3: 2, 3.

The book of Malachi contains the last message of the Holy Ghost to the old dispensation. It was his high honor to close the prophetic scroll 2,300 years ago, before the silence of 400 years, which was to he broken once more, when "God, who at sundry times and in divers manners spake in time past to the fathers by the prophets," should at length speak unto us by His Son.

While he is recognized as one of the prophets of the Restoration, strictly speaking, he came just after the Restoration had been accomplished, so far, at least, as the ecclesiastical and political reorganization of the nation was concerned; and his part was rather to be the spiritual reformer of his times, and to rouse his countrymen from the reaction into which their religious life was falling, and summon them to righteousness and faithfulness to God.

His name signifies "My messenger," and he was indeed the mouthpiece and the messenger of the Holy Ghost to his own age and to ours also, in the very special sense in which these times were typical of our own.

The closing years of the Old Testament dispensation might, very naturally, be expected to correspond to the closing years of the New Testament age. The state of the people in Malachi's day bore a striking correspondence to the age we live in, and his messages to his own generation have a solemn significance to us "on whom the ends of the world are come."

I. MALACHI'S MESSAGES TO HIS OWN TIMES.

The Restoration had been followed by a period of prosperity, and, as usually happens, this had brought spiritual declension and, indeed, a very mournful condition of a religious life.

The moral condition of the people was indicated, as is usually the case, by the prevalence of divorce and the decay of domestic and social purity and righteousness. The wives of their youth were put away without cause, "the daughters of a strange god" were taken into unholy alliances, and the altar of Jehovah was "covered with tears." This was done, not only by the people, but the very priests were foremost in this laxity of morals. Malachi was sent to rebuke their wickedness and to tell them that God hated their "putting away" and their unholy lives, and to call them swiftly and solemnly to righteousness and repentance. Then, along with this, there had grown up a spirit of mercenary selfishness. The very service of the sanctuary had become tainted with it so that the priesthood was a self-interested profession. No man would even shut the doors of the temple without a salary. The old spirit of sacrifice, love, and disinterested devotion was dead; and a lot of time-serving parasites had sprung up, and begun to use the very house of God for their selfish aggrandizement and gain.

Growing out of this mercenary spirit on the part of the priesthood there was on the part of the people corresponding selfishness and stinginess. They withheld the tithes and even tried to cheat the Lord by unworthy and dishonest offerings. "Ye offer polluted bread upon mine altar; and ye say, 'Wherein have we polluted Thee?' And if ye offer the blind for sacrifice, is it not evil? and if ye offer the lame and sick, is it not evil? . . . Who is there among you that would shut the doors for nought? neither do you kindle a fire on mine altar for nought. I have no pleasure in you, saith the Lord, neither will I accept an offering at your hand. . . . Ye said also, 'Behold, what a weariness is it!' and ye have snuffed at it, saith the Lord of hosts; and ye brought that which was torn, and the lame, and the sick; thus ye brought an offering: should I accept this out of your hand? saith the Lord." "Will a man rob God? Yet ye have robbed me. But ye say, 'Wherein have we robbed thee?' In tithes and offerings. Ye are cursed with a curse: for ye have robbed me, even this whole nation. Bring ye all the tithes into the storehouse, that there may be meat in mine house, and prove me now herewith, saith the Lord of hosts, if I will not open you the windows of heaven, and pour you out a blessing, that there shall not be room enough to receive it."

Thus Malachi spoke to the last generation of the Old Testament, and thus he might speak with equal fitness to the last generation of the Christian age. There is the same laxity of morals, the same obliteration of God's sharp distinctions, the same breaking down of the sanctities of home, the same avarice and love of money, the same mercenary spirit in the very work of God with its hired preachers, hired choirs, hired prayers. The very pulpit is an arena for intellectual gymnasts and a field for ministerial ambition. There is the same worldliness and niggardliness in the Church of God, with millions for our luxuries and pleasures, but pittances for God; splendid frescoed ceilings and costly spires, pointing in proud profession to heaven, but less per head from the people of God to send the Gospel to the world than we pay for our table salt or the egg shell in our coffee. Is not this as truly the portrait of our times, as it was of the days of Malachi? And is not this the same picture which the Holy Ghost in the New Testament has left, as of the last days of the present dispensation: "This know also, that in the last days perilous times shall come. For men shall be lovers of their own selves, covetous, . . . lovers of pleasure more than lovers of God; having a form of godliness but denying the power thereof."

Already these times have begun to come, and the messages of Malachi and Paul speak to the compromising Christians of today with a terrible aptness and fidelity. It would, indeed, seem as if the professed followers of God in every dispensation had to be tried and found wanting. Adam first failed in Eden; then the Antediluvian age went out in judgment. The patriarchal family sank into Egyptian slavery. The conquest of Canaan ended in the long captivity of the Judges. The kingdom of David terminated in the fall of Israel and the captivity of Judah. And now the glorious Restoration under Zerubbabel, Ezra, and Nehemiah had fallen back into the worldliness and ungodliness of Malachi's day. Even so shall it be with the closing days of the Christian dispensation. As the pure church of Paul and John became the apostasy of Romanism, even so the church of the Reformation is yet to develop into the Laodicea of the last days; and the signs of Laodicea are not so far to seek already in the spirit of our own times.

But in the days of Malachi there was a faithful remnant, a little Church within the Church, a band of whom the prophet could say: "Then they that feared the Lord spake often one to another; and the Lord hearkened, and heard it, and a book of remembrance was written before him for them that feared the Lord, and that thought upon his name. And they shall be mine, saith the Lord of hosts, in that day when I make up my jewels; and I will spare them as a man spareth His own son that serveth him. Then shall ye return and discern between the righteous and the wicked; between him that serveth God and him that serveth him not."

And so in our own days there is still "the little flock," the church of Philadelphia side by side with Laodicea, waiting for the coming of the Lord. There is a larger remnant than we dream in every dark and sinful generation who have not bowed the knee to the image of Baal. There is today in every church of Christ on earth the strange spectacle of a great, broad mass of professing Christians who know or want to know little of the power of the Holy Ghost, and, within that wider circle, a hidden few, like Enoch, who are walking with God, who are filled with the Holy Ghost, who are watching for the coming of the Lord, and who are the preserving salt of the whole body and the real impelling force of all the Christian activities of the entire church of' Christ today.

Thus the age of Malachi touches our own with a wonderful correspondence, and the closing messages of the Old Testament ring like a trumpet call to the last age of the New Testament church. Let us receive their solemn warnings. Let us rejoice in their bright and blessed promises. Let us be found among the little remnant of holy and waiting ones.

II. THE SPECIAL PROMISE OF THE SPIRIT IN MALACHI.

"There are two special promises in this prophetic book. The first is the coming of John the Baptist. "Behold, I will send my messenger, who shall prepare the way before me." The second is the coming of the Lord himself in His first advent. "And the Lord, whom ye seek, shall suddenly come to His temple, even the Messenger of the covenant whom ye delight in: behold, He shall come, saith the Lord of hosts."This, of course, has reference to the coming of the Lord Jesus Christ in his incarnation and earthly ministry. But the promise immediately unfolds into a fullness of meaning which takes in also the ministry of the Holy Ghost. Indeed, the ministry of Christ and of the Holy Ghost are here so linked together that it is impossible to tell where one begins and the other ends. "But who may abide the day of his coming? and who shall stand when he appeareth? for he is like a refiner's fire, and like fullers' soap: and he shall sit as a refiner and purifier of silver; and shall purify the sons of Levi, and purge them as gold and silver, that they may offer unto the Lord an offering in righteousness." Then, later, there comes a third promise in the next chapter, of the other day that is coming, the other fire that is to consume and burn to ashes all the dross which the fire of the Holy Ghost has not burned away. This, of course, is the day of the Lord's second coming, to be preceded by the ministry of Elijah in some sense, and to bring to Israel's returning sons the rising of the Sun of Righteousness and to the waiting saints of God the day of millennial glory.

It is especially to the second of these promises that our subject holds us, the promise of the Holy Ghost.

1. It is, as we have seen, connected directly with the personal ministry of the Lord Jesus Himself. It is spoken of as if it were all Christ's own work. But we know who it was that brought the refiner's fire and the fullers' soap, the blessed Holy Ghost. Yet it is Christ who "baptizeth with the Holy Ghost"; and when He comes it is Christ He brings, so that it is the one life, the one work, through the two persons of the one God.

2. The work He comes to do is to cleanse and purify. He is the Spirit of holiness. But there are two stages of holiness suggested. The first is cleansing from sin; the second is refining the gold and bringing it to a higher measure of purity and beauty. The Spirit comes to do both these works in the believer's heart. It is one thing to be cleansed from all known sin, but it is quite another to be refined, polished, and transformed into all the fullness of all the good and acceptable and perfect will of God. There is a good, but there is also an acceptable; and then there is the perfect will of God, and the Spirit is longing to bring us up to the highest. The wedding robe of the Bride of the Lamb is represented as not only clean, but bright; that is, glorious and beautiful, like Christ's own transfiguration robes. Iron can be refined until it is more precious than gold. So our hearts can be not only purified but glorified, even here.

3. Corresponding to this double work is the double figure, the refiner's fire and the fullers' soap. The soap is for outward cleansing, the fire is for inward and intrinsic transformation. Fire can penetrate where water cannot reach, and can be used where water and soap are of no avail. Fire can be used to cleanse only that which in its nature is indestructible. The silver and the gold can stand the fire, because they are incombustible. The more you burn them the more you improve them. So the fire of the Holy Ghost can come to us only when we become united with God, and partakers of His divine nature. Then we do not fear the fire. It cannot hurt, but only refines. Beloved, some of us have only

passed through soap and water. God wants our garments fire-touched. Then "the King's daughter" shall be "all glorious within, her clothing of wrought gold," which no flame can deface or destroy.

4. "He shall sit." This is very striking. He does not hurry His work; that is, the work of the fire, the deeper, intenser inworking of the Holy Ghost. There is a baptism of the Spirit, a receiving of the Spirit, a cleansing work of the Spirit which is instantaneous and complete. But there is a later work, the following up, the filling out, the burning in of the Refiner which must take time. God is willing to take the time. Let us be, too. The figure suggests the most thoughtful care. He sits down at the crucible. He does not for a moment leave His precious work. He does not let the fire get too hot, or burn too long. And the moment He can see His face on the molten gold, He knows the work is complete, and the fire is withdrawn. It is a great thing to understand rightly the immediate and instantaneous work of the Holy Spirit in converting the soul, and then in entering it and taking up His eternal dwelling there through our obedience and faith, as our Sanctifier and Keeper; and His more gradual and subsequent work, in developing and filling our spiritual capacity, searching and enlarging us, and leading us on and out and up into all the fullness of the mature manhood of Christ.

How wonderful, how gracious, how kind that He will take such trouble with us, and, with love that will not tire, work out in us to the end "all the good pleasure of His goodness," and make us perfect in every good work to do His will, working in us that which is well pleasing in His sight through Jesus Christ to whom be glory, both now and forever. Amen. Oh, that we might let Him have right of way, and ever cry,

> "Refining fire go through my heart,
>   Illuminate my soul;
>   Scatter Thy life in every part,
>   And purify the whole."

5. Finally, all this is for service. "He will purify the sons of Levi, that they may offer unto Him an offering in righteousness." This is God's great end in all his work of grace. He will not give us the Holy Ghost to terminate upon ourselves; and if He sees that our object in seeking even spiritual blessing and power is our own delight, aggrandizement, or self-importance, we shall be disappointed. But if our purpose is to be like God Himself, channels of blessing to others, and instruments for His use, He will fill us and use us to the fullest measure of our heart's desire. The more we give the more we shall receive, until, like God, our only occupation will be to be a blessing. This is the secret of barren hearts and lifeless churches. They are Dead Seas, that have received without an outlet, until they could hold no more, until even what they had has become a stagnant and unwholesome pool.

Side by side, the blessing and service must ever go hand in hand, according to the ancient promise, "Ye shall receive the power of the Holy Ghost coming upon you, and ye shall be witnesses unto me."

The Old Testament closes with the glorious promise of the Holy Ghost. How wonderfully the New Testament has fulfilled it! Let our lives fulfill it. Let our words and works pass it on until the yet greater promise of His Second Coming shall come to pass, and we shall rise to a richer indwelling of the Holy Ghost and a nobler service in the ages to come than we have ever here been able to ask or think.

We have closed these unfoldings of the Holy Spirit in the Old Testament. We shall next turn, if the Lord will, to the fuller light of the New Testament midday and the dispensation of the Holy Ghost. Oh, if, amid the imperfect light of that ancient dispensation, the Spirit accomplished such glorious results and left such illustrious examples of His grace and power, how much more must He not expect of us, the children of the morning, and the heirs of all His truth and grace! God help us to be worthy of our inheritance and true to our trust.

## Volume 2

## Chapter 1

## The Holy Spirit in the Life of the Lord Jesus Christ

"I indeed baptize you with water unto repentance; but He that cometh after me is mightier than I, whose shoes I am not worthy to bear; He shall baptize you with the Holy Ghost, and with fire." Matt. 3: 11.

These words from the lips of the forerunner intimate that there was to be a great distinction between the old dispensation which he was closing, and the new, which Jesus Christ was about to usher in.

The distinction was to be very marked in connection with the manner and measure in which the Holy Ghost would be poured out upon the people of God and manifested in connection with the work of redemption. The two natural emblems of water and fire are used to denote the difference between the two dispensations.

We have seen that the Holy Ghost was present on earth during the Old Testament age, speaking through the prophets and messengers of God, and working out His divine purpose in the lives of God's chosen agents, and instruments. But the New Testament is preeminently the age of the Holy Ghost, and we might, therefore, expect that there would be a great and infinite difference. The principal difference between the old and new dispensations, with respect to the presence and manifestations of the Holy Ghost, might be summed up in the following particulars.

1. In the Old Testament, the Holy Ghost was given to special individuals to fit them for special service; in the New Testament, the promise is that the Spirit shall be poured out upon all flesh,

and they shall not need to say, one to another, "Know the Lord, for all shall know Him," through the divine unction, "from the least to the greatest." The universal outpouring of the Holy Ghost upon all believers is the striking feature of the New Testament.

2. The Holy Spirit was with men and upon men, rather than in them in the Old Testament. In the New Testament dispensation, the Holy Ghost comes to dwell in us and to unite us personally with God, and to be in us, not only a Spirit of power and a preparation for service, but a Spirit of life, holiness, and fellowship with the Divine Being. It is not the influence of the Holy Ghost that we receive, but it is the Person of the Holy Ghost.

3. This leads us to the third distinction; namely, that under the Old Testament dispensation, the Holy Ghost was not resident upon earth, but visited it from time to time as occasion required. Now the Spirit of God is dwelling upon the earth. This is His abode. He resides in the hearts of men, and in the Church of Christ, just as literally as Jesus resided upon the earth during the thirty-three years of His incarnation and life below.

4. Perhaps the principal difference was this; in the Old Testament age the Holy Ghost came rather as the Spirit of the Father, in the glory and majesty of the Deity, while under the New Testament He comes rather as the Spirit of the Son, to represent Jesus to us, and to make Him real in our experience and life. Indeed, the Person of the Holy Ghost was not fully constituted under the Old Testament. It was necessary that He should reside for three and a half years in the heart of Jesus of Nazareth, and become, as it were, humanized, colored, and brought nearer to us by His personal union with our Incarnate Lord. Now He comes to us as the same Spirit that lived, and loved, and suffered, and wrought, in Jesus Christ.

In a sense, our Master left His heart behind Him, and when the Holy Ghost comes to dwell within us, He brings the living Christ and makes His person real to our hearts.

This must be the meaning of that remarkable passage in John 7: 37, 38, where Jesus said that the Spirit in the believer should flow out like rivers of living water; then the evangelist adds, "The Spirit was not yet; because Jesus was not yet glorified." The Holy Spirit, in the form in which He was to be manifest in the coming age was not constituted until after the ascension of Jesus. Now, He comes to us as the Spirit of Christ. Therefore it, is intensely interesting to us to look at the relation of the Holy Ghost to the person of our Lord in His first baptism and earthly ministry.

This is our present theme. May the Holy Ghost Himself illuminate and apply it to all our hearts!

I. Our Lord was born of the Holy Spirit. The announcement by the angel to Mary connects the Divine Spirit directly with the conception and incarnation of Christ. "The Holy Ghost shall come upon thee and the power of the Highest shall overshadow thee, therefore, that holy thing which shall be born of thee shall be called the son of God." Luke 1: 35.

The human mind cannot fathom this mystery — a holy Christ conceived and born of one who was herself the daughter of a sinful race. We cannot believe in the immaculate Mary, but we can believe in the immaculate Son of God, born of her without sin.

The very fact that she was an imperfect and sinful woman adds to the glory of this mystery and makes it the more perfect type of the experience through which we also come into fellowship with our living Head. For just as Jesus was born of the Spirit, so we, the disciples of Jesus, must also be born of the Holy Ghost; for "except a man be born from above he cannot enter the kingdom of God."

The mystery of the incarnation is repeated every time a soul is created anew in Christ Jesus. Into the unholy being of a child of Adam, a seed of incorruptible and eternal life is implanted by the divine Spirit, and that seed is in itself, through the life of God, holy and incorruptible. Just as you may see in the sweet springtime the little white, spotless shoot, coming from the dark soil and out of the heap of manure, unstained by all its gross surroundings, so out of our lost humanity the Holy Spirit causes to spring forth the life of the newborn soul; and while the subject of that marvelous experience may seem an imperfect being, still he has that within him, of which the apostle has said, "His seed remaineth in him, and cannot sin; because it is born of God." He can sin, but that holy nature implanted in him cannot; it is like its Author, holy, too.

"And so He that sanctifieth, and they that are sanctified, are all of one, for which cause He is not ashamed to call them brethren." Like Him we are born of the Holy Ghost and become the sons of God, not by adoption, but by the divine regeneration.

II. Jesus Christ was baptized by the Holy Spirit. Not only did He derive His person and His incarnate life from the Holy Ghost, but when at thirty years of age He consecrated Himself to His ministry of life and suffering and service, and went down into the waters of the Jordan, in token of His self-renunciation and His assumption of death, the heavens were opened and the Holy Ghost, by whom He had been born, now came down and personally possessed His being and henceforth dwelt within Him.

No one can for a moment deny that this was something transcendently more than the incarnation of Christ. Up to this time there had been one personality, henceforth there were two; for the Holy Ghost was added to the Christ, and in the strength of this indwelling Spirit, henceforth He wrought His works, and spake His words, and accomplished His ministry on earth.

But this also has its parallel in the experience of the disciples of Christ. It is not enough for us to be born of the Holy Ghost, we must also be baptized with the Holy Ghost. There must come a crisis hour in the life of every Christian when he, too, steps down into the Jordan of death; when he yields his will to fulfill all righteousness, like his Master; when he voluntarily assumes the life of self-renunciation and service, which God has appointed for him in His holy will, and when there is added to him, as a divine trust, the Holy Ghost; henceforth it is not one, but two, and then these two are one.

I remember the day when my daughter walked down one aisle of this building, and another walked down the other aisle, and they met at this altar and then they walked back after that simple, solemn ceremony, but not as they came. It was not one person now, but two; yet those two were one, and she leaned her weakness upon his strength and, assuming his name, henceforth looked to him for all the needs of her life.

And so there comes a time when the believer joins his hand with the Holy Ghost, and there is added to his new heart and his Christian experience the mighty stupendous fact of God Himself, and the personal indwelling of the Holy Ghost.

How perfectly this is described in the two sentences in Ezekiel. "A new heart will I give unto you and a right spirit will I put within you." This is the new heart in us. "And I will put my Spirit within you, and cause you to walk in My statutes, and you shall keep My commandments and do them." That is the baptism with the Holy Ghost. And so Peter and the other disciples were born of the Spirit before the day of Pentecost; but Jesus promised them that they should be baptized with the Holy Ghost at the appointed time, and when that day was fully come there was added to their true Christian life the divine personality, the infinite presence and all-sufficiency of God, the indwelling Holy Ghost, who had lived and wrought in Jesus Christ.

Beloved, have we entered into this experience? Have we received the Holy Ghost since we believed, or have we allowed our theological traditions and our preconceived ideas to shut us out from our inheritance of blessing and of power? Let us do so no longer. Let us, with the Master, step down to Jordan, enter with Him into death, rise with Him in resurrection life into the baptism of the Holy Ghost, and then go forth in the fulness of His power and liberty, even as He.

Oh, if the Son of God did not presume to begin His public work until He had received this power from on high, what presumption it is that we should attempt in our own strength to fulfill the ministry committed to us and be witnesses unto Him!

III. No sooner had the Lord received the baptism of the Holy Ghost than He was led up of the Spirit into the wilderness to "be tempted of the devil." This is especially emphasized by the evangelist. It was not the devil that appeared first, but it was the Spirit. In the Gospel of Mark the language is still stronger, and it is said that he was "driven of the Spirit."

Perhaps His human spirit recoiled from the awful ordeal of the wilderness, as it afterwards shrank from the anguish of Gethsemane, and the Holy Ghost pressed Him forward by one of those resistless impulses which many of us have learned to understand, and for forty days His blessing was challenged; His faith was tested; His very soul was tried by all the assaults of the adversary.

He was brought into certain places that seemed to contradict all that He believed, and to challenge all that had been promised to Him. The devil might well say to Him, "Art Thou indeed the Son of God in the midst of hunger, desolation, and wild beasts, and every form of suffering, cast off and neglected even by God, and left in destitution and desolation?"

And then, amid all these perils and privations, suddenly there opened before Him the vision of power and pleasure — the kingdoms of the world and all the glory of them, if He would but yield a single point and accept the leadership of the enemy, who doubtless appealed to His higher nature and represented Himself as an angel of light, or perhaps approached Him through His own form, and all the visions and possibilities of power He might use for the good of men and the benefit of the world.

These and other more subtle insinuations and instigations came to Him on every side and yet, amid them all, He stood unmoved in His obedience to His Father's will and His reliance upon His Father's word, until Satan was driven from His presence, and He came forth more than conqueror. And so the first thing that we may look for, after the baptism of the Holy Ghost, is the wilderness with its desolations and privations. Circumstances will surely come to us, which seem to contradict all that we have believed, and to render impossible the promise of God. Even God will seem to have failed us, and when all is dark as midnight, the vision of help from other sources will come to us, and a thousand voices will whisper to us their promises of sympathy and aid, if we but yield a single point of conscience and give ourselves up to the will of the deceiver. All the temptations of our Master will come to us, the lust of the flesh, the lust of the eye, the pride of life, the temptation to take help from forbidden sources, or perhaps to carry even our faith to the extreme of fanaticism and presumption.

All these will come, but if the Spirit has led us up into the wilderness He will lead us out. If we will but lift our eyes above the tempter to the divine Deliverer, we shall find that even Satan shall be compelled to become our ally; and, more than conquerors, like our Master, we shall take our enemy prisoner and make him fight our very battles.

Let us not fear the conflict; let us not shrink from the testing; let us not count it strange concerning the fiery trial that is to try us; let us not see the devil first, but the Lord always above him, and the Holy Ghost in the midst of our being, our Victor and Deliverer. "When the enemy shall come in like a flood, the Spirit of the Lord shall lift up a standard against Him."

We must first fight the battle in our own soul that we are to fight in the world. David must meet Goliath alone, before he can meet him in the hosts of the Philistines. Jesus must conquer Satan in single combat, before He can go forth to drive him out of hearts and lives. And so we, too, must live out our public service in the private arena of our own spiritual experience, and then repeat our victory in the victory that God shall give us for the lives of others.

Beloved, shall we not trust, through all our tests and trials, and take the Holy Ghost as our Deliverer in the hour of temptation, and our blessed and divine Discipliner, leading us through the ordeal of suffering to the strength of victory?

IV. We next read that Jesus went forth in the power of the Spirit from the wilderness into Galilee. He was not weakened but strengthened by His conflict, and almost immediately afterward we find Him standing in the synagogue at Nazareth publicly declaring, "The Spirit of the Lord is upon me, because He hath anointed me to preach the gospel to the poor; He hath sent me to bind up the brokenhearted, to preach deliverance to the captives, and recovering of sight to the blind, to set at liberty them that are bruised, to preach the acceptable ,year of the Lord." Luke 4: 18, 19.

Henceforth all His teachings, all His works, all His miracles of power were attributed directly to the Holy Ghost. In the twelfth chapter of Matthew and the twenty-eighth verse, we have a very distinct statement of the connection of the Holy Spirit with His miracles of power. "If I by the Spirit of God, cast out demons, then the kingdom of God is come unto you." That is to say, it is the Holy Ghost that casts out demons in us, and this same Holy Ghost is to remain in us and to perpetuate the kingdom of God in the church through the dispensation.

It is a very wonderful truth that it is the same Spirit who wrought in Christ, that He has given to the church to perform her works of love and power.

This was what the Master meant when He said, "He that believeth on Me, the works that I do shall he do also; and greater works than these shall he do; because I go unto the Father." The Holy Ghost in us is the same Holy Ghost that wrought in Christ. We yield to none, in honor to the Son of God. He was truly the Eternal God, "very God of very God." But when He came down from yonder heights of glory, he suspended the direct operation of His own independent power and became voluntarily dependent upon the power of God through the Holy Ghost. He constantly said, "I can of mine own self do nothing." He purposely took His place side by side with us, needing equally with the humblest disciple the constant power of God to sustain Him in all His work. Not that He might be dishonored in His glory and majesty, "For being in the form of God He thought it not a thing to be grasped to be equal with God, but He emptied Himself and made Himself of no reputation, and took upon Him the form of a servant."

And so He went through life in the position of dependence, that He might be our public example and teach us that we, too, have the same secret of strength and power that He possessed, and that as surely as He overcame through the Holy Ghost, so may we.

Oh, what a solemn spectacle it is to see the Son of God spending thirty years on earth without one single act of public ministry until He received the baptism of power from on high, and then concentrating a whole lifetime of service into forty-two short months of intense activity and almighty power!

But He has left to us the same power which He possessed. He has bequeathed to the church the very Holy Ghost that lived and wrought in Him. Let us accept this mighty gift. Let us believe in Him and His all-sufficiency. Let us receive Him and give Him room, and let us go forth to reproduce the life and ministry of Jesus and perpetuate the divine miracles of our holy Christianity through the power of the blessed Comforter.

This is the mighty gift of our ascended Lord. This is the supreme need of the church of today. This is the special promise of the latter days. God help us to claim it fully and, in the power of the Spirit, to go forth to meet our coming Lord.

## Chapter 2

## The Baptism with the Holy Ghost

"*He shall baptize you with the Holy Ghost, and with fire.*" Mat. 3: 11.

This sounds almost like an echo of the last promise of the Old Testament. The voice of "the Messenger" is taken up by "the Forerunner." "He is like a refiner's fire, and like fullers' soap; and He shall sit as a refiner and purifier of silver: and He shall purify the sons of Levi, and purge them like gold and silver, that they may offer unto the Lord an offering in righteousness."

In the last chapter we have seen the relation of the Holy Ghost to the person of Christ. First, He was born by the Spirit, then He was baptized by the Spirit, and then He went forth to work out His life and ministry in the power of the Spirit.

But "He that sanctifieth and they that are sanctified are all of one;" so in like manner we must follow in His Footsteps and relive His life. Born like Him of the Spirit, we, too, must be baptized of the Spirit, and then go forth to live His life and reproduce His work. And so our next theme is the baptism of the Spirit of God through the Lord Jesus Christ.

I. THE BAPTIZER. It is Christ's province to baptize with the Holy Ghost. The sinner does not come first to the Holy Spirit, but to Christ. Our first business is to receive Jesus, and then to receive the Holy Ghost. Therefore, the great promise of the Old Testament is the coming of Christ, while the great promise of the New is the coming of the Spirit.

Jesus received the Spirit from the Father. We receive the Spirit from Jesus. It is necessary for us, in order that we may fully receive the Holy Ghost, that we shall first receive Christ in His person as our Savior and as our indwelling life.

The Father gave the Spirit to Him not by measure and, if He dwells in us, He will bring the Spirit with Him, and He shall dwell in us likewise in the same measure in which He dwells in Jesus.

Our mere human hearts are not fit temples for the Holy Ghost. It is only as we are united to Christ that we are prepared and enabled to receive the Holy Ghost in the fullness of His life and power. It is the Christ within us, that still receives the Holy Ghost.

And so, when our Master was about to leave the world, it is significantly stated that He breathed upon them, and said: "Receive ye the Holy Ghost." The Holy Spirit came upon them through the breath of Christ. This significant action emphasized the fact that the Spirit was imparted to them from His own person and as His own very life. It is true that the act of breathing on them did not bring immediately the residence of the Holy Ghost into their hearts, for this could not be until after the day of Pentecost. But it was meant to connect it with Himself, so that when the Holy Ghost did descend and dwell in them they would receive Him as the Spirit of Jesus, and as communicated to them by the breath and the very kiss of their departing Master.

As we have already seen, the Holy Ghost comes to us as the Spirit of Christ and even as His very heart, the One who wrought in Him His mighty works and repeats them in us.

Would we receive the baptism with the Holy Ghost, let us receive Jesus in all His fullness. Let us draw near to His inmost being, and from His lips let us in-breathe the Spirit of His mouth.

II. THE BAPTISM. What is the baptism imparted to us by Christ?

Sometimes we hear this spoken of as if He baptized us with something different from Himself, some sort of an influence, or feeling, or power. The truth is, the Spirit Himself is the baptism. Christ baptizes, and it is with or in the Spirit that He baptizes us. There is, therefore, one baptism with the Spirit once for all, and, from that time, the Holy Ghost Himself is our indwelling life.

The word "baptize" is significant in this connection. Literally, it might be translated "Baptize you in the Holy Ghost." It is scarcely necessary to say that the word baptize means to immerse, and carries along with it always the idea of death and resurrection. There is something very significant in this in connection with the reception of the Holy Ghost. It means that we are baptized into death, and raised into life, and thus receive the Spirit from on high. Just as Jesus went down into the Jordan, which was the symbol of death, and there received the Heavenly Dove, so we must step down into the death of all our strength and all our life, and, surrendering ourselves completely to Him, rise in newness of life with Christ, and thus receive the Holy Ghost as the seal and source of that new life.

The most important condition of the baptism with the Holy Ghost is that we shall truly die to all our own life, and enter into the meaning of Christ's resurrection. We must be completely submerged, not a hair of our head left; in sight; then when we cease from ourselves we shall enter into God and find that while, in one sense, we have received the Holy Ghost into us, we have in a far greater sense been received into the Holy Ghost. He is too vast and glorious for any soul to exhaust His fullness; therefore, after He has filled and flooded all our being, there is an overflow as boundless as the ocean of immensity, and we are still in that ocean as the element of our inexhaustible life.

It is scarcely necessary to say that the baptism of the Holy Ghost is our union with the living personality of the Spirit. It is not an influence. It is not a notion, nor a feeling, nor a power, nor a joy, into which we are submerged; but it is a heart of love, a mind of intelligence, a living being as real as Jesus Christ of Nazareth, and as real as our own personality.

III. THE SYMBOL OF THIS BAPTISM, FIRE. "He shall baptize you with the Holy Ghost, and with fire." This does not mean that the Holy Ghost and fire are different, or that the baptism of fire is something distinct from that of the Spirit, but simply that the figure of fire expresses more fully the intensity and power of this divine baptism. It means that the soul that is truly baptized with God is a soul on fire. Fire is the most forceful and suggestive of natural elements, and seems made especially to symbolize the Holy Ghost.

1. It is a penetrating element. It goes to the very fibre and heart of things, and is internal and intrinsic in its action. And so the Holy Ghost "pierces to the dividing asunder of soul and spirit, and of the joints and marrow, and is a Discerner of the thoughts and intents of the heart." He searches our inmost being, and requires and produces "truth in the hidden part."

2. Fire is a purifying element. It separates the dross from the gold. It burns up the stubble and purges the vessel from all defilement. It is the type of the cleansing, sanctifying Spirit of God, who alone can purify our sinful and polluted souls and burn up the dross of sin.

3. Fire is a consuming element. It is the most destructive of forces; so the Holy Ghost comes to destroy all that is destructible, to consume all that is corruptible, and to burn out all that is combustible. God wants a people that have been so burned out, that when the testing fires of the great final day shall come there shall be nothing left to consume. It is not only the sinful but the earthly, the natural, the self-bound life, that the Spirit comes to wither, until there is nothing left but the divine and everlasting. "The grass withereth and the flower fadeth; because the Spirit of the Lord bloweth upon it." Do we not want this blessed fire? Shall we not welcome this blessed flame? Are we not weary of the things that wither and decay, and do we not desire the life that cannot pass away; the loves and friendships that shall never say good-bye, and the treasures that shall meet us in the sky?

4. Fire is a refining element. And so the Holy Ghost in the great Refiner. He comes, not only to cleanse, but to improve, to elevate, to mature, to beautify and glorify the soul, and fit our heavenly robes for the marriage of the Lamb. "He shall sit as a Refiner and Purifier of silver." There is an instantaneous and there is a gradual work of the Holy Ghost. There is an act by which He baptizes us into Himself forever. And there is a process in which He sits down beside the crucible, and watches the mol-

ten silver until it perfectly reflects His image, and then He removes the fire and declares the work complete. He comes not only to give us love, but all the gentleness of love; not only long-suffering, but also "all long-suffering with joyfulness;" not only "the things that are pure, and true, and honest," but also the "things that are lovely and of good report." Let us welcome the refining fire. Let us invite Him to sit down in our willing hearts, and finish His glorious work, until we are "all glorious within," our clothing of wrought gold, and our raiment "white and lustrous" for the Marriage Feast.

5. Fire is a necessary element in preparing almost every article of food for our nourishment. We cannot live on raw wheat nor uncooked meat. It must pass through the process of fire to be wholesome and nourishing; so the Holy Ghost prepares the Word of God for our spiritual subsistence. A great many people live on raw and cold theology. It is little wonder that they are spiritual invalids and suffer terribly from bad digestion. A little truth, thoroughly prepared and presented to us by the loving hands of the Holy Ghost, is worth volumes of dry theology and learned exegesis.

The Passover must not be eaten "raw or sodden," but it must be roasted in the fire and properly prepared. The Holy Ghost is as necessary as the blood of Christ and the word of truth. He is a very foolish preacher who tries to preach without Him, and a very foolish Christian who expects to find the truth and the power of God without His blessed anointing and constant illumination.

6. Fire is a quickening element. And so the Holy Ghost is the source of life. What is it that makes the spring, the flowers, and the swarming life of the insect world? It is the warmth of spring, it is the fire of yonder sun. And so the Holy Ghost quickens our whole spiritual being into vitality. Like the mother bird, whose warm bosom incubates the germs of life that she has dropped into her nest, so the Spirit of God vitalizes all our being, and quickens into life and blessing seeds that lay dormant, perhaps, for years. He quickens our spiritual life; He quickens our intellectual

life; He quickens our physical life, and is the source of healing and strength.

7. The Holy Spirit, like fire, melts the rigid heart and molds it into the form of God's holy will, and highest purpose. Without the Holy Ghost we are set in our own ideas, plans, and thoughts; but the soul that is filled with the Holy Ghost is adjustable, both to God and to man. The easiest people to get along with are those most filled with God.

The Spirit is a great lubricator and mellower, and He keeps us adjusted to the will of God, and to the providences of life as they meet us, day by day, in God's perfect order of place and time.

8. Fire is the great energizer and source of power. It is the real secret of the electric current and the throbbing piston of yonder engine. And so the Holy Ghost is the source of all spiritual power. He and He alone can give effectiveness to our lives, and make us tell for God and humanity, and the great purpose of our existence. We need His power in every department of life. He is not only for the pulpit, but for every walk of life. The Holy Ghost will give power to all who will receive it, to make life effective and to make us accomplish the purpose of our being.

The Old Testament age was a life of effort, struggle, and human endeavor. It was man's best with God's help; but God is through with that forever. God is not now trying to get people to do as well as they can, but He is offering to undertake Himself the whole responsibility of their life and work, to enter and possess their hearts, and to be their all-sufficiency. And so we are without excuse if we fail through our own imperfection and ability . God is not blaming us for what we do not do, but for what we do not let Him enable us to do.

"Ye shall receive power after that the Holy Ghost is come upon you;" and we "can do all things through Christ who is our strength."

9. Fire warms, and so the Holy Ghost is the source of love, zeal, and holy earnestness. He sets souls on fire for God, and duty, and humanity. He makes us all aglow with divine enthusiasm. An ordinary mind will accomplish more than a brilliant

one, if it is alive with holy earnestness.

We are living in an earnest age. All the forces of human intelligence are intensely alive. Be in earnest. The world is in earnest. Satan is in earnest. God is in earnest. Redemption is an earnest business and cost its Author every drop of His crimson blood. The Holy Ghost is intensely in earnest. Everything in heaven and earth and hell is in earnest but man. It is an awful thing for a Christian, redeemed by the blood of Christ, and destined to an eternal future of weal or woe, to be frivolous or trifling. O, friend, think, if that day you are wasting were to be cut off the end of your life, instead of the middle, how quickly you would awaken and tremble at the thought of trifling! If every hour you waste were deducted from the sum of your life at the close, how frightful the sacrifice would seem! And yet it is even so. God help us to be intensely aroused to life's solemn meaning!

Now, the Holy Ghost will make us earnest. Indeed, one of His own names is this, "The Earnest of our inheritance until the redemption of the purchased possession." The earnest means the reality. The Holy Ghost is the reality of things, and He makes us real and earnest, too.

10. Finally, fire is a protective element. The eastern shepherd surrounds his fold by night with a little wall of fire, as he heaps up the dry wood of the desert in a circle around his flock, and the wild beasts fear to come within the fiery wall. So God says, "I will be unto her a wall of fire round about, and will be the glory in the midst of her."

The Holy Ghost defends us from the power of evil. A heart on fire with God throws off a thousand temptations. An electric wire, charged with the fiery current, is as mighty as a battery of artillery. A hot stove cover throws off the water that vainly tries to rest upon it. So a heart filled with the Spirit of God is proof against temptation, sin, sorrow, and even disease.

Oh, let us be filled with the Holy Ghost, and we shall carry a charmed life and be preserved from all the powers of earth and hell!

## Chapter 3

## The Wise and Foolish Virgins; or, The Holy Spirit and the Coming of the Lord

"Then shall the kingdom of heaven be likened unto ten virgins, which took their lamps, and went forth to meet the bridegroom. And five of them were wise, and five were foolish. They that were foolish took their lamps, and took no oil with them: But the wise took oil in their vessels with their lamps." Matt. 25; 1-4.

The Gospel of Matthew is the Gospel of the King, and its latest chapters are full of the Master's teachings about His coming. The parable of the virgins is a picture of the attitude of the church at the coming f the Lord, and the necessity of the Holy Ghost in order to prepare us for that great event.

The ten virgins, like the ten servants in the parable of the pounds, represent the whole church. The church is often represented in the Scriptures under the figure of a woman. It is an unnecessary and irrelevant strain to try to make a distinction between the virgins and the bride, and assume that the bride is somewhere in the background of the parable, and in a still higher place than the wise virgins. If that were so, it is strange that the Lord makes no reference to so important a part of the dramatis personae in any of these closing discourses. The truth is, that which is elsewhere represented by the bride is here represented by the virgins. Sometimes the church is called a bride, sometimes a building, sometimes a body, sometimes disciples, servants, virgins; but it is always the same church, and all that is necessary in the interpretation is to simply work out the figure used in each case, consistently with itself, and not to drag in every other feature and accompaniment which a lively fancy may suggest. As well might we try to work out an hypothesis for the mother in the parable of the prodigal son, or to find a meaning for all the figures introduced in the necessary drapery of any of the parables. The Great Teacher has one object in view in this great parable — to show the need of special preparation for the Lord's coming, and we only confuse the mind, and detract from the simple object of the lesson when we try to bring in a whole system of theology.

I. THE POINTS OF RESEMBLANCE BETWEEN THE WISE AND FOOLISH VIRGINS.

1. They were both virgins. They were both separated and pure. It is possible to have a blameless character, to have come out from the world and to be faultlessly right, moral, and correct in our life, and yet be devoid of the Holy Ghost and unprepared for the Lord's return.

2. Both were looking for the coming of the bridegroom. They had all gone out with this one object and were definitely expecting and preparing for him. And so we may fully believe in the doctrine of the Lord's return, may be deeply interested in it, may be personally desiring and expecting it, and yet may be, if we are without the Holy Ghost, unprepared for it, and be found among the foolish virgins at the last.

3. They both Slumbered and slept. The Greek word for 'slumbered', literally means 'nodded'. It vividly describes the drowsiness that gradually creeps over one, until, at last, unwillingly and almost unconsciously, he falls asleep. It implies that, even at the very best, the people of God are more than half asleep. And yet it is a very different thing to doze with the oil in your vessels, than to fall asleep utterly unprepared for your Master's appearing.

4. Both were called just before the Bridegroom came. How gracious it was of the Master to send word to the sleeping virgins! He has promised us that "that day shall not overtake us as a

thief." And even the foolish virgins were awakened at the last moment, and were aware of the Master's near approach. But, alas! it did not avail them now; it was too late to obtain the oil and prepare their dying lamps for the glorious procession that welcomed their King's return.

There was much, very much, in their favor. Just one thing they lacked. But it was enough to prevent their entering in. God help us all to make sure of "that one thing needful!"

II. THE DIFFERENCE. What then was the difference between these two classes of virgins? What was the secret of failure on the part of the foolish ones?

1. Five were wise and five were foolish. It is not enough for us to be earnest and well meaning. God expects us also to be intelligent, instructed, and wise. "Be ye not unwise, but understanding what the will of the Lord is." "See that ye walk circumspectly, not as fools, but as wise, redeeming the time, because the days are evil."

It will be no excuse for us in the day of His coming that we did not know what He expected of us. He has given us full instructions, and to neglect His word is evidence of guilty and careless disobedience. How many are defaulting in their life and service because they do not even understand the truth about their Master's coming, and the Bible is to them a sealed book! God make us wise!

2. The foolish virgins were impulsive, shallow, enthusiastic, and lacking in real solid and lasting qualities. This is indicated by the simple statement that the first thing that the foolish virgins thought about was their lamps, and the first thing that the wise thought about was their vessels and the oil that filled them. The one looked at the transient flame; the other at the abiding source of life and light. The one represents the present people; the other the permanent people with whom we are always coming in contact.

John Bunyan expresses the difference by his two characters of Passion and Patience. The one wanted everything now; the other wanted that which he would have at the end.

3. But the supreme difference between the wise and foolish virgins was the fact that the foolish virgins took their lamps only, and the others took the oil in their vessels. This, we need hardly say, expresses these two great facts and experiences; namely, a Christian life and the baptism with the Holy Ghost. The burning lamp represents the spiritual life which has been kindled by the Holy Ghost; the oil in the vessels with the lamps represents the Holy Ghost Himself, personally received in the consecrated heart.

There is an infinite difference between these two facts. The apostles before Pentecost and the apostles after Pentecost represent this difference.

The vessel, of course, is our personality — spirit, soul, and body; the oil is the Holy Ghost who comes to the yielded and obedient heart to control it, and fill it with the fullness of God. This is the true preparation for a life of holiness and for the coming of our Lord Jesus Christ.

With this we are ready to meet Him when He appears, and although we may have but a few moments to prepare, and may even nod and sleep at times, we have the secret of the Lord within us, and "we shall be found of Him in peace."

This is the great question which God is pressing upon His church today. "Have ye received the Holy Ghost since ye believed?" This is the great mark of distinction between Christians and Christians. Beloved, let us make no mistake, but let us be filled with the Spirit and so "give all diligence to make our calling and election sure."

IV. THE EFFECTS UPON BOTH CLASSES.

1. The wise virgins were ready, and after a few moments of immediate preparation were received to the marriage feast and the joy of their Lord.

2. The foolish virgins woke to find their lamps expiring. "Give us of your oil," they cried, "for our lamps are going out." They were not able to supply their lamps from the vessels of the wise. These needed all the oil they had for the great occasion

which had come, and there was none to spare for the lamps of the other virgins.

It is true that the Holy Ghost is indivisible, and we cannot give part of our blessing to another. If we have Him, we have Him personally and He cannot be separated into parts. We need all His fullness for our own preparation. We may lead others to Him and help them to receive Him, but they must take Him for themselves.

3. We may receive even this blessing too late. It would seem to be implied that the Holy Spirit might still be secured, even at the very moment of the Lord's return, but "while they went to buy, the bridegroom came, and they that were ready went in, and the door was shut."

There will be, doubtless, many spiritual blessings poured out upon the world immediately after the Parousia of our blessed Master, and the translation of His waiting Bride; but it will be too late to enter into the joys of the marriage, and escape the sorrows of the great tribulation. Time is one of the factors in every great question, and it is not only well for us to obey God's call, but it is essential to obey it promptly. The very essence of obedience is, "redeeming the time" — the very point of time — "because the days are evil."

O beloved, let us not lose a moment before we receive the baptism of the Holy Ghost! There is not an hour to spare. We are in solemn days, and we are neither ready to live nor to die, nor to meet our coming Lord, without the Holy Ghost.

There is something very suggestive in this figure of buying. The traders in this case do not represent any body of men who can sell us the Holy Ghost; they simply represent the divine sources from which we receive Him, the divine method which God has provided. There is a sense in which we buy Him by making Him our own. When we buy a thing, it becomes our own property, and so we may receive the Holy Ghost for ourselves and claim Him as our very own.

In the early part of the parable the beautiful original expresses the idea very strongly. "They took their own lamps, and went forth to meet the bridegroom."

There is another sense, also, in which we buy. We must give up something. We must let something go, before we can receive the Holy Ghost. Indeed, we must let all go and then receive Him in His fullness.

A few weeks ago, as we were passing out of a large meeting, a sobbing girl was sitting near the aisle, and asked us to pray with her. Her heart was very heavy. She had come to the Gethsemane of life; she was letting go everything, and some of the things were very dear; but she was true to God and obedient to the heavenly calling. Less than a week afterwards, we were passing away from that place, and a friend came up to greet us and say goodbye. It was the same face, but we scarcely knew her, it was so transfigured. The light of heaven was shining in her beautiful countenance, and the joy and glory of the Lord had lighted up all her face. The sacrifice was past; the resurrection morning had come; she had let all go, and she had received Him.

There is still another sense in which we buy this great blessing. Christ has purchased it for us, and He says to us, "Come ye, buy and eat! yea, come, buy wine and milk without money, and without price." The Holy Ghost is the purchased privilege of every believer. Beloved, come and receive Him, and receive Him at once, that you may be prepared for the trusts of life and the great Parousia.

4. The foolish virgins were excluded from the marriage of the Lamb. All that this means we dare not attempt to explain. That it does mean a difference, a mighty difference between the two classes of Christians, there can be no doubt, and that there shall be such a difference between those who shall meet the Master with joy, and those who meet Him with grief; between those who have confidence, and those who shall be ashamed before Him at His coming, the Bible leaves us no room to doubt.

Just what will be the peculiar privilege of those who enter in, and the severest loss of those who are excluded, it is presumptuous to attempt to define in detail; but it will be loss enough, sorrow enough, to be shut out of anything which our Master had for us; and the soul that is willing just to be saved and forego its crown and a place in the bosom of the Lord, is too ignoble almost to be saved. God write upon our hearts the solemn emphasis of that awful sentence, "the door was shut!"

5. But there was still a more solemn word, "I know you not." They came, they came perhaps with oil. They knocked; they begged for entrance, but He from within only answered, "I know you not." This, as has been shown by Dean Alford, is very different from the more terrible sentence addressed to others, "I never knew you." It is simply an intimation hat they are not in the circle of His intimate personal friendship. He does not exclude them from salvation, but He excludes them from the place of the Bride, and the innermost center of His communion and love.

Beloved, what constitutes a bride? It is not wedding robes nor dowry nor surroundings. It is the heart of love that knows her bridegroom and responds to his affection. It is an interior preparation, and this is the preparation which the Holy Ghost is offering today to the children of God. He is calling out a Bride for the Lamb. He is saying to many a hesitating heart, "Hearken, O daughter, and consider; forget also thy kindred and thy father's house; so shall the King greatly desire thy beauty; for He is thy Lord, and worship thou Him."

The Holy Ghost is bringing those who are willing into a closer fellowship with Jesus, and giving them such an acquaintance with Him that in that day no bolts, nor bars, nor closed doors can keep them from the bosom of their Lord. They know Him and are known of Him; when He appears, His loving smile will recognize them and the magnetic attraction of His presence will draw them in a moment to His heart and His throne.

May God make us willing to receive this blessed preparation that we may be found ready at His coming!

## Chapter 4

## The Parable of the Pounds; or, Power for Service

"Occupy till I come." Luke 19: 13.

Archelaus, the son of Herod, went to Rome to secure, by influence at the court of the Emperor, the kingdom of Judea, and then returned to enjoy his patrimony. Christ used this familiar illustration to represent His return to the Father to receive the Kingdom, and then to return to enjoy it with His followers during the millennial age. This is the frame-work of the parable of the pounds.

The special theme of the parable, however, is the trust committed to His disciples during His absence, and the resources given them to enable them to fulfill their trust. While the Master is representing us and caring for our interests at God's right hand, we are left here to carry on His work and to represent the interests of His Kingdom; to enable us to fulfill this ministry He gives us the necessary resources. These are illustrated by the pound, or mina, given to each of the ten persons. This was a little sum of money worth about fifteen dollars. It represents the resources which God gives to His servants for their work. What are these resources as represented by the pounds?

In answering this question it is necessary to remember the difference between the parable of the pounds and the talents. In the case of the latter, there was a difference in the enduement and endowment of the servants. They had different talents. In the case of the pound, they had an equal allowance. They cannot therefore mean the same thing. If the talents represent our natural gifts of wealth, social influence, or personal intelligence and capacity, then the pound must represent the special enduement of the Holy Ghost given to the people of God and the servants of Christ to equip them for their work.

We are taught most distinctly that spiritual service must come from spiritual enabling. "No man can say that Jesus Christ is Lord except by the Holy Ghost." No man can render any acceptable service to God through natural talent or fleshly energy. The apostles were commanded "to wait for the promise of the Father," and were to "receive power after that the Holy Ghost had come upon them," and then to be witnesses unto Christ, in the power of God.

There is but one divine enabling for service, and that is the enabling of the Holy Ghost. There was but one pound given to each of the servants, and it is the one promise to every true servant of Christ — "Ye shall be baptized with the Holy Ghost."

The same amount was given to each of the servants, and the same Holy Ghost is given to all who will receive Him. We do not receive a part of His Person or power, but we receive Him personally, and have as much of His life and strength as we are able to take. The Holy Ghost is one and indivisible, and there is no partiality whatever in the opportunity which God gives to every one of His consecrated children to serve and glorify Him.

The talents may be quite different. One may be obscure, while another may be in the blaze of publicity; but the same power is given to each one, and the same glory will redound to God through each, no matter how different they appear in the judgment of the world.

This blessed pound is given to every one of His servants. The Holy Ghost is purchased for all who belong to Christ and will yield their lives in surrender and obedience to the divine Spirit. The Apostle has given us the simple condition when He says, "The Holy Ghost whom God hath given to them that obey Him." The promise of Pentecost was not restricted to a few special cases, but the Apostle distinctly states, "The promise is unto you, and to your children, and to all that are afar off, even as many as the Lord our God shall call."

God does not send us warring upon our own charges. He gives to us all that is needful for the trust committed to us. If you should be sent by a great commercial house to carry out a trust for them in some distant land you would expect them to pay your expenses, to provide you your ticket, to give you all necessary introductions, and to equip you thoroughly for your important journey. And when God sends us on His great embassy, He pledges Himself to enable us to carry it out successfully. This promise of power just means — all we need for efficiency. It is sufficiency for efficiency, all personal qualifications, providential workings, and divine enablings that we have a right to expect for the successful accomplishment of the work that is given us to do.

If our work is in the secular realm, we have a right to expect His help and success. If it is in directly spiritual things, we have a right to expect it there. The power is in proportion to the place. God's provision is ample for God's trust. Now the Holy Ghost is the equivalent of all we need for our trust and work.

An English writer, I think Mr. Pearse, tells how he once spoke to a poor woman in a London City Mission, and tried to show her how Christ was the adequate supply for all her need. She could not understand it at first, and then he stopped and began to ask her about her home and her circumstances, and what she needed for her family. Then, handing her a shilling, he said, "Now what would you do with this shilling if you had it?" She told him that she would spend two pence for bread, and a penny for coal, and so on until she had spent the shilling. "So you see," he said, "that this shilling is really not a shilling, but it is coal, and sugar, and bread." "Now," he said, "Christ is the same. Looking at Him in one way He is Christ but in another way He becomes to you peace and joy and salvation and answered prayer, providential help and guidance, supply for all your needs, — everything God can be to you both for time and eternity." The illustration was very simple and beautiful. She understood it and accepted the Savior, who was the equivalent of all her need.

Just in the same sense the Holy Ghost is the equivalent of all things. Therefore, in one place in Luke, He says, "How much more will your Father in heaven give the Holy Ghost to them that ask Him;" and in another place in Matthew He says, "How much more will your Father in heaven give good things to them that ask Him." So this pound is the equivalent of all we need for our work.

Do we need to understand the Bible? He will be Light and Teacher. Do we need unction? He will give the anointing of the Holy Ghost. Do we need faith? He will be to us the Spirit of faith. Do we need sympathy and love to draw souls to Christ? He will be in us, the love of God shed abroad by the Holy Ghost. Do we need power to convict and convert men? He will convict the world of sin and righteousness and judgment, and will accompany our words with His effectiveness. Do we need a power that will cooperate in the circumstances of life? He will make all things work together for us. So the Holy Ghost is just all things, and none of us is excused if ever we fail or come short. God has made provision for all that we require, and He will surely expect us to be faithful and true and to measure up to His high calling.

A Quaker lady was approached, one day, by a friend who begged her to pray for her son, who was going down to destruction through the power of drink. The Quaker lady turned to her and said, "Sister, has thee prayed for thy son?" "Oh yes," she said, "I pray as well as I can, but I'm afraid my prayers are not worth much. I want you to pray, for I believe you know how to pray better than I." "Sister, has thee prayed with thy boy?" she again asked. "Why," replied the lady, "I couldn't pray aloud, I should be embarrassed at the sound of my own voice. Why, you don't expect me to pray in public, do you? I'm a woman." "Sister," said the Quaker friend, "what right has thee to be weak, so that thee cannot pray for thy boy? Thee has the same Holy Ghost as I, to be thy power. Sister, I will not pray for thy boy, till thee prays with thy boy." The lady went away, angry, like Naaman of old, and feeling very badly used; but, like Naaman, she came to her senses a little later, and God began to talk to her, and to make her feel that her friend was right; that she ought not to be powerless; that perhaps her boy was going to perdition through her own weakness and unbelief.

There were many tears and much heart-searching and earnest prayers to God for righteousness and help; at length the Holy Ghost came to her heart, and she began to pray for her boy in faith and love. One night, he came home in a drunken stupor, lay down in his room, and was soon fast asleep. But the Spirit drew that mother to his side, and she knelt and laid her hand on his hot brow, and began to smooth his tangled hair and pray to God that He would touch his heart and save her boy. Suddenly, he awoke, and the Holy Ghost sobered him in a moment. He looked up in surprise, and cried, "Mother! you praying for me? Oh God, have mercy on me," and then he broke down in repentance and prayer for his own soul. God heard those united prayers, and before the night was over that boy was saved, and that mother's heart was filled with the Holy Ghost.

"O sister, what right has thee to be weak?" O brother, why should you be ineffective and powerless? "Ye shall receive power after that the Holy Ghost is come upon you, and ye shall be witnesses unto Me." We have said that the Holy Ghost is given alike to all God's servants. Why then was there such a difference? There is a difference in the way that we use the Holy Ghost. He is given to us to use Him, and this is the meaning of that word, "Occupy till I come."

A similar thought is expressed in the twelfth chapter of 1 Corinthians, where the apostle says, "The manifestation of the Spirit is given to every man to profit withal." He is given to us to "profit," to use, to invest, to exercise the divine gift, and thus to grow; and as we use the Holy Ghost, we become accustomed to using Him, and we have great boldness in the faith and work of God; our efficiency increases and multiplies, until the one pound is worth ten, and the servant hands back his trust, tenfold greater than he received it. This is the reason of the difference between men and men. It is a difference of faithfulness. It is a difference of diligence in improving the trust given them. It is a very solemn thing to receive divine power. God invests Himself in men, and God is a great economist of power and is deeply grieved when we waste His treasures; when we let His power lie idle, or sluggishly neglect the mighty trust that has cost Him so much.

Let us use God's precious gifts. Let us be diligent and faithful in the exercise of spiritual things, and, as we do, our faith will grow; our love will increase, and our usefulness will expand until we shall "bring forth some thirty, some sixty, and some an hundredfold."

The word "occupy" in the original is a very striking one. Indeed, even the English word is quite suggestive. It implies that we do not own our gifts, but that they are simply lent to us, and we use them as the gifts of another. It is not your power. It is not your faith, but His, and He lends to you His own divine sufficiency for the special service required of you; when the service is performed, you are no stronger nor wiser than before. You just quietly depend upon Him for His own personal power for the next service and opportunity.

But the word in the original has a still stronger force. It is a word of affairs. It literally means to be engaged in business affairs. The expression, "trading," used later in the parable, expresses the same idea. There is the deepest emphasis in the expression. The Holy Ghost is not restricted to what we call spiritual things, but He is a great business manager. He is a Spirit of practical wisdom and power. He is an all-round Friend, and He wants to be concerned in all the affairs of our life. Indeed, there is nothing secular, but all things that are given to God are sacred, holy and divine.

It is not necessary, therefore, that you should give up your business and go out of the world to serve Him; but let it be God's business, and then it will always be service. God has no better opportunity for glorifying Himself than to use a man in the secular affairs of life, and be as near to him on Monday as on Sunday; in the workshop as in the holy sanctuary and the secret place.

There are plenty of preachers in the world today, but God wants more practitioners. There are many apostles, but Christ is looking for living epistles. There is nothing that speaks more for God than a life spent in the blaze of the world, yet lighted up with holy and heavenly purity and power. Such lives preach to men, whether they want to hear or not.

We are living in a day when the great men of the world are businessmen. The strongest men of the present century are our railroad kings, our bankers, the founders of our immense corporations and commercial enterprises. These men have gigantic intellects and far-reaching power. Why can they not be as mighty for God as they are for the world? Why can they not be as effective on the Board of Missions as they are on the Board of Trade? They can spend their millions for railways and business corporations; what is to hinder their spending their hundreds of millions to spread the Gospel of Christ? Why should the day not come when men of wealth and successful enterprise shall invest, not a few thousand, but ten, twenty, yes, fifty million, for China, Africa and India? I should not eulogize the man who should come to me and say, "I have twenty million I want to spend for evangelizing Central Africa." I should say to him, "You have done just right, but you have been a long time getting at it."

When businessmen come to understand that this is the nature of entire consecration, we shall see greater things than were seen on the day of Pentecost. Then young men will come forward and consecrate their lives to God, and He will give them the millions that belong to Him to spend as grandly for Him, as the men of the world are laying out their treasures for commercial enterprises and gigantic schemes of selfishness and gain. God help us to "occupy" in these practical ways and days, with a view of His coming!

The most encouraging facts which I know today are just such facts as I have spoken of. There are men in this country who are carrying on great commercial enterprizes for the exclusive purpose of devoting the proceeds on a magnificent scale to the evangelizing of the world, and the giving of the Gospel to all nations.

"Occupy till I come." The object of the Holy Ghost and the object of the consecrated believer must always have direct reference to the Lord's personal return. The business of the Holy Spirit is to prepare Christ's people and the world for His second coming. First, this will be done by the spiritual preparation of our own hearts and lives. The Bride must be made ready, and so the Holy Ghost is working out today a wondrous work of sanctifying grace, in the hearts of the chosen few who are willing to hear His call and to prepare for His return.

But this is not all. Our work is also to have reference to His coming. We are "to occupy till He come." We are to accomplish our ministry with direct reference to the millennial reign of Jesus. Our Christian work is to be shaped and molded by this consideration. Oh, what a difference it would make in our methods of service, if we would make this the standpoint and object of all our work for God! Then we should not have 120,000 ministers among sixty million on this continent, and a few hundred among the vaster millions of China.

Oh, if the Holy Ghost had His way, how many of us He would scatter to the uttermost parts of the earth! I think I see Him going through Scotland, and dismissing a thousand preachers, and saying, "Go to India, China, and Africa." I think I see Him entering a western town, where a dozen churches are competing for the scanty population and trying to establish their separate sects. I can hear Him say, "Shut up three-fourths of these places, and send the men to the neglected and destitute fields where no voice speaks of Me."

How much of our Christian work is standing in the way of Christ's will! How much of our best service is not the service of the Holy Ghost, and is not occupying till He come! How long we have delayed Him even by doing good, and not doing it in His way! But we can be looking for His coming even in our business.

It is very beautiful to notice that in the picture given of Christ's return and the translation of His waiting people, they are found occupied in their callings. It is night in one part of the world, and "two are in one bed;" "one is taken, and the other is left. "It is all right to be in bed when Christ comes, if it is night, far better be there than in sin. It is early morning in another place, and "two women are grinding at the mill." One of them is getting her husband's breakfast ready. It is quite right to be found there, and so she is taken right up from her secular occupation. It is midday in another land, and two are in one field working at their harvest. It is all right to be there, too, if the work is done for God. There is no need for them to hurry home and change their clothes. There is no need to go and fix up things. They are "found of Him in peace, without spot and blameless." And so these toiling farmers are taken right up to be with God, and meet their Lord in the air, and to sit down with the wedding robe at the marriage supper of the Lamb.

How beautiful to know that all that is done for God is sacred! How sweet the old story of the New England Legislature; when the storm came on, and some of the members thought that the day of judgment had come, one of them anxiously moved that the house adjourn. An old Puritan sprang to his feet and said, "Mr. Speaker, if the day of judgment has not come, there is no need for this unbecoming haste; and if it has come, I, for one, prefer to be found at my post. I move that the house do not adjourn." Thus let us "occupy" and be occupied with the Master's work, and for His glory and His approval.

Finally, when He comes there will be a just award. The servant that has faithfully used his enduement of power, receives the Master's commendation and is promoted to higher service. I am so glad that the coming of Christ is not going to end our work. I should not want to meet Him if I had to give up working for the Master. Thank God, we shall have higher service through the eternal years. "Be thou ruler over ten cities." Oh, how much greater is the recompense than the service! A city for a pound; ten cities instead of a hundred and fifty dollars!

All our service here is but a training for that higher ministry. How touching to hear the Master say, "Thou hast been faithful over a very little." The man that had gained ten pounds had done "a very little." The highest service we do for God on earth is but "a very little." We are simply playing at service, or rather going to school at it. We are taking lessons in true ministry. The best we do is but childish and trifling, but it is preparing us for the grand service of the ages to come when, with our Lord Himself, endued with His wisdom, power, and glory, we shall be co-workers, perhaps, amid yonder constellations or, on this green earth, to restore it to the beauties and glories of Paradise again, and to rear the eternal temple for which He is now preparing the precious stones.

The Master does not say that they have been successful, but He recognizes them as having been "faithful." God help us at least to be faithful!

The reward will be in proportion to the fidelity of the servant. The servant that had gained tenfold was rewarded tenfold, and the servant that had increased his investment fivefold received only in proportion. Beloved, we are laying up our treasures. We are carving our eternal destiny. We are preparing our immortal crown. Oh, how the days are telling! God help us to be true!

But alas for the servant who came with his pound wrapped up in a napkin! It was nicely kept. It was a clean napkin, perhaps a costly one. He had taken good care of his salvation. He had nursed his blessing, and he gave it back as good as he got it. But was the Master pleased? Alas, alas, for such a servant! "Take from him the pound, and give it unto him that hath ten pounds." He was not lost. He was not destroyed, as the "enemies" of the Master were. He was deprived. He had some place in the kingdom, but he was forever conscious of an opportunity lost, and a life that never would come again. Beloved, we may save our souls, but lose our lives. We may gain an entrance into heaven, but lose our everlasting crown. God help us to be our best!

Not easily shall that crown be won by any. Even the great apostle did not think rashly of his reward, but straining every nerve and reaching forth unto these things that were before as one that had not yet attained, he used this intense language, "If by any manner of means I might attain unto the resurrection from among the dead." So let us so run that we may obtain.

Beloved, we have an eternity before us. We have an unfading crown to win or lose; we have a life in which to win it, and we have the infinite Holy Ghost to enable us for this mighty competition, for this glorious prize, for this divine trust. God help us to be TRUE!

## Chapter 5

## The Holy Ghost in the Gospel of John

"In the last day, that great day of the feast, Jesus stood and cried, saying, If any man thirst, let him come unto Me, and drink. He that believeth on Me, as the Scripture hath said, out of his belly shall flow rivers of living water. But this spake He of the Spirit, which they that believe on Him should receive: for the Holy Ghost was not yet given; because that Jesus was not yet glorified." John 7: 37-39.

In the first seven chapters of the Gospel of John, we have a very striking progressive unfolding of the doctrine of the Holy Ghost; first, in abstract statements of truth, and then, illustrated in a very significant and beautiful miracle.

I. First, we have the Holy Spirit in relation to the Lord Jesus. In John 1: 32, we see the Spirit descending from heaven like a dove, and abiding upon Him, and in John 3: 34, we are further told that God giveth not the Spirit by measure unto Him.

Up to this time all men had received the Spirit by measure; that is, they had received some of His gifts, influences, and power; but Christ received the Spirit Himself in His personal presence and immeasurable fullness, and since then the Spirit has resided in the world in His boundless and infinite attributes.

Christ first received Him as a pattern for His followers, and then gave Him forth to them, from His own very heart, as the Spirit that had resided in Him, and that comes to us softened by His humanity and witnessing to His person.

Therefore we read in the next place not only of Christ's receiving the Spirit, but of Christ's giving the Spirit. In John 1:33, the great forerunner says of Him, "The same is He which baptizeth with the Holy Ghost." It is Christ that baptizeth with the Holy Ghost. It is through Him we receive the Spirit. It is He who "hath shed forth," as the Apostle Peter says, the power from on high, and the Spirit of Pentecost.

This is the peculiarity of the Holy Ghost as He comes to us in the New Testament age. He comes not only from the Father, but especially from the Son, and through the Son, and He comes to us as the Spirit of the Lord Jesus Christ.

II. We next see the Holy Ghost in relation to the believer; first, He is presented to us as the Spirit of regeneration. In John 3, verses 5 and 6, Christ says, "Except a man be born of water and of the Spirit, he cannot enter into the Kingdom of God. That which is born of the flesh is flesh, that which is born of the Spirit is Spirit."

The very first experience of the Christian life is to receive the new heart from the Holy Ghost. The natural man is unable even to see the Kingdom of God, and is powerless to enter. The Holy Ghost creates in us a new life and a new set of spiritual senses altogether, through which we discern, understand, and enter into the life of God and the spiritual realm. "As many as received Him, to them gave He power to become the sons of God, even to them that believe on His name; which were born, not of blood, nor of the will of the flesh, nor of the will of man, but of God."

Next, we see the Holy Ghost in His deeper, and personal indwelling in the heart. In John 4: 14, Christ said to the woman of Samaria, "The water that I shall give him shall be in him a well of water springing up unto everlasting life." This is the indwelling of the Holy Spirit. It is much more than regeneration. It is the personal incoming of the Spirit Himself, bringing not a cup of water, but a well of water, and establishing in the heart the fountain of life, so that we are henceforth dependent, not upon each other, but upon God only, for the source of our life.

Again in John 7: 37, we have a still stronger expression to describe the interior life of the Holy Ghost in the heart; "If any man thirst, let him come unto Me, and drink." Drinking of the Spirit is more than receiving the Spirit. It is possible for us to receive the Spirit and have Him, and yet not use Him nor drink from the flowing fountain as abundantly as we might.

The Apostle in 1 Cor. 12: 13 uses the same figures where he says, "By one Spirit are ye all baptized into one body, . . . and have been all made to drink into one Spirit." To use the old figure, it is the bottle in the ocean and the ocean in the bottle. It is possible for us to be in the Spirit, and yet not be receiving the Spirit as fully as we need. Drinking is the habit of faith, an exercise of our spiritual senses which constantly renews and quickens our spiritual life, refreshing us and filling us, so that we are glad to pour out our full vessel in service for others.

Then this receiving of the Spirit needs, on our part as well as on Christ's, the using and giving forth of the Holy Ghost to others. And so we read in the next verse, "He that believeth on Me, as the Scripture hath said, out of his belly shall flow rivers of living water. But this spake He of the Spirit, which they that believe on Him should receive." This is the outflow of the spiritual life. This is the evidence that we are filled, because we cannot hold it longer, and now occupy ourselves in imparting the blessing to others. Like Ezekiel's river, it is flowing not in, but out, pouring in streams of blessing through the dry and desert places of life. As soon as our life becomes positive, unselfish, and outflowing, it becomes unspeakably magnified; so that what was a well, in the heart, has grown to rivers of blessing, in the life devoted to God and expended in blessing the world.

The river suggests the idea of fullness, magnitude, and abundance; spontaneous, free, and overflowing, it does not need to be pumped but flows of itself for very fullness. It is the service of a glad, unselfish and loving heart.

God does not want anything that has to be pressed from an unwilling giver. The prayer that is offered God from a sense of duty, the work that is done just because we have to do it, the word that is spoken because we are expected to be ministers and to be consistent with our profession, are dead, cold, and comparatively worthless. True service springs from a full and joyful heart and runs over, like the broad and boundless river. Like the river, too, it runs downward into the lowest places and aims to reach the saddest, hardest, and most hopeless cases. And, like the river, it is a perennial and ever flowing spring, running on amid the changing scenes around it, flowing through the whole course of life, and saying, like the beautiful streamlet as it glides along, "Men may come, and men may go, but I go on forever."

This is the power of the Holy Ghost. It makes us simple, sweet, exuberant, full-hearted, and enthusiastic for God, and our work, and our words are the overflow of a life so deep and full that it brings its own witnesses, and it makes others long for the blessing that shines in our faces and speaks in our voices and springs in our glad and buoyant steps. And it is not merely a river, but rivers. It runs wherever it can find a channel and blesses every life that it touches on its way. Is God thus using us, and has He thus filled us with the Holy Ghost until the fullness overflows?

It is not necessary that we should be always preaching. Indeed, sometimes we are looking too far off for the service that God expects of us. Just at hand we might often find the opening and the channel which would bring blessing to some heart that God has brought into our life, to prepare us for future blessing to a wider circle.

An anxious, earnest Christian woman was crying to God for service and wondering why she was tied up in her home and unable, like other women, to go out and reach a broader place. Her bright little girl was playing beside her and calling in vain to the preoccupied mother to help her with her little doll, which had lost a finger or a garment, and which to her was the central object of life.

Again and again she came to the mother with her little trouble, and the mother, fretted and worried with her own spiritual need, pushed her off, and, at length, rather harshly sent her away and told her not to bother her, as she was busy about higher things. Wearied and disappointed, the little one went off alone into a corner and sat down with her little broken doll and cried herself to sleep.

A while afterward, that mother turned around and saw the little rosy cheeks covered with tears, and the little wrecked doll lying in her bosom, and then God spake to her, and said, "My child, in seeking some higher service for Me, you have broken a little heart of Mine. You wanted to do something for Me. That little child was the messenger I sent, and that little service was the test I gave you. He that is faithful in that which is least is faithful also in more, and he that is unfaithful in the least is unfit for the greater."

The mother learned her lesson. She picked up the little lamb in her arms and kissed her awake; then she asked God and her baby to forgive her, and began from that hour to pour out the love of Christ on every object that came in her way. As she became faithful to do the things nearest at hand, God widened her sphere until the day came when, standing among her sisters, leading the on to higher service and speaking to hundreds and thousands of her fellow-workers, she told the story of her experience, and the lesson by which she learned that God does not need our great service, but simply that we should meet Him in the things that He brings to us, and that we should everywhere be channels of blessing and love.

So let our lives be filled, and then emptied throughout the channels around us. Let us come to Him, and drink and drink again, and yet again, until our hearts are so full that we shall go out to find the sad, the sinning, and the suffering and comfort them with the comfort wherewith we ourselves are comforted of God.

This was the story of the Master. This must be the story of the disciple. We receive that we may give, and only as we give, shall we continue to receive; the more abundantly we impart, the more richly shall we be filled with all the fullness of God.

III. Let us now look at a beautiful object lesson of this double truth in the second chapter of this blessed Gospel. It is the miracle of Cana of Galilee. The evangelist tells us that this was the first of Christ's miracles, and it must have had a special significance. He also tells us that it was a miracle which manifested forth His glory, and this undoubtedly suggests to us that there was some deep lesson back of this miracle, which made it worthy to occupy a place right in the beginning of the deeply spiritual teaching of this wonderful gospel. Indeed, it is a kind of parable and symbol of the whole truth which we have been endeavoring to unfold from the direct teaching of the Lord Jesus Christ in the passages which we have quoted.

1. We see the failure of our natural life, joy, and love, in the exhausting of Cana's wine. Beautiful, indeed, is the bridal scene with its fair and fragrant blossoms, the freshness and beauty of youth, the vigor and nobility of young manhood, the sympathy of innumerable friends, and the bright and sunny hopes and prospects of future happiness. But oh, how soon the vision fails! How quickly the goblet of pleasure is drained, and how often the serpent is left in the dregs, and all that remains is a memory more bitter because of the joy that has turned to sadness!

Alas for life, if this were all! But it is just when the natural fails, that the divine begins. It is just when the old creation dies, that the new creation rises. It is just when Cana's wine is exhausted, that Jesus of Nazareth appears. And now we see in this exquisite miracle the very truths we have been endeavoring to unfold.

2. Next we have the filling of the vessels. The Master's command is, "Fill the waterpots with water to the brim." They were just earthen vessels, waterpots for ordinary use; but they were empty and clean, and all that was necessary was to fill them with pure water. They represent these vessels of our human lives, earthen vessels; but if they are empty vessels and offered to the Master, and if they are filled to the brim with the Holy Ghost, of which water is ever the type, then something will surely come to pass.

They must be full to the brim. A whole heart must receive a whole Christ. The Holy Ghost does not take us by halves, nor will He give Himself by halves. It is the fullness which makes the overflow.

3. Next comes the other and nobler side of the miracle. The filling is the smallest part. What next? "Draw out now, and bear to the governor of the feast." Begin to use the water, and lo! it becomes wine.

Oh! how clear and plain the lesson! It is blessed to receive the Holy Ghost, but it is more blessed to impart Him. And the only way you will know that you have received Him, is by beginning to give Him. You must go forward like the servants of the parable, in faith, and draw out before you see the miracle; but as you bear it to the guests, lo, it becomes wine, and it rises to a higher quality. Both are types of the Holy Ghost, but the wine is the higher. The water speaks of cleansing and fullness, but the wine tells of joy, and love, and life divine.

When we are receiving the Holy Ghost we are only cold water Christians, but when we are pouring forth His fullness in holy service we are drinking of the heavenly wine, and we are made partakers of the Master's own divine and ineffable joy.

It is exactly the same idea expressed later in the rivers of living water, running out, and running over; but it is more than the river. It is the joy and the gladness that turns all life into a marriage feast and a joyful song. Even the world itself is forced to admit, like the ruler of Cana's wedding, that the best wine has come last.

Oh, that we might so live and so minister that men would recognize, even as he, the higher qualities and value of the blessing that He brings! All around us are hearts and lives where the wine of earth has failed, God help us to bring them the heavenly cup, and the divine life of the Lord Jesus Christ, until this poor, starving world shall recognize that we have something better than they, and shall be made hungry by our benignant faces and our overflowing joy.

Now, in conclusion, how are we to receive this blessing? Let us hearken to the message of Mary. "Whatsoever He saith unto thee, do it." It comes to us through some step of obedience to the Master Himself. He will show you the way, and as you obey Him step by step, you will enter into the joy of your Lord. He will interpret every experience and more than realize every anticipation.

But next, you must not forget the other command, "Fill the water pots with water; fill them to the brim." Leave no vacant place in the soul. Hold back no part of your life from Him. Yield a whole heart and fill it with a whole Christ.

And then finally, above all else, go forward and use the gift of His love. "Draw out, and bear to the governor of the feast." Take the life that He has given and use it to comfort the sorrowing, save the lost, help the discouraged, and minister in the name and grace of your blessed Master; as you go forth, the Holy Ghost will go before you, and will work through you, and lead you on from strength to strength, and will multiply you one hundred fold, until, like Ezekiel's vision, the trickling streamlet will become "water to the ankles," "water to the knees," "water to the loins," "water over head, a river to swim in," a torrent of blessing and of power, with the trees of life on either shore, the leaves of healing, and the gladness and the glory of Paradise restored all along your way.

## Chapter 6

## The Comforter

"And I will pray the Father, and he shall give you another Comforter, that he may abide with you forever." John 14: 16.

These three chapters contain Christ's deepest teachings concerning the Holy Ghost.

I. THE NAME, THE COMFORTER. This is not a very happy translation. The Greek word is Paraclete, and it literally means a God at hand, One by our side, One that we may call upon in every emergency. The Latin word, advocate, has the same meaning, One that we call upon or call to us, One ever within call. In this connection, the Holy Ghost is represented to us as the present and all sufficient God. Of course, there is comfort, infinite comfort in all this; but the primary idea is not so much spiritual enjoyment, as practical efficiency and sufficiency for every occasion and emergency that arises.

This is just what the Holy Ghost is — God for everything. God at hand under all circumstances and equal to all demands. Oh, what comfort this brings to our oppressed and struggling life! A God able to make all grace abound to us; so that we, always having all-sufficiency in all things, may abound unto every good work.

II. MODE OF HIS PRESENCE. He shall be in you. "He dwelleth with you, and shall be in you." The presence of God, through the Old Testament and even during the ministry of Christ, was a presence with men; but in the New Testament dispensation and after the coming of the Holy Ghost, it was to be a presence in men.

The Holy Ghost was to become corporately united and identified with the life of the believer, so that He would bring us into direct personal union, and act, not upon us, but in us and through us, becoming part of our very life, and controlling every faculty, volition, and power, from the inmost depths of our being. This is the difference between the two classes of Christians we find today; those who have God with them, and those who have Him in them.

It may not be possible to explain it. It certainly is impossible to make spiritual mysteries plain to any that have not experienced them. It is difficult to explain how the sunshine enters into the midst of the flower and manifests itself in all the living beauties and tints of the blossom; how the water saturates the ground and comes forth again in the leaf, and laden fruit; how the influence and image and personality of a friend becomes a part of our very being, until we think as he thinks, and act under his influence. These are but distant approximations to the blessed mystery of the Holy Ghost's entering, as a Person, into the life and being of a consecrated disciple and controlling every choice, affection, thought and action, and thus fulfilling His own promise, "I will dwell in you and walk in you," "And I will put My Spirit within you, and I will cause you to walk in My statutes, and ye shall keep My judgments, and do them."

III. THE DURATION OF THIS ABIDING. "He shall abide with you forever."

The Holy Ghost comes to stay. He seals the heart into the day of redemption. He takes possession of it to depart no more. We may grieve Him; we may lose the consciousness of His approval; but He has loved us with an everlasting love, and we are kept by His power through faith unto salvation.

There are some who tell us that the Holy Ghost will leave the world at the coming of Christ. This is not the promise of the Master. "He shall abide with you forever." Even when Jesus comes, He will still remain. For through those dark tribulation days, there will be souls on earth that need His consolation, His keeping and His help; He will linger with them through the darkness, and then, through the millennial age, He will cooperate with Christ as He did during the days of His earthly ministry, in bringing this world into harmony with the will of God, and establishing the dominion of righteousness throughout the utmost limits of the creation.

We do not dishonor the work of the Spirit when we pray for Christ to come. The grandest theatre of His work will be in these millennial days, for which we are looking forward with longing and prayer.

IV. HIS RELATION TO JESUS CHRIST. "Whom the Father will send in My name," that is, in My character, to represent Me. He will be "another Comforter." He is to correspond in His relation to us to what Christ was, but He is to be a substitute for Christ, a successor to Christ, and, indeed, more to us than Christ could continue to be. "It is expedient for you that I go away: for if I go not away, the Comforter will not come; but if I depart, I will send Him unto you."

Oh, how precious His presence must be, if it can be more than Christ's presence was! Can we conceive how much Jesus was to these disciples? More than a mother to her child, more than a shepherd to his flock, more than a guide through the pathless desert, more than a pilot on the trackless ocean.

The disciples had leaned upon Him, lived upon Him, and were utterly dependent upon Him for everything, and yet He says, "It is better for you that I go, for One will come that will be more to you than I have been in all these relationships."

Beloved, is the Comforter more to us than Jesus was to His Galilean followers? Ah, then how much more you have to learn of His intimacy and His ministry. Is He to you the Counselor and Companion of every moment, the Leader and the Guide of every step, the Teacher of all you know, the Substance of all you believe, the Source of all your strength and joy and life? This He wants to be. Christ could only be present in one place; but He can be everywhere. Christ spoke to them from outside their natures, He speaks from within. Christ was to a certain extent a physical presence; He in a spiritual, that enters into the deepest life of our being, blends with every consciousness and every thought and every capacity and feeling.

Was He so to supersede and substitute Christ as to displace Him? Not at all. On the contrary, He was to make Christ more real than He had ever been. Here is the great mistake that many are liable to make in their zeal for the honor of the Holy Ghost. They represent Christ as far away at the right hand of God, and they think they honor the Spirit when they exclude the personal presence of the Master.

This was not the way the Savior taught, and this is not the way the Spirit comes. Nay, listen, "He shall testify of Me, He shall not speak of Himself." "I will not leave you comfortless, I will come to you." "At that day ye shall know that I am in the Father, and ye in Me, and I in you."

"He that hath my commandments, and keepeth them, he it is that loveth me; and he that loveth me shall be loved of my Father, and I will love him, and will manifest myself to him. If a man love me he will keep my words; and my Father will love him, and we will come unto him, and make our abode with him."

It is not possible to read these verses and not see that the personal and conscious presence of Jesus Christ is to be ever with His people through the ministry of the Comforter. Indeed, the great business of the Holy Ghost is to stand behind the scenes and make Jesus real. Just as the telescope reveals not itself, but the stars beyond, so Christ is revealed by the blessed Spirit, as the medium of our spiritual vision.

Just as the atmosphere can bring yonder sun down until he is nearer to us here than if we went up into the air to meet him, so the Holy Ghost, God's divine medium for the revelation of spiritual realities, brings Christ from the throne, until distance is annihilated and space has no power to divide.

Surely, if a human telephone or telegraph can sweep at a flash or by a wave of sound across intervening space and bring the distant near, it is not hard for the divine Author of light and life, and all creation, to open a line of communication from earth to heaven, so that we may dwell in the heavenlies, and the living realities of that world be within whispering distance of our quickened souls.

It is even so. Through the telephone of prayer, we may catch the very voice of our absent Master, and be conscious of the heartthrobs of His love; we may even go on into the presence of the spirits of the just made perfect, and almost hear the songs that echo around the throne. Yes, He is with us still, "all the days even unto the end of the age." The presence of the Comforter but makes Him nearer and dearer, and enables us to realize and know that we are in Him, and He in us.

V. THE SPIRIT AS A TEACHER. Not only does He reveal the person of Christ, but He reveals the truth which Christ only began to teach. "He will guide you into all truth, He will teach you all things." "Ihave many things to say unto you, but ye cannot bear them now, howbeit when He, the Spirit of truth, is come, He will guide you into all truth; for He shall not speak of His own knowledge; but that which He shall hear He shall speak."

And so the Holy Ghost, the Author of the Scriptures, is the Illuminator and Teacher of the Word. He makes the truth clear, intelligible, and intensely real, just as you have seen on some great occasion the metal frames, where some grand illumination was to take place; and it seemed to you, in the light of day, that the forms of men and the figures of crowns and stars and processions could be dimly traced in that network of leaden pipes, erected above the triumphal arch, but it was dull and dim to you and made little impression upon your senses or your mind. But wait till evening, till the sun goes down, and a flash of light bursts over that dead framework. Lo! in a moment it is lighted up, and you see the figure of the military hero, the glowing crown with its many colored jewels, the procession of living forms and all the pageant of a grand triumph. The light has done it all.

And so this Holy Book needs to be lighted up by the Holy Ghost, and then we do not read the Bible from a sense of duty; it speaks to us as the living message from our Master, the love letter of our Bridegroom's heart.

Then how gentle and patient the Holy Ghost is in teaching us! He will guide us into all truth. He knows how fast we can go, and He does not cram us; but He unites the word to the action, and the action to the word, and fits His teaching into the framework of our lives, making truth real, day by day, "line upon line, precept upon precept, here a little and there a little," until He has led us on to the graduating class, and fitted us for the more mature tasks of the school of faith.

How much He left to be revealed in the later epistles and the Apocalypse that they could not then endure! And how much truth He keeps back from us, until we are ready not only to understand it, but fully to obey it and translate it into the living characters of our experience!

VI. THE HOLY GHOST AS A REMINDER OF TRUTH. "He shall bring all things to your remembrance whatsoever I have said unto you."

Not only does He teach us, but He quickens our intellect to remember and to learn. He is the Author and the Illuminator of the mind, and He is the Spirit of suggestion. He knows how to bring back forgotten truths in the moment of need. He knows how to suggest the promise in the time of depression. He knows how to say, "It is written," and put into our hand the sword of the Spirit, when the adversary's wiles are trying and perplexing us.

He knows how to "waken our ear, morning by morning, to hear as one that's been instructed, that we might know how to speak a word in season to Him that is weary." He knows how to give the appropriate message for the fitting time, and then to bless it and send it home with lasting power.

Let us trust Him to guide us, to speak through us, triumph through us, and to be our monitor and mother until all the mazes of life shall have been passed.

VII. THE HOLY SPIRIT AS THE SPIRIT OF POWER FOR SERVICE. "He will convict the world of sin, and of righteousness, and of judgment." We can rebuke the world but He alone can convict it.

He can make our expression, our words, our actions, awaken in the hearts of men a sense of sin, and a realization of eternity.

He can bring the message to the conscience and press the will to the great decision, and make our words vehicles for His power. Then He alone can convict of righteousness, and so reveal Christ that it shall not be merely reformation and self-improvement, but true repentance, faith and reliance upon the finished work of Jesus Christ. He can convict the world of judgment. He can pass sentence of death on self, sin, and the world, and separate men from this present evil world for the kingdom of our Lord Jesus Christ.

He can take men out of the power of the prince of this world, and introduce them into the kingdom of God's dear Son. He can give victory over Satan and finish the work which He begins.

Oh, how helpless all our work without Him! Oh, how He waits to show us the great things that He is willing yet to do, not only for us but for the world!

Finally, He is the Spirit of hope, and the promise and the realization of the future. He will show you things to come.

Oh, how this promise was to be fulfilled in the later teachings of the epistles and the Apocalypse, concerning the blessed hope of the Lord's coming! And the same Spirit that has given the light of prophecy, can give the light of interpretation and the life of faith and living hope! He alone can make these things real to us; He alone can center our hopes and hearts in the blessed hope of Christ's coming, and the throne of His Ascension.

It is not enough merely to know that Christ is coming, and to desire it, but it is a great crisis in the life of a soul when it becomes truly centered there, when the source of attraction is removed from the earth to the heavens, and when it learns to live under the power of the world to come. It is one thing to be lifting up the world from the earth side, it is another thing to be drawing up the world from the heaven side. It is one thing to be a man on the earth, living for the glory; it is another thing to be a man in the glory, living for the world. We must be taken out of the world first, and then sent back into it, to be any blessing to it.

The reason that Christ knew how to live was because He did not belong here. The Father had sent Him from heaven, and we must be sent from heaven, too, and work on earth as men that dwell in heaven. Oh, may the Spirit so show us things to come that we shall have our center in the throne of our ascended Lord, and with Him see and live and work to save the world in which, for a little while, we sojourn!

## Chapter 7

## Waiting for The Spirit

"Tarry ye in the city of Jerusalem, until ye be endued with power from on high." "Wait," saith He, "for the promise of the Father, which ye have heard of Me." "And when the day of Pentecost was fully come, they were all with one accord in one place."

These three passages all suggest a single and very definite thought — waiting on God for the filling of the Holy Ghost. The law of time is an important factor both in nature and in grace. There are some operations which are instantaneous, but there are many more that require the lapse of time and the process of development. The principle of vegetation is gradual, unfolding first the blade, then the ear, after that the full corn in the ear. Winter is as needful as spring to fertilize the ground, and the seed must lie silent in the soil until it germinates and springs into the blade and the blossom.

And so, in the spiritual world, there is a place for waiting. God's work of creation was not instantaneous but successive. The promise of the coming Redeemer waited for four thousand years. Abraham waited for the fulfillment of the promise of his son. Moses waited forty years before he could go forth to the great work of His life. Jesus waited for thirty years to begin His public ministry.

The promises of God are for those that wait for Him; and the spiritual life which, in some respects is instantaneous in its operations, in others, is progressive. There is a moment when we definitely receive the Holy Ghost; but there is a preparation for His coming, and a waiting for His fullness for us, just as much as for Jesus and Moses. Doubtless there is a sense in which they waited, which cannot be true of us. For them the Holy Ghost was not yet sent from heaven. The day of Pentecost was the moment of His arrival on earth. Up to that moment He had resided in the person of Jesus, now He was to reside in his Body, the Church, and the earth was to be His home. In that sense we cannot wait for the coming of the Comforter, for He has come and He is here.

But even if the Holy Ghost had come to earth already, that very same command would still have been given to the disciples to wait in the upper room. There was a preparation on their part, just as necessary as the Spirit's coming from heaven to earth. And there is a preparation on our part just as necessary in these days.

It is important, however, that we understand the true nature of this waiting. It is not waiting for the Lord, but it is waiting on the Lord. It is not looking forward to a distant blessing, but it is continuing in the attitude of receiving and claiming the blessing, and giving time for the Holy Spirit to fill the waiting heart with all His fullness.

It is more than expectation of a future blessing. It is rather accepting a present blessing, and yet a blessing so large and full, that it cannot be taken by us in all its completeness in a moment of time, but requires the opening of every vessel of our being, and the continuance of our heart in the attitude of receiving.

The Master is calling us, as He called them to these seasons of waiting, and there are deep reasons in the principles that underlie all Christian experience, which will show the importance and necessity of our thus waiting on the Lord.

I. This season of waiting on the Lord was fitted and designed to mark a great transition in their lives, an epoch of spiritual new departure, an era of the chronology of the heart. God wants His people to have such epochs and such eras.

As we read the records of geology we find that the surface of our globe has been formed by successive layers, between which can be traced successive breaks. There is a stratum of rock, and then there is a stratum of wreck and conglomerate masses, between the layers of previous strata.

It is so in spiritual life. These days of waiting lead us to new planes and new advances. Sometimes it is very desirable that there should be a complete break, that we may get out of the old ruts, and be free to take a higher place, and make a bolder advance.

In music one of the most effective things is the emphatic pause. The word "Selah" in the book of Psalms expresses this pause, and in order to have the effectiveness of such a pause it cannot be too complete a silence. Then the chorus which follows has a double emphasis. And so the Holy Ghost has given us our Selahs in the chorus of spiritual life, emphatic pauses when God wants us to be still and listen to Him, and break away from old ideas and measures, and reach out into the larger fullness of His thought and will.

II. This time of waiting on God was also necessary in order to teach them the greatest lesson of the Christian life — to cease from themselves. The greatest danger about these men was not in what they might fail to do, but in what they might try to do. The greatest harm that we can do is the attempt to do anything at all when we are not prepared, and when we do not understand our Master's will. Suppose a regiment of soldiers should start off without their captain's orders, or their necessary equipment or artillery; the next attempt of the army would be rendered more hopeless by their rash exposure and needless failure.

And so the Master wants to keep us from doing anything, until we are prepared to go forth in His strength and victory. Our hardest lesson to learn is to unlearn, and to know our utter helplessness and wretchedness.

The deepest experience into which they had to enter was self-crucifixion, and crucifixion is the death not only of the evil self, but of the strong and self-sufficient self.

Peter had not yet learned to be still, for before these waiting days were over we find him rushing again to the front, and proposing the election of a new disciple, without the divine direction or recognition. The best that can be said of his work is that it did no harm if it did no good, for God never afterwards seems to have recognized the apostle that Peter led the brethren to choose, but in His own time He called His own apostle.

And so it was necessary that these days should be spent in waiting and learning to be silent, and forming the habit of the suspension of our own activity, and the dependence of our will entirely upon the direction of the Holy Ghost. There are times when the most masterly thing we can exercise is inactivity, and there are times when the most mischievous thing we can do is to do anything at all.

That is a most instructive story that is told of the nervous passenger on board a vessel in a dangerous storm, who was running about the deck in every direction, and asking the captain what he could do to save the ship from going to the bottom; at last the captain, more alarmed by him than by the tempest, fearing that he would drive the passengers into a panic, called him to his side and said, "Yes, you can help me immensely if you will just hold that rope hard and firm; and don't let it go until I tell you!" He eagerly grasped the rope and held it tight and steady until the storm was past, and then he walked about the deck boasting that he had saved the ship, until the captain, hearing of this, came up and, looking at him with a twinkle in his eye, said, "Why, do you know the reason I gave you that rope to hold was to keep you quiet? The only good you did by holding on so steadily was that you were kept from doing any mischief."

Ah, how much mischief we do by doing our own work! How long it took God to teach Abraham to be still! How long Abraham tried to help God to the fulfillment of His own promise! Then he got Sarah into his counsel, and then he took Hagar into partnership, and out of it came Ishmael. Out of Ishmael came nothing but sorrow and hindrance, until, after a quarter of a century had been spent, God quietly fulfilled His own promise in His own way.

How long it took Moses to learn to be still! Forty years he had to wait in the desert until all his young-mannishness had died, and his precocious activity had been changed into modesty and even timidity; then, when Moses shrank back and asked God to send someone else, Moses was small enough and still enough for God to use for His people's deliverance. And so, when he came to the gates of deliverance, his first lesson was to "stand still and see the salvation of God;" to do nothing but wait for Him, and then God stepped upon the scene, and did the work Himself.

God cannot use us until we come to the end of ourselves, and see our utter worthlessness, and helplessness, and then put on His mighty strength, and go forth, crying, "I am not sufficient even to think anything as of myself; but my sufficiency is of God."

III. These waiting days were necessary to enable the disciples to realize their need, their nothingness, their failure and their dependence upon the Master. They had to get emptied first, before they could get filled. Oh, how often they must have thought, as those days went by, of the positions they were now to occupy, the responsibility that was resting upon them, the charge that the Master had committed to them, and their utter inability for it all! How they must have recalled their folly, their unbelief, their strife, their selfishness, their fears, their defeats, and shrunk back into nothingness, and even stood aghast at the prospect before them, until in the very dust they cried to Him for help and strength needed.

And so God wants us to go apart and quietly wait upon Him, until He searches into the depths of our being, and shows us our folly, our failures, our need. There is no wiser nor better thing to do on the eve of a season of blessing than to make an inventory, not of our riches, but of our poverty; to count up all the voids and vacuums and places of insufficiency; to make the valley full of ditches, and then to bring to God the depths of our need for Him to fill.

And it takes time to make this work thorough. It takes time to burn it into our consciousness. It takes time to make us feel it. It is one thing to know in a general way our need and failure; it is quite another thing to realize it, to mourn over it, to be distressed about it, and to be filled with sorrow and shame and that holy zeal and revenge upon ourselves which the apostle tells us is part of true repentance.

In the golden stairway of the Beatitudes, the first promise is to those that are poor in spirit; but there is another step still deeper down on the way to God, and that is "Blessed are they that mourn." It is needful that we shall mourn over our poverty, that we shall realize our need, that we shall be deeply troubled over our spiritual wretchedness, and that we shall come with such hunger that nothing less than all the fullness of Christ can ever satisfy us again.

There are some spiritual conditions that cannot be accomplished in a moment. The breaking up of the fallow ground takes time; the frosts of winter are as necessary as the rains of spring to prepare the soil for fertility. God has to break our hearts to pieces by the slow processes of His discipline, and grind every particle to powder, and then to mellow us, and saturate us with His blessed Spirit, until we are open for the blessing He has to give us. Oh, let us wait upon the Lord with brokenness of heart, with openness of soul, with willingness of spirit, to hear what God the Lord will say!

IV. These days of waiting are important also that we may listen to God's voice. We are so busy that we cannot hear. We talk so much that we give Him no chance to talk to us. He wants us to hearken to what He has to say to us. He wants us on our faces before Him, that He may give us His thought, His prayer, His longing, and then lead us into His better will.

And if He keeps us waiting long, we know the message when it comes will be worth all the delay. "If He tarry, let us wait for

Him." Only a few times did He speak to Abraham. Only a few times did He speak to Paul. But these were messages that will live forever, and their echoes have sounded through all the years, and will resound from the ages yet to come.

Let us wait upon God, not so much in prayer as in hearkening.

V. God wants us to wait upon Him also that we may realize not only our need, but His fullness and His will for us. He wants to show us the vision of the future as well as of the past. He wants to open to us the treasures of His grace, and make us know all the riches of the glory of His inheritance in us.

He wants to lift up our eyes northward and southward and eastward and westward, and then say to us, "All the land which thou seest, to thee will I give it."

He wants to give us the vision of the King in His beauty and the land of far distances. He wants to reveal to us yet unexplored regions of glorious advances in the life of faith. He wants to call us to higher service, and show us mightier resources and enabling for the work of life.

Oh, it is so sweet to wait upon the Lord and dwell on high, to survey the mountain peaks of His glorious grace and look out on the boundless fullness of His promises and His power, and to hear Him say, "Call unto Me, and I will answer thee, and show thee" not merely the things thou hast seen, but "great and hidden things which thou knowest not!"

This is the waiting to which He is calling us today. God grant that these days before us may bring the vision, and then the victory!

VI. Waiting on the Lord is not only a preparation for the Holy Spirit, but is a process of receiving the Holy Spirit. There is a cumulative power in waiting prayer to bring the answer and the blessing, breath by breath and moment by moment. God's blessing is too vast and our capacity is too great to be filled in a moment. We must drink, and drink, and drink again, and yet again, if we would know all the fullness of the river of His grace.

Take an ash barrel, and begin to pour into it a bucket of water, and your whole bucket will be exhausted before the water has made the slightest impression; the ashes will be as dry as at first, and you can pour bucket after bucket, and still the ashes be as dry as ever. It is only when the barrel has been filled that at last you see the first trace of the water you have been pouring in. That ash heap was so dry that it could only be saturated by degrees from the bottom upwards; and it is only when the whole body has been saturated, that the first evidence appears.

And so our hearts are so dry, that we need to wait upon the Lord for days and days before there is any impression. But all the while the dry ground is filling, and the thirsty soil is absorbing, and after the waiting is completed we shall know that it was not in vain; we shall realize that not one breath of prayer was vainly spent; we shall find that every moment was storing up the treasures of His grace and power in the depths of our being.

Beloved, we do not wait enough upon the Lord. We do not spend sufficient time at the Mercy Seat. We allow the rush and hurry of life to drive us off, and we lose time instead of gaining it, by our reckless haste.

Yes, that is an instructive old story about the horseman pursued by his foes, who found his trusted charger beginning to fail in the race, for one of the shoes upon his feet had been detached, and he was slipping upon the rocky path. Suddenly the horseman dismounted at the blacksmith shop, where the two ways met, and although he could see his pursuers over yonder hill, bearing down upon him, yet he waited long enough to shoe his horse. He called to the blacksmith, "Be quick," as he threw him a coin of tenfold value; and the sweating workman filed and hammered and clinched the nails, and did his work fast and well. And when the last nail was turned, and the fugitive leaped into his saddle, the hoofs of his pursuers were thundering just behind him, and he heard their shouts of triumph, as they felt they had secured their prey.

But no! he leaped into his saddle, plunged his spurs into his horse's haunches, and dashed away like the lightning, because he was now prepared for the journey.

Ah yes, he gained by losing time, and would have lost all by going before he was prepared. O, beloved, "Tarry ye in the city of Jerusalem, until ye be endued with power from on high." "Wait for the promise of the Father, which ye have heard of Him." "In quietness and confidence shall be your strength."

Without the Holy Ghost you are unequal to the journey of life; you are unfit for the service of the Master; you are unwarranted in attempting to preach the gospel, or to win a soul for Christ, and you are unprepared for the future which He is immediately opening to you. Oh, let us wait at His feet; let us learn our weakness; let us realize our nothingness; let us get emptied for His filling, and then baptized with the Holy Ghost or filled anew with His utmost fullness; and we shall go forth not to our work, but to His, and find that "He is able to do exceeding abundantly above all that we ask or think, according to the power that worketh in us. To whom be glory now and forever. Amen."

## Chapter 8

## Power from On High

"Ye shall receive the power of the Holy Ghost coming upon you; and ye shall be witnesses unto me both in Jerusalem, and in all Judea, and in Samaria, and unto the uttermost part of the earth." Acts 1:8.

The greatest need of human nature is power. Man is weaker than all other creatures. The tiger's cub is able to take care of itself, but the human being spends one-third of an ordinary lifetime before he reaches maturity.

He is the prey of all the elements around him, and morally he is much weaker still. In his heart are elements of evil that drag him downward, and around him a thousand influences that lead him astray.

There is unspeakable pathos in the cry of a poor, sinning woman who once said in a hospital, as we were pleading with her to do right: "I am not strong enough to be good;" there is infinite comfort in that blessed assurance of the Holy Scriptures, "When we were yet without strength, in due time Christ died for the ungodly."

The gospel is a message of strength. "It is the power of God unto salvation, to every one that believeth." It is the special ministry of the Holy Ghost to give power from on high. How much is signified in this mighty promise? How far have we come short of His fullness? How far may we claim its fulfillment?

We cannot find a better answer than in the book of Acts. This verse is the keynote and the table of contents. Every word in this verse points forward to a whole section of the book which follows.

The first chapter of Acts tell us the story of the power. The next chapters tell us of the witnessing which followed. Then we have the church in Jerusalem. Then we have the gospel in all Judea. Then we have the story of Samaria. And finally, the closing chapters are wholly devoted to the preaching of the gospel unto the uttermost part of the earth.

We shall not attempt now to trace the unfolding of this order through the book of Acts, but shall simply endeavor to illustrate the meaning of this word "power" by the facts and incidents of the story of the apostolic church, as given in the book of Acts, which is really the story of the acts of the Holy Ghost more than the acts of the apostles.

I. THIS IS THE POWER OF A PERSON. The right translation is, ye shall receive not power, but the power of the Holy Ghost coming upon you. It is not your power, but His power. It is not abstract power under your control, but it is a Person, whose presence with you is necessary to your possessing and retaining the power.

He has the power and you have Him. In the science of electricity, it has been found that the best form in which this motive power can be used to run our street cars, is not through storage batteries, but through overhead wires. The power is not stored up in the car, but in the dynamo and the wire, and the car just draws it from above by constant contact, and the moment it lets go its touch the power is gone. The power is not in the car, but in the wire.

And so the power of the Holy Ghost is power from above. It is not our power, but His, and received from Him moment by moment.

In order to receive this power and retain it, there are certain conditions which are necessary. One of them is that we shall obey Him and follow His directions. We can only have His power in the line of His will. The car can only draw the power from the wire in so far as it follows the track. It can have the power to run along the highway, but it cannot have it to run into the neighboring farms and follow the capricious will of the driver. The Holy Ghost is given to them that obey Him, and obedience to the Holy Ghost is a much larger thing than many dream.

It is not merely to keep from doing wrong in some little contracted sphere; but it is to understand and follow the whole will and purpose of God in the use of this divine enduement. We cannot have it to please ourselves. We cannot have it to please ourselves even in the mode of our Christian work. We can only enjoy the fullness of the Spirit, in so far as we use this fullness for the work to which He has called us.

This verse is the measure and the limit of the Spirit's power. He is given that we shall be witnesses unto Christ, both "in Jerusalem, and in all Judea, and in Samaria, and unto the uttermost part of the earth."

We can only know the fullness of the Spirit's power as we use it to give the gospel to the whole world. Only in the line of the world's evangelization and the fulfillment of our great trust can the church of God ever realize the utmost meaning of the promise of Pentecost.

II. IT IS THE POWER OF HOLY CHARACTER. It is not primarily power for service, but it is power to receive the life of Christ; power to be, rather than to say and to do. Our service and testimony will be the outcome of our life and experience. Our works and words must spring from our inmost being, or they will have little power or efficacy. "We must ourselves be true, if we the truth would teach."

The change produced by the baptism of the Holy Ghost upon the first disciples was more remarkable in their own lives than even in their service and testimony.

Peter, the irresolute disciple — always running ahead of his Master, boasting in his self-confidence of what he would do or would not do, and then running away at the threat of a servant girl, transformed into the fearless hero, who stood before the murderers of His Lord and charged them with their crime, and then with lowly spirit and humble heart, going forth to walk in his Master's steps, and at last to die upon his Master's cross with downward head, is a greater miracle in his personal life than even in the wondrous power of his public testimony.

The spirit of unselfish love, that led to the entire consecration of all their means to the service of Christ and the help of one another, was an example that could not fail to impress the skeptical and selfish world. The "great grace" that was upon them all was more wonderful than "the great power" with which they bore witness to the death and resurrection of Jesus Christ. The heroic fortitude with which they endured unparalleled sufferings, "rejoicing that they were counted worthy to suffer shame for the name of Jesus," was an exhibition of power that no man can gainsay, and carried a weight of conviction that nothing can counterpoise.

This is the power which the church needs today to convince an unbelieving world; the power that will make us, not inspired apostles, but "living epistles, known and read of all men." Nothing is so strong as the influence of a consistent, supernatural, and holy character. Many a skeptic, whom all the books in the universe would never have convinced, has been converted by the sweet example of his Christian wife.

Many a missionary among the heathen has found that the failure of his temper and spirit has done more in a moment to counteract all his teaching than years could undo. "He that keepeth his spirit is greater than he that taketh a city." And the power that can surpass the angry word, and stand in sweetness in the hour of provocation in the humble kitchen and laundry, has often become an object lesson to the proud and cultured mistress, until her heart has hungered for the blessing which has made her lowly servant's life a ministry of power, and her humble heart a heaven of love.

III. IT IS THE POWER OF TRUTH. The Holy Ghost works through the Holy Scriptures, and so the baptism of Pentecost was clearly identified with the power of the Word.

The very first thing that Peter did after the Holy Spirit came was to quote the Scriptures, and explain the manifestation from God's own inspired Word, and it was a Scriptural sermon which was used in the extraordinary conversions of that day.

If you will carefully notice the different messages of the apostles, you will find that in every instance they made large use of the Bible, and some of their messages are simply statements of Scripture and quotations from the Old Testament.

The Holy Ghost has given the Holy Scriptures and will never dishonor His own message. The more we know of Him, the more will we honor His Word. The Bible must ever be the foundation of spiritual power, and the instrument of spiritual service; but it must ever be in the power of the Spirit. "The letter killeth, but the Spirit giveth life."

The late Dr. Gordon tells of a Sabbath he spent abroad, on which day he went in the morning to hear a distinguished preacher who was celebrated for his Biblical knowledge. He came home delighted with the clear and brilliant expositions of the truth that he had heard, but chilled with the icy coldness of the message. It was true, clear, Scriptural truth, but as cold as an iceberg.

He went in the afternoon to hear another preacher distinguished for his fervor, and he came back delighted with the earnestness and unction of the preacher but it was a fire of shavings, and there was not truth enough in it to make it lasting.

He went again at night, and heard a third preacher, and he came away not only instructed, but thrilled, because this sermon had been not only an exposition of Scriptural truth, but it had also been alive with the power of God and full of the fire of the Holy Ghost. It was not a fire of shavings, but of substantial fuel, and it left not only a memory of truth, but a glow of warmth that filled his heart with joy and love. This is the power of the Holy Ghost, speaking the truth in love; the Bible ablaze with holy fire; the Word of God dissolved in unction and love, until it can be observed in every fibre of our being, and become the nutriment of our life.

IV. IT IS THE POWER OF LOVE. The baptism of Pentecost was a baptism of love. It brought a love to God that annihilated the power of self. "Neither said any of them that aught of the things which he possessed was his own." Their costliest treasures were yielded up to God. Their wealth, their homes, were held at the service of the church of Christ.

It was love to one another, and they were so absolutely bound together that they formed a corporate body. There was no schism or possible place for the paralysis or mutilation of the whole body of Christ. Today the church of Christ has broken to pieces. Here and there we find a sound member, but the whole body is mutilated and severed, so that it is not possible for the Spirit to flow with undivided and unhindered fullness through the whole; consequently we do not have the gifts of the Spirit in the same measure as in the day of Pentecost. The body is carrying about with it diseased and lacerated members, and it takes the strength of those that are whole to carry those that are broken.

What we need today is the baptism of the Holy Ghost, and then the union will come because of the unity, and we shall not need our platforms and our convocations to bring the body together, but bone to his bone, member to member and heart to heart we shall stand in "unity of the Spirit," and the Church of Jesus will be "fair as the moon, clear as the sun, and terrible as an army with banners."

The baptism of the Holy Ghost will always bring a spirit of love. It will fill the heart with devotion and devotedness to God, with tender consideration for one another, with loving regard for our brethren, with intense longing for the salvation of souls, and with sweetness and charity toward all men.

V. IT IS THE POWER OF SUPERNATURAL GIFTS AND DIVINE HEALING. The name of Jesus, through the power of the Holy Ghost, was efficacious to restore the paralytic at the Beautiful Gate of the temple, and even to raise the dead at the prayer of Peter.

At every great crisis in the apostolic ministry, we find a special manifestation of supernatural power. It was given to emphasize their testimony in Jerusalem. It was specially marked at the opening of the gospel in Samaria. It was still more wonderfully manifested as Peter preached through all Judea. And at every new point in Paul's missionary journey we find "God bearing witness by signs, and wonders, and mighty deeds."

You will notice, however, that the healing of the sick and the working of supernatural power were not primary ends, but rather testimonies to something more important, even the reality and power of the name of Jesus, and the message of mercy through the gospel.

And so, while we must still recognize the supernatural ministry of the Spirit, which never was intended to be interrupted, and ought to be expected yet more wonderfully in these last days before the coming of the Lord Jesus Christ, let us never make the mistake of regarding it as an end, or allowing it to take the place of the higher truths that relate to our spiritual life. At the same time, let us not ignore it. The church is one through all the ages. "Jesus Christ is the same yesterday, and today, and forever"; the Holy Spirit in unchanged, and the constitution of the church is identical with the twelfth chapter of First Corinthians and the plan which God gave at Pentecost.

We cannot leave out any part of the Gospel without weakening all the rest; and if there ever was an age when the world needed the witness of God's supernatural working, it is this day of unbelief and Satanic power. Therefore, we may expect, as the end approaches, that the Holy Ghost will work in the healing of sickness, in the casting out of demons, in remarkable answers to prayer, in special and wonderful providences, and in such forms as may please His sovereign will, to prove to an unbelieving world that the power of Jesus' name is still unchanged, and that "all the promises of God in Him are yea, and in Him, Amen, forever."

Let us not fear to claim His power for our physical as well as our spiritual need, and we shall find that, "if the Spirit of Him that raised up Jesus from the dead dwell in us, He that raised up Christ from the dead shall also quicken our mortal bodies by His Spirit that dwelleth in us."

VI. IT IS THE POWER OF PROVIDENTIAL WORKING. There is nothing more remakable than the manner in which God's providence worked in line with the first disciples, showing that He who dwelt within them was the same God that controls the universe and all the affairs of human life.

How wonderful the providence that brought represtatives from the whole world to meet at Pentecost, and then to receive the power and go forth to their homes in every nation, as witnesses for Jesus!

How marvelous the providence that brought Philip and the eunuch of Ethiopia together down there at the cross roads of the desert, and then sent the prince on to his home in Africa converted, enlightened, and filled with the Holy Ghost, to be a witness for Jesus to his whole nation, and perhaps bring all North Africa to God!

How remarkable the providence that sent Peter to the housetop, and then brought to him the vision that illuminated his mind, enlarged his ideas, and prepared him for his greater commission for the Gentile churches; then, when he was ready, sent, on the very niche of time, the messengers of Cornelius to knock at his door and take him up to Caesarea to preach the gospel to the Gentiles and witness the outpouring of the Holy Ghost at Pentecost!

How wonderful the providence of God that opened the church at Antioch and prepared a new center for Gentile Christianity, in the larger spirit of the cosmopolitan congregation, and then gathered there men like Paul and Barnabas to be the leaders of a wider movement for all the world!

How marvelous the providence that saved Peter from the cruel hand of Herod, opening his prison doors on the very night preceding his intended execution, and smiting Herod down with a hideous disease in the hour of his presumptuous purpose to destroy the Church of God!

How extraordinary the providences that followed Paul through his wondrous life, opening his way from land to land, and making storm and tempest, and even the very viper that sprang upon him, to work for the cause of Christ!

And still the same God rules in the same realm of Providence. Still the Holy Ghost within us can control the circumstances around us. Still the march of events will keep time to the leadings of the Spirit. And the man that walks in the Holy Ghost shall have a charmed life and be immortal till his work is done, and he will find that winds and waves and fierce and cruel men, and even Satan's very emissaries shall be forced to become auxiliaries to His purpose, and work with Him for the furtherance of the Gospel.

And so God has shown in the lives of men like Arnot, in Africa; Paton, in the New Hebrides; George Muller, in Bristol, and many a humble missionary of the cross who has dared to trust the mighty promise of the ascending Master, the permanent value of His words, "All power is given Me in heaven and in earth, and lo, I am with you all the days, even unto the end of the age."

VII. IT IS THE POWER FOR GUIDANCE. The Holy Spirit gives power for guidance. He directed them. He led their steps. He sent Philip to Samaria, and down to the desert to meet the eunuch. He sent Peter to the housetop and then to the home of Cornelius. He restrained Paul and Silas from preaching in Bithynia and Ephesus, and then He sent them to Macedonia, to give the gospel to Europe.

Step by step He was the Guide of all their ways, and He is still our Counselor and Guide; and if we will trust Him and acknowledge Him in all our ways, He will direct our steps and lead us into all the fullness of our Father's will.

VIII. IT IS THE POWER FOR THE GOVERNMENT OF THE CHURCH. There is nothing more wonderful than the oversight of the Holy Ghost in the church of the apostolic age. He was its recognized Leader and Head. He directed its councils, and was acknowledged as its President. He controlled its disciples, kept out unworthy members, and preserved it from the touch of the world.

How solemn and awful His dealing with Ananias and Sapphira! How suggestive the solemn statement "of the rest, durst none join themselves unto them"! Oh, if the Holy Ghost is in the Church, the world will not have to be kept out; it will be only too glad to stay out.

Alas, that day should have come when learning, genius, influence and worldly power should be recognized in the house of God, and the world should be sought by sinful compromises and unholy attractions, and the church should be baffled and hindered by the "mixed multitude" that she has no power to keep away. God is trying to show His ministers and people that He is adequate for all the needs of His work, and any pastor and church that will fully recognize Him, shall always be prospered and blessed, spiritually, financially, numerically, influentially, and every way.

Oh, that God would show His Church her true power and glory, and that she might again be the woman "clothed with the sun, with the moon beneath her feet!"

IX. IT IS THE POWER OF CONVICTION OVER THE HEARTS OF MEN. The power of the Holy Ghost is not always a conscious power on our part. It is marked chiefly by effectiveness in reaching the hearts of others. On the day of Pentecost, it was the power to convict the consciences of men, and to influence and control their actions. "They were pricked to the heart, and they said, Men and brethren, what shall we do?"

It is not always the highest excitement that indicates the strongest power. The great question is, "What is the effect upon the hearts and lives of men?" When Demosthenes used to speak in Athens, the people forgot all about Demosthenes, and said, "Let us go and find Philip." It put the "go" into them. And so when the Holy Ghost is present in power He leads to results.

The speaker may be very calm, and have little consciousness of the power, but in the audience are men and women who are brought face to face with God; and the truth is "manifested to every man's conscience in the sight of God," and a Voice within says, "Thou art the man." The will is led to decide and choose for God, and men turn from sin and yield themselves in entire surrender. This is the power we want — the power that "will convict men of sin, and of righteousness, and of judgment;" not the power of great machinery, of thrilling eloquence, melting pathos, and marvelous preaching and singing but the power that quietly moves upon the hearts of men, in their workshops and in their homes, until they are constrained to give themselves to God.

X. IT IS THEPOWER TO SUFFER. Perhaps there is no more remarkable manifestation of the power of the Holy Ghost, in the early church, than the sweetness and grandeur with which they endured all things for Jesus'sake. Beaten with stripes and humiliated before the council, they came together, not to condole with each other or show their bleeding wounds, but to rejoice "that they were counted worthy to suffer shame for the name of Jesus."

Hunted out of Iconium by a mob of respectable women, pelted with stones and hooted from the community, the "disciples were filled with joy, and with the Holy Ghost." Theirs was a gladness that did not recognize their sufferings, but lifted them above persecution, and counted it but part of their coronation.

And so the power of the Holy Ghost will give us the heroism of endurance and enable us, like our Master, for the joy set before us to endure the cross, despising the shame. It will bring about a spirit of self-denial and holy sacrifice; it will make it easy for us to let go things and give up things "and endure all things for the elect's sake," and to say with the great apostle, "Yea, and if I be offered upon the sacrifice and service of your faith, I joy and rejoice with you all."

XI. IT IS THE POWER FOR SERVICE. Finally this was the power for unwearied, earnest and effective work. It was a power that could enable Paul, in a single lifetime, while supporting himself by his own manual labor, unsupported by any missionary society or church, and without the facilities of our railroads, steamboats, telegraphs and means of communication, to girdle the globe and preach the gospel everywhere, and say in words of superlative triumph, "So that from Jerusalem, round about unto Illyricum, I have fully preached the gospel of Christ."

O, beloved, we are living in an earnest age, and surely the Holy Ghost ought to produce earnest men today. God give to us this power for work that will multiply our lives until they measure up to the extraordinary opportunities, and to the marvelous intensities of these last days on which the ends of the world are come.

Oh, for a race of Pauls! Oh, for an army of Gideons! Oh, for a band of heroes! Oh, for the baptism of the Holy Ghost in all the meaning of Pentecost and in all the highest thought of Christ Himself!

## Chapter 9

## Filled with the Spirit

"They were all filled with the Holy Ghost." Acts 2: 4. "Be not drunk with wine, wherein is excess; but be filled with the Spirit." Eph. 5: 18.

These words imply that there is a difference between having the Spirit and being filled with the Spirit. These disciples, on the day of Pentecost, had, in some measure, received the Spirit previously. The Lord Jesus must have meant something when He breathed on them and said, "Receive ye the Holy Ghost." And the disciples to whom the apostle wrote the Epistle to the Ephesians had already been "sealed with that Holy Spirit of promise," which was the earnest of their inheritance until the redemption of the purchased possession; but they were not filled with the Spirit.

What this difference is we may not be able to state explicitly or accurately. Our theories and definitions may be at fault, and it is probably unnecessary that we should understand all about it theoretically. The most important thing is that we should feel after it until we find it; that we should long for it and press forward to receive it. It is very probable that many a soul is converted without being distinctly conscious of the process at the time, and that many a Christian receives the gift of the Holy Ghost when he is stumbling after it and reaching out for it in the darkness and the dimness of spiritual trouble. And so we may not know all about this, but we may earnestly desire it and persistently seek until we find it. All divine conditions transcend our understanding, and our most real, intense and important experiences often come to us by processes which we ourelves could not explain.

The most familiar operations of the natural world afford a forcible illustration of this distinction. We all easily understand the difference between the shallow stream and the overflowing river. In both cases there is water, but in one case it is a feeble current, while in the other it is an overflowing stream that drives the innumerable wheels of the factories along the shores. The power all comes from the fullness which causes the overflow.

We can easily understand the difference between a boiler full of water and a boiler full of boiling water. In the one case it is cold water which fills, but which has no power; in the other it is the water converted into steam, driving the wheels of the mighty engine and carrying the cars across the continent along the iron track.

That single degree of temperature makes all the difference in the world between power and impotence. The Scriptures of truth bear out this distinction with the greatest possible clearness and force.

In writing to Timothy, the Apostle Paul says, in the first chapter of the second epistle and sixth verse, "Wherefore I put thee in remembrance that thou stir up the gift of God, which is in thee by the putting on of my hands. God hath not given us the Spirit of fear; but of power, and of love, and of a sound mind."

The gift was already bestowed and fully recognized, but it was like an expiring flame — the embers of the fire were falling into ashes, and the flame was almost dead. The word used is re-kindle, stir up the fading embers, rekindle the fire — be filled with the Spirit.

Again, in 1 Corinthians 12: 7, we read, "But the manifestation of the Spirit is given to every man to profit withal." This word "profit" expresses the whole difference between receiving the Spirit and being filled with the Spirit. Every one may receive the Spirit, but only a few "profit withal"; that is, improve the gift, develop it, exercise it, and reach its utmost fullness.

All this is perfectly unfolded in the beautiful parable of the pounds, Luke 19. The one pound given to each servant is the special enduement of the Holy Ghost, power for service; but the improvement of the pound, in each case, is different, according to the diligence and fidelity of the servant. And so the outcome of each life is different, and the final reward bears the same proportion. It is a wonderful and solemn truth and places an awful responsibility upon every one of us for the right use of God's spiritual gifts, and especially that Gift of gifts, the blessed Holy Ghost Himself.

In the twelfth chapter of First Corinthians and the thirteenth verse, we have another remarkable statement: "For by one Spirit are we all baptized into one body, whether we be Jews or Gentiles, whether we be bond or free; and have been all made to drink into one Spirit."

It is one thing to be baptized into the one body by the Spirit; it is another thing to drink into that one Spirit. The first is an act; the second is a habit. The first brings us into a relationship; the second is the true use of that relationship, the drinking of His fullness until we become filled, and the habit of abiding in His fullness so that we are always filled.

Once more, the same truth is very beautifully taught in the story of the widow and her pot of oil, already referred to in connection with 2 Kings 4: 1-7. That little pot of oil represents the Holy Ghost; but the outpouring of the pot of oil into all the vessels which the widow borrowed from her neighbors, illustrates the fullness of the Spirit, as we receive Him into all the needs of our life, and into all the circumstances which God's providence brings to us as opportunities for the development of our spiritual life and the richer fullness of the Holy Ghost.

So many have the Holy Ghost confined in a little pot of oil and hidden away on the shelf of a cabinet. God wants us to go out into all the needs of life, and pour that divine fullness into every vessel that comes to us, until our whole life shall be a living embodiment and illustration of the all-sufficiency of Christ.

II. Let us now inquire what are some of the effects and evidences of the filling of the Holy Ghost.

1. To be filled with the Spirit, in the first place will bring us the fullness of Jesus. The person and work of the Holy Ghost must never be recognized apart from the person of Christ — to do this is sure to lead us into Spiritualism. Natural religion recognizes the spirit world. Spiritualism is full of it. The priestess of Apollo was called the Pythoness, because she inhaled a spiritual influence until her whole body became swollen like a python, and her whole being was alive with intense spiritual force; but it was the spirit of evil; it was a spirit apart from the person of Christ and the true God.

The Holy Ghost never comes to us apart from Jesus. He is the Way to the Father, and He is the Way from the Father to us; and the blessed Spirit when He comes witnesses not of Himself but of the Lord Jesus Christ. Let us be very careful of this. It is possible to become inflated with a spiritual influence, and yet to ignore and even disobey the Lord Jesus Christ, and to be led into pride, self-sufficient sentimentalism, and even sin.

The object of the Holy Ghost, like that of an artist, is to picture Jesus upon the canvas and make Him real to us, while the blessed Actor Himself is, in a measure, out of sight.

The more we are filled with the Holy Ghost, the more we recognize Christ, depend upon Christ, live upon Christ alone. Therefore this very word "filled" is used in connection with Him.

In Colossians 2: 9, 10, we have these two remarkable relative verses, "In Him dwelleth all the fullness of the Godhead bodily, and ye are complete in Him." Literally translated, it reads, "In Him dwelleth all the fullness of the Godhead in a bodily form, and ye are filled with Him." God fills Jesus; Jesus fills us. Christ is the ideal man, the pattern of what a man should be, and God has put into Him all that humanity needs to be to satisfy Him; therefore, in order that we should be true men, we must relive His life, reproduce His personality, receive Him, grow up into

Him, and live Him in all the completeness of His glorious life.

So we read, "Of His fullness have all we received, even grace for grace." We ourselves are insufficient for every situation, and the great business of the Holy Ghost is to bring us up to the situations of life and show us our insufficiency, and then reveal to us Christ and bring Him into our life as the supply of our needs. So in connection with that wonderful promise of the Holy Ghost in the fourteenth chapter of John, the true sequel is, "I am the Vine, ye are the branches. Abide in Me and I in you. He that abideth in Me, and I in him, the same bringeth forth much fruit; for apart from Me ye can do nothing."

This is the life into which the Holy Ghost brings us, the life of personal union with and constant dependence upon the Lord Jesus Christ. To be filled with the Spirit, then, is to be filled with Christ, and so live that our constant experience and testimony will be, "I live; yet not I, but Christ liveth in me: and the life which I now live in the flesh I live by the faith of the Son of God, who loved me, and gave Himself for me."

2. To be filled with the Spirit will exclude the life of self and sin, and will, of course, bring us into a life of holiness, righteousness and obedience.

We read in Exodus 40: 34, 35, that "when the cloud of the glory of the Lord filled the tabernacle, Moses was not able to enter into the tent of the congregation; because the cloud abode thereon, and the glory of the Lord filled the tabernacle."

This is the true picture of a Spirit-filled man. The indwelling and in-filling of the Holy Spirit excludes self and sin. There is no room for Moses when the glory of God fills our being.

3. The filling of the Holy Ghost will bring us joy and fullness of joy. "These things have I spoken unto you," the Master said after He had given us the promise of the Spirit, "that My joy might remain in you, and that your joy might be full." And so the apostle prays that "the God of hope may fill us with all joy and peace in believing, that we may abound in hope through the power of the Holy Ghost."

The fullness of the Spirit must crowd out pain, doubt, fear and sorrow, and bring the joy of Christ to fill our being. What is it that makes the melody in an organ? It is not the touch of skillful fingers only on the keys, but it is the filling of the pipes by the movement of the pedals. I may try in vain to play the most skillful tune, unless the organ is filled; and so our songs of praise are dead and cold until the breath of God fills all the channels of our being. Then comes the heart-song of praise and the overflowing fountain of gladness.

4. So all the fruits of the Spirit come from the Spirit-filled heart. "The fruit of the Spirit is love, joy, peace, longsuffering, gentleness, goodness, meekness, faith, temperance." These are all fruits or, at least, the fruit of the Spirit, and spring spontaneous from the fullness of the Holy Ghost.

When, a few years ago, I stood at Hebron and looked at the pool of David and saw it overflowing, my friend turned to me, and said, "This is the token by which we know that the valleys of Judea are filled with water, and its plains will be covered with fertility and luxuriance. The rains have been abundant because the pool of David is full at Hebron, and the sources of irrigation are ample."

And so when the heart is full of God, the life will be full of godliness. Spontaneously and sweetly will spring up all the fruits of righteousness, holiness and blessing, and "the desert shall rejoice and blossom as the rose."

5. Again, the Holy Ghost can fill our minds and understandings with knowledge and light, and control our thoughts with harmony and sweetness and strength. The peace of God that passeth all understanding will keep our hearts and minds, and our thoughts will be stayed upon Him, and "brought into captivity to the obedience of Christ."

6. Yes, our very bodies will feel the fullness. The Holy Ghost is a true tonic for physical energy and perfect health. The fullness of the Spirit is the elixir for body and brain and being. To be filled with His blessed life will make our feet spring, our nerves

steady, our brain strong, our circulation regular, and our whole being at its best for God and holy service.

7. Then, also, our very circumstances keep time to the blessed fullness of the heart within.

Like the widow's pot of oil that flowed out into every vessel, so the presence of God touches everything that comes into our life, and we find that all things work together for good to us if we love God and fulfill His purpose.

Our circumstances will become adjusted to us, or we become adjusted to our circumstances, and the whole of our life, "fitly framed together," will become vigorous, and full of power and blessing.

8. The blessing will no longer be expended upon itself; but we shall have enough and to spare; it will overrun until there is not room to receive it, and the residue will become the inheritance of a suffering world. These are the lives God uses, and God cannot use us until we are running over.

It was when Cana's water was poured out that it was changed from water into wine. It was when Ezekiel's river ran from the sanctuary to the desert that it grew deeper and broader and fuller. And it is when our lives are lost in self-forgetting love that we know all the fullness of God.

III. HOW MAY WE BE FILLED?

1. We must be empty.

I have a phonograph into whose sensitive gelatine cylinders I dictate my literary work. One busy day, I dictated a large amount of matter, filling up every cylinder. I spent nearly two days getting through a great amount of literary labor, and felt very much relieved that it was off my hands.

But when my typist proceeded to copy the messages which I had spoken to these cylinders, she could not understand the words, they were all jargon and confusion. The reason was very simple. I had neglected to shave off the former dictation before giving the new message. I had really dictated a lot of matter into ears that were already filled and, therefore, it had made no impression. My work was lost, my labor was in vain. But I learned a lesson that was worth all it cost, and that is, that we must be empty before we can be filled. God cannot speak His messages into full ears. The Holy Ghost cannot pour His fullness into those who are already full.

2. We must be hungry. For "He hath filled the hungry with good things, and the rich hath He sent away empty." The caravans on the burning desert, when they cannot find the accustomed well of water, let loose the thirsty harts and they sweep over the burning plains, panting with thirst, until they find the water brooks.

And so the hungry heart always finds the living bread, the thirsty soul is always filled with water. There is nothing that finds God so quickly as an earnest soul. We always find Him when "we search for Him with all our hearts."

3. We must be open if we would be filled. "Open thy mouth wide and I will fill it." We must be free from prejudice and preconceptions of truth that shut us up from God's voice. We must be adjusted so as to catch His whisper and understand His will.

4. We must receive as well as ask; we must believe as well as pray; we must take the water of life freely; we must know the secret of drinking the living water, if we would be filled.

5. We must wait upon the Lord. The heart is too large to be filled in a moment; the soul is too great to be satisfied with a mere mouthful. "They that wait upon the Lord shall renew their strength." We must "continue in prayer"; we must be much at the throne of grace; we must learn the secret of communion as well as supplication; and as we thus wait upon the Lord, we shall be filled until we shall find it a luxury to give forth our blessing to others.

6. And finally, if we would be filled, we must learn to give as well as receive; we must empty our hearts, that they may be refilled. God is a great economist and He loves to bless those who make the best use of their blessings, and become in turn a source of blessing to others.

The Holy Ghost is given for service; God cannot bless a selfish soul; and there is no selfishness more odious in His sight than that which can hoard God's spiritual blessing, and let others die in ignorance of the gospel, and suffer through selfish neglect.

"The liberal soul shall be made fat, and he that watereth others shall be watered himself." In this blessed work of winning the lost and giving the gospel to the world, we shall find our own rich reward, and "the fullness of the blessing of Christ."

## Chapter 10

## The Holy Spirit in the Epistle to the Romans

"But ye are not in the flesh, but in the Spirit, if so be that the Spirit of God dwell in you. Now if any man have not the Spirit of Christ, he is none of his." Rom. 8: 9.

We approach, in this great epistle, a spiritual temple, and from its illuminated windows there shine out the beams of lofty and divine truth. It is so glorious that it needs only to be stated to bring its own illumination and vindication. This, the greatest of the epistles, presents to us the doctrine of the Holy Ghost with a symmetry and fullness quite as remarkable as the unfolding of the other doctrines which it contains.

I. First, we have the witnessing Spirit. In Romans 1: 3, 4, the Lord Jesus Christ is said to have been "of the seed of David according to the flesh, and declared to be the Son of God with power, according to the Spirit of holiness, by the resurrection from the dead."

The Spirit of holiness has been interpreted to mean the divine nature of Jesus Christ, but it is quite proper and, indeed, a more simple interpretation to apply it directly to the Holy Ghost as a divine Person, witnessing to the divinity of the Lord Jesus Christ, by raising Him from the dead according to the will of the Father.

The Holy Ghost was ever the witness to Christ's divinity, and the Spirit Who had so distinct a part in the offering up of His sacrifice (for it was "by the eternal Spirit that He offered Himself to God without spot") had surely as important a part in

His resurrection. This is the first view we love to take of the Holy Spirit, as the Witness of Jesus, and especially of the risen Jesus, the living Christ, and the divine Lord.

II. We next see the Holy Ghost as the Spirit of life and holiness. In Romans 8: 2, we read, "The law of the Spirit of life in Christ Jesus hath made me free from the law of sin and death."

This is the first work of the Holy Ghost in sanctifying the soul. Let us carefully notice the place where this comes in. It is subsequent to our justification by faith and our surrender to Christ in death and resurrection. Then the Holy Spirit comes and takes possession of us and breathes into us the life of the Lord Jesus Christ. This becomes a new law of life and power in our spiritual being, and this new law lifts us above and sets us free from the old law of sin and death.

Just as the law of life lifts us above the law of gravitation, and the power of my will can raise my hand in spite of that physical law which makes dead matter fall to the ground, so the Holy Ghost, bringing Christ as a living presence into my heart and life, establishes a new law of feeling, thinking, choosing, and acting, and this new law lifts me above the power of sin and makes it natural for me to be holy, obedient, and Christ-like.

III. We see the Holy Spirit operating in the mind as well as in the spirit, and we read in the next paragraph, verses 5 and 6, "The minding of the flesh is death, but the minding of the Spirit is life and peace." The Holy Spirit enters the mind and disposes it to the will of God, so that we choose the things that He chooses, and think God's thoughts after Him.

We mind the Monitor Who dwells within us; we listen to the voice that speaks to us; we follow His directions, and "we walk not after the flesh, but after the Spirit."

IV. The Holy Spirit is next revealed as the Spirit of quickening and healing in our mortal flesh. In verse 11, "If the Spirit of Him that raised up Jesus from the dead dwell in you, He that raised up Christ from the dead shall also quicken your mortal body by His Spirit that dwelleth in you."

The Holy Ghost is the source of physical as well as mental and spiritual life. The human body consists of more than the outward frame. There is the inner mechanism of nerves, and, inside of that, the vital fluids and currents which quicken, energize, and impel the whole material organism.

Inside of all this is the principle of life, and inside of this is the Holy Ghost in the consecrated believer. He is most distinctly represented to us here as a vital force in our material being, a source of life, quickening, exhilaration and physical energy for those that know Him and obey Him. He is the Spirit that raised up Christ from the dead, and He dwells in our mortal bodies as a quickening life. This is not the immortal body of the resurrection, but the mortal frame of the present life which feeds upon the divine life. And this is the secret of living on the life of God.

It is thus that our bodies are the temples of the Holy Ghost, and our frames are the members of Christ, and partake of the life of our living Head.

V. The Holy Spirit, as the guide and director of our Christian life, is very clearly presented to us in the next few verses. "Therefore," adds the apostle, "we are debtors, not to the flesh, to live after the flesh. For if ye live after the flesh ye shall die: but if ye through the Spirit do mortify the deeds of the body, ye shall live. For as many as are led by the Spirit of God, they are the sons of God."

We are to "live after the Spirit"; we are to obey our divine Guide; we are to follow our heavenly Leader; we are to yield ourselves to the Mother and the Monitor who comes to direct our pathway.

Christian life is not a mere moment of blessed transformation, but it is a life of continual abiding and obedience. Step by step, we must walk with God and maintain the attitude and habit of dependence and holy obedience. The Holy Spirit never wearies of the care of our life, and we should never weary of His loving jealousy for us. This is the secret of peace and gladness constant obedience and a hearkening spirit that waits to catch the whisper of His will and obey His every word.

VI. In this passage we have another most important truth; namely, that the Holy Spirit is the Spirit of crucifixion. He is the One that mortifies our evil nature and holds us in the place of death and resurrection life. The attitude of the Christian life is that of reckoning ourselves dead, indeed, unto sin.

This attitude must be maintained as a habit, and there are constant occasions when the old life will seek to reassert itself and must be held steadily in the place of death. This is what is meant by "mortifying our members," and this can only be done by the Holy Ghost. If we attempt it ourselves we shall be everlastingly in the attitude of attempted suicide, and we shall never reach the place of peaceful death. The reason so many ghosts are walking around is because so many people have tried to die in their own strength, and have got up in the same strength, and walk about as the apparitions and shadows of the old carnal life.

The Church of God is full of these uncanny spirits, these live corpses, these resurrected ones; and they are very sad looking objects to themselves and to everybody else. The true secret is to be so full of the Holy Ghost that, like the autumn leaves which drop off by the coming of the spring, our old life shall be kept in the place of death by the expulsive power of divine love and Christ's indwelling life.

VII. The Spirit of sonship is also clearly unfolded in this beautiful paragraph: "As many as are led by the Spirit of God, they are the sons of God." The Holy Ghost brings us into the same relation with the Father as Jesus Christ, the divine Son. We are made partakers of His Sonship through His indwelling life, and the prayer of the Master becomes fulfilled in us and through us, "that the love wherewith Thou hast loved Me, may be in them and I in them." It is because He is in us that the Father loves us with the same love that He loves the Son, and we dwell in the blessed consciousness and confidence of this place of child liberty and love.

We are called the first born ones. We are all first born ones, even as He is the First Born One and the Only Begotten. We partake of His very Sonship; and as the bride shares the bridegroom's family and home, so we enter into all privileges, immunities, glories, and prospects of Christ's own glorious life. "Behold, what manner of love the Father hath bestowed upon us," and the Spirit hath brought to us, "that we should be called the sons of God."

Beloved, have we received power thus to become the sons of God, and does the Spirit, not of adoption, but of Sonship, cry out instinctively from our inmost being, "Papa, Father," our own dear Father, His Father and our Father, His God and our God?

VIII. The Spirit of hope and anticipation of the coming glory is next seen. And so we read in verse 23, "And not only they, but ourselves also, who have the first fruits of the Spirit, even we ourselves groan within ourselves, waiting for the adoption; to wit, the redemption of our body."

That is, the Holy Spirit awakens the consciousness and brings the earnest of the coming glory, and calls forth our eager longing and outreaching for it. Just as the embryo birdling in its shell, when the time for its birth draws near it, presses through the restraints that confine until at last it bursts the fragile shell and leaps forth into liberty and life to breathe the air of the great world, and soon to leave the firmament on eagle's wings, so the Spirit-filled heart has in it the bud and the embryo of a transcendent future, and it stretches out even now its nascent wings, and groans within itself for the coming glory.

Who is there of all the disciples of Christ who has not some time felt the birth-pangs of a grander life and the prophecy of a future transcending all we know of power and blessing?

We have not only the conception and anticipation of this glorious future, but the apostle says we have "the first fruits" even now. The Spirit of God in our hearts is the prophecy and promise of the coming age of more glorious spiritual life when we shall be like Him, and clothed with His perfections and something of His wisdom and power, we shall share His throne forever.

The touches of divine healing that have thrilled our mortal frame are but the foretaste of the resurrection hour, when we shall sweep up into the fullness of our eternal manhood, and these mortal frames shall be as beautiful, as glorious, as pure, and as strong as His glorified body on the throne.

What we have seen of answered prayer, of power over nature, of victory over circumstances, of divine life even in this limited sphere, these are but anticipations and earnest-payments of the time when we shall inherit the kingdom which Adam lost, and share man's destined dominion over the whole creation.

And so the Holy Spirit in us is teaching us the millennial song, is waking up in us the pulses of the resurrection, is illuminating before us the vision of the coming glory, and is calling us out to prove even here our celestial wings.

And as the parent eagle teaches her little ones to fly, moment by moment and effort by effort, luring them from their soft nest, bearing them on her mighty wings, so the Mother Dove is teaching us to spread our wings upon the higher air and press forward into a little of our future inheritance.

Oh, let us not be disobedient to these heavenly visions! Let us not repress these outreachings. Let us not quench these immortal fires. And let us not cramp and stunt, and crush out the heavenly inspirations and aspirations which carry with them not only the prophecy, but the vital power of an endless and boundless life.

IX. In the twenty-sixth verse we have the Holy Spirit as the Spirit of prayer. "Likewise also the Spirit helpeth our infirmities; for we know not what to pray for as we ought; but the Spirit itself maketh intercession for us with groanings which cannot be uttered. And He that searcheth the hearts knoweth what is the mind of the Spirit, because He maketh intercession for the saints according to the will of God."

This is the deep mystery of prayer. This is the delicate divine mechanism which words cannot interpret, and which theology cannot explain, but which the humblest believer knows even when he does not understand.

Oh, the burdens that we love to bear and cannot understand! Oh, the inarticulate outreachings of our hearts for things we cannot comprehend! And yet we know they are an echo from the throne and a whisper from the heart of God. It is often a groan rather than a song, a burden rather than a buoyant wing. But it is a blessed burden, and it is a groan whose undertone is praise and unutterable joy. It is "a groaning which cannot be uttered." We could not ourselves express it always, and sometimes we do not understand any more than that God is praying in us, for something that needs His touch and that He understands.

And so we can just pour out the fullness of our heart, the burden of our spirit, the sorrow that crushes us, and know that He hears, He loves, He understands, He receives; and He separates from our prayer all that is imperfect, ignorant and wrong, and presents the rest, with the incense of the great High Priest, before the throne on high; and our prayer is heard, accepted and answered in His name.

X. The Spirit of service is His attribute. The Holy Ghost is next represented as the Spirit of power for consecrated service. In the twelfth chapter of Romans and the first verse, there is a singular and beautiful force in the use of the Greek word "paraclete."

The expression, "I beseech you, therefore, brethren by the mercies of God" literally means, "I paraclete you by the mercies of God"; that is, not I, but the Holy Ghost beseeches you, that ye present your bodies a living sacrifice, holy, acceptable unto God, which is your reasonable service. This is the Holy Spirit's message to the saved and sanctified children of God, and this is the true power for consecration and service.

We may so identify ourselves with the blessed Paraclete, that our appeals and messages to men shall not be ours but His, and we can say, "I Paraclete you"; in the name of the Holy Ghost, beseech you. Thus our words and works will come to men with the authority and the power of the Holy Ghost.

XI. The Spirit of gladness is revealed in Romans 14: 17. "The kingdom of God is not meat and drink; but righteousness, and peace, and joy in the Holy Ghost." Romans 15: 13. "Now the God of hope fill you with all joy and peace in believing, that you may abound in hope, through the power of the Holy Ghost."

The Holy Spirit is always the Spirit of gladness, and the Spirit of gladness and hope is essential to power for service and effective testimony for Christ.

XII. The Spirit of missions is His Spirit. The crowning revelation of the Holy Ghost in this sublime epistle is the Spirit of evangelization for the whole world. It is very beautiful that in this, the most doctrinal of all the epistles, the most profound theological treatise on justification, sanctification and the purposes of God ever written by inspired hands, should be these closing words respecting the ministry of the Holy Ghost for the evangelization of the whole world. But how could it be otherwise from such a soul and such a hand as Paul's?

Listen to these inspiring words: "I have written more boldly unto you, as putting you again in remembrance, because of the grace that was given me of God, that I should be the minister of Jesus Christ unto the Gentiles, ministering the Gospel of God, that the offering up of the Gentiles might be made acceptable, being sanctified by the Holy Ghost. I have therefore my glorifying in Jesus Christ in those things which pertain to God. For I will not dare to speak of anything save those which Christ wrought for me, for the obedience of the Gentiles by word and deed, through mighty signs and wonders, by the power of the Spirit of God; so that from Jerusalem and round about unto Illyricum, I have fully preached the gospel of Christ; yea, so have I strived to preach the gospel, not where Christ was already named, lest I should build upon another man's foundation; but as it is written, To whom He was not spoken of, they shall see; and they who have not heard shall understand." Rom. 15: 15-21.

To the glowing heart of Paul the work of missions was just the offering up of the Gentile world as a great living sacrifice to God, sanctified by the Holy Ghost. To present this offering to God was the glorious and all absorbing service of his life, and in this he had claimed and received the mighty power of the Holy

Spirit; so that his soul could truly say, "through mighty signs and wonders from Jerusalem round about unto Illyricum, I have fully preached the gospel of Christ." He could not rest in the beaten tracks of old and occupied fields, but pressed forward to the regions beyond to tell the story of divine love and grace, where Christ had not been named.

In an age when all our methods of international communication were unknown, when there were no railroads, steamboats, telegraphs, nor missionary societies, this lone man preached the Gospel, from land to land, until he could say of this vast region of the known world that circled round Jerusalem, he had so fully preached the gospel of Christ that no place was left in those parts, and that he was now at length at leisure to visit his friends in Rome and do some home mission work.

Wherever the Holy Ghost has possession of our hearts and lives, this will be the impulse that will possess us, and it will be the practical outcome of our consecration, until we shall have given the gospel as a witness to every tribe and tongue, and the purpose of the Christian Dispensation to gather out of the Gentiles a people for His name shall be accomplished, and the Lord Himself shall come.

Oh, may the Holy Spirit help each of us, from the study of this wonderful epistle, to understand His meaning for us and for our times, and to rise from the grandest truths of the gospel to the grandest work of the ages!

## Chapter 11

## The Holy Spirit in the First Epistle to the Corinthians

The First Epistle of Paul to the Corinthians unfolds the doctrine of the Holy Ghost in a number of distinct paragraphs, bringing out four different aspects of the truth, that are full of practical significance.

In the second chapter we have the Holy Ghost presented as the source of mental illumination and the Spirit of wisdom and revelation. In the third and sixth chapters we have the Holy Spirit in His indwelling in our spirit, and His sanctifying power. In the sixth chapter we have the Holy Spirit dwelling in our body and uniting us to Christ. And in the twelfth chapter we have the Holy Spirit constituting the whole body of Christ and uniting it, filling it with life, and enduing it with power for service.

I. THE SPIRITUAL MIND. 1 Cor. 2: 6-16.

The last verse of this wonderful chapter expresses the particular truth of which the whole chapter is an unfolding — "We have the mind of Christ." The Spirit is here represented as the Quickener of the mind, and the Source of mental illumination, and the Revealer of spiritual truth. There are three distinct and important thoughts in the chapter. The Holy Spirit is the Revealer of super-natural truth.

1. In the first place, the Spirit is the revealer of sources of knowledge. For "eye hath not seen, nor ear heard, neither have entered into the heart of man the things which God hath prepared for them that love Him. But God hath revealed them unto

us by His Spirit; for the Spirit searcheth all things, yea, the deep things of God."

There is much that eye hath seen, but there are truths beyond our natural vision just as wonderful as this world of light and beauty, when it is suddenly revealed to a man who has always been blind, and whose vision is restored. His first thought is, "How beautiful, how wonderful! Why didn't you tell me of this before?"

And so there are spiritual truths, and there is a world of higher vision which God has for the quickened spirit, and which our natural senses never could discover; and when we see it in the light of His revealing, we wonder we never heard of it, and we think everybody ought to see it.

There are things which ear has heard, the words of eloquence and wisdom, the notes of melody and harmony; the whisper of affection, the voices of nature and human love; but there is a higher realm whose messages of heavenly truth and divine love ear hath never heard. There are words of tenderness and wisdom which the Shepherd's voice is waiting to speak to those who know it, and the Holy Ghost is longing to give to "him that hath an ear to hear what the Spirit saith unto the churches."

There are thoughts and truths which human hearts have conceived, wonderful creations of the human imagination, wonderful conceptions of the human soul, wonderful inductions from human observation and perception, wonderful systems of thought and philosophy. But there are deeper and higher truths for the heaven-taught soul which will fill the ages to come with wonder and rapture. "In Him are hid all the treasures of wisdom and knowledge," and some day we shall know, even as He, all the secrets of truth. But He cannot speak them to us until we are able to hear them. This is the province of the Holy Ghost. Some of these truths He has revealed to us in the Holy Scriptures, but this is but a primary revelation for the present age and, as we shall know Him better, He will lead us on and up to all the heights and depths of knowledge in the cycles of eternity.

"For the Spirit searcheth all things, yea, the deep things of God." Like a mother who is searching through her wardrobe to find what will fit the ages of her children, like a teacher who is wisely discriminating, and determining just what class he can put the pupil into according to his progress, so the Holy Ghost is searching constantly to find how much we can stand; how far He can advance us; how fully He can reveal to us "the mind of Christ," and He is often disappointed, because as babes, we are unprepared for His higher messages.

2. We need more than supernatural truth, we need a supernatural mind to receive it. And so the next thought presented here is the Holy Spirit's ministry in giving to us the mind of Christ, and a supernatural power of reception. "For what man knoweth the things of a man, save the spirit of man that is in him? even so the things of God knoweth no man, but the Spirit of God."

You may repeat this sermon to the little canary bird that sings in your chamber, and he may bend his little head in earnest attention and try to take in your thought and meaning, but you will find that he has not grasped it. His little mind is not equal to your higher thought; he has only the mind of a bird, while you have the mind of a man. In order to make him understand you, you will need to put your mind into his brain.

And so when we bring our little mind up to the great thoughts of God, we are inadequate; we cannot take them in. Your canary may have a bigger head than your neighbor's canary; it may know one or two notes of song; it may have a few little tricks that others have not learned; it may be an educated, a cultivated, a professional bird; but it is only a bird. And so your philosopher, your man of science, your scholar, may know a few intellectual tricks, which the common mind is ignorant of; but he has only a human mind, he cannot take in the things of God without divine illumination.

This is the reason why "the wisdom of the world is foolishness with God." "But," He adds, "we have received the Spirit which is of God, that we might know the things that are freely given to us of God." "We have the mind of Christ."

This is the stupendous truth which revelation holds out, that we may have a divine capacity in order to understand a divine revelation. The Holy Ghost does not annihilate our intellect, but He so quickens it and infuses into it the mind of Christ, that it is practically true "that old things have passed away, behold, all things have become new."

He can give us the power to cease from our own thoughts, and He can put into us His divine thoughts. He can make the truth real and living, so that it glows and shines with the vividness of intense realization. He can enable us to grasp it, to feel it, to remember it, and to understand it. He can light up the page until it glows as the firmament of stars at night or as the sunshine of the day that makes all objects plain. He can stop our foolish and vain imaginations and "bring every thought into captivity to the obedience of Christ." Blessed baptism for our poor wandering minds! Blessed "peace of God that passeth all understanding," that can "keep our thoughts" as well as our hearts by Christ Jesus! Blessed sight as well as light that the blind can have!

Therefore, in that beautiful and symbolical Gospel of John, where every act of Christ was an object lesson, we find that, after He had revealed Himself as the Light of the world, He immediately healed the blind man and restored his sight, as much as to say, "It is not only light you need, but vision." He came "that they which see not might see, and that they which see might be made blind!"

3. There is one more thought still, and that is the insufficiency of human wisdom to know the things of God. "The natural man receiveth not the things of the Spirit of God; for they are foolishness unto him: neither can he know them, because they are spiritually discerned."

The natural man here is not, of course, the fleshly man, but it is literally the physical man; that is, the soul man, the intellectual mind, the cultured mind, the mind of the philosopher. It is not for want of human education that men do not know the truth of God, but it is for want of spiritual organs. Therefore it is that "the wisdom of this world is foolishness with God, and He taketh the wise in their own craftiness." Therefore it is that scholarship and genius and even ecclesiastical authority so often fail to grasp the deeper spiritual truths of the gospel, and even oppose and hold up to ridicule and scorn the things that God hath revealed to them that love Him.

And so, beloved, when you find the gifted and the influential, even in professors' chairs and sacred pulpits, opposing the truths that are dearer to you than your life, and that you have seen in the living light of God, do not wonder; do not feel provoked; do not answer back according to their folly; but pray for them; pity them and, as you have opportunity, let the light of the truth they do not know shine into their hearts. Let them feel the touch of your love. Let them see the tears of your deep and earnest compassion. Let them behold the glory that shines through your face and life, and some day they will become hungry for the secret of the Lord which you have found.

When Apollos preached in Ephesus the wonderful wisdom of the schools, Aquila and Priscilla heard him and saw his great lack. They did not criticize him and denounce him, but they lovingly prayed for him; they gently brought to him the deeper truth, and God opened his heart to receive it.

And Oh, men of culture, men of self-confidence, you will never find the truth by your processes. You cannot understand it without the divine revelation. You are blind, and dark, and doomed, unless God will give you light. Oh, lie down in humility, abasement, and helplessness, at His blessed feet; confess your blindness, and cry to Him like Bartimeus of old, "Lord, that my eyes may be opened"! And you, too, shall receive spiritual sight, and behold wondrous things out of his law.

II. THE INDWELLING OF THE HOLY GHOST AS OUR SANCTIFIER.

1 Cor. 3: 16, 17: "Know ye not that ye are the temple of God, and that the Spirit of God dwelleth in you? If any man defile the temple of God, him shall God destroy; for the temple of God is holy, which temple ye are."

1 Cor. 6: 11: "And such were some of you; but ye are washed, but ye are sanctified, but ye are justified in the name of the Lord Jesus, and by the Spirit of our God."

Here we have the Holy Spirit as the indwelling presence of the sanctified heart, and, indeed, as the source of its sanctification and preservation. This is the mystery of godliness — God dwelling in the temple of a human soul. It is not merely that the temple is made holy, but, being separated and sanctified, it is made the abode of God Himself, and He lives in it His own glorious life. "I will dwell in them, and I will walk in them."

The apostle appeals to the Corinthians with the question, "Know ye not ?" The power of this blessed relationship is in knowing it, recognizing it and living under its power. There are many glorious facts, which, if we but knew them, would revolutionize our lives. For ages the world lived on the edge of the profoundest secrets of science and nature, and because it knew them not, it never entered into their power; but when it knew the secret that was locked up in the lightning and the steam, then all the forces of our modern commercial and industrial life at once came upon the scene of human life.

And when we know that we have within us the in-dwelling presence of God, we become at once partakers of His omnipotence. When we know that we have within us the power that can lift us above every temptation, difficulty and sorrow, we become partners in the power of God, and we go forth with the shout of a conqueror.

0, beloved, many of you are living in poverty, defeat and disappointment, when you might be conquerors and millionaires — spiritual millionaires! Only claim your rights, only touch the wire that is throbbing with electric fire, only draw upon the bank account which is deposited in your name, only use the resources that belong to you, only know and prove your full salvation, and you shall go forth as the victorious sons of God, and conquered difficulties shall fall beneath your feet, and you shall march forth, shouting, "Thanks be unto God, who always causes us to triumph in Christ Jesus."

III. THE HOLY SPIRIT FOR OUR BODY.

1 Cor. 6:19. "What! know ye not that your body is the temple of the Holy Ghost which is in you, which ye have of God?"

This is a different truth from the one that we have been considering, at least it is a different measure and degree of the same truth. The Holy Ghost not only fills the heart, but He fills, or wants to fill, the body, too. He wants to have us surrender to Him every physical organ and member, and possess it, fill it, and quicken it with His divine life. He is the Former of our body as well as the Father of our spirit, and He is able to impart to every part of our frame the very life of the risen Christ. And when He fills the body and makes it His temple, He unites it with Christ. Then also the thirteenth and the fifteenth verses become true, "The body is for the Lord, and the Lord is for the body." "Know ye not that your bodies are the members of Christ?"

Then He introduces us to that mysterious and glorious relationship where we call Him Husband, where we are wedded to the very life of our beloved Lord, and where He imparts to our vital being and our physical organism His own resurrection life and strength.

This is a relationship as pure and holy as the very heart of God. It cannot be compared with any human relationship; it is infinitely above it. It is a fellowship in the Holy Ghost so delicate, so sacred, so pure, that the faintest image of earthliness would defile it. But it is as real, as actual, as satisfying, as the most tender and intimate of human affections; and, indeed, all we know of earthly love and earthly joy is only its imperfect type and shadow. It is the source of physical quickening for the consecrated body. It makes our bodies the members of Christ. It brings into every part of our being His very life; it makes Him to us our

Life and Living Bread. It translates into actual experience His wonderful words, "As the living Father hath sent Me, and as I live by the Father, so he that eateth Me, even he shall live by Me."

This is a love and a life that "none but he that feels it knows." But He will teach it to the consecrated and obedient heart, and He will give to us even here a foretaste of that blessed fellowship above where we shall sit down at the Marriage Supper of the Lamb, and live forever on His own divine life.

Then we are also taught that this indwelling of the Holy Ghost in our body, and this union of our frame with the personal Christ will bring entire sacredness, dedication, and consecration to all our being. "Ye are not your own, for ye are bought with a price; therefore, glorify God in your body which is God's." The reading of the Authorized Version is wrong here. The word spirit is not found in the original. He is speaking exclusively of our physical life. It is our body that is bought with a price. It is our body that is not our own. It is our body in which we are to glorify God.

And how shall we glorify Him but by letting Him live in it, look through it, and work in it for others, until our whole physical life shall be an expression of God's grace and fullness, and He shall look through our holy lives, and walk in our springing steps and shine in our glowing faces and speak in our living, loving tones, and be revealed to men in all we think and say and do.

Oh, what a sacredness it gives to life to receive it breath by breath and moment by moment from Him!

They tell of a poor Chinese woman who had refused to accept Jesus from the missionary nurse that waited upon her. She was dying of an ulcerated arm, and when the doctor said that if she could get anyone to give up his flesh and blood to be transfused into this shrunken and diseased member she might be healed, she sent for her son and asked him if he would let the doctor take the pieces of flesh and the drops of blood from his arm to be infused into his mother. He refused, and then she broke down in deep sorrow and discouragement.

One day the missionary nurse found her weeping and sat down by her side and asked her if she would allow her to give her flesh and blood to heal her. She was deeply moved at the offer, and although she protested that, it was too much to ask, yet she allowed the operation to be performed. Day by day she continued to improve, and at length the arm was healed, and a white patch of pure flesh and skin covered the place where the ulcer so long had consumed her flesh.

One day the missionary nurse saw her weeping again and looking at her healed arm with strange tenderness. She asked her what was the matter, and the native woman said, "Teacher, I have been looking at this white spot on my arm, and thinking you gave me your flesh and blood to heal my poor diseased body. Why could you do it?"

And the teacher said, "It was only for love of Jesus, because He gave His life for me."

The poor Chinese woman wept afresh, and looking up, she said, "Teacher, I want your Jesus. If He can make you love me that way, when my own son refused to save me, I want Him to be my Jesus, too." And that poor Chinese woman was brought to Christ by the love of a missionary who could give her very flesh to her.

O, beloved, as I look at these veins that were once so dark with the currents of disease, and think of Him who not only gave His life for me, but who every morning freshly gives it to me, how can I live for myself; how can I live for the world; how can I prostitute to sin these God-given powers; how can I but feel, as this text has said, "I am not my own, I am bought with a price, I will glorify God in my body which is God's"?

God help us so to receive the life of Jesus, and so to give it forth in holy, consecrated service for Him, and for the world, which can only be brought to Him by the living pattern of His great love, and by the indwelling of His own wondrous life, through the Holy Ghost which is given to us!

# Chapter 12

# The Holy Spirit in the Body of Christ

"For by one Spirit are we all baptized into one body, whether we be Jews or Gentiles, whether we be bond or free; and have been all made to drink into one Spirit." 1 Cor. 12: 13.

The whole of this wonderful chapter is devoted to the unfolding of the profound truth that the church is the body of Christ, and that the Holy Ghost is the life of the church, constituting and sustaining its union with Christ, the living Head, and clothing it with divine power and efficiency for its holy ministry.

I. THE HOLY GHOST CONSTITUTES THE BODY OF CHRIST.

"For by one Spirit are we all baptized into one body." The church is not an organization. It is an organic life; it is a living body constituted by the Holy Ghost, and united to Jesus Christ, its life and living Head. Eve was created in the person of Adam, at first, and then, afterwards was taken from him by the special act of God, and united to him as his bride. So the Church is taken out of Christ by the Holy Ghost, and then given back to Him in divine union, as His glorious Bride.

Each individual member is thus called and created anew in Christ Jesus and, one by one, the Lord adds to Himself and to His Church such as shall be saved. No other power can constitute a church. Men may be added to organizations, but this does not make them the body of Christ. The union must be vital; the work must be divine. It is called a baptism. This word expresses the deep truth of death and resurrection. It is by the death of our natural life and the resurrection life of the Lord Jesus Christ, that we become incorporated into His glorious body and united with His life as the great Head of the Church.

Everything pertaining to the natural life is incongruous with the true Church of Christ. The greatest curse of the church today is the carnal element that still adheres to it through unsanctified men. The greatest need of the Church of the Lord Jesus Christ is to be baptized into death through His cross, and raised into His divine life. This the Holy Ghost alone can do. This He is doing, member by member and moment by moment, as the days go by, gathering out of every people and kindred and tongue, a body for the Lord, a Bride for the Lamb. And when the last member shall be gathered and the Bride shall be complete, the Lord will come and unite His body to its waiting and glorified Head.

So those alone belong to the true body of Christ, who through the Holy Ghost, have passed through death into resurrection. "For by one Spirit are we all baptized into one body."

II. THE HOLY GHOST SUSTAINS THE LIFE OF THE CHURCH.

The apostle adds in the same verse, "We have all been made to drink into that one Spirit." It is one thing to be baptized into the body, it is another thing to drink of the ocean into which we have been plunged.

The Holy Ghost becomes the vital element of our new life. In Him we live, and move, and have our being. As the bird lives in the air, as the fish lives in the sea, as the flower lives on the sunshine, so we live in the element of the Holy Ghost; and, as we drink of His fullness, our life is maintained and grows into the maturity of Christ.

This is the secret of being filled with the Spirit, and this is the source of fruitfulness and life. Have we thus been made to drink into that one Spirit? He has to make us drink. He has to make us so hungry and thirsty that we will fly to Him for His life and love. He has to press us into the hard emergency, so as to constrain us to receive His fullness. And thus He is watering, nourishing, filling, and perfecting His glorious workmanship, and preparing it for the maturity of the body and the fullness of Christ.

III. THE HOLY GHOST UNITES THE BODY.

"For there is one body," not two, "and as we have many members in one body, so also is Christ."

1. He unites us to Christ the Head, and then He unites us to one another in Him. Each individual is connected directly with the Lord Jesus Christ, as the source of his individual life, and from Him life must come to every member and extremity of the body.

But He needs His Church just as much as His Church needs Him. What is a head without a body? What is a body without a head? And so the Church here is called by a very solemn name, "So also is Christ." The Church is spoken of as Christ; the Head in heaven is Christ; the body on earth is Christ. It represents Him; it stands for His merits, rights, and name, His holy character, and vital power. It is filled with His life; its holiness is His presence; its physical strength is derived from His resurrection life, and all its power is just the working out of the ascended Lord. He is still working through it, and continuing to work, as He began on earth, and we can look up, and say, "As He is, so are we also in this world." All our sufferings He shares. The most tender cords of sympathy bind us to Him. When His disciples are persecuted and hurt, His heart from the throne is thrilled with sympathetic pain, and He cries, "Why persecutest thou Me?"

2. But not only so, the Holy Ghost unites the members also together. "Therefore if one member suffer, all the members suffer with it; if one member be honored, all the members rejoice with it." Weakness or disease in any portion of the human body affects the whole; so the morbid sickly condition of so many members of the Church of Christ today affects the whole body, and holds back the strength of Christ's cause from accomplishing results which He has a right to expect.

Therefore it is a very solemn thing to be responsible for schism or separation in the Church. When we do we sin against the heart of Jesus, we sin against the Holy Ghost, we sin against the very body of Christ. Therefore it is not only necessary to keep from offences, injuries, and attacks upon the body of Christ; but we must also maintain a healthful spiritual condition, or we shall defile the whole body by sympathetic contact. And, therefore, if we are filled with the Spirit, we shall have a very tender, compassionate and sympathetic heart toward Christ's Church, and shall be solicitous and sensitive for her welfare and prosperity. It will be our joy, like the great apostle's, "to be offered upon the sacrifice and services of her faith," and to "fill up that which remains of the sufferings of Christ for His body, the Church;" sharing with the blessed Head the needs of His people, bearing one another's burdens, and so fulfilling the law of Christ.

IV. THE HOLY GHOST ENDUES AND ENABLES THE BODY OF CHRIST FOR ITS VARIOUS MINISTRIES.

This is the special theme of this chapter and all we have said leads up to it.

1. Every ministry, in order to be effectual, must be inspired and made efficient by the Holy Ghost. No man can rightly say that Jesus Christ is Lord, save by the Holy Ghost. God cannot use secular and natural gifts apart from the Holy Spirit. "If any man speak, let him do it as the oracle of God; if any man minister, let him do it as of the ability that God giveth, that God in all things may be glorified through Jesus Christ." It is not splendid talent, it is not deep culture, that constitute efficiency in the body of Christ, it is simply and absolutely the power of the Holy Spirit. It is a divine ministry and must have a divine equipment.

2. We are also taught that every member of the Church may have the Holy Ghost for service; for "the manifestation of the Spirit is given to every man to profit withal"; that is to say, the Holy Ghost is no respecter of persons, but is ready to endue and enable every servant of Christ for the work to which he is called, and the place in the body to which he is appointed.

This blessed enduement is not for apostles, prophets, miracle workers, teachers, special officials, merely, but for every member of the Church of God. Every part of the body is necessary and important, and, as the apostle reasons very beautifully from human physiology, the weakest and humblest members of the human frame are often most highly honored; so also, in the Church of Christ, God uses and honors the weakest and the lowliest, filling them with His own enabling, and thus glorifying His own grace.

3. There is infinite variety. As in the human body, every member has his separate office, and the unity is enriched by the diversity which it harmonizes. God does not want any man to copy another, but each to be himself, with God added.

Our ministries are determined in some measure by our place in the body, by our environment, by the circumstances and providences amid which we are placed, by leadings, and natural instincts and preferences, and by the gifts both of nature and of grace. Just where we are, the Holy Ghost waits to equip us, enable us, and fit us for higher usefulness, and most efficient service.

He names a number of these gifts. Some are called be apostles, some prophets, some evangelists, some pastors and teachers, some workers of miracles, some counselors, some just helps, and some governments; but you will notice, that the helps come before the governments, and the teachers come before the miracle workers. It is not brilliancy that God recognizes, but service; and if you cannot be a wonder worker, you can be at least a little lamp to give light to the path of some traveler, or you can be an armor-bearer to stand beside some other worker and help along.

4. Each of these gifts of the Holy Ghost is administered by the Holy Ghost Himself. The man, who is used as an instrument, does not receive the glory and is not recognized as the worker, but simply as the instrument. And so we have the significant expression, "All these worketh that one and the self-same Spirit." It is the Spirit that works, and the man is just the vessel through whom He exercises His sovereign and Almighty grace.

As Richard Baxter has put it so wisely, "Each of us is just a pen in the hand of God, and what honor is there in a pen?" While we recognize this we shall be saved from all self-consciousness, egotism, and elation, and we shall lie in the dust at His blessed feet, hidden and empty vessels, in the place where He can use us best.

5. There is one other thought of great significance, and that is, that as the servant uses the gift, it grows. "The manifestation of the Spirit is given to every man to profit withal." As we wisely use and faithfully improve the gifts of the Holy Ghost, they grow in effectiveness and we become more and more used and honored of God, until He may be pleased to add to us not only one, but many gifts, as we covet earnestly the best gifts, and He shall multiply the fruit of our service by thousands and tens of thousands, so that, in the day of recompense, our seed shall be as the stars of heaven and our crown shall be brighter than their supernal light.

What a solemn truth it is to have God Himself as our Enabler, our Enduement for service! Yes, He has given to us a crown to win; He has given to us a life in which to win it; He has given to us an age of extraordinary opportunities, and He has given us the Holy Ghost to work out in our lives the highest possibilities of existence. God help us to be true to our tremendous trust, and to our brief but infinite opportunities, through the grace of the Lord Jesus Christ and the power of the blessed Holy Ghost.

## Chapter 13

## The Holy Spirit in Second Corinthians

"Now, He which stablisheth us with you in Christ, and hath anointed us, is God; who hath also sealed us, and given the earnest of the Spirit in our hearts." 2 Cor. 1: 21, 22. "Forasmuch as ye are manifestly declared to be the epistle of Christ ministered by us, not written with ink, but with the Spirit of the living God; not in tables of stone, but in fleshy tables of the heart." 2 Cor. 3: 3. "But we all, with open face beholding as in a glass the glory of the Lord, are changed into the same image from glory to glory, even as by the Spirit of the Lord." 2Cor. 3: 18.

These three verses present to us five striking and instructive symbols of the Holy Spirit; jewels, they are, of holy metaphor, flashing celestial light from their faces, and speaking of the deepest truths of Christian experience.

1. THE ANOINTING.

"He which stablisheth us with you in Christ, and hath anointed us, is God."

The figure of anointing runs through all the Scriptures, and it is crystalized in the very name of Christ and Christian. Christ means the Anointed One, and the Christian is the Christ-one, or the one that has been anointed with the Holy Ghost. We see it in all the ceremonies of the Old Testament. Especially was it employed in the setting apart of the three great officials of the Old Testament; the prophet, the priest, and the king.

Prophets were anointed that they might be set apart as witnesses and messengers of the will of God, and so we are God's witnesses and messengers. Priests were anointed to stand between God and the people, and make intercession in behalf of others; and so we are anointed as God's holy priesthood, to come near into His presence, to worship at His feet, to present the incense of faith, love, and devotion, to bear upon our hearts the sufferings, sins, and needs of others, and to share the priesthood of our glorified Master. And kings were anointed to rule in the name of God, and to stand in glorious majesty representing Jehovah to the people; and so we are a royal priesthood, kings and priests unto God and His Father; and, possessing the Holy Ghost, ours shall be a regnant life, victorious over self and sin, triumphant over temptations and difficulties, and glorious in the dignity of our high calling.

For this threefold ministry we are anointed of the Holy Ghost. Only the Holy Spirit can fit us for so high a calling, and He is given to every follower of Jesus who is willing to receive and obey Him.

The figure of anointing is used with still more wide and beautiful significance. It speaks of holy gladness. " Anointed with the oil of gladness above our fellows." "Thou anointest my head with oil, my cup runneth over." It is the symbol of healing, "anointing with oil in the name of the Lord; and the prayer of faith shall save the sick, and the Lord shall raise him up."

This anointing is the privilege of the humblest believer, and of the most unworthy sinner that is willing to receive Jesus and be baptized with the Holy Ghost. There is no more beautiful figure of the anointing, in the Old Testament, than the story of the leper in the book of Leviticus. A poor outcast, unworthy and sinful, he was brought unto the priest in his helplessness and misery; then he was touched with the blood, washed with the water, disrobed, and cleansed; and then he was clothed upon in the garments of holiness; the blood of the oil touched the tip of his ear, his thumb, and his foot, and he, too, became an anointed one.

So, still, the most helpless, hopeless, and worthless may receive the very highest gift of the Lord Jesus Christ, the blessed Holy Ghost, and say with the apostle, "Now He which stablisheth us in Christ, and hath anointed us, is God"; and then go forth to say with the Master, "The Spirit of the Lord is upon me; for He hath anointed me to preach the gospel to the poor, to bind up the broken-hearted, to proclaim deliverance to the captives, the recovering of sight to the blind, and set at liberty them that are bruised, to preach the acceptable year of the Lord."

II. THE SEAL.

The seal is associated with all the relics of antiquity and all the customs of business in every age. It is used first to authenticate and certify; and so the Holy Ghost certifies the believer, putting the stamp of God upon him, giving to him the witness of his acceptance and the assurance of His full salvation.

Next, the seal is the token of ownership; and so the Holy Ghost sets us apart, stamping us as the property of God, and marking us as no longer our own, but the purchased possession of Jesus Christ, bought by His blood, bound to live for His service and glory.

Again, the seal is the expression of reality. It cuts its impression in the wax and makes it real, tangible and enduring; and so the Holy Ghost makes the things that we have known, real, and turns into actual experience that which was before but theory. He makes truth real; He makes Christ real; He makes divine things facts in our consciousness and our blessed experience.

Finally, the seal transfers the image and the Holy Ghost imparts to our receptive hearts the very image of Jesus Christ, and leaves the stamp of His character upon our lives.

You cannot, however, affix the seal to the hard and settled wax. It must be soft and melted; then the impression is easily made and becomes fixed and abiding; and so God has to soften our hearts before He can seal them. Oh, the blessedness of brokenness! The Holy Spirit is ever seeking to melt our rigidness into tenderness, so that He can impress upon us the stamp of His ownership and His image, and make us the representatives of Christ to all who see and know us.

The sealing of the Holy Ghost is a very definite and explicit act. In the Epistle to the Ephesians we are told exactly when it occurs. "After ye believed, ye were sealed with that Holy Spirit of promise." We first yield ourselves, and then we believe and receive the Holy Ghost by a definite act of committal and faith; then His work begins.

We come and set our seal to the divine covenant; for "he that hath received Him, hath set his seal that God is true." And then, on our seal, which we have affixed with our trusting, trembling hands, the Holy Ghost comes and puts down His mighty seal upon us, the double stamp is given, and we are fully sealed unto the day of redemption. Beloved, have you received the anointing, have you been sealed by the Holy Ghost?

III. THE EARNEST.

This is also a very significant word. It has been reproduced in almost all languages from the original Hebrew. The very same Hebrew word reappears in the Greek language and in other tongues.

It represents the first installment in the purchase. When I buy a piece of land, I make a payment on the signing of the contract, and the seller is bound by my payment to make good to me the deed in due time, and I am bound to follow it up with the complete payment. It is a first installment, a part payment, binding the whole transaction.

It has still another sense closely akin to this. In Oriental countries and ancient times, the seller, also, gave a first installment, as well as the buyer. Taking a little handful of soil from the land purchased, he put it into a bag and handed it to the purchaser as a pledge of the whole property's being transferred to him in due time. It was the very same soil as he had bought, though only a portion of it, but it was the guarantee that all the rest should be duly transferred.

So the Holy Ghost is to us the payment in part, and the pledge in full, of our complete inheritance. He is the first fruit of the harvest, He is the first portion of the inheritance. He brings into our heart and life the very same blessed reality which heaven will complete; the only difference will be in measure and degree. And so we have the double earnest. First, we have Him in our hearts as the earnest of the spiritual inheritance which heaven will bring. But a little later, in the fifth chapter and the fifth verse, we have a little different phase of the earnest. "Now He which hath wrought us for this very thing is God, who hath also given us the earnest of the Spirit." Now, the very thing of which Paul is speaking there is not our spiritual inheritance, but our physical inheritance in God. It is the resurrection body, it is the glory which Christ is to bring, when we shall be clothed upon with our house which is from heaven, and he clearly states here that the Holy Spirit is the earnest of this, also.

What can this mean but the blessed truth and the still more blessed experience to many of us — the Holy Ghost's imparting to the body the very principle of the resurrection life, quickening it, exhilarating it, strengthening it, inspiring it with divine life and vigor, lifting it above disease and pain, and anticipating, in some little measure, the glory of the resurrection.

IV. EPISTLES OF CHRIST.

"Forasmuch as ye are manifestly declared to be the epistle of Christ ministered by us, written not with ink, but with the Spirit of the living God; not in tables of stone, but in fleshy tables of the heart." 2 Corinthians 3:3.

We have here a new figure of the Holy Spirit as the great Recorder transcribing Christ and His character and life upon the living tablets of human hearts and lives. It is a beautiful figure; each of us is represented as a volume published to the world, and carrying to men the message of Christ. It is the only volume that many ever read. It is the Bible bound, not in Russia, nor Morocco, nor cloth, but in human lives. This is the work of the Holy Ghost, and this is the highest ministry of every consecrated life. Beloved, are we thus revealing Christ to the world? Are we thus carrying the living message of His love and will to men and women around us? Are we written on by the finger of the Holy

Ghost? Oh, how sacred were those holy tables of stone on which God's own fingers recorded the ancient law, and which He deposited for safe keeping in the Ark of the Covenant! How much more sacred the tables on which the Holy Spirit is now inscribing the very life of Jesus, and entrusting to the keeping of our consecrated lives!

God help us to receive the message and then to publish it so truly, so sweetly, so wisely and so consistently, that it may be known and read of all men, and that it shall minister Christ to a world that will not read His Bible, and does not know His grace. As has been happily said, "Each of us is either a Bible or a libel." God help us to be living epistles of Jesus Christ in the power of the Holy Ghost.

V. PHOTOGRAPHS OF JESUS.

"But we all, with open face beholding as in a glass the glory of the Lord, are changed into the same image from glory to glory, even as by the Spirit of the Lord." 2 Cor. 3: 18.

This is the last of these metaphors of the Spirit, and it carries the thought to a beautiful and perfect climax. We are not only books, but we are illustrated books; we are not only epistles of Christ, but we are photographs of Christ. In the center of the volume of our life is a living picture, which the Holy Ghost is ever perfecting, and in which He is revealing to the world the very glory of Jesus.

The idea is very striking, and exquisitely fine. We are represented as gazing with fixed look upon the face of Jesus Christ, and, as we gaze, His likeness is reflected in our countenance; the Holy Ghost is taking a picture of Jesus, not on a sensitive plate, as in our photographic art, but on a human face, and the face becomes a living illustration to the world of the glory of our Lord.

In order that this picture may be perfectly taken, we must keep our own face steadfast, and our eye fixed upon Him, and as we do so His glory is reflected in our countenances, and His very image is reproduced in our faces. It is also necessary that we must gaze with open face. There must be no veil nor cloud between. As in the photographer's art, the little covering must be removed from the face of the camera in order that the impression may be taken; so the world, the flesh, and every obstruction must be put aside, and with unclouded face and single eye we must look steadfastly to Him; and as we become occupied with Christ, and abide in His fellowship, His glorious likeness is reproduced in us, and we stand before the world, not only living epistles but living likenesses, of our blessed Lord. Sublime conception! We are illustrated volumes, revealing to the world our blessed Savior, even as He revealed to the world His glorious Father.

It was His to be the brightness of the Father's glory and the express image of His person. It is ours to be the image of His glory and the express image of Him. As He represented God, so we are to represent Christ, and men will know Him by what they see of Him in us.

This is the blessed work of the Holy Ghost. He is the Artist that stands behind the canvas and brings out the glorious, heavenly picture. Not only so, but He makes a living picture. We are not stereotyped and put away in a cabinet, but the picture is renewed from day to day, and each day should be brighter than the past. It is "from glory to glory," even brighter and brighter until it shall be lost in the light of heaven. It is not even "from grace to glory." We are to reach the stage of glory, and then go on "from glory to glory" in increasing luster forever.

Beloved, have we understood these things? Oh, may the Holy Ghost enable us to realize and fully prove the blessed meaning of these five heavenly symbols of the Holy Ghost — the anointing, the seal, the earnest, the living epistles, and the living photograph of the Savior's face! Amen.

## Chapter 14

## The Holy Spirit in Galatians

"If we live in the Spirit, let us also walk in the Spirit." Gal. 5: 25.

The Galatians were the Scottish Highlanders of ancient times and the ancestors, also, of the hot-blooded race that transferred the name of Gaul from the Province of Galatia to ancient France.

They were a warm-hearted and generous people, quick to receive the teachings of Paul, and quick also to be led astray by the false teachers that followed him. And so we find him warning and pleading with them, with his warm-hearted enthusiasm, against the seductions of the Judaizing party, who had begun to lead them back from the simplicity of Christ to the entanglements of the law.

The theme, therefore, of the Epistle, suited to the condition of the Galatians, is FREE GRACE. In opposition to the misleading men who were seducing them from the liberty of the gospel, he reiterates, again and again, the freeness of the grace that saved them at the beginning, and that now must still sanctify and lead them all the way through.

And so this thought gives tone to all the apostle's references to the Holy Spirit in the epistle. These references are by no means few or unimportant, and they are all touched with the complexion of this glorious theme, the freeness of the Gospel and, of course, inferentially, the freeness of the Holy Ghost.

I. The Holy Ghost is received by faith and not by the works of the law. "O, foolish Galatians, who hath bewitched you? This only would I learn of you. Received ye the Spirit by the works of the law, or by the hearing of faith?" Gal. 3: 1, 2.

The Holy Ghost is just as freely given as the blood of Jesus and the justifying righteousness of God through Christ. The Holy Ghost is promised just as salvation is promised, and received just as salvation is received, by simple faith in the blood of the Lamb, and the act of appropriating the blessing to ourselves. Not by our surrendering, not by our consecration, not by our sufferings or crucifixions, but by simply believing, do we receive this great gift of Jesus Christ, the blessed Holy Ghost.

He is not given because we deserve it; He is not given because we have suffered; He is not given to those who struggle, but He is freely given to those who freely receive Him, on the simple promise of God, and by child-like trust in His grace and love.

We must trust the Holy Ghost as well as Jesus. We oust speak to the rock and bid the waters flow. If we strike it with our violent hands and our struggling self-efforts we shall only keep back the blessing which we seek. Let us believe; let us receive the Holy Ghost.

II. Our whole Christian life must be sustained and maintained by the Holy Ghost through the same simple faith by which we first began. And so we read again, Galatians3: 3: "Are ye so foolish? having begun in the Spirit, are ye now made perfect by the flesh?"

Oh, how many are so foolish! They begin as hopeless sinners at the foot of the cross, taking all as the sovereign gift of divine mercy, and then they begin to build up a sort of reputation and condition of self-constituted strength and try to sanctify themselves by their own set of credentials, crucifixions, and ineffectual struggles. It is, indeed, utterly foolish and vain. We need the same grace to keep us as saves us at first. "By whom also we have access by faith into this grace wherein we stand."

Our Christian life is just a succession of the simple acts of faith with which we first began. "As ye have received Christ Jesus the Lord, so walk in Him." And the Holy Ghost is essential to sustain and maintain all the exercises of spiritual life by His own divine efficiency and spontaneous working to the very close of our Christian life.

O, beloved, have you been so foolish? Cease your hard and vain endeavors, and simply abide in Him. Be filled with the Spirit, and the fruit will take care of itself.

III. Our Christian service and our power for service through the Holy Ghost are by simple faith and the free grace of God in Christ. And so we have the next appeal in Galatians 3:5. "He, therefore, that ministereth to you the Spirit, and worketh miracles among you, doeth He it by the works of the law, or by the hearing of faith?"

Yes, the very ministry, for which the Holy Ghost enables us, must be done in simple faith and dependence upon His gracious gifts. The Holy Ghost in His power for service, is given just the same as in the beginning, in the name of Jesus, in the exercise of divine mercy, and by simply believing God and taking Him at His word. According to our faith is it unto us. "He that ministereth the Spirit"; here is not some man, but it is God. It is Jesus that ministereth the Holy Ghost and He does it to them that believe and as they believe. Would we then have this deeper fullness, we must believe in the Holy Spirit; we must receive Him by implicit trust in the promises of God.

IV. We have the Holy Spirit next presented as the sum of all the blessings that come to us through Christ and the great covenant with Abraham on which the gospel is founded in Gal. 3:13, 14, "Christ hath redeemed us from the curse of the law . . . that the blessing of Abraham might come upon the Gentiles, that we might receive the promise of the Spirit through faith."

The promise of the Spirit, therefore, is the substance of the covenant with Abraham and the supreme blessing of Christ's redemption. And as the covenant with Abraham was purely one of faith and not of works, long antecedent to the dispensation of law, so the Holy Ghost must be as freely given as all the other blessings of the gospel. The inference is quite justified that if we have not received the Holy Ghost we have not inherited the full blessings of the covenant with Abraham, and the full purchase of Christ's redemption.

The Holy Ghost is just the Agent who applies to us the redemption purchased by Christ, and without Him the cross becomes but a vain possibility to us, and the gospel an unfilled promise.

Beloved, have you received the promise of the Spirit? Other promises are called the promises, but this is called THE PROMISE; it is the one all-embracing promise that includes all the rest, and without it all the rest are vain. Oh, let us claim the promise of the Father, and the inheritance of faith in all its blessed fullness!

V. THE SPIRIT OF SONSHIP AND OF CHRIST.

The Holy Ghost is next presented, in this beautiful epistle, as the Spirit of the Lord Jesus Christ dwelling in our heart through our union with Him, and bringing us into His very sonship, and the fellowship of His inheritance. "Because ye are sons, God hath sent forth the Spirit of His Son into your hearts, crying, Abba, Father." Gal. 4: 6.

This sonship is the peculiar promise of the New Testament, the peculiar privilege of those who are united to the person of the Lord Jesus Christ. This is not the sonship that comes by virtue of our creation; this is not even the sonship that comes by virtue of our regeneration and God's begetting us as His children, but this is a new and higher sonship, that comes by virtue of our union with Jesus Christ, and it brings us into His very relationship to the Father.

He is the only begotten Son, the First Born, and we also are first born ones, and called "the church of the first born ones who are written in heaven." It is in His very sonship and with His very heart within us, that we look up and say, "Abba Father;" it is a double Fatherhood, a twofold experience, born of His very heart and then wedded to His Only Begotten Son. Oh, what manner of love the Father hath bestowed upon us, that we should be called the sons of God! We are the sons of God, and "we know that when He shall appear we shall be like Him." We are no longer servants, but sons and heirs of God, through Christ.

Beloved, have we received power thus to become the sons of God and to let the Holy Ghost work in us our high calling?

## VI. THE HOLY GHOST AS THE SPIRIT OF SANCTIFICATION AND VICTORY. GAL. 5:16.

"This I say then, walk in the Spirit and ye shall not fulfill the lusts of the flesh. For the Spirit," that is, the Holy Spirit, "lusteth against the flesh, and the flesh against the Spirit, and these are contrary the one to the other: so that ye cannot do the things that ye would."

A single letter here sheds God's own perfect light upon the exposition of this verse, and that is the capital with which we spell the word Spirit. It is the Holy Spirit that resists the flesh, and He alone can overcome it and exclude it, and as we "walk in the Spirit, we shall not fulfill the lusts of the flesh."

Here is God's great secret of holiness; not fighting sin, but being filled with God. It is the old principle of the expulsive power of a stronger force and a supreme affection. Just as water excludes air from that tumbler when it is filled with water; just as light excludes the darkness when the room is lighted, so the indwelling of the Holy Ghost excludes the presence and power of sin.

It is the old question of struggling to sanctify our wives, and fighting the flesh to keep it down, on the one hand, or rising with God above it and dwelling in that higher, holier element, where we are removed from its control. It is the question whether we shall try to cleanse the swamp of its filth and its abominable creatures, or whether we shall fly above it, and dwell in the pure light of heaven with the Holy Ghost, where its miasmas cannot reach us, and its serpents cannot crawl.

It is the old fable of the cleansing of the Aegean stables by spades and carts and scavengers, or the simple and better way of letting the current of the mighty river flow through that stable until it sweeps all its impurities away and turns its banks into a paradise of loveliness. In a word, it is the glorious privilege of sanctified, not by works but by free grace, not by self effort, but by simple faith in the indwelling presence and power of God.

VII. THE FRUIT OF THE SPIRIT.

This naturally follows from the previous thought, and it is exquisitely brought out in the next few verses, where we have the works of the flesh in their manifold forms. First, the acts of impurity; then, the sources of impurity; then, the idolatry to which impurity leads; then, malignity and hate in all their forms, pouring out toward men the evil that had already separated from God, and finally, the awful excess of crime and sensuality into which it brings men.

In contrast with this dreadful picture He gives us "the fruit of the Spirit, which is love, joy, peace, longsuffering, gentleness, goodness, meekness, temperance, faith."

These are not fruits, but fruit. It is all one fruit. We have not a great many things to do but just one, and that one thing is to love; for all these manifestations of the fruit are but various forms of love. Joy is love exulting; peace is love reposing; longsuffering is love enduring; gentleness is love refined; meekness is love with bowed head; goodness is love in action ; temperance is true self-love, and faith is love confiding, so that the whole sum of Christian living is just loving. And we do not even have to love, but we only have to be filled with the Spirit and then the love will flow as a fountain, spontaneously, from the life within. It is all free grace; it is all the fullness of an inexhaustible stream, the artesian well that pours from the boundless depths, and flows in floods of blessings on every side.

Oh, how easy is this life, how delightful, how true, how glorious!

VIII. OUR PART IN RECEIVING THE SPIRIT, AND CO-WORKING WITH HIS WORKING. GAL. 5:25.

"If we live in the Spirit, let us also walk in the Spirit." Is there then nothing for us to do but just lie passive in His hands while He works in us? Oh, yes; there is much for us to do. We must "walk in the Spirit;" we must co-operate with God; we must keep step with our blessed Companion; we must follow as He leads the way.

It is the habit of constant dependence and obedience; and as we thus walk with Him, He will be manifested in us and will fill us with His fullness and work out in us the fruition of His life.

There are things to do, but they are to be done at His leading and at His enabling. There are attitudes to be maintained, but they are as natural as the steppings of a little child that holds its mother's hand, and walks by her side through the great city, where it knows not a single street or number. It is not our walk so much as our Companion. It was not Enoch so much as the One with whom Enoch walked. And yet Enoch had to keep step with His blessed Friend and, as we thus abide in Him and walk in Him and follow Him, we shall know all the fullness of His love, and will follow on to know the Lord.

IX. THE ATTITUDE OF THE SPIRIT FILLED MAN TO THE WEAK AND ERRING. GAL. 6:1.

"Brethren, if a man be overtaken in a fault, ye which are spiritual, restore such an one in the spirit of meekness, considering thyself, lest thou also be tempted."

Is this life in the Spirit to make us proud and self-sufficient in our attitude to others? No, it will make us tender, compassionate and full of sympathy to the faltering ones, who stumble by our side. It is the spiritual man that is to restore the erring, and even he, with all his experience, is to consider himself, "lest he also be tempted," and to know that he is just as weak and frail as his brother.

It was when Peter had reiterated his love and had been accepted anew of his Lord after the deep and humbling lesson, that he received, as his highest trust, the command to feed the feeble sheep and the helpless lambs. So, as we are filled with the Spirit, it will be the spirit of gentleness, the spirit of patience, the spirit of compassion, the spirit that will restore the erring, and seek and save the lost.

Finally, the Spirit, in relation to the future; sowing to the Spirit, reaping to the Spirit.

What is the bearing of all this present life on the life to come? It is very real; it is very solemn; it is very lasting. "God is not mocked: for whatsoever a man soweth that shall he also reap. He that soweth to the Spirit shall of the Spirit reap life everlasting, and he that soweth to the flesh shall of the flesh reap corruption."

Oh, how the days are telling! We may scatter the thistle down; we may throw our precious seed in the depths of sin, but there shall be a sad reaping bye-and-bye; or, we may sow seeds of patience and trust, of holy suffering, and unselfish service, and bye-and-bye we shall reap if we faint not.

Oh, ye that trifle away the precious hours and opportunities of these days, some day you will wake to find how much you have lost! Some day, when, with a converted soul and a consecrated life, you long for holy usefulness and oh, how you will mourn that you wasted your youth and lost the opportunities that would have fitted you for glorious work for God until it is too late!

O, ye who seem to see no fruit now, go on! Sow to the Spirit and wait; "Cast your seed upon the waters, and you shall find it after many days." And some day, in yonder heaven, you will know what this promise means, "I have called thee, that thou shouldest plant the heavens." Some day as you see the avenues of glory planted with the trees of righteousness and blooming with the flowers of Paradise, an angel voice by your side may tell you that these were the sowing of years of faith and patience, these were the seeds of faith and prayer, of sacrifice and obedience, that you planted long ago.

Pray on, beloved. You are planting seed in heavenly soil, and some day your rapturous soul shall embrace the answer. Suffer on, patient soldier of the cross. It may not be given to you to serve; it may not be given to you to preach the Gospel; it may not be given to you to do the work for which you would gladly give all the world; yours is to stand bravely, truly, in the ordeal of pain, misconstruction, irritation, uncongenial surroundings in the household, in the business office, in the place of terrible temptation. Be true. You are sowing to the Spirit, and some day you will reap the amaranthine flowers and fruits of glory.

You shall have your crown. Nothing that the Spirit breathes can ever die. Nothing that the Spirit plants can ever perish. Sow on. Weep on. Wait on. Hold on. It may be weeping now, it will be rejoicing bye-and-bye. It may be sowing now, but it will be reaping bye-and-bye.

## Chapter 15

## All the Blessings of the Spirit, or the Holy Ghost in Ephesians

"Blessed be the God and Father of our Lord Jesus Christ, who hath blessed us with all the blessings of the Spirit in the heavenlies in Christ Jesus." Ephesians 1: 3.

This is the text of the whole Epistle to the Ephesians. That epistle is an unfolding of "all the blessings of the Spirit." This is the true translation of the passage.

There is a great difference between the blessings of the Spirit and spiritual blessings. This is a case where a single noun is worth a hundred adjectives. The person of the Holy Ghost is worth more than all His gifts.

The blessings unfolded in this epistle are said to be "in the heavenlies"; that is, in the higher realm and element where we dwell in Christ, above the natural life, and in fellowship with the heavenly world.

The apostle's theme, in this sublime epistle, is the higher blessings of the Holy Ghost, which He makes known to those who enter into the fullness of Christ, May the Holy Spirit Himself enable us to see and enter into all the blessings of the Spirit!

I. THE SEALING OF THE SPIRIT.

"In whom, after ye believed, ye were sealed with that Holy Spirit of promise, which is the earnest of our inheritance until the redemption of the purchased possession." Ephesians 1:13-14.

We have already spoken in a former chapter of the seal and earnest of the Spirit, and it is not necessary to enlarge upon them here. The seal is the mark of ownership, reality, certainty and resemblance, the earnest is the first installment and pledge of the full inheritance. The Holy Ghost, when He seals us, makes real and sure to us the blessings of our inheritance and stamps us with the image of Christ; and, as the earnest, He gives to us the promise and the pledge of all the fullness of our future heritage.

This promise is the privilege of every disciple, and it may be claimed and received, by simple faith, the moment we believe. It is recognized not as the crowning experience of Christian life, but rather as its beginning.

Beloved, have we been thus set apart and stamped as the purchased possession of God, and made to know in our inmost experience the hope of our calling, and the foretaste of our future glory?

II. THE SPIRIT OF ILLUMINATION.

The Holy Ghost next opens our inner eyes, and reveals to us the vision of our high calling and our full inheritance. This is given at great length in the sublime passage, Ephesians 1:15-23. This is the apostle's first prayer for the sealed ones of whom he has already spoken.

He asks for them, that the Holy Ghost may be to them the "Spirit of wisdom and revelation in the knowledge of Him." This is a special divine revelation beyond the power of human intellect in its own natural wisdom and strength. It is not only that new truths are unfolded and illuminated but new spiritual vision is given to understand and realize them. The eyes of their understanding are to be enlightened. This should rather be translated, "the eyes of your heart." It is the deeper spiritual nature that is here referred to, the very core of our being, and the fountain of our thoughts and conceptions of divine things.

It is not through our cold intellect, but through our spiritual instincts, that we are to understand the heavenly vision. There are things that "eye hath not seen, nor ear heard, neither have they entered into the heart of man; but God hath revealed them unto us by His Spirit." There are humble Christians who could not spell a word of two syllables or explain a single rule of grammar, who have thoughts and conceptions of God, and raptures of heavenly joy, for which an angel would gladly leave his throne.

The object of this vision is: first, "that ye may know what is the hope of His calling." This means the glorious purpose for which He has called us, as an object of delightful hope and expectation, that we may know our high destiny and be thrilled with the joy of its anticipation.

Next, He prays that we may know "the riches of the glory of His inheritance in the saints." The word "know" in all these clauses, means, in the original, to know fully, to know to the utmost. The "inheritance in the saints," means that glorious work of grace which Christ is fulfilling in the hearts of His people, and which is yet to be consummated in the eternal glory, when we shall sit with Him upon His throne, and share with Him, as His glorified Bride, His eternal kingdom. This is the inheritance for which He Himself gave up His primeval throne, and for which we count all things but loss.

The apostle prays that the sealed ones may catch the vision of this glorious inheritance in its present and future possibilities, and may fully know all the riches of its glory. This will take the glow from every earthly picture and from every worldly prospect, and this will make sorrow light and things present seem like empty bubbles and worthless dreams. Still further, he prays that they may fully know "what is the exceeding greatness" or rather the surpassing greatness of His power, or, as the Greek expresses it, "His `dynamite,' to us-ward who believe."

It is not merely joy and glory that the vision unfolds, but actual and practical power. There is nothing we so much need as power. We are ever coming into conflict with forces too strong for our human weakness. We are fighting a ceaseless battle and we are inadequate for the weakest of our foes and the smallest of our difficulties. We are "without strength," and the deepest need of our heart is for spiritual power. But there is for us all the power we need, treasured up in Him who said, "All power is given unto Me in heaven and in earth." The word here used for power has received a new significance through the progress of modern science.

The terrific force expressed by "dynamite" is here represented as the figure of the spiritual power that the holy Ghost wants to show us and impart to us, if we can only see and receive the surpassing greatness of His "dynamite" to us-ward who believe. But we must see it, and believe it, or we cannot have it.

What is the difference between the nineteenth century, with its blaze of light and its resources of mechanical power, and the fifteenth century with its slow and tedious processes of toil? What is the difference between our Empire Express sweeping over the land at sixty miles an hour, and the poor Indian savage on his snow shoes, travelling in a month the distance that now we can cover in a day? There was just as much power in nature then as now. The hidden forces of electricity and of steam were all in existence then, as much as today. Ah, the difference was, he did not know it, and we do. And so there are stored up in Christ spiritual forces surpassingly greater than the dynamite or the electric engine; but millions of Christians go stumbling, groaning, and defeated through life, because they do not know the riches of the glory of their inheritance.

What right have we to be weak? What business have we to fail? What excuse have we to be ignorant with such a treasure house of blessing stored up at the throne of grace, and at the call of faith and prayer?

And then he gives us an object lesson of all this in the resurrection and ascension of the Lord Jesus Christ. This is not a mere theory but an accomplished fact. All this power has been actually proved and tested, and what was true once can always be true again. What was fulfilled in the life of Jesus can be fulfilled in each of us. And so he prays that our vision may be quickened and enlarged, so that we can see the working of his mighty power, as it was wrought "in Christ when he raised him from the dead, and set him at his own right hand in the heavenly places, far above all principality, and power, and might, and dominion, and every name that is named, not only in this world, but also in that which is to come: and hath put all things under his feet, and gave him the head over all things to the Church, which is his body, the fullness of him that filleth all in all."

All his surpassing power has been already exemplified in the resurrection of Christ. It burst for Him the fetters of the tomb, rent asunder the sepulcher, shattered the Roman seal upon the stone, scattered the terrified soldiers that guarded the tomb, and brought forth the risen Lord in all the glory of His immortal life. Not only so, it raised Him far above the empty tomb, far above the earth itself, up through the air, and the fields of space, past the planets and the constellations, yonder to the Central Throne, where He sat down in the place of honor and power, at the right hand of the eternal God.

It exalted Him far above all government and power and might and law and every name that is named, both in the present age and in all the ages to come. Think of all the names you know; think of all the powers you fear; think of all the foes you dread, He is far above them all.

And He is there not for Himself but for you. He is Head over all things for His body, the Church. His very business there is to use His power for us. His eternal occupation is to represent us. He is as much in need of us as we are of Him. He is but a head without us; for we are His body; we are the complement of His life; we are the other half of His being, and when He helps us He helps Himself; when He blesses us He is more truly blessed. Therefore we may confidently claim the boundless fullness of His blessing and know that all that is true of Him may be just as true of us, for "as He is, so also are we in this world."

To see this vision is to be omnipotent. May the Holy Ghost anoint our eyes and show us His glory!

III. THE SPIRIT OF ACCESS AND COMMUNION.

Having seen the glory of our ascended Lord, we are next admitted by the Holy Spirit, in access and communion, into His presence. "For through Him we both have access by one Spirit unto the Father." The door is open now, and we can go in and out with the freedom of children, gazing upon His glory and drawing from His fullness, strength for weakness, and grace for grace.

This is by the Spirit. It is He who gives to us the sense of need, the spirit of prayer, the confidence to come, the witness of acceptance, and the blessed fellowship of constant communion. We are to "pray in the Holy Ghost,"and as we follow His suggestions, and breathe out His groanings, and aspirations, our God-given prayers will reach the throne and come back to us in blessing.

IV. THE INDWELLING SPIRIT.

But now we have a far grander vision. We have seen the glory yonder, within the heavenly gates, and amid the splendors of the throne. We have had permission to enter through the open doors of prayer, and gaze upon it, and draw from its stores of grace. But now the Holy Ghost brings it all down to us, and puts it into our very heart and being.

The heaven above becomes the heaven within; the Savior enthroned at God's right hand becomes the enthroned Lord of our heart and being, and God Himself removes His tabernacle from heaven to earth, and dwells in very deed with men, and in the temple of the believing heart. This is the next stage of the Spirit's working in this sublime epistle. It is twofold; first, in the whole Church as the body of Christ, Ephesians 2: 21, 22. "The whole building fitly framed together groweth unto a holy temple in the Lord; in whom ye also are builded together for an habitation of God through the Spirit."

Then also it is fulfilled in the heart of each individual Christian, Ephesians 3: 16-19. "That He would grant you, according to the riches of His glory, to be strengthened with might by His Spirit in the inner man; that Christ may dwell in your hearts by faith; that ye, being rooted and grounded in love, may be able to comprehend with all saints what is the breadth, and length, and depth, and height; and to know the love of Christ which passeth knowledge, that ye might be filled with all the fullness of God."

The essence and substance of this prayer is, that we may be filled with all the fullness of God, and that Christ may dwell in our hearts by faith, so fully that we shall "know the breadth, and length, and depth, and height" of His measureless love.

Now for this the Holy Ghost has to strengthen us and prepare us. In our ordinary condition, we could not stand the glory and power of such a blessing. It would be like putting a charge of powder that would fill a cannon into a pocket pistol, and the only effect would be the explosion and destruction of the pistol. If God were to give us all the power for which we sometimes ask him, it would destroy us. We should be so lifted up with self-consciousness and self-importance that we should be ruined, or else we should be crushed by the weight of glory. Therefore, He prays, first, that we may be strengthened with might by the Spirit in the inner man, so that Christ may dwell in the heart by faith.

Just as the maker of that cannon strengthens it at the breech, doubling the thickness and strength of the metal where the pressure is heaviest, and gradually tapering it to the muzzle, that the resistant power shall be equalized to the strain, so the Holy Ghost prepares us to be the vessels of His grace and power. Perhaps the maker of that cannon experimented for many years before he got the quality of the metal and the strength of the barrel perfectly adjusted to his purpose. Perhaps he often broke it up and recast it, before he dared to put the stamp of his establishment upon it, and trust it in the battleship of his country. And so the Holy Ghost has to work long and patiently with us, and often to break us, over and over again, before we can be fully trusted with His highest commissions, and stand the exceeding weight of glory which He wishes to put within us, and upon us. Let us not be afraid of His mighty love, nor shrink from the pressure of His wise and mighty, molding hand.

In the vision of Daniel the empires of the world were represented under the magnificent image of a figure with a head of gold, shoulders and arms of silver, trunk of brass, and legs of iron. It was a very splendid-looking form of grandeur and power, but the end of it was that it was broken to pieces, and scattered like the chaff of the summer threshing floor. The secret all lay in this, that as the image descended toward its feet, the strength of the iron was mixed with miry clay, and the feet, on which its grand form rested, were no better than clods of mud.

Many a grand looking life has no better support than this, and all the work that rests on mixed materials must go to pieces in the hour of strain. God is taking the clay out of us. He wants men and women made of unmixed steel, that will stand the pressure of the power that He means to give them, and the glory with which He is yet to clothe them.

The truth is, God blesses every one of us as much as He can and fills us as full as we can hold. The trouble is, some of us cannot hold much. As we yield ourselves to His gracious working, He will fill us more and more with all the fullness of God. Christ shall be to us an indwelling presence, and we shall "comprehend with all saints what is the breadth, and length, and depth, and height, and to know the love of Christ which passeth knowledge." For He "is able to do exceeding abundantly above all that we ask or think," and the only limit is, "according to the power that worketh in us."

Dr. Boardman tells of a lady in London, to whom this passage came with such convicting power that she felt she could not rest until God had made it real to her. She knew that she had never received exceeding abundantly above all that she asked or thought, and she just went to her Father, and asked Him to make His word true to her, and told Him that she would never cease until this verse had become her actual experience.

She waited upon God for many weeks, and when she came back she told her pastor that her prayer was answered, and God had revealed Himself to her in a manner far exceeding her highest thought. But she said that He had shown her that there was so much more yet for her to receive, that He had raised her thought as far above her blessing, as her blessing had been above her former thought. And so He was leading her on from glory to glory, and as each new capacity was filled it was enlarged and filled again.

This is indeed true ; and so we may all have exceeding abundantly and be kept forever in that strange paradox of the spiritual life, ever satisfied and yet ever hungering and thirsting for more.

V. THE LIVING OUT OF THE HOLY SPIRIT IN OUR DAILY EXPERIENCE.

All this beautiful inward experience would be but a holy mysticism if it did not have a direct practical hearing on our common life. And so we have in Ephesians 5: 9, 10, 17, 18, the practical bearing of all this upon our everyday life. "For the fruit of the Spirit is in all goodness and righteousness and truth; proving what is acceptable unto the Lord. Wherefore, be ye not unwise, but understanding what the will of the Lord is. And be not drunk with wine, wherein is excess, but be filled with the Spirit." This is to be the habit of our daily life, and as we are thus filled with the Holy Ghost, our lives will be filled with goodness, righteousness, and reality.

We will not be shams and professions, but blessed expressions of the divine life within, and our whole being, inspired with a divine exhilaration, shall overflow in gladness, goodness, sweetness, unselfishness, and blessing, to all with whom we come in contact.

VI. THE OVERCOMING LIFE THROUGH THE HOLY GHOST.

The last picture in the epistle carries us forward to the closing and crowning experiences of the Christian life. It is a scene of conflict and fierce temptation. We are "wrestling with principalities and powers, the rulers of the darkness of this world, with spiritual wickedness in the heavenlies." These throng the thickest at the very gates of heaven. Think it not strange that we should find such beings and such conflicts in the heavenly places. That is just where they love to concentrate their forces, and turn us back at the very portals of glory. Let us not be "terrified by our adversaries, which is to them an evident token of perdition, but to us of salvation, and that of God." We have seen these principalities before in this epistle. They are the powers of which we were told in the first chapter, that Christ was "far above them."

They are conquered foes, and in Him we are already "more than conquerors."

But how shall we meet these terrific forces? Thank God for the Holy Ghost again. "When the enemy shall come in like a flood, then the Spirit of the Lord shall lift up a standard against him."

First, we have the sword of the Spirit, Ephesians 6: 17. "And take the helmet of salvation, and the sword of the Spirit, which is the Word of God." This was Christ's weapon in the conflict when He met the adversary in the wilderness, with the repeated word, "It is written." And when the devil, surprised at the power of this heavenly sword, picked it up and began to use it himself by quoting Scripture, Christ took the other edge of it, and struck him back the last fatal blow by His answer, so sublimely wise, "It is written AGAIN."

The Holy Ghost has given us this Word, and He is not likely to ignore it in His own manifestations to our hearts. Indeed, it is His purpose that we shall live out every particle before we pass from this earthly stage to the life beyond. It is He, and He alone, that can make it the sword in our victorious hands, suggesting to us the promise or the reproof or the command which we need for each new situation, and then arming it with the fiery point and piercing edge, that will cut through all the devil's disguises and make us always to triumph in the battle of life.

Then we have the prayer of the Spirit in the eighteenth verse. "Praying always with all prayer and supplication in the Spirit, and watching thereunto with all perseverance and supplication for all saints." This is our next victorious weapon; and the most remarkable thing about it is, that the principal part of the prayer is not for ourselves at all, but for others. It is when, like wise generals, we turn the position of our foe and attack him directly, by praying for others, that we compel him to retreat and let us alone; and, as we become occupied with the high and holy thoughts of unselfish love and prayer, we forget the troubles that were crushing us and the temptations that were pressing us and we are lifted clear above the battlefield, into those heavenly places where the serpent's fangs cannot reach us, and the devil's fiery darts cannot come.

## VII. WHAT SHOULD BE OUR ATTITUDE TO THIS HEAVENLY FRIEND?

We have it beautifully expressed in Ephesians 4: 30. "Grieve not the Holy Spirit of God, whereby ye are sealed unto the day of redemption." It is not said that we make Him angry, or drive Him away; but we grieve Him, disappoint Him, and cause Him pain.

He has set His heart upon accomplishing in us, and for us, the highest possibilities of love and blessing; when we will not yield to His wise and holy will; when we will not let Him educate us, mold us, separate us from the things that weaken and destroy us, and fit us for the weight of glory that He is preparing for us, His heart is vexed, His love is wounded, His purpose is baffled; and if the Comforter could weep, we would see the tears of loving sorrow upon His gentle face.

Just, as a mother fondly longs for the highest education and success of her child, and feels repaid for all her sacrifices and toils when she beholds her noble boy in the hour of his triumph; just as a loving teacher spends years in the training of his pupil, and when, at last, some day, that successful student is rewarded with the highest prizes and the acclamations of the university, he takes his favorite in his arms with a joy far greater than as if the triumph were his own, so our blessed Mother God is jealously seeking to work out in our lives the grandest possibilities of immortal existence; and, some day, when that blessed Spirit shall take us by the hand and present us to Jesus as His glorious Bride, "without spot or wrinkle or any such thing," the joy of the Holy Ghost will be greater than our own.

Oh, let us not disappoint Him! Let us not grieve Him. Let us not hold back from Him. Let us not sin against His forgiving, longsuffering love. "Grieve not the Holy Spirit of God, whereby ye are sealed unto the day of redemption."

## Chapter 16

## The Holy Spirit in Philippians

"For I know that this shall turn to my salvation through your prayer, and the supply of the Spirit of Jesus Christ." Phil. 1: 19. "If there be therefore any consolation in Christ, if any comfort of love, if any fellowship of the Spirit, if any bowels and mercies, fulfill ye my joy, that ye be like-minded, having the same love, being of one accord, of one mind." Phil. 2: 1-2.

The Epistle to the Philippians is the sweetest of the Pauline letters. It is the unfolding of his inmost heart and of his tenderest relations, to the most fondly-loved of his spiritual flocks. No other church e as quite so dear to him as the little band at Philippi, who were the first seal of the beginning of his missionary work on the continent of Europe. He could say to them truly, "I have you in my heart. Ye are all partakers of my grace. I thank God for your fellowship in the gospel, from the first day until now."

But it is not only the expression of a hallowed human love; it is also the embodiment of all that is most mellow, mature and delicate, in the Christian spirit and temper. It is the ripeness of the mellow fruit, just ready to fall from the branch; it is the bloom on the peach, delicate as the rainbow tint, and soft as the wing of an angel. There is something about its tone that can be understood only by the finer senses of the deepest and highest Christian experience.

While the great Epistle to the Ephesians is like the tabernacle building, with its deeper and deeper unfolding of truth and life, the Epistle to the Philippians is like the sweet incense on the golden altar and in the holy place.

There are only two references to the Holy Sprit in this epistle, but these two are in perfect keeping with the structure and spirit of the whole epistle.

I. THE SUPPLY OF THE SPIRIT.

The word for "supply" employed here is a very unusual one, and has a special and strongly figurative significance. It is the Greek word, Epichoregos, and it refers to the Epichoregos, or chorus leader in ancient Greece. On a great festival occasion it was customary for a certain man, as an act of public generosity and also a distinguished honor to himself, to provide for the public entertainment of the people by an elaborate musical exercise, consisting of a great many pieces, a great variety of music, musical instruments and performers; it was his business to supply all that was necessary for this performance, to meet all the expenses of the occasion, to secure all the performers, instruments, assistants, etc., and see that everything was supplied and also to lead the chorus. From this old word, our expressions chorus, and chorus-choir are derived. Now this word conveys the idea of supplying, but also of supplying especially the parts in a musical chorus; and it carries along with it the idea of something harmonious and glorious. It is a very abundant supply and it brings a very triumphant result.

This word is used in a remarkable passage in the first chapter of 2 Peter, "Add to your faith courage, knowledge, temperance, godliness, brotherly kindness, charity." This word "add," is the same Greek term, Epichorego. It means, "chorus into your faith and life these beautiful graces"; bring them all into tune, and work them out in harmony and praise, so that your life shall be a doxology of joy and thanksgiving. And then, at the close of that paragraph, the word reappears, "For so shall an entrance be ministered unto you abundantly into the everlasting kingdom of our Lord and Savior Jesus Christ." Literally it might be translated, "So an entrance shall be chorused unto you." That is, the very graces that were wrought into your earthly life and attended you as a heavenly choir shall wait for you at the gates of heaven and sing you home to your coronation. The love and gentleness, the faith and patience that you exercised in your earthly pilgrimage shall be waiting yonder, as a train of musicians, and shall celebrate your victory and your recompense.

Now this is the word used in the passage in Philippians, "the supply of the Spirit of Christ Jesus." The Holy Ghost is the choir leader, and He is bringing into the apostle's life all the supplies of grace he needs to make his life not only tolerable but triumphant, and turn everything into a chorus of praise.

The apostle had just been telling us before of the peculiar trials through which he was passing and the subtle foes that were distressing and harassing him, by even preaching the very Gospel that he loved so well, for contention and strife, "Supposing," he says, "to add affliction to my bonds." Yet so abundant was the supply of the Holy Ghost, as the Choir Leader of his victorious life, that he rose above their jealous hate, turned the very trial into a triumph and was enabled to bring blessing out of the devil's blows and to exclaim in a chorus of praise, "What then, notwithstanding every way, whether in pretense, or in truth, Christ is preached; and I therein do rejoice, yea, and will rejoice; for I know that this shall turn to my salvation," that is, my complete and full salvation, "through your prayer and the supply of the Spirit of Jesus Christ."

And so for us, beloved, the Holy Ghost is able to provide so fully, that

"Ills of every shape and every name,

Transformed to blessings, miss their cruel aim."

This was to turn to his salvation. He does not, of course, mean his literal deliverance from condemnation, but that deeper, fuller life in Christ which is all comprehended in complete salvation. It is one thing to be "saved as by fire"; it is quite another thing to be saved to the uttermost.

Now the apostle says that this is to come to him "through their prayer." We can help each other to the deeper and fuller supply of the Spirit of Christ Jesus. If our heart is open to receive the blessing, the prayers of others reach us and add to the measure of our fullness.

Every breath of true prayer accomplishes something and makes some addition to the measure of blessing that we ask for ourselves and others. There is no greater service that you can render to a true child of God than to pray for him in the Holy Ghost, and in that deep divine love that brings you into a common touch with his life and needs. Especially is this true of those who stand in public places to represent Christ to others, and who must receive, first, the stores of blessing which they are called to impart. Let us pray for them and we may be very sure the blessing will come back to us. To keep up the figure of the text and the imagery of the chorus, our prayers are just the breath which fills the mighty organ and swells the strain that bursts from every pipe and every note.

II. THE COMMUNION OF THE SPIRIT. PHIL. 2: 1, 2.

This passage is a very exquisite one. It touches the most delicate shades of Christian feeling. It speaks of "consolation in Christ," the tenderness of His comforting love. It speaks of the "comfort of love," the sweet and healing balm of sympathy and holy affection. It speaks of the "fellowship of the Spirit," the communion of the saint with God, and with his brethren in the holy Ghost. It speaks of "bowels of mercies," the finer chords of spiritual sensitiveness, which thrill responsive to every touch of pain or joy in each other's hearts. There is something about it so refined and exquisite that the rude, coarse mind cannot grasp it, and it is literally true, "that none but he that feels it knows."

It is especially of this third phrase that we are to speak — "If there be any fellowship of the Spirit." The Greek word is Koinonia, which might be literally translated, in common. It really means to have things in common.

1. It is used first of our fellowship with God. "Truly, our fellowship is with the Father, and with His Son, Jesus Christ." "The communion of the Holy Ghost."

Our communion with God is the basis of all other communion. And communion with God is not merely external worship and articulate prayer but it is really oneness with God, and having everything in common "with Him." Just as oil and water cannot mix, just as iron and clay cannot blend, so there can be no communion between God and the sinful soul. We must be reconciled to Him; we must be at one with Him; we must be conformed to His image and partakers of His very nature and filled with His Holy Spirit.

There must be in us the organ of intercourse. It is not enough to have a telegraph wire reaching your office from the distant city, but you must also have a battery here in order to receive the message of the wire. And so we must have with us the spiritual organs of communion with God, in order to enter into His fellowship.

We may have such fellowship. The Holy Ghost is the channel and organ of this communion. He is at once the electric current that conveys and the battery that interprets the message both ways. "Through Him we have access unto the Father." We can pour out our heart into His and He can pour in His heart into ours. We can ask Him for the things we need and get them. But more than all the things we get, is the answer of His own heart to ours. And more than all the words which He speaks to us, or we speak to Him, is the deep and silent communion of the heart that is in accord with His holy will, and living in the consciousness of His delightful presence.

It is not necessary to be always speaking to God, or always hearing from God, to have communion with Him; there is an inarticulate fellowship more sweet than words. The little child can sit all day long beside its busy mother and, although few words are spoken on either side, and both are busy, the one at his absorbing play, the other at her engrossing work, yet both are in perfect fellowship. He knows that she is there, and she knows that he is all right. So the saint and the Savior can go on for hours in the silent fellowship of love, and he be busy about the most common things, and yet conscious that every little thing he does is touched with the complexion of His presence, and the sense of His approval and blessing.

And then, when pressed with burdens and troubles too complicated to put into words and too mysterious to tell or understand, how sweet it is to fall back into His blessed arms, and just sob out the sorrow that we cannot speak!

"Too tired, too worn to pray,
  I can but fold my hands,
  Entreating in a voiceless way
  Of Him who understands.

"And as the weary child,
  Sobbing and sore oppressed,
  Sinks, hushing all its wailings wild
  Upon its mother's breast,

"So on Thy bosom, I
  Would pour my speechless prayer;
  Not doubting Thou wilt let me lie
  In trustful weakness there."

2. This also includes our communion with one another. "The fellowship of the Spirit" means fellowship in the Spirit with spiritual minds. Thank God for the article in the creed which binds together the Church of every age and clime, "I believe in the communion of saints."

This must, of course, be first of all, communion in the Spirit. It is not the fellowship merely of natural affection but it is the communion of hearts that have a divine life in common. Of course, it is dearer and closer with those that are dearest to us but, even in the case of our nearest friends, our love must be transformed or it cannot be lasting or bring us into spiritual communion.

Then it is communion in the truth, and the closer our agreement in the truth, the closer will be our communion in the Spirit. Therefore as God leads us on to deeper teachings and higher truths, He intensifies our fellowship.

We can remember the time when we were first saved and were brought at once into the same fellowship with all others that were saved. Our little note was "Jesus saves me," and every saved man was a brother beloved. We just wanted to take him by the hand and tell him we were brothers. But it was just one little in the chorus. It was the soprano, and soprano alone makes very thin music.

After a while we learned the deeper basis of sanctification, and then we got a new note, and a new part to our song. And our music grew richer, and our harmony fuller.

We can remember the first time we met another Christian who had also learned the blessed truth of Christ our Sanctifier. He was not only a brother, but he was doubly a brother. And oh, how delightful it was to find one that could understand our deeper feelings and teachings in the Spirit, and how much closer was our communion in the fullness of the truth!

After a while we added a third part, the triumphant tenor of divine healing, and the Lord's supernatural life in our body. Shall we ever forget the first time we were thrown into the society of those who understood and believed these things? We had been standing alone, misunderstood, misrepresented, perplexed, and as we found some other heart that was treading the same lone way and living in the same blessed experience, it was a threefold chord, and a divine fellowship.

And yet there is one more part in perfect music, the soft suggestive undertone of the alto, that carries our thoughts afar and wakes up the chords of memory and hope. And so we came into the fourth truth of this blessed gospel — the Coming of our Lord, and the glorious hope of His return. Need I say that this brought a deeper fellowship still with those who stand together in this holy expectation as the waiting Bride of the Lamb? And so God makes us one in the fullness of the truth. Let us not lightly think of any truth which He has given us, or fail to be true to His testimony and our mutual fellowship.

Then again, we have fellowship not only in the truth, but in the life of the Spirit. All the platforms in the world will not make us one without oneness of heart. The fourfold gospel is not any better than the thirty-nine articles without the Holy Ghost. The true secret of Christian union is the baptism of the Spirit and the fullness of the life of Christ in all who believe.

And this is the fellowship of prayer. It makes us sensitive to each other's needs and burdens and it binds us all together, like travelers in the mountains, so that if one falls the others hold him up, and if one suffers all suffer together.

Let us ask God to show us all that this ministry means for us and for His servants; let us each be so "fitly framed" in the body of Christ, that we shall carry upon our hearts the very ones the Spirit would assign to us, and the very burdens which He would have us share with them.

Finally, it is fellowship in service. We are called together for a common testimony and a common work in these last momentous days. It is not accidental that the Holy Spirit has given us a common experience and has led us out in similar lines of truth and life. He is preparing a mighty spiritual movement in these last times for the special preparation of the Master's coming, and we cannot miss His special calling without great loss to ourselves, and great hindrances to His purpose for our lives and for His church.

W hen God brings into our life a special experience of truth and blessing, we cannot go on as heretofore, but there is always some special ministry and testimony for which we have been prepared, and we are to stand together for the propagation of these present truths, and the help of other lives that need the very blessing that has come to us.

How solemnly some of us feel that if we had faltered in our testimony, when God first spake to us these deeperthings, not only should we have lost the best work of our life, but multitudes of other lives might have missed their blessing, too.

Whatever else we do, beloved, let us be true. Let no coward fear, let no compromise with popular opinion and halfhearted respectability make us falter in our high calling, or be faithless to the bonds of fellowship in the little flock that the Master is preparing for His kingdom.

"If there be, therefore, any consolation in Christ, if any comfort of love, if any fellowship in the Spirit, if any bowels and mercies, fulfill ye my joy, that ye be like-minded, having the same love, being of one accord, of one mind."

## Chapter 17

## The Spirit of Love

"Your love in the Spirit." Col. 1: 8.

This is the only reference to the Holy Spirit in the Epistle to the Colossians. The theme of this beautiful letter is the fullness and glory of Jesus. But Jesus cannot be glorified without recognizing the Holy Ghost; and so we have this brief reference to the blessed Spirit. But brief as it is, it shines like a heavenly pearl, reflecting the deepest and most important truths concerning the blessed Comforter.

The apostle had just been visited by Epaphras, one of the ministers of the Colossian Church, and he had reported to him the condition of that Church. It was all summed up in one sentence, "He declared unto us your love in the Spirit." This seems to have been the one characteristic of this Colossian Church; it was full of love. Its fellowship was perfect, its union unbroken; its members were filled with charity, unselfishness and consideration for one another. There were no gossiping tongues; there were no slanderous rumors; there were no misunderstandings and quarrels; there were no criticisms, murmurings and bad feelings, but all were joined together in harmonious love and beautiful cooperation in the testimony, work and worship of the Church. And this was manifestly a divine unity. It was "love in the Spirit." It was not mere partisanship, nor personal friendship; it was not because they were clannish, and united in little cliques of personal favoritism, but it was all so heavenly, so holy, so Christ-like that it was evidently the prompting of the Holy Ghost. And so, as the apostle hears of it, he exclaims with thanksgiving and deep joy, "We give thanks to God, and the Father of our Lord Jesus Christ, praying always for you since we heard of your faith in Christ Jesus, and of the love ye have to all the saints, for the hope which is laid up for you in heaven."

Would to God that this beautiful picture might be more frequently repeated. Let us look at it as a pattern of true Christian love and an illustration of the choicest and noblest work of the Holy Spirit.

There is plenty of love in the world and always will be. It is the secret of every romance, the theme of every poem, and the center of every play that has ever touched the heart of humanity, or charmed the ears of men. It lies back of all that is heroic in national history. It gilds every record of patriotism and glorifies every home alter and fireside. But there is a great difference between the love of nature and "love in the Spirit."

I. Natural love is an instinct and a passion; the love of the Spirit is a new creation and the fruit of the supernatural life imparted by the Holy Ghost, when the soul is born from above. The natural heart knows nothing about it. Human love may only be a little higher in measure, degree and character than the instinct of the mother bird over her young, or the fondness of the lioness for her cubs. It is born of earth and with earth it will pass away. But the love of the Spirit descends from above. It is part of the nature of God and it must last forever. It is the kinship of a heavenly family and the bond of an eternal home.

II. Natural love is selfish in its nature and terminates upon its own gratification; divine love is unselfish and reaches out to the good of its object. And therefore the strongest affection born of earthly passion may turn to the bitterest hate, if it is crossed and disappointed. It can strike down, with the deathblow of vengeance, the one for whom it would have given its life, when that one awakens its jealousy and resentment. Divine love on the other hand, forgets itself, and seeks to bless its object.

It does not love for the sake of the pleasure of loving, nor for the sake of the pleasure the loved one can afford; but it loves in order to bless and help and elevate and it shrinks from no sacrifice even the sacrifice of its own happiness, if it may accomplish its high purpose for its object.

III. Natural love is based upon the attractive qualities of its object; divine love springs from something within, and is the outflow of an irresistible impulse in itself. Mere human love is attracted by the goodness and loveliness of the one it loves, fancied or real. But divine love can seize upon the most unlovely, can love it into loveliness, and can keep on loving through an impulse in its own heart, when everything in the circumstances would render it impossible. And so, "God commendeth His love toward us, in that, while we were yet sinners, Christ died for us."

We see a faint approximation to this kind of love in true motherhood. Who ever saw a mother yet that did not have a "beautiful baby?" Others might not see it but she sees it. And even when that babe is decrepit, feeble and fretful, and a source of constant trial and strain, instead of lessening, it intensifies that maternal affection. Night and day it is her joy to minister and suffer and serve; and when that little sufferer passes out of her life, her loss is all the greater because it cost her so much, and she knows not how to get on without the frail and feeble dependent one, which was almost her very life.

God loved us because of something in Himself and so if Christ is dwelling in us, we shall love because of the Christ within us, and we shall love even the unworthy and the unlovely, because He loves them, even when we cannot love them for themselves.

IV. Natural love is sensitive and lives in the sunshine of responsive affection, but divine love is long-suffering, patient, and true, in the darkest hour of suffering and wrong. The very element of divine love is suffering. In the sublime picture given in First Corinthians, the thirteenth chapter, love begins her march by "suffering long," and ends by "enduring all things," while in the center stands the signal, "love is not provoked." The whole environment of her being is suffering and wrong. She can suffer without being unkind and endure without being hard. Her sublimest example is the Son of God in the midst of His cruel foes; the more they wronged Him, the more He felt that they needed His love and the more He longed to suffer that He might bless and save them. This is ever the spirit of Christian love.

A few weeks ago, when half a score of martyrs fell in Southern China, one of the survivors, in speaking of that hour, said that when they were all expecting death, the only consciousness which she remembered was the intense joy and love which seemed to be breathed into their hearts from the very gates of heaven. And when the tidings reached their friends in England, there was no word of resentment, even from those who loved them best, but a still deeper longing to go forth in yet diviner love and save men from the ignorance and the blindness which could make them perpetrate such a crime.

The love that blesses those that bless us is only earthly, "do not even the publicans the same?" But the love that reaches out to those who can make no return, the love that blesses them that curse us, and prays for them that despitefully use us and persecute us, and would die for those that would take our very life, this is the love of God; this the Holy Ghost alone can produce in the heart.

V. Natural love is fitful; divine love is abiding and everlasting. Natural love depends either upon our moods or the moods of those we love. But divine love is the eternal Christ within us, loving on the same through good and ill forever. Oh, how much we need to pray, "Search me, oh God, and see if there be in me any evil way, and lead me in the way everlasting!"

Do we not want the affections that shall be forever? Are we not tired of having our heartstrings torn? He is able to give us His own everlasting love.

VI. Natural love is exclusive, partial, and partisan; divine love is comprehensive and universal, like the very heart of God. It does not love its favorites, but it loves for love's sake all that need to be loved. It does not ignore the closer ties and fellowships of life. It does not love all alike with the same affection nor even with the same degree; but it loves each in the place where God has fitted him and her into our life, and loves all in due proportion and world-wide sympathy.

It gives the husband a deeper affection to the wife, who has her peculiar place in his heart. It gives the friend a yet more delicate and special bond of fellowship with the one that fits into the closest sympathy and fellowship of the heart. But it has room for every fellowship, every tie, and every friend, each in his true place, and all in perfect symmetry, and fullness. Like the broad bright sunshine, it goes wherever there is room, and it goes most quickly where there is largest room. Like the blessed Master, it has the John, that leans upon its breast, and the Mary, that enters into its deeper confidences; but it has also the Peter who, in his place, is loved as truly, the Thomas, who finds the sympathy he needs, and the little child, that lies in His bosom with confiding delight. This is the love of God.

Human love becomes antagonistic and dislikes those who are not within the charmed circle, but God's great love has a universal fairness, justness, and rightness, and yet a sweeter tenderness, and a finer delicacy in its every heart-throb and holy tendril, than the finest sentiment of human affection.

VII. Human love is intemperate; divine love is moderate and self-restrained. The petulant, passionate mother, in one moment can hug to her bosom her beloved child with passionate affection, and in the next can pour out the fierce invectives of wrath upon his head. The impulsive father can love his boy so intemperately and indulgently, as to be unwilling to deny him the wishes and gratifications which he knows may cost him his character and his future life. True love restrains and even dares to displease, that it may do even greater good in the end to its object. And thus God loves us, even to wounding us that He may heal, and chastening us, that He may save.

Thus it was that Joseph loved his brothers, restraining the bursting affection of his heart, while he sternly stood off from these guilty men, and brought them to repentance; and then, when they saw their wrong, he was the first to forgive, and help them to forget; throwing himself upon their bosom, with passionate intensity he cried, "Be not grieved nor angry with yourselves, it was not you, but God."

This is divine love, a thoughtful, sober, far-seeing devotion, brave enough to wound that it may heal, and to correct that it may save.

VIII. Human love lives by sight; divine love walks by faith. And so we read, "love believeth all things, hopeth all things." When it cannot see the quality of loveliness in its object now, it prays that God may place it there, and it believes in the answer to its prayer, and acts as if it were already fulfilled; and then hope joins hands with faith and looks out into the future, until the vision becomes a present realization, and it covers its object with all the glory of that which some day is to be.

Thus God loves us. He sees us, not as we are today in our unworthiness and sin, but as we shall be, some day, when we shine forth as the sun in the Kingdom of our Father, and reflect the glory and the beauty of our Savior's face; and this is what He recognizes and delights in. He treats us every moment as if we were already glorified. He sees us "in heavenly places in Christ Jesus." He "believes all things, and hopes all things" for us, and purposes to fulfill all things in us. This is the love with which we should bless our friends. Thus should we pray for them, believe for them, and see them in the light of God and heaven; and thus our love will lift them up to its own vision, and realize in them its own holy purpose.

IX. Human love is human; "love in the Spirit" is the love of God within us. It is the love of the Holy Ghost Himself, filling and flowing in our hearts. It is not the best that we can feel, or say, or do, but it is the very heart of Christ reproduced in us. And so it has been well said that the thirteenth chapter of First Corinthians is just a photograph of Jesus, and the true way to read it is to insert Christ instead of love, and then to transfer to it our hearts and lives and insert Christ instead of self in our experience. Then, indeed, it shall be true that "Christ in us suffereth long and is kind; Christ in us seeketh not His own; Christ in us envieth not, is not puffed up; Christ in us rejoiceth not in iniquity but rejoiceth in the truth; Christ in us is not provoked; Christ in us beareth all things, believeth all things, hopeth all things, endureth all things, and never faileth."

And so we are thrown back again upon Him, and constrained to sink out of self into Christ, and to say, "Not I, but Christ that liveth in me." This is the purpose of the Holy Ghost, to show us our insufficiency and Christ's all-sufficiency and, step by step, to transfer the living picture to our lives and reproduce the living reality in our experience.

This, then, is "Love in the Spirit." The blessed Spirit of Love has come down from heaven to teach us this crowning lesson of righteousness, holiness, and divine conformity. For "God is love, and he that dwelleth in love dwelleth in God, and God in Him," Love is the fulfilling of the law. Love is the sum of all goodness. Love is the essence of holiness. Love is life.

The Holy Ghost has come to train us in the school of love. Day by day He leads us out into some new lesson as we are able to bear it. And when things seem hard and trying, it is just another class in the school of discipline, another opportunity of putting on Christ Jesus and learning either the patience, or the long-suffering, or the gentleness of love.

An injured bishop was once complaining to Francis De Sales how a brother had wronged him, lied about him, and tried in every way to defame him; the good saint listened and assented, saying, "Yes, my brother, it's all true; it's very wrong; it's very unkind; it's very unjust; it's very cruel;" and then he added, "but there is another side to it." "But," said the Bishop, "do you mean to say that there is any excuse or reason to justify this?"

"Not on his part, my brother, but there is on the other side of the question, a still higher reason for it, and it is this: that God has let all this happen to you, and all this to be said about you, to teach you the lesson that is worth more to you than even your good name, and that is to hold your tongue when people talk about you, which it is very evident you have not yet learned."

The good Bishop saw the lesson, and silently received it. Would to God that we might see in everything our Master's hand, our Teacher's lesson, our Father's love. Life would become to us a school of love, and we so sweetly perfected in this highest grace, that nothing could part us but, above the hand of every enemy we should see the hand of love more richly blessing us and making "even the wrath of man to praise" God, and minister to our perfection. Then, perhaps, we should some day be able to say, like one of the Medieval saints, "It is so sweet to love my enemies that if it were a sin to do so, I fear I should be tempted to commit that sin, and if it were forbidden by the Lord, I fear it would be the greatest temptation of my life to disobey that commandment."

God, give us the "love of the Spirit," and say to us afresh the new commandment : "Love one another, as I have loved you."

## Chapter 18

## The Holy Spirit in Thessalonians

"For our gospel came not unto you in word only, but also in power, and in the Holy Ghost." 1 Thess. 1: 5. "Having received the word in much affliction, with joy of the Holy Ghost." 1Thess. 1: 6. "God hath from the beginning chosen you to salvation through sanctification of the Spirit and belief of the truth." 1 Thess. 2: 13. "Quench not the Spirit." 1 Thess. 5: 19.

The first three of these four passages present to us three aspects of the work of the Holy Ghost; as the Spirit of power, of joy, and of holiness, and the last passage presents the practical side of the question and the solemn danger of our quenching the Holy Ghost.

I. THE POWER OF THE SPIRIT.

The apostle attributes the conversion of the Thessalonian Christians to the power of the Holy Ghost. His work among them was accompanied with extraordinary manifestations of the Spirit's convicting and converting power. Speaking of it again, the apostle says, "Yourselves, brethren, know our entrance in unto you, that it was not in vain; when ye received the word of God which ye heard of us, ye received it not as the word of men, but, as it is in truth, the Word of God, which effectually worketh also in you that believe."

So wonderful was their awakening and turning to God, that he could say of them: "From you sounded out the word of the Lord, not only in Macedonia and Achaia, but also in every place your faith to God-ward is spread abroad; so that we need not to speak anything. For they themselves show of us what manner of entering in we had unto you, and how ye turned from idols to serve the living and true God; and to wait for His Son from heaven, even Jesus, which delivered us from the wrath to come."

These wonderful results the apostle attributes entirely to the power of the Holy Ghost, accompanying the word of God, and giving it such authority that they received it, not as the word of man, but as a direct message from the living God.

This is the first element in the power of the Spirit, that it takes the worker and the speaker quite out of view, and brings the hearer face to face with the authority of God.

This is what Paul means, when he says that his word came to them with much assurance. This means, literally, much boldness. He spoke to them as a messenger direct from heaven, and they so received him. His message was not with wisdom of words, nor studied rhetoric, but with divine authority. How much of our preaching is with words only — logical words, rhetorical words, well-uttered words, perhaps pathetic words, words that move to tears or to enthusiasm, but only words!

The Holy Spirit's power leads men beyond all forms of expression, to the substance of God's great message of repentance and salvation, and the necessity of immediate decision and obedience. It makes people do something, and do it at once and forever.

The word for power here is dynamite. It is the kind of power that breaks up things. It breaks up the conscience and convicts it of sin. It breaks up the heart and melts it to repentance. It breaks the will into surrender and choice. It breaks the fetters of sin, the habits of life, and the bonds of Satan.

Not only does it speak to men in much assurance, but it produces in them the same assurance. It makes them to know that God is speaking, to know that they are sinners, to know that they are lost, and then to know that they are saved.

Beloved, have we felt this convicting, converting, transforming power? Fellow-workers, is this our reliance, our supreme and sole dependence for the salvation of men, and the service of our King?

## II. THE JOY OF THE SPIRIT.

One of the first results of the conversion of the Thessalonians was the spirit of joy. "Ye received the word in much affliction, with joy of the Holy Ghost."

The spirit of gladness is one of the immediate fruits of the Holy Ghost. The new life is essentially a joy-life, banishing the very elements of sorrow and gloom, and bringing us into the light of an everlasting sunshine.

The joy of the Holy Ghost is not a natural emotion and it is not dependent upon favorable circumstances or pleasant surroundings. In the present case, their joy is in an immediate contact and contrast with much affliction. They had everything to try them — persecution, the loss of friends, the danger of even death itself; but the very extremity of their affliction only developed a deeper and diviner joy.

So it ever is. Christian life is an everlasting paradox; sorrowful yet always rejoicing; poor yet making many rich; having nothing, and yet possessing all things.

It is an inexplicable mystery. The world cannot understand it; the world cannot give it, and, thank God, the world cannot take it away. We cannot understand it ourselves. It is a song in the night, that gives no other reason for its singing than that the song is there. It is a fountain in the desert, that flows from no visible source, and empties into no earthly outlet, and runs according to no prescribed channel. It is an artesian well that bursts from the rocky depths, and flows on without the mechanism of pumps, or endless chains, or human buckets, or hands. It is glad, just because there is a gladness there that came from heaven and belongs to heaven and lives in heaven forever.

It is a blessed heritage. It is a fortune to its possessor, even amid the depths of penury. It is an antidote to temptation and sin. It lifts us above the power of evil and holds us in the impregnable heights of peace and victory. It is a balm for sickness and pain, and a holy elixir for nerve and brain and every outward ill. It is an inspiration for service, and gives an irresistible emphasis to our appeals to the sin-sick and sorrowing world; it is vain to call the lost and weary to the gates of mercy, when the telltale countenance, the tired manner, and the sepulchral tone assure them, that they are happier than we. The joy of the Lord is our strength, not only for holiness, but for health, and happiness, and holy influence on other hearts and lives, and in all our work for God and man.

Beloved, open your heart and receive the joy of the Spirit.

III. THE SANCTIFICATION OF THE SPIRIT.

The first thing that strongly impresses an ordinary and candid reader of this verse is the strong and universal language in which sanctification is here spoken of as an essential part of our salvation.

It is stated in the most unambiguous language that we are "chosen to salvation through sanctification of the Spirit and belief of the truth." We are not chosen to salvation irrespective of our spiritual condition, but we are chosen to those conditions; and one of the essential conditions is sanctification of the Spirit.

How any man or woman can expect salvation, and yet be indifferent to his sanctification, is very hard to understand. The salvation consists largely in the sanctification itself, for thus, and thus alone are we saved from the virulent and soul destroying power of sin.

Sanctification is here attributed to the Holy Spirit. It is His work, not ours; it is as much a part of the free grave of God in Christ as our justification and forgiveness. In the previous epistle, fifth chapter, twenty-third verse, its nature is very fully expressed in the apostle's prayer: "The very God of peace, or the God of peace Himself, sanctify you through and through; and I pray God your whole spirit and soul and body be preserved blameless unto the coming of our Lord Jesus Christ. Faithful is He that calleth you, who also will do it." God Himself must do this work, and He does it through t he blessed Holy Ghost.

The word, sanctify, has three specific meanings; namely, to separate from, dedicate to, and fill with.

First, we must lay off, and separate from, the old life of self and sin. There are some things we cannot consecrate to God, but we must lay them down. The old sin-offering could not be laid on the altar — it was unclean, because the sin of the people had been transferred to it; it must be carried outside the camp and there burned with fire in the place of judgment. And so we cannot consecrate our sin and our sinfulness to God. We must renounce it; we must lay it off; we must die to it; we must be separated from it.

Then, secondly, comes the dedication to God. This is the place for consecration. This is the place for the burnt-offering. That was laid on the altar and accepted as a sweet-smelling savor. And so when we have separated from our sinful self, we offer our new life in Christ to God in entire dedication, and He accepts it as a sweet savor. But even then it is nothing but a consecrated will, a mere possibility, an empty vessel, clean, but empty still, and the very power to make the consecration worth anything to God, must come from God Himself. He has the vessel, but He must fill it and keep it full. And so this is the third meaning of sanctification. It is the filling of the Holy Ghost, who takes our consecrated will, our clean and empty vessel and all the possibilities of our new and yielded life, and so unites them to Jesus, and fills them with the very life of Jesus, that we just live out the life of Christ from day to day, and we shed forth the fullness which the Holy Ghost supplies within.

Our life is not our own, but "of His fullness have we received, even grace for grace."

Now this is the sanctification of the Spirit. It is His peculiar province thus to sanctify the souls that have been justified through the grace and the blood of Christ.

First, He shows the soul its need of sanctification, its inherent and hopeless sinfulness, and its utter inability to bring a clean thing out of an unclean, or live a holy life, with an unholy heart. Next, He shows us God's provision for our sanctification in the free gift of Christ, the efficacy of His atonement for the death of our old self, the power of His blood, and the willingness of the Holy Spirit to undertake this work, to cleanse our heart, and to dwell within it. Then He leads us to the next step — a glad and full surrender and committal of our soul to Him for this blessed work, an unreserved separation from all evil, and an equally unreserved dedication of our all to God, and to His perfect will.

Then He accepts us, and makes real the transaction into which we have entered; by full surrender and appropriating faith, He puts to death our old life of self and sin and He enters and dwells within our consecrated heart, uniting us to Jesus, filling us with His own all-sufficient grace and presence, and leading us henceforth moment by moment, in constant dependence upon His glorious grace.

In one sense, this work is instantaneous; it has a definite beginning and a moment in which we count it all eternally settled. In another sense, it is progressive, as He leads us on from step to step, from strength to strength, from grace to grace, from glory to glory, even as by the Spirit of the Lord.

As each new revelation of light comes, He calls for new obedience and new advances; yet while we walk in the light, we are fully accepted according to the light we have, and counted holy and well-pleasing in His sight.

It is after we receive His sanctification and enter into perfect union with Him, that our real growth begins; and the church of Christ has yet to learn the depths and heights and lengths and breadths of the fullness of life in the Spirit, as the providence of God makes new situations for the obedient disciple from day to day, and the Holy Ghost fits us into them by His all-sufficient grace.

IV. THE PRACTICAL APPEAL.

"Quench not the Spirit."

In view of these three blessed aspects of the Spirit's work, how tender and solemn the appeal: "Quench not the Spirit"! While this primarily refers to the Church collectively, it may also be true of the believer individually.

It is possible for us, as private Christians, so to misunderstand, hinder, and disobey the loving leadings of the gentle Holy Ghost, that we shall quench His holy fires and disappoint His great purposes of love.

I do not say that a soul that truly believes in Jesus Christ will be lost at last, but, beloved, it may lose very much of what salvation ought to mean. It is one thing to be lost; it is another thing to lose our crown, and our Father's highest will; the Scriptures are full of loving warnings against the danger of coming short of our full inheritance, and losing aught of our full reward.

The Holy Ghost is like a sensitive lover. A woman's heart is not won by a violent assault, but by the gentle approaches of respectful, sensitive, and considerate love; and, at any point along the way, she can check and chill the advances of the heart that woos her, until, at last, she quenches the love that would have laid all at her feet. And so the Holy Ghost comes to us, with respectful and gentle monitions. He will accept no sacrifice which is not freely given, He will require no obedience that is not gladly rendered. But He does ask us for sacrifice and obedience as the proof of our love, and He does place us in situations of perplexity and trial, through which alone we can receive the training which His love designs for us.

Now here it is that disobedience and refusal may come in. We may shrink from His gentle leading; we may refuse the trial through which He would bring us to some glorious victory; we may choose the easier path, and shun the dreaded cross; but, in so doing, we grieve the Holy Ghost; we arrest our own progress; we compel our God to wait until we are ready to go forward with Him, and after a while we may so wear out His patient love, that He shall find us unfit to receive the blessing He designed for us, and while we may not lose our soul, we shall be rejected from our crown.

There are souls that have lost something out of their life forever, and, perhaps, have become so hardened that they do not even know what they have lost.

It is possible to take a piece of iron, red-hot, and then plunge it into the water and cool it, and do this so many times, that, at last, the very metal scales off like ashes, and the temper and substance of the iron is corroded and destroyed.

It is possible to wear out our hearts by disobedience and repeated chills of divine love, until, at last, there is nothing left but dross.

Oh, let us be careful how we play with the voice of God, and the infinite, everlasting gentleness and love of the mother heart of the Holy Ghost! "Quench not the Spirit."

You may do it by disobedience; you may do it by distrust; you may do it by self-indulgence and cowardly softness; you may do it by yielding to temptation; you may do it by going into the world and selling your birthright for a mess of pottage; you may do it by petulance, irritation, an angry look, a hasty word; you may do it by impatience and rebellion against the hand of God. Let us be careful. Resist not the Spirit. Grieve not the Spirit. Quench not the Spirit.

And, finally, we may quench the Spirit in others. We may hinder the work of God in human souls. We may hold back the Church of Christ from victory. We may paralyze the whole body by keeping one or two members in a state of chronic disease.

So Moses, Joshua, and Caleb were kept back for forty years by Israel's unbelief. So the Church is kept back today from the fullness of Pentecostal power, by the weakness of so large a part of the body of Christ. And so, many a soul is cramped, or chilled, or even seduced from God's high purpose and the Spirit's holy calling by the mistaken love, or the thoughtless and unholy influence of some one that called himself a friend.

God saves us from the fearful guilt of not only sinning, but causing others to sin. God help us to fan the flame of divine life and power in our own and other hearts, until it shall burn, not only with the light of Pentecost, but as the beacon watch fire of the Advent Morning.

## Chapter 19

## The Holy Spirit in the Epistles of Paul to Timothy

In the pastoral and personal letters of Paul to his son in the gospel, Timothy, we have five important references to the Holy Spirit. We shall consider them in their logical order.

I. The Holy Spirit in relation to the person and work of Jesus Christ. 1 Timothy 3: 16, "Great is the mystery of godliness: God was manifest in the flesh, justified in the Spirit."

The reference here is, no doubt, to the witness of the Holy Ghost to the incarnate Son of God. This was given not only by the announcements that preceded his birth, and by the supernatural manifestations of the Holy Ghost that accompanied and followed it, but especially at His baptism, when the Spirit of God publicly descended and abode upon Him, bore witness to His divine Sonship, and united Himself with His person, becoming henceforth the enduement of power for His ministry and work. Henceforth the Holy Ghost continually bore witness to Jesus Christ by manifesting the power of God in His words and work.

It was through the Spirit that He spake His messages; it was through the Spirit that He cast out demons and healed the sick; it was through the Spirit that He offered Himself without spot to God and stood victorious in the conflict and suffering of the cross; it was through the Spirit that He overcame the power of Satan, not only in the wilderness, but in the final conflict; it was through the Spirit that He presented His perfect sacrifice at the throne of His Father, and it was through the Spirit that He rose from the dead "declared to be the Son of God with power, according to the Spirit of Holiness, by the resurrection from the dead."

And then the Holy Ghost still further justified His claim, by coming down as He had promised, and taking up the work that He had begun, and bearing witness to the ascended Lord in the ministry of the apostles, in the organization and work of the Church, and in all the miracles of grace that have followed through the Christian age. Jesus is justified by the Spirit, who witnesses to Him as the Son of God, the Savior of the world, and the faithful and true Witness in all His promises and claims.

Wherever the Holy Ghost still comes, He will always be found witnessing to Jesus, and honoring the Son of God.

II. The Holy Ghost in relation to the Holy Scriptures. 2 Timothy 3: 16, "All Scripture is given by inspiration of God, and is profitable for doctrine, for reproof, for correction, for instruction in righteousness; that the man of God may be perfect, thoroughly furnished unto all good works."

The Holy Ghost is here presented in relation to the Word of God. It is His own word and, wherever it comes, He witnesses to it and honors it. The man who knows the Holy Ghost best will know his Bible best, will love it, will live upon it, and will use it as the weapon of his work and warfare.

The expression here used literally means "God-breathed," "every Scripture God-breathed is profitable for doctrine, for reproof, for correction, for instruction in righteousness." The Holy Scriptures are the breath of God. Just as He breathed into man the breath of life, and man became a living soul, so He has breathed into the Word His own life, and it is the expression of His thought, His mind, and His heart. Just as you breathe upon the window-pane, and the vapor clouds it, so God has breathed upon the page, and lo, His very thought and heart are there, not as dead letters, but as the living message of His love.

We recognize this holy book as the very Word of God. It is not a volume of valuable historical records, ethical principles, and sublime poetry; but it is a direct message from heaven speaking to man with the authority of His Lord; as we so receive it, believe it, and put our whole weight upon it; it becomes real, and the Holy Ghost witnesses by its actual effect upon our hearts and lives that it is, indeed, the true word of the eternal God.

Then it becomes profitable to us; in the first place, for teaching, giving us true views of God's will and of the things we most need to know; next, for conviction, as the word literally means, for reaching the conscience, and showing us where we are wrong. Then it becomes the word of correction, or direction, not only showing us the wrong and making us conscious of it, but showing us the right and how to enter into it. And, finally, it is the word of "instruction in righteousness," building us up, as the word literally means, and carrying us on into the maturity of Christian manhood. Thus the man of God becomes mature in his own experience, and thoroughly furnished unto all good works, for the help of others and the service of His Master.

The man of God must live by the Word of God, and the Holy Ghost never will pass by or lightly esteem the Word that He has given. There are two extremes. The word without the Spirit is dry and dead, but the Spirit without the word is incomplete. Let us honor the Holy Scriptures; let us study them; let us habitually use them, search them, feed upon them, incorporate them into our lives, and use them as the weapon of our warfare against Satan, and for the souls of men.

III. The Holy Spirit's message for our own times. All this Word is the Spirit's message, but He has given some messages in these epistles explicitly for our own times. And so we read, 1 Timothy, 4:1, "Now the Spirit speaketh expressly, that in the latter times some shall depart from the faith, giving head to seducing spirits, and doctrines of demons."

This is more elaborated in the second epistle, third chapter, the first to the fifth verses. "This know also, that in the last days perilous times shall come, for men shall be lovers of their own selves, . . . having a form of godliness, but denying the power thereof."

When we want to print a passage with peculiar emphasis we underline it, and our printer sets it up in italics. When we want to emphasize it a little more, we put two or three lines under it and then he sets it up, not in italics, but in capital letters, and sometimes in large capitals.

Now this is the way the Holy Ghost has written these verses. It is His emphatic, italicized, double capital-lettered message to the men of today, to the closing days of the nineteenth century and the first moments of the twentieth century. "He speaketh expressly." It is His message to us, and it is His emphatic message that we do well to hear.

It is not a sentimental and rose-colored message, glowing with poetry and complacency; it is a solemn warning of danger and holy fear. It speaks in no ambiguous tones. Its voice is, "Take heed," "Look out," "Beware." It tells us not of days of universal liberty and Christian influence; it speaks not in the eloquent language of our modern apostles of progress, recounting the spread of the Gospel, the increase of the professors of Christianity and the advent of the speedy Millennium of our age; but it tells us that, as the days hasten to their close, they shall get darker and more dangerous still; not glorious times, but "perilous times"; times of seducing spirits; times of strong delusion that would believe a lie; times when the light within us shall be darkness; times when the most dangerous elements will be in the very Church of God, and on the part of those who have "a form of godliness, but deny the power thereof"; times when the men that seem to be the most upright, the most self-denying, "abstaining from meats, and forbidding to marry," and apparently the very impersonations of self-sacrifice and the highest morality, shall be the very leaders of Satanic delusion and monstrous iniquity.

These times are upon us already. The vista is opening; the century is closing with lurid clouds on every side. Was there ever a spectacle so humbling and so heart-breaking as the heavens are looking upon today? Thousands and tens of thousands of helpless Christians butchered like cattle in the shambles, and outraged by brutal lust, at the bidding of a sovereign ruler of Europe, and with the tacit consent of six great powers who control ten millions of soldiers! All this going on for weeks and months and years, under the light of heaven and the eyes of diplomacy, and men threatening to go to war about every trifle, and not a sword raised, nor a protest uttered, against these outrages and butcheries! Surely, human government is an utter failure. Surely, the best of our kingdoms and kings are as the potter's clay. Surely, weakness and wickedness have joined hands. Surely, God is showing the utter incapacity of man to rule this earth, and the utter need of the coming of the Prince of Peace and the mighty King, who shall judge the people with righteousness and the poor with judgment. He shall judge the poor of the people, and save the children of the needy, and break in pieces the oppressor. He shall deliver the needy when he crieth, the poor also, and him that hath no helper. He shall spare the poor and needy, and save the souls of the needy. He shall redeem their souls from deceit and violence, and precious shall their blood be in His sight.

Oh, for that blessed King to come! The whole creation groans, the persecuted Armenian cries, and the saints under the altar plead, "How long, oh Lord, how long?" The Spirit speaketh expressly that these things are to be so, and the very fact that they are becoming so is light even in the darkness, and the first streak of dawn in the black sea of night.

Thank God the morning is at hand. Let us listen to the Spirit's voice, let us watch and pray and be ever ready.

IV. The Holy Spirit as the Christian's enduement for life and service. 2 Tim. 1:6, 7, "Wherefore I put thee in remembrance that thou stir up the gift of God, that is in thee by the putting on of my hands. For God hath not given us the spirit of fear; but of power, and of love, and of a sound mind."

Here we have, first, a distinct recognition of the Holy Ghost, definitely given. God hath given the Spirit not of fear, but of power, etc.

The tense employed here in the Greek is always emphatic; it is the aorist tense, and it expresses an act that has been definitely done at a fixed moment in the past. It is not a progressive experience; it is not a gradual approach to something, but it is something done, and done at once, and done once for all. In this sense the Spirit is given. It is the crisis hour in the life of the believer, when the Holy Ghost is thus received as the enduement for life and power in all our spiritual need, and according to all the fullness of the Master's promise.

Beloved, have you thus definitely received the gift and the promise of the Father? Many promises you have claimed, but has the promise been thus made real to you? What reason can you give that it is not so? Oh, do not let another hour pass until at His feet you definitely surrender yourself, and receive Him according to His Word!

But again, we notice that even after receiving the Holy Ghost there is much for the believer to do. And so Timothy is entreated and reminded to stir up the gift of God, which is in him. The word here used is a metaphor, and describes the rekindling of a sinking fire. The flame of divine life and power is declining, or, at least, it is undeveloped and incomplete, and it is to be revived, rekindled, and stirred up.

Now the Holy Ghost when given to us is a divine investment for us to improve, and as we use, develop and improve it, it multiplies in our hands. It is the pound in the parable, which may be increased to ten pounds. It is the pot of oil in the widow's story which may be poured out into all the vessels of the house and all the vessels of the neighborhood, and increased as it is used. It is the water in Cana's vessels which may be emptied into the vessels and poured out to the guests until it becomes wine, abundance of wine, enough for all the needs of the occasion.

The Holy Ghost may thus be stirred up and developed or He may be neglected and left to decline and languish, until, instead of being God's mighty dynamo, and all sufficient power, He becomes but a protest against our unfaithfulness and our negligence.

Beloved, let us stir up the gift of God that is in us. Let us take away the ashes from the declining fire. Let us put on the coal and the fuel of living truth. Let us set on the draught by prayer, and let it burn until it warms the household of Christ and becomes a light and a benediction to a perishing world. And, as we stir up the gift of God that is in us, it becomes to us the Spirit of power, of love, of courage, and of a sound mind. And so we have the fourfold fullness of the Holy Ghost represented in these strong words.

First, He is not the Spirit of fear, which is just another way of saying that He is the Spirit of courage. We must have courage to begin with, or we shall never be able to press on to any of His other gifts. We must have courage to deny ourselves and suffer, to say "No" to our wills and our craving self-indulgence, and to let go everything that hinders His highest will and our highest blessing.

We must have courage to believe what God says, and to confess that we believe; and we must have courage to go forward and obey His bidding and enter into all fullness.

Secondly, He is the Spirit of power. Courage without power would but throw our lives away. Courage combined with power will make us invincible. The Greek word for power is dynamite. He is the dynamite that accomplishes results, and breaks down all barriers and all hindrances.

Beloved, have you this power? Is your life telling? Are your purposes accomplished? Are your prayers effectual? Are your lives victorious, or are you baffled and thrown back by waves on every shore and by every billow or opposing rock? God hath given us the Spirit of power. Stir it up. It is not your power; it is the Spirit of power. It is the indwelling Holy Ghost. The mighty cable is running beneath your street; attach your ear to it, and it will carry any weight that you place upon it. Power is there, anyhow, and if you do not use it, it only runs to waste.

Thirdly, He is the Spirit of love. Courage without power is ineffectual frenzy, and courage and power without love would be despotic and monstrous cruelty. It needs love to give beneficence to the power and direct it for the good of others. So the Holy Ghost gives us the Spirit of love, which turns all our purposes and all our accomplishments into benedictions. It is not our love. We come to the place continually where we cannot love, but it is His love. It is Almighty love; it is love to the unlovely and distasteful; it is the love which in Him forgave His enemies and prayed for His murderers.

But there is yet another element needed in this four-fold enduement. We need the Spirit of wisdom, the Spirit of a sound mind, or, as some have translated it, the Spirit of discipline. This is the Spirit that holds all our powers in equilibrium, keeps us in perfect balance, and enables us to turn all forces, all resources and all opportunities to the best account.

Mere power and courage without wisdom might throw themselves away, and even love, without a sound mind, might become a misguided sentiment, and at last defeat its own purpose. And so the Holy Ghost is the Spirit of practical wisdom, restraining, directing, and controlling all our thoughts and purposes and actions, so that we shall accomplish the highest and best results.

Now this is not our wisdom. It is not common sense. It is not a sound judgment and a level head, as men speak. But it is the indwelling Holy Ghost, training us, and disciplining us, restraining us, and educating us to understand His thought, to follow His leadings, and to walk in His will.

It is sometimes different from the counsels of human wisdom; but it is always safe, always best to obey God. The wisdom of Paul and Silas would have led them to stay in Ephesus, Bythinia, and Asia; but the wisdom of the Holy Ghost sent them into Greece and Europe, for God foresaw what it meant to evangelize that great continent of the future. The wisdom of the flesh would have held back almost every bold enterprise of faith and courage which the Church of God has ever made; but the wisdom of God was justified in His children, as they went forward at her bidding, and were strong in God's command.

The Holy Ghost is equal to all our situations. Let us trust Him. Let us obey Him. Let us follow His wise and holy training, and He will lead us in a safe way wherein we shall not stumble.

Now the essence of this enduement consists in the proportion of all its parts. It is not courage alone, nor love alone, nor wisdom alone, nor power alone. Mere wisdom would make us hard and cold, but wisdom set on fire with love and energized by power will enable us to bless the world.

The lion is the emblem of courage; the ox is the symbol of strength; the man is the emblem of love; and the eagle with her soaring vision is the type of wisdom, all blended in the one Spirit of courage and love and of a sound mind.

With such a divine provision, beloved, why should we be afraid? Why should we be feeble? Why should we be harsh, or tried? Why should we be foolish or fail? Let us stir up the gift of God which is in us, and put on the strength, the life, the might of the Holy One, and go forth, insufficient in ourselves but all-sufficient in His boundless grace.

V. Finally, we have the Holy Ghost represented here as the power Who will enable us to keep our sacred trust. 2 Timothy 1:14, "That good thing which was committed to thee keep by the Holy Ghost which dwelleth in us."

The words, "good thing committed to thee," are the same as the apostle uses in the previous verse, where he speaks of that which "I have committed unto him." Literally, it means, my deposit. There are two deposits; there is one deposit which we have put in the keeping of Christ, and we know He is able to keep it; it is our precious soul; it is our eternal future; it is the momentous interests of our life beyond.

But He has also given a deposit to us. God has invested a trust in us that is as dear to Him as the trust that we have committed to His keeping — it is His glory; it is His testimony; it is His kingdom on earth, "the good thing which was committed to us." Oh, shall we keep it, and hand it back untarnished and glorious and approved when we shall meet Him?

Thank God, the Holy Ghost is given us to enable us to keep it — "that good thing which was committed to thee keep by the Holy Ghost which dwelleth in us."

Not only does He take care of His end, but He comes also to take care of ours. Blessed Friend, Blessed Helper, Blessed Substitute, Blessed All-Sufficient One, we receive Thee; we lean upon Thee; we commit to Thee Thy trusts to us, as well as our trusts to Thee; and in Thy wisdom and in Thy might and in Thy love, and in thy All-mightiness, we go forth to finish the work committed to us, to watch and work for our Lord's appearing! Amen.

# Chapter 20

# Regeneration and Renewal

"He saved us by the washing of regeneration, and the renewing of the Holy Ghost; which he shed upon us abundantly through Jesus Christ our Savior." Titus 3: 5, 6.

This passage gives us a grand view of the plan of salvation. First, the apostle tells us of our former condition, when "we were sometimes foolish, disobedient, deceived, serving divers lusts and pleasures, living in malice and envy, hateful, and hating one another."

Next, he tells us of the source of our salvation. Negatively, it was "not by works of righteousness which we have done," but, positively, "it was according to His mercy that He saved us" through the kindness and love of God our Savior.

The work of salvation is altogether divine. "Mercy shall be built up forever." It was mercy that saved us, and it is mercy that keeps us saved. We shall never get beyond the divine mercy. A poor Indian, once, when asked how he got saved, took a little worm and put it on the ground, and then built a fire of dry leaves around it. The worm caught the smell of the fire and felt its dangerous heat, and began to flee, but only met another wall of fire on the other side, and so went from side to side in terror and despair; until at last, finding no way of escape, it gathered itself up in the center of the circle and lay there helpless and dying. Then the Indian stretched out his hand, picked it up and saved it. "That was the way," said he, "that mercy saved me." It is according to His mercy that He has saved us, and it is mercy every day that fulfills in us all the fullness of that great salvation.

Then He tells us of the special steps. "By the washing of regeneration, and renewing of the Holy Ghost; which He shed in us abundantly through Jesus Christ our Savior; that, being justified by His grace, we should be made heirs according to the hope of eternal life."

This seventh verse does not mean that justification follows regeneration. The Greek tense implies that it precedes it. "Having been justified by His grace" is the true force of the tense. God takes us as sinners and justifies us through His grace the moment we believe, and then He regenerates us and gives us the Holy Ghost and leads us forward into all the fullness of His grace, and on to the blessed hope of our eternal inheritance.

We have, however, only to deal in this connection, with two steps in this scale, "the washing of regeneration and the renewing of the Holy Ghost."

I. REGENERATION.

This literally means "the laver of regeneration." The Greek word really refers to the laver in the ancient tabernacle. You know that in the court of God's ancient sanctuary there were two objects of deep interest. The first was the altar of burnt offering where the sinner came and, transferring his guilt to the sacrifice, received atonement through the blood; the next was the laver, or fountain of water, where he saw his defilement in its mirrored sides, and then cleansed them in its flowing stream. The first represented the blood of Christ; the second represented the Holy Spirit in His regenerating work. This court was open to all the people. It represented the free, full provision of the gospel for the sinner, the justifying, redeeming work of Jesus, and the regenerating grace of the Holy Ghost.

And so the laver of regeneration represents the primary work of the divine Spirit in quickening the soul that, is dead in sin, and bringing it into the life of God. The Bible is full of this. The sinner is constantly represented as dead in trespasses and sins. It is not merely a matter of light. It is not enough for him to form good resolutions and accomplish moral reformations. It is life he needs. And, therefore, we read, "If any man be in Christ, he is a new creation; old things have passed away; behold, all things have become new."Therefore, the Lord Jesus says to Nicodemus, "Except a man be born. again, he cannot enter the kingdom of God." Therefore, the prophet Ezekiel says of the coming salvation, "I will take away the hard and stony heart out of your flesh, and I will give you a heart of flesh. A new heart will I put within you, and a right spirit will I give unto you." This is the laver of regeneration, this is the indispensable work of the Holy Ghost in conversion.

Last night I knelt beside a dying bed. It was a dear lad who had for months been dying, but had no one to lead him to the Savior. That day a dear friend had for the first time told him of Jesus and tried to lead him through the narrow gate.

As I knelt by his side, with his weak brain, and sinking body, I felt how impossible it was for me to make him understand his need in this change.

He had never done anything very wrong, and he had no deep sense of outward sin, but God helped me to show to him that "that which is born of the flesh is flesh" and that his natural heart could not enter the family of heaven any more than the little kitten upon the hearth, or the canary in the cage, could be a member of my family or enter into my sympathies, joys, and conceptions.

Then, as his heart felt his need of this great change, it, was easy to lead him to Jesus and to offer him the free gift of eternal life through Jesus Christ our Lord, and to tell him that he could take it in a moment as the gift of God's great love. Then it was that the blessed Holy Ghost came to our relief, and showed His almighty new-creating power.

Never shall I forget the strange sweet flash of eternal light that shone across his countenance for a moment, as he accepted that gift and with all his heart said, "I will," and then threw his head upon my breast and his arms about my neck, and for a long time lay there, while I prayed, and he entered into the bosom of everlasting love.

When I left him, all was peace and the sweetness of heaven; and in the early morning he passed through the gates into the city, and those that were by his side told us how, just before he passed through, God gave to him a vision of the opening heavens and the chariot that was to bear him home; and the dear family, who knew not God and scarcely understood these wondrous things, were unspeakably touched with the message of divine grace that had come to him, and through him to them, from the gates ajar.

This is the laver of regeneration. O precious friends, you cannot enter heaven without this new heart! You cannot see the Kingdom of God without this divine life, You cannot come into it without this divine touch. You cannot bring it to yourself. You cannot work it up by struggling and by effort. Thank God, there is a better way. "As many as received Him, to them gave He power to become the sons of God, even to them that believe on His name; which were born not of the flesh, nor of the will of man, but of God."

O, sinner, come to the laver of regeneration! Let your hard and stony heart bow at the feet of Jesus. Receive Him; come to Him with all your hardness and helplessness, with all your lack of faith and feeling; and He will take away the stony heart, and give you a heart of flesh, He will plunge you in the laver of regeneration, and then lead you on into all the fullness of His grace and glory.

II. THE RENEWING OF THE HOLY GHOST.

After we have received the new life it needs to be sustained; it needs to be cherished, matured, built up, and led on into all the fullness of Christ. This is the work of the same blessed Mother God that brought us first into life. This is what is meant by the renewing of the Holy Ghost.

1. First, it suggests the daily dependence of our life. We are not supplied in a moment for a lifetime. We have no store of grace for tomorrow. The manna must fall each day afresh; the life must be inhaled breath by breath; we must feed upon the liv-

ing bread day by day. It is not at our command, but all derived from Him.

We must abide in Him, and He in us, "for apart from Him we can do nothing." Our store of grace is not a great reservoir, but just a little water pipe carrying enough for the moment and ever passing on. And so we must learn to live in constant communion with Jesus and constant fellowship with the Holy Ghost.

He is only too glad to have our fellowship. He does not weary of our oft returning. He longs to have us come to Him and keep coming again and yet again, and "He is able to save to the uttermost," or rather, forevermore, "all that keep coming unto God by Him, seeing He ever liveth to make intercession for them."

2. The language implies our spiritual freshness. We cannot live on old food and stale bread; but God's supply for us is perpetually fresh and new. "I will be as the dew unto Israel" is His own blessed figure. It does not rain always, but the dew comes every night and sparkles every morning upon the flower and the leaf. It comes gently, quietly, not in the rush of the tempest, to wash out the tender plant, in the supply which refreshes without disturbing. And then it comes in the hottest weather and the most trying times. Indeed, the dew does not fall, but rises; it is always in the air and is absorbed by the plant just as its condition is fitted to take the moisture that is always floating in the atmosphere. The Holy Ghost is always within reach, if we are in condition to receive and absorb Him. Oh, let us drink in the dew of His grace and live in the renewing of the Holy Ghost!

What a beautiful figure of this was given in the rod of Aaron, which, when placed within the holy sanctuary, budded, and blossomed, and bare fruit. So the rod of faith, and prayer, and holy priesthood, and communion, bears fresh buds, blossoms, and ripe fruit, continually.

Still more beautiful was the figure of the water that flowed through the desert for the supply of Israel's thirst. Once it was struck at Horeb and opened its bosom for the flowing stream, but ever after that the river was there to supply their needs. And so, when they thirsted again, God sent them back and bade Moses not to strike the rock, but "speak," said He, "to the rock, and it shall give forth its waters." Moses made the mistake of striking it, but the waters were there and flowed all the same, and God's faithful grace was still supplied.

And yet again, when they came into the boundless desert, there was nothing but the fiery sand beneath them and the burning sun above them. But again the water was there. All they had to do was to gather in a circle, and dig with their spades a well in the desert, and then gather around it and sing their song of faith and praise; and lo, the waters gushed forth, and their need was all supplied.

This is the renewing of the Holy Ghost. Thus He supplies our daily needs. Thus He waits to meet the cry of faith. Thus He loves to answer the song of praise, and flow through all our being with His glad and full supply, until "the wilderness and the solitary place shall rejoice, the desert (of life) shall blossom as the rose." This is what the Apostle Peter meant when he spoke of the "times of refreshing that should come from the presence of the Lord," before "the times of the restoration of all things," which Christ's advent shall bring. We are in "the times of refreshing," and we are waiting for the times of restitution. Oh, let us take the blessing! Oh, let us claim the fullness! Let us receive the renewing of the Holy Ghost. Let us enter into the mighty promise, "I will make you and the places round about you a blessing; and I will cause the shower to come down in his season; there shall be showers of blessing."

3. There is one more thought suggested by this expression. The Greek word here used is employed once only besides in the New Testament. We find it in that remarkable passage in the twelfth chapter of Romans, where the apostle says, "Be not conformed to this world, but be ye transformed by the renewing of your mind."

It is well known that the expression there should be translated, "Be ye transfigured by the upward renewing of your mind."

It is the same word as here used for "renewing," and it is connected there with the figure of transfiguration.

The thought of the apostle here is that the Holy Ghost is leading us on to our transfiguration. It is not merely grace, but glory, that He wants to bring us into. It is not enough to be regenerated, we want also to be glorified. It is not enough to go to the laver of regeneration. Let us enter in through the door, and then go in and out and find pasture. Let us pass in to the golden lamps of the Lord. Let us feed upon the table of shew-bread with its sweet frankincense. Let us breathe the odors of the incense that fill the sanctuary. Let us have "boldness to enter into the Holiest by a new and living way;" and there, in the light of God's Shekinah presence, there, under the wings of the cherubim, there, in the innermost presence of God, let us anticipate the glory of the life beyond, and go forth with its radiance upon our brow to shed its blessing upon a dark and sorrowful world.

The Holy Ghost wants to transfigure our lives just as truly as He transfigured Christ's. Two and a half years of that blessed life of ministry had passed. He, too, had been born of the Spirit. He, too, had been baptized in Jordan's banks. From the opening heavens the Holy Dove had come down to rest upon Him. He had gone forth, in the power of the Spirit, into the conflict with Satan in the wilderness, and the service of love through the villages of Galilee.

But now He was going down into the deep valley of Kedron, into the shame of the judgment hall, into the dark, sad conflict of Gethsemane, into the mystery of the cross, into the awful place of God's forsaking for the sins of men, into the deep, cold grave. And He needed more. He needed the glory as well as the strength of God. And so He went up to Hebron's height that night, and was clothed upon with the glory of His primeval throne, and His Advent reign; and then, in that glory He went down from the mountain to cast out the demoniac at its foot, to triumph over persecution, rejection and every adversary, to endure the cross, despising the shame, and to be the Conqueror of sin and death.

So we read that, after this, there was a strange majesty in His mien, "and as they saw Him, they were amazed, and as they followed, they were afraid." O, beloved, we, too, are entering upon strange and solemn times! Dark clouds are round about the horizon, lurid lightnings are flashing from the sky; solemn mutterings are heard upon the air; there are signals of a crisis; everything is troubled; days of solemn meaning are drawing nigh.

We need more than we have had. We need to pass from grace to glory. We need the transfiguration life as well as He. We need to look from Hebron's height above the valley of humiliation and suffering, away to the sunlit hills of the Advent glory. Oh, shall we be transfigured, too? And then shall we go forth, like Him, to triumph over Satan, sin and death, to shed the light of His glory around us, to stand unmoved amid the perils and convulsions of our time, to meet our coming Lord, proving "all that good, and acceptable, and perfect will of God."

Let us come apart with Him like the three disciples of old. Let us rise to an exceeding high mountain apart. Let us not fear the shadows of the night, and the cloud of the glory as we enter in; and we, too, shall know something of the meaning of His mighty promise, "The glory which Thou gavest Me, I have given them, that they may be one, even as We are One."

## Chapter 21

## The Holy Spirit in the Epistle to the Hebrews

There are five special references to the Holy Ghost in this epistle.

I. THE HOLY SPIRIT IN RELATION TO CHRIST'S DEATH. Hebrews 9: 14. "How much more shall the blood of Christ, who through the Eternal Spirit offered Himself without spot to God, purge your conscience from dead works to serve the living God?"

We have seen that the Holy Ghost was connected with the whole life of the Lord Jesus Christ. Through His overshadowing He was born the incarnate Son of God. Through His baptism He was anointed for His special work. Through His leading He was brought into the wilderness to be tempted of the devil, and then led forth in victory. He anointed Him to preach the gospel. He cast out demons through the Holy Ghost. All through His life the Spirit was in partnership with Him, and He condescended to be dependent upon Him for divine strength and grace even as we His disciples.

But now we see the Holy Ghost in the last hour of His life, ministering on the Cross of Calvary, and taking part in the last and most important act of the Master's whole life. "Through the Eternal Spirit He offered Himself without spot to God." The blessed Comforter was with Him in that dark, lone hour. He strengthened Him for His agony in Gethsemane, and upheld Him so that He could not die before His time nor sink under the power of the devil.

He sustained Him in sweetness, gentleness, and spotless righteousness, through the awful ordeal of shame and suffering, in the judgment hall and the Roman praetorium. He stood with Him in the anguish of the cross, when all others forsook Him, and when even His Father's face was turned away. To the very close of that great sacrifice, the Holy Ghost ministered, suffered and sustained, and then presented that offered life before the throne of God, as a perfect and spotless sacrifice for sin, and a sufficient ransom for every sinner's life.

Blessed Holy Ghost, how much we owe to Him, even for the Cross of Calvary, and the great Atonement! And just as He was with the Master in His crucifixion, so will He be with the disciple. He will enable us, likewise, to die to self and sin. It is only through the Holy Ghost that we can be truly crucified. "If we through the Spirit do mortify the deeds of the body, we shall live." But if we try to kill ourselves, we shall only be like poor Nero, who stabbed his body a hundred times, but never dared to stab himself to death. Would we die with Jesus and rise into all the fullness of His endless life? Let us receive the Holy Ghost, and let Him love us into death and life eternal.

Then, if even these mortal lives should be laid down, before the coming of our Lord, the same blessed Paraclete that was with our dying Lord, will overshadow our last couch of pain, and, on His mighty wings of love, will bear our departing soul across the lonely voyage, to the bosom of the Father, and present our spirit without spot before the Throne of God. Blessed and eternal Spirit, our Mother God and Everlasting Friend, oh, how much we owe to Thee!

II. THE HOLY GHOST AS THE WITNESS OF THE NEW COVENANT. Hebrews 10:15. "Whereof also the Holy Ghost is a witness; for after that He had said before, This is the covenant that I will make with the house of Israel, after these days, saith the Lord, I will put my laws into their hearts, and write them on their minds, and I will be their God, and they shall be my people, for I will be merciful to their unrighteousness, and their sins and their iniquities will I remember no more."

This is the Gospel revealed by the Holy Ghost to Jeremiah, in the dark and declining days of ancient Judaism, when, through the broken windows of the earthly temple, the prophet's vision looked to the light of a better morning.

This ancient covenant, so gloriously revealed to Jeremiah, is three times repeated in the Epistle to the Hebrews; and it must, therefore, be entitled to the greatest significance and weight. It is, indeed, the very essence of the Gospel. It breathes the spirit of the New Dispensation.

Under the old economy the law was written upon tables of stone. Here it is written upon our minds and upon our hearts. Thus it is made a part of our very nature, thought, desire, choice, and being. It is the instinctive and spontaneous impulse of our very life, and it is as natural for us to love it and to do it, as to live and to breathe.

We all know the force of the great law of love. How much do you suppose it would cost for that father and husband to hire the woman who nurses his children, and takes care of his home? What amount of money could purchase her toil and labor, as she lives by his side, shares his fortunes, and works herself to death for these helpless little ones? No earthly consideration could induce her to undertake this charge, no law except the law of force could make her such a slave. Yet there is another law, the law of love, and God has written it upon every mother's heart; and by the drawing of that sweet law of love, she leaves her father's house, her luxurious home, her comfortable surroundings, and goes forth with the man she loves, to share his fate, to toil by his side, to nurture his children, to work early and late for these helpless little ones, unwearied, unconscious of any sacrifice and only too glad to be able to pour out her very life to make them happy. Ah! this is the law upon the heart! This is the way the Spirit of God puts into us the will of God and makes it our choice and our delight.

Therefore, the Holy Ghost was given at Pentecost on the exact anniversary of the giving of the law. Pentecost and Sinai are the two ordinances in the calendar of the ages that correspond with each other. The first was the law written upon stone; the second was the law in the living power of the Holy Ghost in human hearts nod lives.

Beloved, have we learned this secret of life and power? Do we know the divine covenant, the indwelling Spirit, and "the law of the Spirit of life in Christ Jesus," making us "free from the law of sin and death," and "fulfilling the righteousness of the law " not only by us, but "in us"?

Then it is added, "I will be your God, and ye shall be my people." We do not become His people first, thus constituting Him our God; but He first becomes our God, and we are His people. The mother is before the babe, and it is her motherhood that constitutes its childhood. It is because she is its mother, that it is her child. And so God calls us, chooses us, saves us, fills us, and we respond to His love and become His willing, obedient children.

Then our sins are not only forgiven, but forgotten. We are lifted above every cloud of condemnation, and it is true for ever, "their sins and their iniquities will I remember no more."

Beloved, have we entered into this New Covenant by the Holy Ghost, and are we walking under the spontaneous and all-impelling impulses of the indwelling Holy Ghost?

III. THE HOLY GHOST IN RELATION TO THE SUPERNATURAL SIGNS AND OPERATIONS OF THE GOSPEL. "God also bearing them witness, both with signs and wonders, and with divers miracles, and gifts of the Holy Ghost, according to His own will." Heb. 2: 4.

The apostle gives us in this passage a vivid picture of the preeminence of the "great salvation" of the Gospel as compared with the law. The dispensation of Moses was introduced by angels and by men, but the Gospel has been "spoken to us by the

Lord," and repeated by those who were sent directly by Him, and then confirmed to us by the Holy Ghost Himself.

The passage refers not only to the signs and wonders of the early chapters of Christianity, but to the supernatural power which God has promised to every age and stage of the dispensation, to confirm to an unbelieving world the divine reality of God's great message. The Holy Ghost is still present in the Church, and is still giving the confirmatory signs, not only by His miracles of grace in the hearts of men, but by His miracles of Providence in the Church and in the world and His miracles of power in the bodies of those who trust Him.

Beloved, do we know these signs, and are we proving them to the world? Is this gospel still a living power, and its own great witness? Who is there among us that has not seen enough to make us know and feel that it is the power of God? "How shall we escape if we neglect so great salvation?"

IV. THE HOLY GHOST IN RELATION TO OUR IMMEDIATE DECISION FOR GOD. "Wherefore, as the Holy Ghost saith, Today if ye will hear His voice, harden not your hearts." Heb. 3:7, 8.

This is always the Holy Spirit's message to men. It is always a present message, an urgent message, and demands an immediate decision. Back of it, He is always pointing to that solemn story of the wilderness, when God's chosen people came forth from bondage under His mighty hand, and advanced under His glorious leadership to the very gates of Canaan. Then, in one fatal moment, they faltered, doubted, disobeyed and went back to nearly half a century of failure, disappointment, and a dishonored death. Just for a single day they stood upon that narrow isthmus, and then they took the wrong step, and lost all by indecision. Oh, how sad, how desolate these wilderness years, ever moving but going nowhere; toiling, suffering, but accomplishing nothing, simply marking time, waiting for the sad inevitable hour that should close their disobedient lives!

Beloved, there are still such lives, there are men and women who have missed their opportunity. They have disobeyed their high calling, and have gone back from the gates of promise. They are simply marking time and finishing a life whose one sad echo will be forever, "Alas, what might have been!"

This is true of the sinner. There is a moment when he must decide or perish. The Holy Spirit's message to him is always, "Today, while it is called today," for it may not be all the day; it may be a golden moment on which eternity hangs, "Today, while it is called today, if ye will hear His voice, harden not your hearts."

It is also His message to the disciple, for each of us comes up to the gates of the Land of Promise, to the point of a great decision, to the place for entire consecration, to the Jordan's bank where the Holy Ghost is waiting to descend upon us if we will dare to step down into the waters of death and self-dedication. And there comes a moment when there is no time to lose. It is NOW OR NEVER. Oh, if it is such a moment with any of us today, beloved, "while it is called today, harden not your hearts"!

Yes, and even after we have received the Holy Ghost there are crisis hours in consecrated lives. There are great doors of service offered; there are great openings for higher advances; there are sacrifices to be dared, advances to be made, promises to be claimed, victories to be won, achievements to be undertaken; but they will not wait for us. Like harvest time, they are passing by, and the Holy Spirit's message to us is, "Redeeming the time because the days are evil."

It is not merely the time, it is the point of time, ton kairon, the very niche of time. We have not days for it, but only moments. The days are evil, the moment is golden; let us seize it while we may. God help us, beloved, to understand that message, and to let that blessed Guide and Friend lead us from victory to victory, and at last present us faultless in the presence of His glory with exceeding joy.

V. THE HOLY GHOST IN RELATION TO THE BACKSLIDER. There are two very solemn passages in this epistle in relation to the backslider.

"For it is impossible for those who were once enlightened, and have tasted of the heavenly gift, and were made partakers of the Holy Ghost, and have tasted the good word of God, and the powers of the world to come, if they shall fall away, to renew them to repentance; seeing they crucify to themselves the Son of God afresh, and put Him to an open shame," Chapter 6:4-6.

"Of how much sorer punishment, suppose ye, shall he be thought worthy, who hath trodden under foot the Son of God, and hath counted the blood of the covenant, wherewith he was sanctified, an unholy thing, and hath done despite unto the Spirit of grace?" Chapter 10: 29.

Time and space will not permit us to enter fully on the exposition of these verses, but a few remarks may throw sufficient light upon them to prevent their being a stumbling-block to sincere and trembling hearts.

In the first place, it is quite certain from other Scriptures, that there is mercy and forgiveness for every sinner who is willing to accept the mercy of God through the Lord Jesus Christ. Again and again, the infinite mercy of God to the penitent sinner has been repeated and reasserted, until no sincere penitent need ever doubt his welcome at the throne of grace. "All manner of sin and of blasphemy,"our Savior has said, "shall be forgiven unto men."

In the next place, the sin of the persons referred to here is no ordinary sin. It is not a mere fall, but it is "falling away," and falling away so utterly that the backslider wholly rejects the very blood of Christ through which he might be forgiven, and throws away the only sacrifice and hope of mercy. He crucifies to himself the Son of God afresh; he puts Him to an open shame; he tramples upon His blood, and he defies and does despite unto the Spirit of grace.

The difficulty of his salvation arises not from any limitation of God's mercy, but from the fact that he utterly rejects God's mercy, and the only way by which it could be manifested through the Lord Jesus Christ.

In the third place, the case supposed is not necessarily an actual case. It may be of the nature of a warning and a supposition, and the very warning is given in order to prevent it from becoming a fact. The mother cries to her child, "Come back from the edge of the precipice or you will be killed," but this does not imply that the child is to be killed. It is the very means by which it is saved from death. God's warnings are not prophecies, but they are His loving way of keeping back that which otherwise would happen. And so the apostle adds, "we are persuaded better things of you, and things that accompany salvation, though we thus speak."

Finally, in the Revised Version there is a little word of comfort and hope in the sixth verse. Instead of "seeing they crucify to themselves" the translation is, "so long as they crucify to themselves the Son of God afresh." It implies that in a certain spiritual condition they cannot be saved nor forgiven, but it also implies that so soon as they abandon that condition, and become penitent and accept the blood of Christ, the mercy of God is still free and full.

There is, therefore, no reason to infer from these very solemn warnings that any penitent soul need despair of being forgiven. At the same time, the warning is so solemn that we would not for one moment weaken its tremendous force. For we never can tell, when we begin to go back or even look back, where we are going to stop. That which seems but a trifling fall may become a "falling away," and may end in the rejection of Christ and the defiance of God. Our safety lies in heeding the solemn warning, "The just shall live by faith, but if any man draw back, My soul shall have no pleasure in him. But we are not of them who draw back unto perdition, but of them that believe unto the saving of the soul."

The story is told of a man who advertised for a coachman. Among those who came were two who seemed to him to be particularly bright. He took them aside and asked them how near they could drive to the edge of a precipice without falling over.

The first candidate answered that he could go within half an inch and had frequently done so, just shaving the edge and feeling perfectly safe. He then asked the other the same question. "Well, sir," replied the man modestly, "I really cannot tell, because I have never allowed myself to venture near the edge of a precipice. I have always made it a rule to keep as far as possible from danger, and I have had my reward in knowing that my master and his family were kept from danger and harm."

The master had no difficulty in deciding between the two candidates. "You are the man for me," he said, "the other may be very brilliant, but you are safe."

Ah, friends, let us not play with danger, trifle with sin, nor venture so close to the edge of the lake of fire that we may not be able to return! The Holy Ghost, as our loving, jealous Mother, is guarding us from harm by these very warnings. Like the Pilgrims in the Palace Beautiful, who went on their way saying, as they had looked at the wonderful visions of the palace, "These things make us both hope and fear," so, in a wise and holy fear as well as a bright and blessed hope, lies the balance of safety and the place of wisdom. Thus walking in His love and fear, may we be kept by the Holy Ghost until that glad hour when we, through the eternal Spirit, too, shall offer ourselves, without spot, to God.

## Chapter 22
## God's Jealous Love

"The Spirit that dwelleth in us lusteth to envy." James 4: 5.

In the marginal reading of the Revised Version, we find this verse translated: "The Spirit that He hath made to dwell in us yearneth over us unto envy." A still more happy rendering is, "The Holy Spirit, that dwelleth in us, loveth us to jealousy."

This is a little gem in a mass of rocks, a little flower in a wilderness, a little bit of poetry and sacred sentiment embosomed in the great epistle of common sense. One would almost as readily expect to see a rose in a wilderness or a blossom on a glacier, as to find this exquisite little bit of sentiment in the epistle of the most practical of all the apostles.

For James has really struck the keynote of the entire system of revelation. This is the golden thread that runs through the whole Bible, from the bridal of Eve to the Marriage of the Lamb. The love life of the Lord — this is the romance of the Bible, and the golden chain of Revelation.

The story of Rebekah is a kind of idyl, setting forth the whole idea in her romantic wooing and wedding. Just as Abraham sent his trusted servant to bring a bride for Isaac, and just as old Eliezer faithfully discharged that trust, finding, wooing, and then bringing home the beautiful Rebekah, and at last presenting her to the arms of Isaac, waiting for her in the eventide; so the Holy Ghost has been sent by the Father to call from this sinful world a Bride for His beloved Son, and, having called her, to bring her home, to educate her, to robe her, and gradually to prepare her for her glorious meeting with her Lord, in that sublime event which is to be the consummation of the age — the Marriage of the lamb.

Now, the Holy Spirit is represented in this passage as loving us to jealousy, and holding us sacredly to our blessed Bridegroom and Lord. In the context we read about the friendship of the world and the sin of adultery. The true reading of this passage, "Ye adulterers and adulteresses," is simply, "ye adulteresses." It is wholly in the feminine gender. He is not speaking about the earthly marriage bond, but about the fidelity of the Bride of the Lamb to her heavenly Lord. The Church is represented throughout the Scriptures as a wife, and the sin of unfaithfulness to Christ as spiritual adultery. Therefore, it is the adulteress that is mentioned here, and she is asked in the most solemn manner, "Know ye not that the friendship of the world is enmity with God? Whosoever, therefore, will be the friend of the world is the enemy of God."

Compromise with the world is unfaithfulness to Christ and adultery in His sight. It is in this connection that our text is introduced. "The Spirit that dwelleth in us loveth us to jealousy." He is constantly guarding our loyalty of heart and our single and unqualified devotion to Christ alone.

Now, the Spirit which is given to each of us is holding us true to Christ. He first wins and woos us to Christ and then holds us true to Him, and leads us on until we shall be prepared to meet Him at His glorious coming.

This figure could be much better understood in eastern countries and ancient times than now. Almost every Oriental marriage has a go-between, a friend of the bridegroom and the bride, who arranges the preliminaries, and brings the parties together, just as Eliezer brought Rebekah to Isaac. This is the high mission of the Holy Spirit, and in its discharge He is so true to Christ that the least spot upon our holy character, the least compromise in our allegiance and devotion awakens in His heart a holy jealousy. He has devoted Himself to bringing about our union with Jesus, and to fitting us for it in the highest possible measure.

This is the purpose of all His dealings with us, this is the meaning of all the discipline of our life, to call us to Christ, and then qualify us for our high calling, as the Bride of the Lamb.

I. First, He seeks and finds us, and brings us to Jesus in conversion. He sees in us those qualities which God created for Himself, and which Satan is prostituting for our shame and ruin, and He sets His heart on winning us for our heavenly Lord.

This will explain the fact that must often have occurred to many of us, that God revealed Himself to us in mercy many a time before we knew Him as a Savior, and a Father, and answered many of our prayers when we really had no claim upon His promise. He was wooing us to His love. He was trying to make us understand that He was seeking us. He was presenting to us the jewels of Isaac that we might be drawn from the gifts to the Giver and led to listen to His overtures of grace. He was treating us in advance as His friends and His children. He was leaping over the intervening years of sin and unbelief, and anticipating the hour when we should love Him, and weep with bitter sorrow that we did not sooner understand and accept His love to us.

O, beloved, He is calling some of you now! He is longing for you with a jealous love. You belong to Him by God's eternal purpose, you will some day love Him and live for Him with all your heart, and then you would give the world to be able to undo the years of your present sin and folly. Oh, let Him reach your hearts; let Him win your affections; let Him draw you to His bosom and make you His beloved!

II. But secondly, even after we come to know Him as a Savior, He is pressing us forward to a deeper union and a closer fellowship. We have come to Him for refuge from judgment, and from guilt; we have accepted Him as a Deliverer from condemnation and from fear; we have fled for refuge, like the little bird pressed by the storm upon the deck of the passing steamer; but He wants us closer; He wants us to put away our doubts and fears, and to enter into His confidence and fellowship. And so the Holy Ghost is loving us into the life of entire union with Jesus and unreserved consecration to Him.

Thousands of Christians know Him only as a shelter between them and their guilt and danger; He wants to take them into the innermost chambers of His heart and make them partakers of His deepest love. And so the Holy Spirit is wooing the children of God, and drawing them to the very bosom of Jesus. He is saying t o them "Hearken, Oh daughter, and consider, forget thy kindred and thy father's house; so shall the King greatly desire thy beauty: for He is thy Lord, and worship thou Him."

He wants us to turn away from every earthly idol, and give Him our whole heart, that He may give us His in return, and make us the partakers and the heirs of all His riches and His glory. This is what consecration means. This is what the baptism of the Holy Ghost is. In this His jealous love is calling some, even as they read these lines.

III. But even when we thus yield ourselves to Christ in full consecration and receive Him by the Holy Ghost as an indwelling Savior and the Ishi of our heart, we have only begun Rebekah's homeward journey, and the Holy Ghost, like Eleazar, has to lead us on through all the way, educating and preparing us for our meeting with our Lord.

And all through this life of discipline and experience, He is still loving us with a ceaseless and tireless devotion, and pressing us forward with jealous solicitude into God's highest and best will. And so He becomes our Sanctifier. He is preparing our wedding garments and fitting them to us, so that the King's daughter shall be "all-glorious within." "She shall be brought unto the king in raiment of needlework." She shall be robed not only in garments white, but garments bright, the wedding robes of the Marriage of the Lamb.

When we receive Christ as our Sanctifier, there is a sense in which we are wholly sanctified from the beginning. We have accepted all the will of God, and God counts us fully obedient. Our will is utterly surrendered and His will is our unqualified choice. But oh, how much there is for us yet to learn, how much more light, how much more realization, how all these things have to be wrought into the very fibre of our being! As that young lady takes the pattern of embroidery that has been stamped in its minutest details upon the fabric, in one sense she has the whole pattern from the beginning. But now she goes to work with worsted, and silk, and threads of gold, and puts in many a stitch, with patient, delicate needle. She works into that pattern every tint and color and costly material, until it is not only a stamped pattern on the canvas or the silk, but a beautifully inwrought figure with every tint of the rainbow, and with all the brilliant sheen of satin and silk, and silver and gold, and perhaps with precious pearls skillfully wrought into the glowing design. So the Holy Ghost stamps the image of Christ upon us from the beginning; He then goes to work to burn it in and work it in, until our clothing shall be of wrought gold and finest needlework. So He is loving us to jealousy in His deeper work of sanctifying grace, sensitive to every spot, guarding against every slip and failure, and aught that could mar the fullness and perfection of God's great purpose of grace within us.

Some day we shall thank Him for His love, when we stand with the glorious Bride of the Lamb, presented faultless before the presence of God with exceeding joy, while the wondering universe shall come to see the Bride, the Lamb's Wife, with robes more radiant than all the gems of earth and colors more glorious than a thousand rainbows or a thousand suns.

No thoughtful mind can fail to appreciate the importance and the reality of this deeper work of the Holy Ghost. It is one thing to have love, but it is another to have the love that suffereth long and is kind; that never faileth; that is not provoked. It is one thing to have patience, but it is another to "let patience have her perfect work that we may be perfect and entire, wanting nothing." It is one thing to have forbearance and longsuffering, but it is another thing to be "strengthened with might unto all patience and longsuffering with joyfulness." It is one thing to have the things that are just and right, but it is another thing to have the "things that are lovely and of good report," not only the useful and the necessary, but the beautiful and the decorative qualities of Christian life. It is one thing to have the graces of the Holy Ghost in form; it is another to have them in maturity. It is one thing to have the grapes of June or July; it is quite another to have the mellow purple fruit of September or October, ripe and ready for the vintage.

We have seen the Holy Ghost thus leading on a soul, here adding a touch, there subtracting an excess, there deepening a line, there ripening and mellowing a quality. Silently, gradually, day by day and moment by moment, we have seen the picture growing more complete, more symmetrical, more deep, and full of strange indescribable expression, until at last we felt somehow that the work had been wrought into the depths of life, and that the soul was ripe and ready for the Master's coming.

IV. Along with this work of sanctification, there is also a work of separation, and crucifixion. That anything may grow, something must die. He is separating us from the influences of the alien world, and the thousand forces that could distract or counteract His gracious purpose. It is here that His jealous love is most manifest. It is here that He has often to break our idols, and sever the cords that bind us, which would weaken our character, or hinder our highest growth. But the deeper and higher we are to grow, the narrower must our range of earthly sympathy become. And so He has not only to separate from sin, and from the ungodly and unholy world, but to separate us from a thousand things that touch the life of self, and that enter in as hindrances between us and our Lord's highest purpose.

We may not see it ourselves, but He sees it, and He loves us too well to let it hurt us. It may be some dear friend; it may be some innocent and what we regard as an absolutely holy affection. But He may see that that love, or that friend is taking His place, and instead of becoming an attachment to the Head, it becomes a barrier between us and our living Head. Instead of a fruit-bearing branch it becomes a parasite, drawing away our life, or a prop on which we lean instead of rooting more strongly in Him, and so He gently detaches us from it.

It may be that our ambition, or our literary taste, or our fondness for some artistic delight, our beautiful home, our refined friendships, our higher pursuits in the lines of aesthetic taste, are absorbing much of the strength of our life and making Him and His work less. And, so the flashlight falls upon this, and the surgeon's probe detects it, and the deep cathode ray goes through the very flesh and bone, till it reaches the very intents of the heart, and brings to light the hidden danger; then He tests our loyalty and love and calls upon us to surrender it to Him.

Yes, it may be even our Christian work that is absorbing our affection and enthusiasm and leaving Him out. It may be for an idea or an ambition that we are working, rather than for our Lord, and so His jealous love sometimes must destroy the vision that He may save His child. We are reminded of the apprentice boy, who saw his master gazing intently at the beautiful fresco that he had just completed upon the ceiling, and gradually stepping backwards to admire it, until he was on the very edge of the scaffold and another movement would have dashed him to the pavement below. Suddenly the faithful apprentice dashed forward, seized the painter's brush and dashed it over the beautiful fresco, daubing it, and destroying it with one ruthless blow.

The master sprang forward with a cry of agony, but in a moment he stopped and looked at the pale, trembling boy, pointing with his finger backward to the scaffold where he had stood, and then he understood it all. He took the boy into his arms and in a paroxysm of tears he embraced him, and thanked him that he had spoiled his work and saved his life.

So the blessed Holy Ghost has marred the vision of our past, and has desolated the hopes of our future that He might save us for something better. Let us trust Him to the end; let us let Him love us as much as He wants to; let us never doubt His faithful will, nor question the commandments which are "for our good always."

V. The jealous love of the Holy Ghost is also educating us, and seeking to enlarge our vision and our thought, so that He can better fit us to be the eternal companion of our glorious Bridegroom. He is trying to make us understand the majesty of His purpose, and to bring us into partnership with Him in His glorious plans to save the world, and in the ages to come, to lead out His redeemed ones into the highest and grandest services for the universe. His heart is often grieved and disappointed, to find us so narrow, so self-bound, so unable to enter into His glorious purposes, and His eternal designs.

There is a sad story told of a young couple who became betrothed in early life. Afterward the young man went to college, and acquired a liberal education, and then went abroad and traveled for years in a foreign country, finishing his studies and widening his views of life and men. All the while they kept up their correspondence and their engagement, and at last one day he came back to meet his beloved and claim her as his bride. But, alas, he found that while he had grown, she had remained stationary. He loved her still, and her whole life was bound up in him. But she was not able to understand him; she was not able to enter into his higher thoughts and plans, and she was not able to be the companion of his magnificent mind. He wedded her, but more and more, from day to day, he saw that the breach was widening. Her horizon was no wider than her neighbor's fence and her neighbor's farm; her world was scarcely bigger than the kitten on the hearth, the lambs that gamboled in the field, and the milk-pan and kitchen range.

He never told her, and she scarcely understood the shadow that had fallen upon his life, but, day by day, he pined and wasted away, until at last he died of a broken heart.

Ah, friends, our beloved Bridegroom with His glorious mind, His sweeping vision of the universe and His mighty purpose, not only to redeem this world, but to glorify His Father's name in every star and constellation of yonder space through His redeemed ones by-and-by, must often be grieved to find us so slow to understand Him!

You sit down in your corner grocery to make a petty fortune; you work away at your farm in order to make a scant living and some day have a farm for your boys, and you get absorbed in your little circle, and perhaps your little bit of a church. You never think of the great world that is waiting to be saved, the millions that have never heard of Jesus, or the high purpose of His heart to make you, with Him, the queen not only of the millennial years but of the whole redeemed universe. Let us rise to meet His thought; let us get out beyond our self-bound, earth-bound life, and enter into His plan for the world, and speed His glorious coming, and His mighty purpose for all mankind.

VI. And so again, the Holy Ghost is leading us out, and developing our faith and thus preparing us for the higher life of the world beyond. For faith is just the wings by which we are some day to sweep across the abyss and soar amid the heights of the ages to come. Even after we receive the Holy Ghost we are content to move on in small planes and small circles, and we do not want to be disturbed or pushed out to harder, higher things; therefore, the Holy Ghost has to come and just compel us by His love to develop into spiritual strength and energy of which we thought ourselves incapable.

"As an eagle stirreth up her nest, fluttereth over her young, taketh them, beareth them upon her wings, so the Lord alone did lead Him." And so He stirs up our nest and pitches us out in mid air, helpless and defenseless orphans, and we think that it is to destroy us, but it is only to constrain us, that we may strike out the little wings of faith and learn to fly in the great unseen. And when we get a little weary, He stretches out His mighty pinions and bears us up again until we are ready for another lesson. And so through hardship, through the discipline of trials, through new circumstances into which He brings us, through difficulties for which we feel unequal He is developing us, throwing us upon Him, teaching us to claim His grace and educating us for the higher energies, and the nobler manhood of the life to come. Oh, how He delights in us when we yield to Him! How disappointed He is in us when we refuse! How sad when the clay will not let the Potter fashion it, and He has to throw it aside! Beloved, let us trust His love, and yield to His high and holy purpose of love and blessing.

VII. Finally, the Holy Ghost is yearning for our higher usefulness, and training us for service. The life of God is an unselfish life; the employment of the ages to come will be wholly benevolent and self-forgetful. Our service for Christ today is a great investment through which we are laying up treasures beyond, that are to constitute our everlasting riches and reward. And so the Holy Ghost is pressing us forward to make the most of present opportunities; He is trying to get us to plant the seeds of usefulness and to invest the things that we hold dear in sacrifice and service, which yet will bear immortal flowers and plant the heavens with trees of righteousness and fruits of glory.

## Chapter 23

## The Holy Spirit in the Epistles of Peter

There are three important truths respecting the Holy Spirit presented in the Epistles of Peter.

I. THE SPIRIT OF INSPIRATION.

In 2 Peter 1:21 we are told that "the prophecy came not by the will of man, but holy men of old spake as they were moved by the Holy Ghost." This is a very explicit statement of the doctrine of inspiration. They were not giving their own opinions; they were not writing by the impulse of their own will. Sometimes they said things that were contrary to all their natural preferences and attachments, as for example, when Samuel pronounced his judgment upon the house of Eli, or when Jeremiah uttered his awful warnings against his dearly loved people and country.

But they were "moved by the Holy Ghost." The Greek word 'moved' is a very strong one, and in the Revised Version is translated "borne." They were swept along by a mighty impulse which carried them far beyond themselves. They did not always even understood their own predictions, for in 1 Peter 1:10, we are told that "the prophets have inquired and searched diligently, who prophesied of the grace that should come unto you: searching what, or what manner of time the Spirit of Christ which was in them did signify, when It testified beforehand the sufferings of Christ, and the glory that should follow."

Daniel tells us that he heard but understood not, his own vision. Sometimes they saw the vision of a glorious King, sometimes of a bleeding Lamb. But they did not always fully comprehend what it all meant, nor when it was all to be fulfilled. It loomed before them as a glorious vista of far reaching promise, but there was many a cloud upon the vision, and all they clearly knew was that "not unto themselves, but unto us they did minister" these wondrous revelations of truth.

In the next verse the apostle speaks of the Holy Ghost, not only in the message of the prophets, but in the message of the ministers of the gospel, as these truths are now preached unto us by the ambassadors of Christ, "with the Holy Ghost sent down from heaven." The ancient prophet was the organ of the Spirit, but the minister of the gospel has the very presence and person of "the Spirit sent down from heaven," accompanying his message and giving authority and power to his word; so that when we speak the message of God, we speak in the very name of God, and those who hear are responsible for rejecting or receiving, not the word of man, but the very word of the living God.

II. THE SPIRIT OF SANCTIFICATION.

1 Peter 1: 2, "Elect according to the foreknowledge of God the Father, through sanctification of the Spirit, unto obedience and sprinkling of the blood of Jesus Christ." The Apostle Peter fully believed in the sovereignty of God, and in the divine purpose of election ; but he did not believe in any foreordination apart from personal sanctification. The truth is, there are two ends to the divine purpose. On yonder side the cable is fastened to the throne, and hidden from our view is the inscrutable and inaccessible light of God; but on this side the cable of divine mercy is within our reach, and we may fasten it around our own hearts through faith in the Lord Jesus Christ, and the indwelling of the Holy Ghost, so that we may make our calling and election sure, and know that we belong to the heavenly family.

The word "through"should rather be translated "in" sanctification. Holiness is the element and atmosphere of the divine calling, and as we are found there we must be inseparably linked with Him; and apart from this spiritual condition, we have no right to rest in any theological dogma or ecclesiastical form. Let us leave the theology of it to God, and let us make the practical application sure.

Let us carefully notice the form of expression here used. It is not sanctification by the Spirit, but sanctification of the Spirit. There is a great difference. Sanctification by the Spirit might leave us crystalized into a sanctified state, like the wax when the stamp is withdrawn, or like the clock wound up to go by its own machinery. But sanctification of the Spirit is not a self-constituted state, but a sanctification which consists in our union with the Spirit, and makes and keeps us dependent upon His indwelling life and power every moment. We are not sanctified apart from Him, but only as we are filled with Him, and abide in Him continually. We are but the vessel, an empty shell which He must fill, and keep ever freshly filled by "the renewing of the Holy Ghost."

The Greek genitive expressed by the preposition 'of' indicates the most intimate connection between our sanctification and our possession of the Holy Ghost. Beloved, have we the Spirit as our Sanctifier and our Life? Have we something more than holiness, even the Holy One Himself to "dwell in us and walk in us," and ever "cause us to keep His statutes and judgments and do them?"

Again, the sanctification of the Spirit brings us the "sprinkling of the blood of Jesus Christ." Now, the blood of Jesus Christ means the life of Jesus Christ, and the life of Christ has always a twofold application. First, the life of Christ was given for us through the shedding of His blood and the atonement of His death on Calvary. But the life of Christ is also given to us by His union with us and abiding in us.

This latter sense is the one covered by the "sprinkling of the blood." We read in the twenty-fourth chapter of Exodus, that when Moses was about to take the leaders of Israel up into the mount, he offered sacrifices of oxen, slaying the bullocks and pouring out half of their blood upon the altar, thus signifying the shedding of Christ's blood for us in the offering of His sacrifice upon the cross. But the other half of the blood he took in basins and carried it up unto the Mount, sprinkling part of it upon the people and the book of the covenant; and, thus sprinkled with blood and accompanied by the blood, they went up into the very presence of God, and were received into His love and favor. Instead of the thunders and lightnings which yesterday made Mount Sinai a scene of terror, the blue heavens without a cloud covered them as a celestial dome, and Jehovah received them into His presence chamber, feasted them as princely guests at a royal banquet, and, it is added, "upon the nobles of Israel he laid not His hand; but they did eat and drink, and they saw God."

Now, the sprinkled blood in this beautiful type is quite different from the shed blood poured out upon the altar; it represents the life of Christ imparted to us, and making us fit for His presence and fellowship. This is the work of the Holy Ghost. He brings us into living union with the person of Jesus and reproduces in us the very life of Christ.

We believe this is the meaning of the strong expressions used so often respecting the life and blood of Jesus. We are said to be "saved by His life." Again, the "blood of Jesus Christ His Son," that is, the life of Jesus Christ, "cleanseth us, or keeps cleansing us from all sin." So again, in the sixth of John, it is by eating His flesh and drinking His blood that we have eternal life, and that life is nourished from day to day. Beloved, do we know the sprinkling of the blood of Jesus, and are we living upon His life?

There is another beautiful type in the Old Testament throwing much precious light upon this striking figure. It is the account of the red heifer in the nineteenth chapter of the Book of Numbers. We will pass by the other applications of this remarkable type, and refer only to the sprinkling of the water of separation. When any one in the camp of Israel had become defiled by the touch of the dead, or by contact with uncleanness in any way, it was provided that he should be cleansed and restored by sprinkling with the water of separation. This water was made out of the ashes of the heifer that had been sacrificed and then burned, and preserved in a sacred place for this purpose. Water was poured upon it and then, with a bunch of hyssop, the unclean person was sprinkled and cleansed.

Now, we know that the water which you make out of ashes is known as lye, and it is pungent and cutting in its operation as caustic or fire. The sprinkling that came in this way upon the unclean would not be likely to be forgotten. It was a cleansing that would cut to the core, and burn to the bone. And so the work of the Holy Ghost is not always soft and complacent, but often most searching and consuming. He brings home to our hearts the application of the death of Christ, until it takes us into actual fellowship with His death, and makes us also willing to die to the sinful or selfish thing which He has revealed in our natural life.

There is, therefore, a sense in which the sanctifying work of the Holy Ghost is at once immediate and progressive. There is a moment in which we actually enter into personal union with Jesus and receive the baptism of the Holy Ghost. In that moment we are fully accepted, and are fully sanctified up to all the light we have. But as the light grows deeper and clearer He leads us farther down, and farther on, at once revealing and healing every secret thing that is contrary to His perfect will, as we are able to bear it, and bringing us into perfect conformity to the very nature and life of Christ.

It is somewhat like the operation of the limestone brook upon the wooden branch that is left lying in the flowing stream. Day by day, the limestone held in solution is deposited in the open fibers of the wood, until after a while the wood has been changed to stone and, while retaining its natural form, its substance has been transformed into the nature of the stone. So there is a sense in which the Holy Ghost holds the life of Jesus Christ in a kind of solution, and imparts it to us, until we become perfectly conformed to the very image of our glorious Pattern and Head.

Once more, the sanctification of the Spirit leads to "obedience." It is not all theory and experience, but it is intensely practical and real. It runs into our daily lives in the home, the factory, and the store. It makes us better men and women, and compels the world to testify to its genuineness and reality. And then it becomes so easy. It is not the obedience of effort, but the spontaneous and joyful outflow of life and love. He not only dwells in us, but He also walks in us. "And what the law could not do in that it was weak through the flesh," "the law of the Spirit of life in Christ Jesus," does accomplish, "making us free from the law of sin and death, that the righteousness of the law might be fulfilled in us, who walk not after the flesh, but after the Spirit."

III. THE SPIRIT OF GLORY.

1 Peter 4:14, "If ye be reproached for the name of Christ, happy are ye; for the Spirit of glory and of God resteth upon you." The work of the Holy Ghost is more than cleansing. It is also glorifying. He comes not only to make our garments white, but lustrous, like the transfiguration light and the marriage robe.

In the ancient tabernacle there were three sections. The first represented salvation; it was the Court where the worshiper came to the altar and the laver for the atoning blood and the cleansing water. The second was the Holy Place, the chamber where the priests had their home, and where they dwelt with God amid the light of the golden lamps, feeding upon the sacred bread and frankincense, and breathing the fragrant odors that arose in clouds of incense from the golden altar of intercession. This represented sanctification, communion, fellowship, the life of abiding in personal union with the Lord Jesus Christ. But there was another chamber farther in. It was the Holy of Holies, the sacred presence chamber of God, where the Shekinah glory shone between the outstretched wings of the heavenly cherubim. This was God's image of the glory. This represents, of course, the future glory of our heavenly home and the millennial day for which we are waiting. But This also represents the beginning of that glory into which we may enter now. For the Holy Ghost is the earnest of our future inheritance, and He brings its foregleams and foretastes to us here.

That inner chamber, in the days of Moses, was shut off from view. Only the high priest might enter it, and he but once a year. But the veiling curtains were rent asunder when Jesus died, and the glory was opened wide for us to enter in. And so we read the divine invitation, "Having, therefore, boldness to enter into the holiest by the blood of Jesus, by a new and living Way, which He hath consecrated for us, through the veil, that is, His flesh, let us draw near with a true heart, in full assurance of faith." Yes, we may enter into the glory even here. "The glory which Thou gayest Me, I have given them," is our Savior's parting bequest. Not only does He give us His peace and His love, but He gives us His glory, too, and into its heavenly radiance we may enter now. "Whom having not seen, we love, in whom though now we see Him not, yet believing, we rejoice with joy unspeakable and full of glory." "Not only so, but we glory in tribulations also." "If ye be reproached for the name of Christ, happy are ye; for the Spirit of glory and of God resteth upon you."

It is difficult, if not impossible, to make this intelligible to any one who has not been initiated into the alphabet of heavenly things. It needs spiritual senses and instincts to comprehend it. But almost every child of God has at one time or other, been touched with some thrill from the Spirit of glory. Perhaps it lighted up the closet of prayer until it became the gate of heaven. Perhaps it touched your sorrow with a light that transfigured the night into morning and the shadow of death into the light of heaven. Perhaps it came when Jesus healed your body and gave you the first fruits of the resurrection. Perhaps it comes to you sometimes when you sit and think of the cross behind you, the Christ within you, and the home before you, and you scarcely know whether you are in the body or out of the body. But the blessed Spirit is ready to bring it to us just where we need it most.

It would seem as if its congenial sphere was the place of suffering, persecution and reproach. It would seem as if, when earth's barometer goes down to the lowest point, heaven's sunburst always comes most brightly through the tempest clouds. It is "in tribulation" "we glory"; it is "when reproached in the name of Christ" that "the Spirit of glory and of God rests upon us."

But let us be very sure that we are reproached "in the name of Christ," as the passage should be translated. Let us not suffer, as the passage suggests, because of our own foolishness or sin, as transgressors or busybodies. But, standing in the name of Christ, living in His high and holy character, representing Him and resembling Him, let us not fear if trials come, and storms of sorrow fall. The cloud will be but His background for the rainbow. The pillar that loomed by day as an enshrouding mist, will glow by night like a celestial fire;

"And sorrow touched by God grows bright
With more than rapture's ray,
As darkness shows us worlds of light
We never saw by day."

## Chapter 24

## The Holy Spirit in the First Epistle of John

One is impressed with the limited number of direct references to the Holy Ghost in the great epistle of the beloved disciple in comparison with his references to the person of the Lord Jesus Christ.

There are only four or five passages in all this long letter, in which the blessed Paraclete is mentioned by name, but Christ is referred to over and over again. One is led to inquire why this should be. And perhaps the answer suggests a deep and beautiful truth. John was so saturated with the Holy Ghost that, like the Holy Ghost, who never witnesses of Himself, He was constantly thinking of Jesus, and witnessing of Him. The very fact that he was not directly referring to the Spirit was the best evidence that he was in the Spirit, and that he was occupied, as the Holy Ghost always is, in thinking of Jesus and glorifying the Son of God.

And so, beloved, as we are most full of the Holy Ghost we shall be most occupied with Jesus; so that we will not think so much of our own experience or of the glorious Friend within us as the face of Jesus and the depths of His heart of love.

There are, however, several very important references to the Holy Spirit in this epistle. Before we take them up in detail, it is necessary that we should explain our silence respecting one of the verses in this epistle which bears most direct witness to the Holy Ghost.

It is the well known passage, 1 John 5: 7: "There are three that bear record in heaven, the Father, the Word, and the Holy

Ghost; and these three are one." This verse which contains so direct and theological a testimony to the doctrine of the Trinity is undoubtedly spurious. It is not found in any of the early manuscripts, and by the consent of the highest scholars of our age it has been omitted from the Revised Version, and was undoubtedly added by some transcriber, who had more zeal for theology than discernment of the mind of the Spirit and the order of thought in this chapter. The verse is quite irrelevant in the place where it is introduced, and it is by no means necessary to prove the divinity, either of the Son or of the Holy Ghost.

I. THE HOLY GHOST AS THE DIVINE ANOINTING.

"But ye have an unction from the Holy One, and ye know all things. But the anointing which ye have received of Him abideth in you, and ye need not that any man teach you; but as the same anointing teacheth you of all things, and is truth and is no lie, and even as it hath taught you, ye shall abide in Him." 1 John 2:20, 27.

We have previously referred to the symbol of oil, and he figure of anointing, with reference to the Holy Spirit. The idea of this passage is substantially the same as in the passages formerly referred to. The word is a little different. It is not so much the anointing as the unction, the 'chrism' which is here mentioned.

We need not remind our readers that this word 'unction' or 'anointing' is the same word from which the Christ comes, so that "anointed one" just means 'Christ one'. We read in the previous verses of the anti-Christ and of the many anti-Christs who shall come. In contrast with these are 'the Christ ones'. The Holy Ghost is raising up Christ men. The word Christian is derived from this root, but it is not entirely satisfactory. A Christian is one that is somehow connected with Christ, but a 'Christ one' is one that is united with Christ and represents Him, being, in fact, a second edition of Him, and representing the very life of Christ among men.

Now this was the great mission of the Holy Ghost — to set apart the Christ, and make Him the great pattern for all future men. Having accomplished this work in the glorification of Jesus, He is now reproducing the Christ, in the 'Christ ones', and calling and training the disciples of Jesus to represent the Master and repeat His life through the Christian dispensation.

We have already called attention to the use of anointing in setting apart prophets, priests, and kings, and to the special significance of the name of Christ in relation to His threefold office as our Prophet, Priest, and King. In like manner we are anointed to be prophets, priests, and kings of the Church of God, to be God's witnesses to men of His will and work, to be God's intercessors for men, and to be God's kingly ones, victorious over self and sin, and waiting to share with our blessed Head the kingdom of the millennial age.

Now the Holy Ghost calls us to this high ministry and fits us for it. The anointing here spoken of is described as a divine gift, "Ye have an anointing." The verb here is quite emphatic. It means we have received a special gift, and we know we have received it. Beloved, have we received the divine anointing, the Holy Ghost?

His work is here referred to especially in two aspects; as a Teacher, and as a Keeper. As our Teacher He brings to us the mind of God through the Holy Scriptures. The language here used does not imply that we are inspired as the apostles and prophets of the Lord, to know the will of God apart from the Holy Scriptures. It does not mean that we are not to receive the message of God from human lips; but it does mean we are not to receive any message as the word of man, but, even when we are taught by the ministers of Christ, we are to receive them as the messengers of God, to compare their word with God's Holy Word, and only to receive it as it is the voice of God, speaking to our conscience in the Holy Ghost.

But this anointing not only teaches us, but keeps us abiding in Him. The great object of this blessed presence in our hearts is to unite us to Christ, and to keep us ever dependent upon Him and close to Him, so that "when He shall appear we may have confidence and not be ashamed before Him at His coming." So let us receive Him; so let us abide in Him; so let us represent our blessed Lord. And in the age of anti-Christ let us be not only Christians but Christ ones, standing for our Lord on earth as He ever stands for us in heaven.

II. THE INDWELLING SPIRIT.

"And hereby we know that He abideth in us, by the Spirit which He hath given to us." 1 John 3: 24. "Hereby know we that we dwell in Him, and He in us, because He hath given us of His Spirit." 1 John 4:13.

It is not so much, however, the indwelling of the Spirit that is here referred to, as the indwelling of Christ through the Spirit. The object of the Holy Ghost is to reveal and glorify Jesus and make Him personal and real in the life of the believer.

This is not a matter of faith, but it is a matter of knowledge. "We know that He abideth in us." It is real to our consciousness, it is satisfying to our hearts. Christ is to us a personal presence, claims our affection, and satisfies all our need, while the Holy Ghost just ministers Him to us, and holds us in abiding communion with Him as the source and substance of all our life for spirit, soul and body.

We shall never rightly understand the Holy Ghost so long as we terminate our thought upon Him. The Scriptures always lead us on beyond every subjective experience to the person of the Lord Jesus Christ Himself.

III. COUNTERFEIT SPIRITS.

"Beloved, believe not every spirit, but try the spirits, whether they be of God, because that many false spirits have gone forth into the world." 1 John 4:1. The great ambition of the devil is to counterfeit the Holy Ghost. He has always had many counterfeits and many anti-Christs, but as the age draws to a close "the spirits of wickedness in heavenly places" will grow thicker and "the wiles of the devil" will become more subtle and deceiving.

Already we can discover the beginning of that age of Satanic delusion which is to close the present dispensation and gather the hosts of evil to "the great battle of the Lord God Almighty." Often he comes in the disguise of good and as an angel of light, and God has warned us to be watchful and to "be not deceived."

The Apostle John gives us the supreme test, and that is the witness these spirits bear to the Lord Jesus Christ. When any spiritual influence terminates upon itself and does not directly lead us forward to the Lord Jesus Christ and to glorify and vivify Him, we have good reason to be doubtful of it. Any spiritual experience that rests chiefly in the experience and in its delightfulness or significance, is very apt to prove another spirit. The Holy Ghost always witnesseth to Christ.

This passage gives us a still more discriminating touchstone by which we may detect some of the spirits that have gone abroad in our own day. "Every spirit that confesseth not that Jesus Christ is come in the flesh is not of God; but this is that Spirit of anti-Christ of which we have heard that it should come," and which even in John's day was in the world.

This is the spirit that denies the material world and theactual physical incarnation of the Lord Jesus Christ, making the story of creation a beautiful allegory and the account of Christ a fiction, discarding the doctrine of sin and atonement and the actual crucifixion of Christ as a substitute for sinful men.

It is not necessary to name the plausible and wide-spread error which is abroad today, which tells us that there is no material world, that there is no material body, that there is, therefore, no physical basis for disease, that everything is ideas and mind, and that all we have to do is to think rightly, and everything else will be right, for pain is only an idea in the mind and if we refuse to believe in the pain it will cease to exist, and healing will follow as a matter of course. This is neither Christianity nor science, but it is the false spirit which John predicted eighteen centuries ago, and one of the harbingers of the final anti-Christ.

But there are many more abroad. There is real danger among those who know the Holy Ghost, that they should become absorbed or lifted up in their own self-consciousness, and thus be separated from Christ and the truth. Satan is trying to get us on a pinnacle of the temple that He may cast us down into some wild fanaticism or presumption. If we are God's true children he cannot kill us, but he can break our backs and disable us for the battle of the Lord. He can mar our testimony, cause our good to be evil spoken of, and make us so extravagant and ridiculous that we shall not commend our testimony to thoughtful and well-balanced men. May God give to us "the spirit of a sound mind," as well as of "love and power."

IV. THE SPIRIT OF VICTORY.

"Ye are of God, little children, and have overcome them; because greater is He that is in you than he that is in the world." 1 John 4:4.

The secret of victory is to recognize the Conqueror within and the adversary as a conquered foe. John does not say we shall overcome, but he says we have overcome them, because He that is in us is "greater than he that is in the world." "Hethat is in us" has already conquered, and He leads us on to His own victory. We are to meet the enemy as already subdued and, like Joshua and the hosts of Israel, to put our feet upon the necks of the giants and look into their faces with defiance. Satan has power only when he can make us dread him. He flees before the victorious faith and holy confidence.

At the same time, John fully recognizes the power of him that is in the world. "We are of God," he says later, "and the world lieth in the wicked one." It lies in his arms, a helpless captive, taken alive at his will. He is the power that controls it, and, although it may look sometimes like a very cultivated, beautiful and civilized world, yet the principle that lies at the root of all its progress and power is human selfishness and, therefore, godlessness. Christ is not yet the sovereign of all the world. He is the sovereign of His people's hearts; He is in them; Satan is in the world. But the heart in which He dwells is already victor, and goes forth to every conflict with the battle cry, "Thanks be unto God who giveth us the victory through our Lord Jesus Christ."

## V. THE WITNESSING SPIRIT.

This is the last aspect under which the Holy Ghost is presented in the Epistle of John. "It is the Spirit that beareth witness, because the Spirit is truth. And there are three that bear witness in earth, the Spirit and the water and the blood, and these three agree in one," 1 John 5: 6, 8. The three witnesses who agree upon earth are the Holy Ghost, the water of baptism, and the blood of Jesus Christ which we commemorate in the Holy Supper, and which we recognize as the atonement for our sins, and the purchase of our redemption. It is of the witness of the Spirit that we are called, however, to speak here.

1. The Holy Ghost witnesses first through the Word, and this is John's argument in this passage. He says, "If we receive the witness of men, the witness of God is greater: for this is the witness of God which He hath testified of His Son; for God hath given us eternal life, and this life is in His Son." Then he goes on to say that if we receive not this witness "we make Him a liar, because we believe not the witness which God hath given of His Son." This is the message of the Gospel. It is the Holy Ghost that speaketh. It comes to men as God's witness and He declares to the sinner that God hath given to us eternal life, that this life is in His Son, and that if we accept His Son, we have life. Now our duty is to believe this witness, and to believe it implicitly and immediately; the moment we do believe it, it becomes true for us, and we are included in the objects of this great salvation. This is where faith must commence, by taking God's witness and believing His Word respecting our own salvation through Jesus Christ.

2. The Holy Ghost next witnesses in our hearts that that which we have believed is true for us and real to us. "He that believeth on the Son of God hath the witness in Himself." The moment we believe the Word, that Word becomes effectual in our hearts and brings us into the actual experience of peace and salvation. The Word comes first and then the inward witness. We cannot receive the Holy Ghost's assurance of our acceptance of salvation, until we believe on the simple Word of God that we

are accepted and saved, simply because we have come to Christ as He commanded us, and we are not cast out as He promised. Then the soul enters into a real and conscious peace and a delightful assurance, based upon God's Word and repeated by God's Spirit to the individual conscience, that we are the children of God.

3. The Holy Ghost witnesses to our deeper union with Christ and our divine Sonship. When the disciple fully yields himself to God, he is sealed with the Holy Ghost; the Spirit of Sonship is shed abroad in the heart, and Jesus Christ is made personal and real to the soul. The Spirit of God testifies to our union with Him. And so Christ has said, "At that day"; namely, when the Spirit of God comes, "ye shall know that I am in the Father, He in me, and I in you." This is the sealing of the Spirit. This is the wedding ring forever authenticating the marriage of the soul to its Beloved.

4. The Holy Ghost witnesses to God's acceptance of our prayers. This follows in 1 John 5: 14, 15, "And this is the confidence we have in Him, that, if we ask anything according to His will, He heareth us. And if we know that He hear us, whatsoever we ask, we know that we have the petitions that we desired of Him."

5. The Holy Ghost witnesses to our service, and gives us the seal of power and usefulness. "God also bearing witness unto them with signs and wonders, and divers miracles, and gifts of the Holy Ghost, according to His own will," Hebrews 2: 4. We go forth to the service of Christ and the Holy Ghost bears witness to our service. He gives us power for service; He gives us souls for our seals; He makes our words effectual, and He makes our fruit "remain" for His glory and our own eternal joy.

Every servant of Christ who is baptized with the Holy Ghost has a right to expect the witness of the Spirit to his work. Just as of old, "they went forth and preached everywhere, the Lord working with them and confirming the Word with signs following," so still we have a right to expect "the signs following."

Sometimes they are spiritual signs, in the conversion of souls; sometimes they are physical signs, in the healing of the body; sometimes they are circumstances of marvelous import, in answered prayer, difficulties removed, signal providences of God, and the manifesting of God's approval and blessing. So God has set His seal upon the missionary work of our day. So God has set His seal upon the testimony of those who have dared to claim the fullness of the gospel, and enter into all the riches of their inheritance. So God will set His seal upon every life that is fully consecrated and fully yielded to Him.

Beloved, claim the witness, expect the power; do not be satisfied without His seal to your testimony.

6. The Holy Ghost not only witnesses to us, but witnesses through us. The special object of His coming upon us is that we shall be witnesses unto Jesus. "Ye shall receive the power of the Holy Ghost coming upon you, and ye shall be witnesses unto Me, both in Jerusalem, and in all Judea, and in Samaria, and unto the uttermost parts of the earth."

This is the great ministry of the Spirit, to witness through the disciples of Christ to the Church, to the world, and especially to the heathen.

Beloved, have we, as we read these words, the consciousness that we have been true to our testimony? Have we stood for Christ in our home? Have we spoken to all in our household fearlessly and fully the witness of Christ Jesus? Can we say that we are "pure from the blood of all men?" Are we known in our business and social circles as uncompromising friends of Christ? Have we dared to speak in the Church of Christ in every proper and becoming way the message and the witness of the Master? Is our position known? Are we out and out for Christ, and is it our joy and privilege, as opportunity is afforded, to bear witness to the unsaved, of Him who is able to save to the uttermost? And shall we some day find waiting for us a chorus of loving hearts that shall be our eternal crown and seal?

A few weeks ago, the writer had the great joy of standing in a pulpit before a large congregation, and hearing the pastor of that great Church rise and tell his people that more than twenty years before, he had been led to Christ by the one who now stood by his side, although this fact had never yet been known to this one, whom he introduced to his people as, under God, the instrument of his salvation and usefulness. As our heart thrilled with humble gratitude to God for such a privilege, we seemed to see the vision of a time when, in yonder heavenly world, one and another might come forward and greet us and lead us to the throne and tell the blessed Master that He had used us to bring them to God, and we for the first time should meet and know the children from many lands that the Holy Ghost had made seals of our ministry. O beloved, will anyone there be waiting and watching for thee? Have you some surprises in store at God's right hand when you shall "rest from your labors and your works shall follow you?"

Let us receive the fullness of the Spirit first, and then we cannot but give Him. Let Him witness in you and to you, and then He will surely witness through you. Oh, let us be so fully given to Him, that He can possess us and control us, and then can use us to reproduce in others blessing which we have received!

In a frontier Indian mission station, a little girl, one day, came to her teacher and said, "Teacher, will you let me do something?" The teacher asked her what she wanted to do. She said, "I want to give myself away to you, because I love you," and kneeling down by her side and putting her two hands in the teacher's, she said, "I give myself to you, because I love you." And the little heart just swelled with gladness, as she threw herself into the arms of her teacher, so glad to be owned and loved.

A few days afterwards she asked the teacher how she could consecrate herself to Christ. She had heard about it, but didn't understand it. The teacher said, "Darling, just give yourself away to Jesus as you gave yourself away to me."

A light came into the little face, and kneeling down again beside her teacher, she clasped her hands, and looking up with holy reverence, said, "Jesus I give myself to You, because I love You;" and then the Holy Ghost came down and she knew she was sealed His own forever.

She had a very wicked father in a distant station, a cruel, brutal man who refused to listen to the gospel. She began to pray for him, and one day she asked the teacher if anything could be done to save him. "Why," said her teacher, "write to him and tell him that you have given yourself away to Jesus, and ask him to do the same." The little letter was sent with many tears and prayers. Days and weeks passed by, but nothing seemed to come out of it. She did not know but he was fiercely angry and waiting for some terrible revenge. But one day he appeared at the mission. He had walked fifty miles, and was tired and broken, and tears were running down his face. He asked for the teacher, and then he requested to be baptized. He said he had come "to give himself away to Jesus," and amid the rejoicings of his little one, and all at the station, the rough, brutal, wicked man gave himself to Jesus and became a humble follower and fearless witness of the Savior he had hated and despised.

Beloved, shall we let Him have us, and then shall we let Him use us likewise?

## Chapter 25

## The Holy Spirit in Jude

"These be they who separate themselves, sensual, having not the Spirit. But ye, beloved, building up yourselves on your most holy faith, praying in the Holy Ghost, keep yourselves in the love of God, looking for the mercy of our Lord Jesus Christ unto eternal life." Jude 19-21.

The Epistle of Jude, like the Apocalypse which follows it, is written for the last times. It draws a striking contrast between the first and last chapters of human history, especially in the forms of wickedness which prevailed at the beginning and will return at the end, and it records a prophecy of the Lord's return uttered by Enoch in antediluvian times, and soon to be fulfilled in the times in which it is our lot to live.

In the present passage, Jude describes two classes of men and draws a strong contrast between them. They resemble each other, but the one is the counterfeit of the other. The forms of wickedness that are to be most dangerous in the times of the end, are not those marked by open defiance of God, but those that shall be cloaked under a form of godliness without the power, and be Satan's counterfeits of the Holy Ghost. Let us look first at the counterfeits, and then at the genuine people.

I. SATAN'S COUNTERFEIT PEOPLE.

"These are they who separate themselves, sensual, having not the Spirit," Jude 19. This is an unhappy translation. The word sensual, as used in current speech, means immoral, gross, licentious and openly wicked. The Greek word does not convey this impression. The word sensuous would benearer to it, but even this is too strong. The word natural is better, and it is so translated in the second chapter of First Corinthians — "the natural man." The only way to convey the true conception is to anglicize the Greek word, and call it "psychical." It is derived from the Greek word 'psyche,' meaning the soul. It describes the intermediate part of human nature. Man, according to the philosophy of the Bible, is a trinity like his Creator, consisting of spirit, soul, and body. The spirit is the higher nature, that which knows God, distinguishes between right and wrong, and is capable of religious affections, emotions, and exercises. The physical is the other extreme. It is the material organism indwelt by the soul and spirit, and the instrument of its desires, purposes, and operations. Intermediate between these two is the soul, the natural mind, the seat of the affections, the understanding, the tastes, that which loves and hates, that which thinks, that which can be cultivated, and which has at once its lower passions and its finer tastes. The psychical man is the man that is controlled by this department of his being.

There are three conditions in which we may live. First, we may be controlled by our lower nature, our animal existence, our body and its gross appetites. This is pure sensuality. Secondly, we may be controlled by our tastes, by our intelligence, by our affections and passions, by our psychical nature. Thirdly, we may be controlled by our spiritual nature.

The psychical man is the man that is controlled by his natural mind, whether its tendencies be high or low. He is the man born of his mother, descended from Adam, inheriting a fallen human nature, and acting entirely from its promptings. He may be a very refined man, a very intellectual man, a very intelligent man, a very affectionate man, a man full of domestic virtues and patriotic fire, but he is a natural man.

Now all these three departments of our nature are fallen and under the curse. Our body is subject disease and death. Our soul has become self-centered and has wound about itself and its own gratification, a watch spring around its center. And even our spirit is fallen; the conscience is deranged; the will is enfeebled and wrongly directed, and our highest aspirations and intuitions are under the influence of wicked spirits and unholy motives.

It is not enough for us to subject each or all the departments of our nature to any one of them, even to the spirit, because our natural spirit is fallen, too. Some people think that all that is necessary is to crucify the body, to put it into a cage, feed it on herbs and roots, deny it every gratification, and sometime it may lose its evil propensities. This has been proved to be a monstrous failure. The moment the restraint has been removed, it has sprung back to all its former tendencies. You may crush it, but you cannot destroy its evil trend.

Some again tell us that all we need is to exterminate the soul, to crucify our human passions, our earthly affections, our natural tastes and desires, and become cold, abstracted, and spiritual. Well, the devil is a spirit, but he is the most wicked of spirits. The monk in his cell, shut off from every earthly thought, desire, and affection, may be the incarnation of wickedness, Jesuitism, cruelty and unholy ambition.

God's remedy is to yield up the whole man — spirit, soul, and body to God, hand it over to death, and then receive a new creation, a converted body, a regenerated soul, a new spirit in the glorious work of a complete conversion. But even this is not enough; for even when converted, we will, if left to ourselves, relapse again, and therefore we need not only a new heart and a new spirit, but the HOLY SPIRIT to enter and keep the new man, to garrison the heart and mind, to hold the citadel, to dwell and walk within us, and "cause us to keep His statutes."

Now, the apostle says of these men that they have not the Spirit. They have a substitute for it, and it is their own spirit, or rather their own soul, their carnal mind, their human wisdom, their cultivated nature. They are psychical men.

Well, the generation has not passed away, the world is full of them still. What is Theosophy? What is Christian Science? What is much of our modern preaching? What is the religion of culture? It can weep under the pathos and eloquence of the preacher; it can even preach under the impulse of impassioned eloquence until the people weep, but both preacher and people may be but psychical men after all. Perhaps they weep today in the church, and will weep tomorrow in the theater. When the French were shedding streams of human blood in the terrible revolution of a hundred years ago, they were spending their evenings in the theater of Paris shedding floods of tears over sentimental plays. There is a great deal of counterfeit feeling even in modern religion.

The sublime oratorio may lift your soul to raptures of delight; the perfect harmonies of the classic hymn may charm your cultivated taste, but this is not religious feeling. Nay, you may even bow beneath the magnificent arch of yonder Cathedral, and in its dim religious light you may feel a kind of awe that you think is worship, but it is pure sentiment, and you can go out from all this to live for self and sin. It is mere psychology. It is only the kindling of the human mind. Thus heathen idolatry rouses its votaries to intensest feeling and overpowering enthusiasm.

Thus poetry, art, music and eloquence in every age have charmed and thrilled the human mind. But it is only human feeling after all, and has nothing to do with the work of the Holy Ghost. The power of the Spirit reaches the conscience and convicts it of sin, enlightens the understanding, and reveals the differences between right and wrong, and the beauty and authority of the will of God. It touches the will, and crucifies it to its own selfish choice, and then conforms it in glad surrender to the will of God; it controls the whole life in simple and practical obedience and service. There may be far less sentiment and feeling, "but by their fruits ye shall know them."

We have to guard against the counterfeit, and not mistake the psychical for the spiritual, for the "natural man (the psychical man) receiveth not the things of the Spirit of God, neither can he know them, for they are spiritually discerned."

The natural man, of "flesh and blood, cannot inherit the Kingdom of God." The Adam race cannot enter the eternal home, but through death to life we must pass into the resurrection of Christ, and through His spiritual life, born of the Second Man, the Lord from heaven, we share His eternal inheritance.

"He that saveth his life [psyche] shall lose it, but he that loseth his life for My sake shall keep it unto life eternal." We must lay down this self-life even in its sweetest and highest forms. Shall we lose it forever? Nay, we shall receive it back in resurrection power, and in the ages to come shall have a grander culture and a nobler satisfaction forever. Some day God will clothe us with the rainbows and cause us to shine as the sun in the Kingdom of our Father, and He will give us a mind, a capacity, a test to appreciate and enjoy it, too, and yet hold it only for His glory.

II. THE SPIRITUAL MAN.

"But ye, beloved, building up yourselves on your most holy faith, praying in the Holy Ghost, keep yourselves in the love of God, looking for the mercy of our Lord Jesus Christ unto eternal life."

1. The spiritual man is a man of faith. Faith is the foundation of the Christian life and character, and on this foundation we build up ourselves. We can grow no wider than the foundation. We can advance only "according to our faith." We are to "add to our faith courage, knowledge, temperance, godliness, brotherly kindness and charity," and all the graces of Christian life. They are to be taken by faith and, step by step, we are to go forward by successively receiving from the fullness of Christ, "from faith to faith," from grace to grace, from day to day.

The spiritual man is a man of love. "Keep yourselves in the love of God." While faith is the foundation, love is the element in which we grow and live, and so Christ has said, "Abide in My love." It is the congenial atmosphere of our life and growth. Love is life, and only as we keep ourselves in the love of God and dwell in the cloudless communion of His fellowship, can we grow.

3. The spiritual man is a man of hope. He has a glorious outlook; he has a heavenly horizon; he has an infinite vision. From

day to day the vision grows larger, and the inspiration grander. There can be nothing glorious without hope, and the higher the hope the mightier its inspiration.

Ours is a glorious hope, an infinite hope, looking out on the eternal years and reaching up to the very heights of God. And as we live under the influence of this blessed hope, we are raised to a majesty and grandeur that dwarfs all petty earthly things and gives sublimity to our life and character.

4. The spiritual man is sustained and upheld in his life of faith, and love, and hope, by the prayer of the Holy Ghost. This is the power that impels his life; this is the inspiration that upholds his faith, and hope, and love; this is the force that continually supplies the strength of his whole. The Holy Ghost has come to undertake the whole care and responsibility of the consecrated life. He takes His place there as the Pilot upon the deck to bring the vessel into the harbor; as the Contractor for that building, providing all necessary supplies for its erection an completion; as the Teacher and Trainer of some important school, undertaking the whole discipline of that young and precious life; as the Mother, undertaking the care and oversight of her precious child; as the Commander-in-Chief for some great campaign, with his eye and hand on every detail of the conflict — so the Holy Ghost sits down as the Author and Finisher of our spiritual life. He is looking forward every moment to the glorious consummation. He has understood, as we cannot understand, God's glorious plan for us. He sees us every moment as we shall be when we shine forth like the sun in the kingdom of our Father. He comprehends the perils that surround us, the defects within us, the temptations without us, and all the possibilities and disabilities of our life, and He has determined to carry us through in spite of all to the glorious consummation.

Now He does this through the ministry of prayer. He takes us into partnership with Him in the work of our own development and full salvation. He does not work upon us as the potter upon the plastic clay, but He works with us and requires our cooperation with Him; so, as each need arises, He gently lays it upon our own heart; He whispers it to us as a breath of prayer, or a burden of desire, and He leads us out to present it to the Father in the name of the Lord Jesus Christ. Thus, step by step, moment by moment, He prays out in us every need of our own life, every need of our work, every need of the other lives that He lays upon us, and the Father sends the answer in the name of the Lord Jesus Christ.

There is not a moment in the believer's life when the Holy Ghost is not vigilantly, tenderly watching over him,, and guarding him with more than a mother's care. And if we were only more sensitive to understand, more quick to hear, more ready to respond, our lives would be one ceaseless breath of prayer, and everything would come to us through the blessed channel of the Spirit's intercession. Then truly we would "pray without ceasing," and "in everything give thanks," and "wait upon our God continually." Then we should never miss a single hint, suggestion, or ministry of prayer; but we would be in perfect touch with our blessed Guide and have the continual consciousness of His approval, and the sense of meeting His highest, fullest thought.

This, beloved, is the secret of many an experience which you have not perhaps understood. This is the explanation of that depression that sometimes falls upon your heart and brings the tears gushing to your eyes, or makes you bury your head in your hands and pour out a supplication which you cannot comprehend. He sees some need, some peril, which you cannot comprehend, and He is praying against some evil which some day you will know. When you are about to take a false step, to enter upon a wrong path, to miss some important call, or to be deceived by some subtle wile of Satan, He is there to pray the prayer within you which may be only a groan that cannot be uttered; but if you are wise you will yield to it, and you will answer to His touch. Often it is a prayer for some other life, some soul in peril, somebody in dire distress or disease, some cause that needs assistance, some wrong that needs resistance, some need of the Master's heart which He is letting you share with Him.

Oh, to be more sensitive to His voice, and more obedient to the prayer of the Holy Ghost! Then we should miss nothing of His highest will, and your life would be all sunshine in the presence of the Lord.

Now, what is the prayer of the Holy Ghost?

1. The Holy Ghost lays upon us the desire and burden of prayer. Sometimes we understand it; sometimes we do not. Sometimes it is a joyful consciousness of spiritual elevation; sometimes it is an unutterable and inarticulate groan. Sometimes it is a definite sense of need, a consciousness of personal defect, or a heart-searching sense of our own emptiness and failure. It is a blessed thing to "hunger and thirst after righteousness." The sense of need is the shadow side of the blessing. Let us thank the Holy Ghost when He gives us the burden of prayer.

It was God's highest commendation of Daniel of old that he was "a Man of Desires," and it is the promise of God that if we delight in the Lord "He will give to us the desires of our heart."

2. The Holy Ghost enables us to pray according to the will of God. He gives us direction in our prayers. He saves us from wasting our breath and asking at random. He illuminates our mind to understand the Scriptural foundations of prayer, and makes us understand the things that are agreeable to the will of God, enabling us to ask with confidence that it is His will, and that we have the petitions that we desired of Him.

Mr. George Muller often says that it takes him much longer to decide what he is to pray about, than to obtain the answer to his prayer when he does present his petition.

3. The Holy Ghost gives us access into the presence of God. He creates for us the atmosphere of prayer. He gives us the sense of the Father's presence. He leads us to the door of mercy and steadies our hand as we hold out the scepter of prayer, and reveals to us that inner world of divine things which none but he that feels it, knows.

4. The Holy Ghost enables us to pray in the name of Jesus. He shows us our redemption rights through the great Mediator,

and coming in His name we can ask even as He, and humbly, yet confidently claim, "Father, I thank Thee that Thou hast heard me, and I know that Thou hearest Me always."

5. The Holy Ghost enables us to pray in faith, "for He that cometh unto God, must believe that He is, and that He is the rewarder of those that diligently seek Him."

He enables us when we pray to "believe that we receive the things that we ask," and to rest in the Master's word, without anxiety or fear. He witnesses to the heart the quiet assurance of acceptance and He sustains us in the trial of our faith which follows, enabling us still to trust and not be afraid.

6. The Holy Ghost enables us to pray the prayer of love, as well as the prayer of faith. The Holy Ghost leads us into the dignity and power of our holy priesthood, laying upon us the burdens of the Great High Priest, and permitting us to be partakers of "that which remaineth of the sufferings of Christ for His Body, the Church." In this blessed ministry we are often made conscious of the needs of others, and permitted to hold up some suffering or tempted life in the hour of peril; and we shall find some day that many a life was saved, many a victory won, and many a blessing enjoyed through this hallowed ministry that reaches those we love by way of the throne, when we never could have reached them directly.

When we become wholly emancipated from our own selfish cares and worries, and fully at leisure for the burdens of the Master, the Spirit is glad to lay upon us the needs of the multitudes of God's people, and the burdens of the whole Church and Kingdom of Christ, so that it is possible to have a ministry as wide as the world, and as high as that of our great High Priest, before the Throne.

7. The Holy Ghost leads us into the spirit of communion, so that when we have nothing to ask we are held in the blessed silence and wordless fellowship in the bosom of God. This should become the very atmosphere of our being.

Finally, as we thus "pray in the Holy Ghost" we shall be enabled to "build ourselves up on our most holy faith," we shall "keep ourselves in the love of God," and we shall "look" in heavenly vision "for the mercy of the Lord Jesus Christ unto eternal life." And the benediction of this beautiful epistle shall be fulfilled in our lives. "Now unto Him who is able to keep you from stumbling, and to present you faultless before the presence of His glory with exceeding joy, To the only wise God our Savior, be glory and majesty, dominion and power, both now and forever. Amen."

## Chapter 26

## The Sevenfold Holy Ghost

"I was in the Spirit on the Lord's day." Rev. 1: 10. "The seven Spirits which are before his throne." Rev. 1: 4. "And before the throne seven lamps of fire, which are the seven Spirits of God." Rev. 4: 5. "Having seven horns and seven eyes, which are the seven Spirits of God sent forth into all the earth." Rev. 5: 6.

The book of Revelation is the last message of the Holy Ghost to the Church of Christ. It was given after the first generation of Christians had passed away, and only John was left of all the immediate followers of the Lord. Christ had been half a century in heaven, and He came back once more to visit the Apostle at Patmos, and give the final unfolding of His will to His followers of these last days of the dispensation. It is peculiarly, therefore, the message of Christ to us; and it is called in the Apocalypse itself, the message of "the Spirit unto the churches."

In the passages that come before us now we have a picture of the Holy Ghost Himself as He came to John in this Apocalypse.

I. THE SEVENFOLD FULLNESS OF THE SPIRIT.

The seven Spirits which are before the throne cannot mean any created spirit, for it would be blasphemy to associate any lower beings than divine persons with the Father and the Son in the ascription of glory and worship given to the Trinity in this passage.

It is evidently the Holy Ghost represented as a sevenfold Spirit. Seven, the number of perfection, is used to denote the perfect fullness of the divine Spirit in His attributes and works. He is the Spirit of all power and wisdom, all life and love, all grace and fullness, all that we can ever need for the fulfilling of life's duties and the accomplishing of God's perfect will for each of us.

We might stop to specify the seven great attributes of the Holy Ghost, as the Spirit of Light, the Spirit of Life, the Spirit of Holiness, the Spirit of Power, the Spirit of Joy, the Spirit of Love and the Spirit of Hope; but when we have named these seven glorious aspects there are yet as many more that we might still name, for, like the love of Jesus, the love and grace of the Holy Ghost pass our knowledge.

Can you think of anything you need for your spiritual life, your physical being, or your service for God and man? You can find it in the Holy Ghost. Is there any place where you have failed, or others have failed? That is just the place that He is equal to with the grace that never fails. "He hath given to us ALL THINGS THAT PERTAIN TO LIFE AND GODLINESS," and "He is able to make all grace abound unto us, so that we always, having all sufficiency in all things, may abound unto every good work."

Then the mention of the seven Spirits in connection with the seven Churches would seem to suggest the beautiful truth that there is a separate aspect of the Holy Spirit for each separate Church. He is not the same to all; He is direct and specific in His relation to His Churches and to His people, and the whole of His love and grace is given distinctively to each one. Just as a fond mother with a dozen children gives her whole heart to each of her children, so the Holy Ghost gives Himself to each of us specifically, and you and I can press up to the place where John lies upon the Redeemer's breast, and dare to call ourselves the "disciple whom Jesus loved."

Beloved are we fully proving the sevenfold Holy Ghost?

II. THE FULLNESS OF THE SPIRIT OF LIGHT.

"Seven lamps of fire before the Throne." Rev. 4:5.

This is a picture of the fullness of the Spirit of light. It comes in the midst of a scene of grandeur and terror. A door is opened in heaven, and John beholds the throne of the eternal Jehovah, surrounded with the insignia of majesty and the manifestations of God's avenging wrath and power.

Judgment is about to begin upon a wicked world, and the spirits of wickedness that have so long possessed it. There are voices of thunder and lightnings of wrath gleaming from the central throne, but in the midst appear these seven lamps of fire, shedding their benignant light upon the lurid scene, and immediately all is transformed. Before the throne is a sea of glass like unto crystal, and the scene of judgment becomes changed to one of peace. And then "the Lamb in the midst of the throne" appears, and the songs of the whole creation arise to God and to the Lamb.

These seven lamps before the throne remind us of the vision of Zechariah in the fourth chapter of His prophecy, representing the Holy Ghost as the sevenfold light of the Church, and the oil of that supplies the ever-burning lamps. We have no other light but the Holy Ghost, and His is perfect light, sevenfold effulgence, shining upon every mystery, every perplexity, and every step in life's pathway.

He gives to us the light of the Holy Scriptures, revealing the mercy of our Lord Jesus Christ for our salvation, and the will of God for our conduct. He is the light of life, giving guidance in our pathway, and showing us how to walk through the tangled mazes of life. He is the Light that searches and reveals our heart, and then shows us the precious blood that cleanses, and the promise suited for every time of need. He is the perfect Light that never deceives, that never exaggerates, that never evades or hides the most painful truth, that never changes, fails or leaves us in darkness.

And He is not only the Light, but He is also Peace and warmth, He is "a burning," as well as "a shining Light." He gives life as well as light, power as well as direction, love as well as truth, and when we receive His light we become also "burning and shining lights," and our lives will be living illustrations of the truths that we profess and the principles that we hold.

III. THE HOLY SPIRIT AS THE SOURCE OF PERFECT SIGHT.

"Having seven horns and seven eyes which are the seven Spirits of God sent forth into all the earth." Rev. 5 : 6.

This is the most sublime vision of the Lord Jesus Christ in the whole book of Revelation. As the evangelist stands looking into heaven, he beholds a scroll containing, it would seem, the purpose and the will of God for the future ages, sealed. No man in earth or heaven was able to open the scroll, or loose the seals. Suddenly an angel turning to him, explained that the mystery was about to be solved and that One had been found that was able to loose the seals and open the scroll. It was the Lion of the tribe of Judah, who had prevailed to loose the seals "and open the book."

As John stood looking for the Lion, lo! it was a Lamb, bearing the crimson marks of suffering and death, and yet, on closer inspection, wearing also the insignia of infinite power and wisdom, for he had seven horns and seven eyes, the types of perfect power and perfect knowledge.

These seven eyes represent the seven Spirits of God, that is the sevenfold Spirit of God, sent forth into all the earth. We need more than light; we need sight to see the light, the power of an inward illumination, the creation and quickening of a new set of spiritual senses that can take cognizance of the new spiritual realities that the Holy Ghost reveals, and that can recognize the person and the presence of the Lord Jesus, whom it is the Spirit's great delight to make manifest. And so the Holy Ghost is represented here as the eyes of Christ, the eyes of God within us for our illumination.

This suggests the beautiful expression in one of the Psalms, "I will guide thee with Mine eye." God gives us His very eyes, and in His light enables us to see all spiritual truth and all divine realities. Therefore, it is quite significant that when our Lord Jesus Christ had revealed Himself in the Gospel of John as the light of the world, He immediately follows His beautiful teaching by healing a blind man, thus suggesting to them that what they needed was vision, even more than truth. And then He proceeded to tell them that He had come into the world, "that they which see might be made blind, and they that were blind might see, "and that their very confidence in their own wisdom was the cause of their blindness and their inability to understand His teaching.

This is what the Holy Ghost brings to us, the vision of the Lord, power to see divine things as God sees them. Not only does He give us the knowledge of the truth, but the realization of it. Not only does He reveal to us the promises, but He enables us to appropriate them. Not only does He show us the living bread and the flowing water of life, but He opens our mouths to drink, and gives us the taste to receive and know the blessedness of these things. Not only does He speak to us; He speaks through us, thinks in us, gives us divine instincts and intuitions, and enables even our own sanctified judgment to act under His influence and by His suggestion, so simply and yet so perfectly that it is not so much God speaking to us, as God speaking through us, and "working in us to will and to do of His good pleasure."

These seven eyes, we will notice, are the eyes of the Lamb as well as the eyes of the Holy Ghost. Perfect unity between the Spirit and the Son is most strikingly expressed in this strong and sublime figure. The seven horns represent the power of the enthroned Christ and the seven eyes represent the wisdom of the indwelling Holy Ghost. Between these horns and eyes, between the infinite power of Jesus and the infinite wisdom of the Holy Ghost how can we ever fall or fail?

Let us ever recognize the Holy Ghost as the Spirit of Jesus, and let us ever honor the slain Lamb, as we honor the Holy Ghost.

Again, the eyes of the Lord are represented as "sent forth into all the earth." The Holy Ghost is operating not from heaven, but from earth. The infinite wisdom of God is present with His Church to direct, guard, and energize all her work for Him, until the mystery of redemption shall be accomplished, until the seals of the scroll shall all have been opened, and the vision all fulfilled in the glorious return of the Lord Jesus Christ as the Lion of the tribe of Judah.

IV. IN THE SPIRIT ON THE LORD'S DAY.

Having given us this account of the fullness of the Holy Ghost, he next speaks of His relation to us. John says, "I was in the Spirit." Observe he does not say — "The Spirit was in me." This is also true but the other expresses a greater truth. A Spirit so sevenfold, so vast in His resources and attributes, is too large even for the whole of the human heart, therefore, he becomes an ocean of boundless fullness in which we are submerged and in which we dwell. As we listen to the expression it seems as if we were standing beside a spring, and we drank from it until we were filled. Then it still kept flowing on until it became a pool, and then an ocean, a great and boundless flood into which we were plunged until we could find neither fathoming line nor shore, but laved [washed] and drank, until we were lost in the ocean of His infinite fullness. This is the divine conception. The Holy Ghost is the very element and atmosphere in which we live, as the mote in the sunbeam, as the bird in the air, as the fish in the sea, as our lungs in the ether whose oxygen we inhale, and on whose breath we live. Not only are we filled with the air by a single inspiration, but the air is all around us still, and we can breathe and breathe and breathe again, and yet again, until it becomes the source of our ceaseless life, and only limited by our capacity to receive it.

It is our privilege not only to be thus in the Spirit in seasons of holy rapture and special elevation, but we may dwell there, abiding in Him and He in us, so that it shall be true, indeed, in a spiritual sense "in Him we live and move and have our being." Then will every day be "the Lord's day"; then will all life be one ceaseless Sabbath of holy rest and heavenly fellowship, and every place be a sanctuary, every season a Sabbath, and every moment a heaven of peace and joy and love.

"Come blessed, holy, heavenly Dove,
  Spirit of light and life and love,
  Revive our souls we pray,
  Come with the power of Pentecost,
Come as the sevenfold Holy Ghost
And fill our hearts today."

## Chapter 27

## The Spirit's Last Message to the Churches

"He that hath an ear, let him hear what the Spirit saith unto the churches." Rev. 3: 22.

The seven letters of the Lord Jesus to the seven churches of Asia contain the last message of the Holy Ghost to the Churches of the Christian age. These messages were not addressed to the Apostolic Church; for all the apostles except John were already in heaven, and the first two generations of Christians had passed away. In a very peculiar sense these epistles represent the message of the risen Savior and the Holy Ghost to the Churches of the last days and our own times. While they are the words of the Lord Jesus Himself, they are also represented, in that perfect unity which the Scriptures constantly recognize between the Spirit and the Son, as the words which the Spirit saith unto the Churches.

A short circuit through the western part of Asia Minor would take one in the order of these epistles from Ephesus to Smyrna, and thence to Pergamos, Thyatira, and the other cities mentioned. It has been supposed by many thoughtful interpreters, that these Churches represent in chronological order the successive conditions of Christianity from the time of John to the end of the age. This is doubtless true to a certain extent.

Ephesus, strong in its orthodoxy, zeal and Christian work, represented the Church immediately after the apostolic age. Smyrna, persecuted and suffering, represented the next epoch of persecution and martyrdom. Then came the reaction of Pergamos, the prosperous and worldly Church with its greater perils and temptations representing the period of Constantine, when Christianity was the established religion of the State, and the world had ceased to oppose and exchanged her persecuting frown for the fawning smile of seductive pleasure.

The Church at Thyatira represents the next stage, the rise of spiritual corruption, and especially of the Romish apostasy. This is naturally followed by Sardis, a condition of entire spiritual death, which well represents the darkness and death of the middle ages.

Philadelphia follows, feeble, but true, loyal to Christ's word and name, and receiving His approval and benediction. This represents the Reformation era, the cause of that and the revival of spiritual life and power under Luther, Cranmer, Knox, Doddridge, Baxter, and the religious life and deeper spiritual movements which have been going forward, in a blessed minority of the Churches of Christ, during these later centuries.

There is yet one picture more, it is the Church of the Laodiceans, rich, prosperous, self-satisfied, widely respectable, but thoroughly lukewarm, indifferent, and deeply offensive to the heart of the Lord Jesus Christ. He stands as One outside the door, knocking for admission, warning of coming judgment, and soon to return again and sit down upon His Millennial throne. Surely this represents the Church of today, and the still more worldly Church of the immediate future, the last age of Christianity before the coming of the Lord.

Now, while the picture is chronologically true, at the same time each of these Churches represents a condition of things that is permanent and perpetual to the time of the end. While Ephesus represents the first ages of Christianity, yet it is found all the way through. While Philadelphia represents the dawn of the Reformation, yet the spirit of Philadelphia runs on, and the representatives of true revival and vital Christianity are found to the close, and so all these Churches are concurrent as well as successive.

They represent seven conditions of Christianity which may almost always be found in some quarter of Christendom, and to which the Holy Ghost is speaking His last solemn message of warning, reproof, or promise. Let us look at them in this light.

## I. THE SPIRIT'S MESSAGE TO THE STRONG CHURCH.

The Church at Ephesus was a strong Church. It was full of good works. "I know thy works," and not only thy works, "thy labor" — works that cost something, "and thy patience " — works that are continuous. It was an orthodox and a jealous Church, which stood firmly for what it believed to be the truth, and it withstood without compromise all that was false and counterfeit. "Thou hast tried these that call themselves Apostles, and are not, and hast found them liars." This is a very high testimony, and one would think that a Church of which the Master can say so much, must be considerably in advance even of the average standing. But the Lord is not satisfied with Ephesus. The Spirit's message is one of the deepest searching and condemnation. Our English version poorly expresses the emphatic meaning of this condemnation. It is not "I have somewhat against thee," but rather "I have against thee." I have so much against thee, that if thou dost not change this cause of offence and reproof I cannot bear thee; I will not suffer thee; "I will come unto thee and remove the candlestick out of its place, except thou repent."

What was this grave charge? What was this solemn omission? "Thou hast left thy first love." It was the lack of love, the lack of fervor, the lack of devotion to the person of the Lord Jesus Christ. They had the active and the orthodox element, but they had not the heart life, without which all these are but empty forms, and for which Christ will accept no substitute.

You do not marry a wife to do your cooking and washing as an African savage, but to be your companion, and to give you the devotion of her heart. If she were to excuse her want of love, by the fact that she had so much work to do, you would tell her that a servant could do your work, but only a wife could give you the love for which your heart longs. This is what Jesus asks from His Church, and He will take nothing else instead.

What is this first love? Is it the intense demonstrativeness which we manifest at our conversion, that glad overflowing, perhaps over-effervescent devotion of childhood, which passes into sober and earnest but quiet habits of faithfulness and obedience? And are we to accept His reproof if we do not always feel the excitement of our first experiences? Certainly not. First love does not mean the love we have first had when we were converted, because He wants us to have something better as the days go by. It is not first in the order of time, but it is first in the order of importance. He means the love that puts Him first, the love that gives Him the supreme place, the love that makes Him the first waking consciousness, and the last thought as we fall asleep at night, the supreme joy of all our being, the gladly accepted sovereign of our will and all our actions, and the One apart from whom we have and want nothing; the first and last of our heart's affections, and our life's aim. This is what Christ expects, and without this love our noblest liberality, our loftiest zeal, our busiest work, is but a sounding brass, a tinkling cymbal, and a disappointing mockery to His loving heart.

This is the first and the last message of the Holy Ghost to these seven Churches. Jesus wants your love. A dear Christian friend once passed through a peculiar experience. It seemed to her as if Christ was not satisfied with her life, and so she began to plan for more work. She added another Sunday School class, another Ladies' Society, a few more hours of laborious work, and still she was not satisfied. Month after month the hunger grew, and the sense of disappointment only increased.

At last she threw herself before Him, and said, "Lord, will you not show me what it is You want? What more can I do to please You?" And then a gentle voice seemed to whisper to her, "It's not more work I want, but more love, and I want you to work less and love Me more." And as she let herself fall into His loving arms, and learned to lean upon His breast, and sit like Mary at His feet, while Martha was bustling around with her busy work, she found that what the Master wanted was her heart, and her first love. "He that hath an ear, let him hear what the Spirit saith unto the churches."

II. THE SPIRIT'S MESSAGE TO THE SUFFERING CHURCH. Rev. 2: 8-11.

The Church in Smyrna was a martyr Church. It represents the suffering people of God in every age. It is not always outward fire. There is a keener pain in the white heat of inward trial, and there are sorrows still for human hearts to bear, as piercing as in the martyr days. What is the Spirit's message to the suffering church? "Be thou faithful unto death, and I will give thee the crown of life." Do not get out of your trouble as easily and as quickly as you can by any possible means, but rather be faithful in your trouble, be faithful even if it kills you; be faithful not until death, but unto death, faithful even at the cost of death itself. The great temptation to the tried ones is to regard deliverance from trouble as the principal thing.

How noble the example of the men of Babylon in contrast with this! "If it be so," they said, "our God is able to deliver us, and He will deliver us out of thy hand, oh king; but if not, be it known unto thee, oh king, that we will not serve thy gods, nor worship the golden image which thou hast set up." That is the true attitude of faithfulness, to stand like Christ in the wilderness, refusing the devil's help, until God Himself shall set us free, or accept the sacrifice at its fullest cost. This is the greatest need of today, the backbone and the royal blood of self-sacrificing loyalty to principle and to God. When the Holy Ghost can find such men and women, He can accomplish anything by them.

III. THE SPIRIT'S MESSAGE TO THE WORLDLY CHURCH. This is represented by Pergamos. Rev. 2: 12-17.

This Church dwelt where Satan's seat was, and Satan's throne is in the world. Its special danger was the doctrine of Balaam, the temptation to go to worldly banquet with the great and influential, to eat of things sacrificed to idols, and to indulge in unholy pleasure, holding the doctrine of the Nicolaitans — the form of godliness, and yet the liberty to sin.

This is the peculiar temptation of the Church of today, to hold on to God with one hand, and to the world with the other, to compromise sterling principle for the approval of the influential and the great, to go to their feasts, keep in touch with social amusements, to retain their influence and approval, and yet pretend to be true to God. In contrast with the forbidden bread, and the forbidden love of this present evil world, the Holy Spirit offers something better — the hidden manna of the heavenly banquet, and the everlasting love of the Lord Jesus Christ, represented by the white stone with the new name written upon it, which no man knoweth save he to whom it is given.

Let us refuse the temptation of the world's bread and the world's friendship, and some day we shall sit down in His banqueting house, and His banner over us will be love as He receives us to the Marriage of the Lamb, and gives us the rapture of His own love, one thrill of which would compensate for an eternity of earthly delight.

Beloved, is He speaking to some of you? Is the world plausibly trying to win you to a worldly life? "He that hath an ear, let him hear what the Spirit saith unto the churches."

IV. THE SPIRIT'S MESSAGE TO THE CORRUPT CHURCH.

Thyatira represents the age of corruption, and the counterfeit life of the wicked one. The striking phrase found in this epistle — "the depths of Satan" — well represents the abominable mysteries of the Papacy, and the kindred perils which are gathering around the church in these last days, through Satan's counterfeits and the false life of Thyatira.

This will doubtless increase as the age draws to its close. There will be false prophets; there will be visions, illuminations, revelations, "osophies"and "isms" yet more and more.

In opposition to these, the Holy Ghost has given us a safe criterion in this epistle, "I will put upon you none other burden, but that which ye have already, hold fast till I come." This settles the whole question. There is to be no new revelation, no new

Bible, no new authoritative voice from heaven. We have it all now in the Holy Scriptures, and all we have to do is "that which we have, hold fast till He come."

These men come to us with their theosophies and their revelations, telling us, as the serpent told Eve, of higher life and loftier spiritual planes; but it is the false, elusive light of the lamps of the pit. In answer to it, we have only to hold up the word of God, and all these illusions will be exposed, even as the sunlight not only chases away the darkness of the night, but eclipses the feeble torchlight glare.

In contrast with all this, how glorious the promise which the Spirit gives to the faithful overcomer! In opposition to the devil power which the adversary offers, and the false light of his revelations, the Lord Jesus says, "I will give him that overcometh power over the nations in the millennial kingdom, at My second coming and the true light of the Morning Star," the power and the light which are from above, and which shall be forever. O, beloved, are any of us turning our eyes to the false delusive torchlights of error, fanaticism, superstition and a false mysticism? "He that hath an ear let him hear what the Spirit saith unto the churches."

V. THE SPIRIT'S MESSAGE TO A DEAD CHURCH.

Sardis represents the culmination of all that has gone before, a Church which has a name to live, but which is really dead. What is His message to such a Church? Alas! it is useless to speak to a dead Church, but He can speak only to the remnant that is still alive within it. And to these He says, "I have a few names, even in Sardis, that have not defiled their garments; and they shall walk with me in white, for they are worthy."

If God has placed you in such a community, you can stand faithful; you can live in vital connection with Him, and you stand as a true confessor of Christ where all around are dead. And to such He gives a glorious promise; "He that overcometh, the same shall be clothed in white raiment; and I will not blot out His name out of the book of life, but I will confess his name before My Father, and before His angels." "He that hath an ear, let him hear what the Spirit saith unto the churches."

Beloved, be true, though you stand alone, and someday you will hear your name confessed before the Father's throne.

VI. THE SPIRITS MESSAGE TO THE LITTLE FLOCK OF FAITHFUL ONES.

The Church in Philadelphia meets nothing but words of approval from the Lord. It is the little Church, it has but little strength, but it has been faithful in two respects. It has been true to Christ's word and loyal to His name. It holds its testimony clear and true to the word of God and the holy Scriptures, and in contrast with ecclesiastical names and outward forms, it recognizes and honors the name of the Lord Jesus Christ. The holy Scriptures and the living Christ, these are its testimonies. It is easy to recognize the true evangelical flock of Christ by these signs in all the ages, and especially in these last days.

In contrast with higher criticism, down grades and latitudinarian views, are we standing, beloved, for the simple authoritative, unchanging Word of God? In contrast with all other names are we standing for the person, the divinity, the glory, and the all-sufficient grace of the living Christ, and proving the power of Jesus' name?

Then for us also the Spirit speaks these mighty promises: First, "an open door" of service, that none can shut; secondly, a part in the glorious translation of the bride at the coming of the Lord. "I will keep thee from the hour of temptation that is coming upon all the world, to try them that dwell on the face of the whole earth"; thirdly, a place of permanence and honor in the new Jerusalem, a part in the Millennial kingdom of our Lord, where we shall stand, as pillars in His temple, bearing the name of the new Jerusalem, and the new name Jesus Christ, identifying us with Him in His personal love and glory forever.

O beloved, in view of this high calling and these glorious truths, let us be true, and "he that hath an ear, let him hear what the Spirit saith unto the churches."

## VII. THE SPIRIT'S MESSAGE TO AN INDIFFERENT CHURCH.

There is something awfully suggestive in the fact that the Church of the Laodiceans is spoken of quite differently from all the others. Even Sardis was recognized as His Church; but this last Church is not His Church, but theirs. It is the "church of the Laodiceans," and He seems to say to it, as He did to His own Israel of old, "Behold your house is left unto you desolate."

You have not wanted me to control, you may have your Church if you will. The very name Laodiceans means "to please the people." It represents a popular Church, and a timeserving age. It is a very large, wealthy, powerful Church; it is rich, increased with goods, in need of nothing. It is also a self-satisfied Church. The reports of its membership, its finances, its missionary organizations are very flattering. It is doing a great deal of work; it is spending a great deal of money, and it is thoroughly satisfied with its own progress and prosperity, but alas! in the eyes of its Lord, it is "the poor, the miserable, the blind, and the naked one." He is represented as excluded from its interior, and standing knocking at its door as a stranger, He is uttering His last solemn warning and appeal, and telling of chastening and judgment about to come upon it. He is counseling it to buy of Him the gold of true faith, the white raiment of divine holiness, the eye-salve of spiritual illumination.

But alas, the saddest and the most solemn part of all this picture is, that it represents the last stage of visible Christianity, the Church at the end of the age and at the coming of the Lord!

Beloved, can it be possible that the Church of our fathers, the Church of the reformers, the Church of the martyrs, could ever become such a Church? Ah, ask yourselves did not the Church of Paul and John become the apostasy of Rome?

What is the real secret of all this? "Thou art lukewarm," — respectable indifference; the same cause which led to the rejection of Ephesus, only aggravated and intensified; the want of heart; the want of love; the want of enthusiasm; the want of Jesus Himself within. The Church that has lost the spirit of revival, the Church that has lost the simplicity of fervor, the Church that looks upon religious experience as sentimentalism, fanaticism, and extravagance, clothed in a stately respectability and self-satisfied complacency, folds her arms, and says, "I am rich, increased with goods, and have need of nothing," while Jesus is standing at the door, and the last judgments are about to fall.

And now the Master turns from the Church of the Laodiceans, and His last message is not to the Church, but to the individuals in it, who are willing to stand out from its indifference, and to be spiritual overcomers. "If any man will hear my voice, and open the door. I will come in to him, and will sup with him, and he with Me." "To him that overcometh will I grant to sit down with Me in My throne, even as I also overcame, and am set down with My Father in His throne."

It is to the individual the promise is given. Yes, even if the Church should become apostate, one by one we can stand true to God, and still may win our crown.

There are two promises: First, we must receive the Christ within; secondly, we shall sit down with Him upon His throne. The Prince comes to us now in disguise. Soon He will come in all His glory to know those who have stood with Him in these days of trial and rejection, Oh, in view of that great day, God help us to be true!

It is said that Ivan, of Russia, used sometimes to disguise himself and go out among his people to find out their true character.

One night he went, dressed as a beggar, from door to door, in the suburbs of Moscow, and asked for a night's lodging. He was refused admittance at every house, until at last his heart sank with discouragement to think of the selfishness of his people. At length, however, he knocked at a door where he was gladly admitted. The poor man invited him in, offered him a crust of bread, a cup of water and a bed of straw, and then said, "I am sorry I cannot do more for you, but my wife is ill, a babe has just been given her, and my attention is needed for them." The emperor lay down and slept the sleep of a contented mind. He had found a true heart. In the morning he took his leave with many thanks.

The poor man forgot all about it, until a few days later, the royal chariot drove up to the door, and, attended by his retinue, the emperor stopped before the humble home.

The poor man was alarmed, and throwing himself at the emperor's feet, he asked "What have I done?"

Ivan lifted him up, and taking both his hands, he said "Done? you've done nothing but entertain your emperor. It was I that lay on that bed of straw; it was I that received your humble but hearty hospitality, and now I have come to reward you. You received me in disguise, but now I come in my true character to recompense your love. Bring hither your newborn babe." And when the child was brought to him, he said, "You shall call him after me, and when he is old enough, I will educate him and give him a place in my court and service." Giving the man a bag of gold he said, "Use this for your wife, and if ever you have need of anything, don't forget to call upon the poor tramp that slept the other night in that corner."

As the emperor left him, that poor man was glad indeed that he had welcomed his king in disguise. The day is coming when amid the splendors of the advent throne, we would give worlds for one glance of recognition from that royal eye.

And we shall be so glad when, amid the myriads of the skies, we shall see His loving smile and meet His recognition and hear Him say, "Come, ye blessed of my Father, sit down upon My throne. You were not ashamed of Me when I came to you in disguise. Now I have come to confess you before My Father and His holy angels."

He that hath an ear, let him hear what the Spirit saith unto the churches."

## Chapter 28

## The Holy Spirit's Last Message

"The Spirit and the Bride say, Come." Rev. 22: 17.

This is the last message and the last mention of the Holy Ghost in the New Testament. It is usually interpreted as an appeal to the sinner to come to Christ, but it is really a prayer on the part of the Spirit and the Bride, for Christ to come back again, in His promised second advent. It is answered by His gracious message, "Behold, I come quickly," and the response of the apostle and the church, "Even so, come Lord Jesus, come quickly. Amen."

It is very striking and beautiful that the last word of the Holy Ghost in this great Apocalypse, which is devoted to the unfolding of the Lord's return, should be a cry of prayer to Him to come. The great business of the Holy Ghost since Christ's ascension has been to prepare for His return. The two last messages of our departing Master, recorded in the first ten verses of the Acts of the Apostles, are the promise of the Holy Ghost and the promise of His second coming. Between these two promises lies the whole Christian age, and the object of the first is to fulfill the last.

The Holy Ghost has now unfolded the prophetic vision, and as He closes it until the end of time, He pours out one ardent prayer and unites the beloved Bride of Jesus in it, "Come Lord Jesus." And then He sends the message forth to all around and adds, "let him that heareth say come." And, turning to the world and the sinner, He utters the last message of inviting mercy to come to Jesus. "Let him that is athirst come, and whosoever will let him take the water of life freely."

This passage suggests the connection of the Holy Ghost with the Lord's return.

I. The Holy Ghost has given us the predictions of Christ's second coming. It was He that whispered to Enoch the first testimony respecting the advent in antediluvian times. It was He that gave to dying Jacob his vision of Shiloh's reign. It was He that revealed, even to double-hearted Balaam, the glory of the latter days, until he longed to have a part in it. It was He that enabled Job to speak of the day when in his flesh he should behold his living Redeemer and see Him for himself and not for another. It was He who inspired the heart of David to sing so often and so sublimely of the Prince of Peace, whose name should endure forever and whose sway should reach from shore to shore. It was He who gave to Isaiah his prophetic fire, and revealed to Daniel and Zechariah the panorama of the ages. Through the lips of the Master on the side of Olivet He foretold the fall of Jerusalem and the end of the Age.

It was He who taught the early Church this blessed hope, as the comfort of her sorrows and the inspiration of her labors. It was He who gave to the first apostolic council at Jerusalem its clear outline plan of the Christian age, and revealed to Paul the great apostasy, and the glorious messages of the advent in the Epistles to the Corinthians and Thessalonians. And now to the last of the apostles, He has unfolded with a clearness far surpassing all former visions the glorious truth of the Lord's return, and as He sums it all up He turns heavenward in one last prayer, "Come, Lord Jesus, come quickly."

By and by, when we read this book in the light of heaven, we shall find that every incident and detail of the Lord's return has been unfolded. Much of it we have misunderstood; much of it may remain somewhat obscure until the time of the end, but nothing has been left unsaid that we need to know to fit us for the meeting with our Lord. The Holy Ghost has made the testimony clear and plain. One word of every twenty-five of these New Testament Scriptures is about this great theme.

He is a very foolish man who reads his Bible without seeing it, and who misses the benediction pronounced in this very book, on "him that readeth and on them that keep the words of the prophecy of this book."

II. The Holy Ghost has interpreted and illuminated the prophetic Scriptures.

It is not enough to have the prophetic word, we need some one to enable us to understand it.

Daniel uttered these advent visions, but he dimly comprehended them, and was told to seal them up until the time of the end. But he was also told that, as the end drew near, the wise should understand, and this is just what is happening today.

The most remarkable sign that we are in the last days and that the mystery of the ages is about to be finished, is the wondrous light which the Holy Ghost has shed on the interpretation of prophecy in our time.

Mistakes there have doubtless been; obscurities still there are; much yet remains to be made plain, but the great landmarks of the future are clear and plain, and the church of Christ knows enough to be able to be true to her trust and ready for the coming of her Lord.

The brightest and soundest scholarship of the age is on the side of pre-millennial truth. The light of science has become tributary to the interpretation of the Holy Scriptures, and the truth respecting the Lord's coming has been so widely published and so simply illustrated and proclaimed, that no earnest Christian today need be in darkness with regard to that day. Nor need the most illiterate and simple disciple of Christ shrink back from the study of prophecy because it is mysterious and obscure. The Holy Ghost will make it plain, and will bless us in its study, as we earnestly read and faithfully keep the words of this prophecy.

II. The Holy Ghost is preparing for the Lord's coming by awakening the desire and expectation of Christ's return in the hearts of His disciples.

When the Lord Jesus was about to come to earth for the first time, His faithful people were waiting for redemption and for the consolation of Israel, and at the proper time, they were there to welcome Him. It needed no special note of invitation to bring Simeon and Anna to the temple when the infant Jesus was to be presented there; but, through the simple and unfailing guidance of the Holy Ghost, they were both on time, and Simeon took the holy Babe in his arms and blessed Him, and Anna went forth from that joyful scene, womanlike, to tell of His coming "to all that waited for redemption in Jerusalem."

And so will it be at the last. Christ's Simeons and Annas will be waiting too. And already they have caught the first rays of dawn, the first intuitions of the Bridegroom's drawing near.

As the hour draws near this will become more uniform and universal among the little flock, and when He appears His Bride will not be left "in darkness that that day should overtake her as a thief," but she will be found ready and waiting to go forth to meet Him.

This blessed hope, which is taking possession of so many of our hearts, is one of the signs of our time, and its sympathetic throb is felt even among the votaries of false religion, who, with an instinct that they cannot understand or explain, are also looking for the appearing of some great One in the present generation.

Sometimes these holy intuitions are truer and more unerring than the conclusions of our science and philosophy. The little bird makes no mistake when, following an impulse in its little heart, it spreads its wings on the air and sails away to southern lands as winter is coming on. It knows that the springtime is there and it finds it true.

The little fellow was right as he stood holding the string of his kite which had gone far out of view in the lofty firmament, when the boys laughed at him and told him it was gone, who answered firmly, "No; 'taint neither, it's all right. I know it 'cause I feel it pull."

Ah, beloved, can you feel it pull? And, although worldly wisdom may scoff, and human ambition may plan for the coming generations, and the self-centered world roll on around its little axis, yet our eyes are upon the east, and our hearts tell us with an intuition that we know is true that the coming of the Lord draweth nigh.

It is the blessed Holy Ghost. Let us listen to His whisper; let us catch his full meaning; let us, as the day draws near, be found "bending ourselves back," and "lifting up our heads" and, like the bird upon the branch, with fluttering wings and uplifted eye waiting for the signal of its mate, let us be ready at His earliest call to rise to meet Him in the air.

IV. The Holy Ghost is preparing for Christ's return by the spiritual enrobing of His children.

The call is going forth. "The marriage of the Lamb is come, and His wife hath made herself ready; and it was granted to her that she should be arrayed in fine linen, clean and bright, the fine linen is the righteousness of the saints."

The Holy Ghost is preparing a people today for the coming of Christ. There is a marked movement in all sections of the Christian world for an entire consecration to Christ, that we may receive the baptism of the Holy Ghost and be transformed and conformed to Christ.

This is the very time that the Bridegroom is near at hand. When the Bride is found robed and ready, her Lord will not be long behind. This is one of the special religious movements of our time. Call it by what name you please, sanctification, the second blessing, the higher Christian life, the baptism of the Holy Ghost, entire consecration — it is the call of God today to His own people, and it is the precursor of the Master's coming.

Our Lord's beautiful parables of the wedding robe and the ten virgins are founded on this great truth, the need of special preparation for the coming of the Lord. In the former parable it is personal holiness that is implied, and in the latter the indispensable need of the baptism of the Holy Ghost. Both these qualifications are freely given in the grace of God. To the Bride it is "granted that she should be arrayed in linen, clean and bright." She does not have to make her own apparel but simply to put on the beautiful garments of her King, and like Rebecca of old, go forth arrayed in the robe which He has given, and covered with his veil to meet Him with acceptance at His coming.

Beloved, have we received the wedding robe? Have we made sure of the oil in our vessels with our lamps? Are we arrayed in raiment not only "clean" but also "bright," not only without the stain of sin, but with all the beauty and glory of the priestly garments? There is an inner and an outer robe. The inner robe must be spotless, the outer must be glorious. This is why the Holy Ghost is leading us through the discipline of life.

The word for "white" here in Revelation means bright, and it is the same word used about the transfiguration garments of our Lord. Beloved, let us put on the white robe and the beautiful garments, and, through the grace of the Holy Ghost, be robed and ready for His coming.

V. The Holy Ghost gives the earnest of the resurrection.

We have already referred to this in former chapters, in connection with the physical life of Christ manifested in the believer through the Holy Ghost. This is an anticipation of the resurrection life. This is a foretaste and first fruit of the physical glory which is awaiting us at his coming.

Divine healing, rightly understood, is just the life of Jesus Christ in our mortal flesh and a foretaste of the resurrection. It is the work of the Holy Ghost to "quicken our mortal body" as He dwelleth in us. Beloved, do we know this supernatural life? And are we thus already tasting the fountain of immortality which is to supply our life eternally from its exhaustless spring?

VI. The Holy Ghost is working in the providence of God among the nations, to prepare for the coming of Christ.

The wonderful events of our time are the beginning of those overturnings which are to bring in the kingdom of Christ and His millennial reign. The Ancient of Days is already working among the nations, and through the power of the Spirit of God is breaking down the barriers and opening up the highway for Christ's return. The same Holy Ghost that of old touched the hearts of heathen kings and made them God's instruments in accomplishing His purpose, is calling out today the various providential agencies which are but part of God's plan for the approaching end of the age. Surely, the extraordinary events that are so rapidly happening around us in every quarter of the globe are full of portentous meaning.

The wonderful progress of knowledge, the running to and fro of men, with their commercial activities and their methods of transportation and communication by land and sea, wars and rumors of wars disturbing the whole political realm, revolutions and upheavals of society and political institutions — all these are full of meaning and promise, and through them all moves the steadfast purpose of the Holy Ghost, whose "eyes run to and fro throughout the whole earth," and whose hand is moving men to the fulfillment of His higher will.

VII. The Holy Ghost is enabling and sending forth the disciples of Christ to fulfill their great trust in witnessing for Christ and evangelizing the world.

This is His greatest work of preparation for the coming of Christ. In direct connection with the promise of the Spirit is the great commission, "Ye shall receive the power of the Holy Ghost coming upon you, and ye shall be witnesses unto Me, . . . unto the uttermost part of the earth."

And so today we witness the mighty workings of the Holy Ghost in sending out the message of the gospel to the neglected at home and the heathen abroad. The Holy Spirit is more than a delightful sentiment in the believer's heart. He is a mighty influence of practical, missionary zeal and world-wide evangelization, and the heart in which He is saying, "Come Lord Jesus, come quickly," will always be heard crying, "Let him that is athirst come, and whosoever will, let him take the water of life freely."

Beloved, if we are truly filled with the Holy Ghost and longing for the coming of Christ, we shall be active witnesses and workers in preparing for Him. We shall be found faithful to our trust wherever God has placed us. We will be soul-winners at home, and if we cannot go abroad we will help others to go and give the gospel quickly to all the world.

How much of our religious life is comfortable sentimentalism, taking the pleasant part, enjoying the selfish luxury, doing as much Christian work as is agreeable, and yet knowing little or nothing of the ceaseless self-sacrificing and intense devotion of the Lord Jesus Christ to finish His work and bring this revolted world back to His Father!

O, beloved, are we wholly in earnest? Have we, too, "a baptism to be baptized with, and are we straitened until it be accomplished?" Are we going forth "as much as lieth in us" to give the gospel of the Kingdom to all nations that the end may speedily come?

Perhaps, dear brother, as you read these lines, God may be calling you to go forth and call home the lost disciple who shall complete the number of the Bride and then bring back our adorable Redeemer.

Nay, perhaps, dear sinner, as you read these lines, you may be the soul for whom Christ is waiting to complete His glorious Bride, as He calls, "Whosoever will, let him take the water of life freely."

There are three little words that seem sweetly linked together here. The first is "come, Lord Jesus," that is the Spirit's cry, and that will be the cry of every one who is filled with the Spirit. "Let him that heareth say, Come."

The second is, the word, "Go." If we are truly saying "come, Lord Jesus," we will go with the Gospel of salvation to the lost at home and the heathen abroad. And the third is the same word, "COME" again. For this will be our message, as it is the Spirit's, to a lost and dying world. "Come to Jesus." "Let him that is athirst come, and whosoever will, let him take the water of life freely."

It is said that when Queen Victoria first visited Scotland, it was arranged that the tidings of her arrival should be signaled from Edinburgh, and by beacons on the mountain tops should be flashed all over the land until it reached from Leith to Stirling, and Stirling to Inverness, and Inverness to distant Caithness, and from mountain to mountain, the beacon blazed forth its joyful welcome, "The Queen has come."

So this text seems to be a cry from the watchtower. Oh, let us haste to plant the watch fires on all the mountain tops of earth; let us station the watchmen for the morning; let us as make ready for the beacon blaze; and, some sweet morn, the nearest watcher shall catch the signal, flash it from post to post, and tower to tower, and land to land, till all around the globe he that heareth shall say "Come," and the shout shall go up from the meeting ranks of earth and heaven, "THE LORD HAS COME." EVEN SO COME LORD JESUS, COME QUICKLY.

www.ingramcontent.com/pod-product-compliance
Lightning Source LLC
Chambersburg PA
CBHW070520010526
44118CB00012B/1036